ACKNOWLEDGEMENTS

The musical examples quoted from Stravinsky's works are referred to in detail in the *List of Works* which begins on p. 313.

Extracts from books are published by permission — details of sources are given in *References* and *Bibliographical Sources* at the end of this book.

Music examples from the following works are reprinted by kind permission of Boosey & Hawkes Music Publishers Ltd:

Petrushka, Le Rossignol, Oedipus Rex, Symphony of Psalms, Le Sacre du printemps, Persephone, Orpheus, Mass, The Rake's Progress, Septet, Three Songs from William Shakespeare, In Memoriam Dylan Thomas, Canticum Sacrum, Agon, Threni, Movements, Epitaphium, Double-Canon, A Sermon, A Narrative and a Prayer, The Flood, Abraham & Isaac, Elegy for JFK, Variations, Requiem Canticles.

Musical examples from *Berceuses du chat, Les Noces, Renard, Quatre Chansons russes, Histoire du soldat, Three Pieces for Solo Clarinet* and *Les Cinq doigts* reproduced by permission of the publisher and copyright owner J. & W. Chester/Edition Wilhelm Hansen London Ltd., these copyright works are specifically excluded from any blanket photocopying arrangements. Those from *The Firebird* are reproduced by permission of Messrs B. Schotts Soehne, Mainz, Germany, and their London agents, Messrs Schott & Co Ltd.

The following credits are applicable to extracts from books:

Those from *Memories and Commentaries* and *Dialogues and a Diary* are reprinted by permission of Faber & Faber Ltd and the University of California Press. Those from *Themes and Episodes* by Igor Stravinsky and Robert Craft are reprinted by permission of Faber & Faber Ltd and Alfred A. Knopf, Inc. Those from *Stravinsky: the Chronicle of a Friendship 1948–1971* by Robert Craft are reprinted by permission of Alfred A. Knopf, Inc. Those from *Stravinsky in Pictures and Documents* are reproduced by permission of Simon & Schuster, Inc.

CONTENTS

I

Keys to Stravinsky

STRAVINSKY'S MUSIC HAS been universally known, recognized, and celebrated from the moment it first appeared, and is still celebrated as the most glorious this century; even so, it remains one of the most secret of arts. Yet, compared with the 'hermetic' language of his contemporaries from Schoenberg to Boulez, no other composer has expressed himself in so clear and pure a manner. Nor has any other composer aroused such conflicting passions or given rise to so many scandals, misunderstandings, and such violent polemic, or so puzzled the world by his many metamorphoses. Has his music been understood for what it is? Has it not rather been both hated and loved for something that it is not? A hundred years after his birth, as the storms which raged over 'contemporary music' fade away, Stravinsky still remains an enigma.

His work belongs chronologically to the twentieth century, yet stands alone. It has systematically sidestepped our 'accelerated' process of musical history, and remained aloof from it even when it seemed prompted by the same ideas. It found kinships in every historical epoch — from the earliest days of polyphony to our own time — and in every tradition. But it upheld no doctrine and founded no school. Its only antecedents were those which it deliberately chose, claiming a sovereign freedom, either to assimilate or to invent. It has no posterity, only at most epigones. In René Char's words: 'What he has left us cannot be found in any Will.'

Solitary — and provocative: its successive renunciations challenged and puzzled its admirers as much as its fiercest opponents. Complex and shifting — 'protean', as it has been called — does it not defy every attempt to grasp its profound unity, to understand it as the work of a single artist making his own way through the anguished journey of the twentieth century?

*

The generation that came to maturity after the Second World War have made musical history a conscience, a mission, a warranty and a weapon. They had been presented with a picture of 'history being

written' by the just men and the martyrs — Schoenberg, Webern,
Varèse — whose path they must 'ineluctably' follow without
equivocation or deviation of any kind, and without looking back,
under pain of being considered (or indeed considering themselves)
'useless'. How could it have been otherwise? The forging of a gen-
uinely contemporary language with the world in ruins and an
exhausted musical language finished off by Schoenberg and gifted by
Webern first with the grace of silence and then with a new breath of
life — this demanded nothing less than total commitment. The
generation that submitted itself to this revolutionary discipline was to
give birth to something more, and better, than a new grammar — a
whole new conception of music and a sharing of intellectual concepts
— a common idea that was to spread all over the world and then
gradually to recede, after enriching the liberty and independence of
the individual with a radical experience that all had shared.

To the obsessive idea of history as a progression and musical
evolution as determined by necessity, Stravinsky opposed his own
conception of history as *permanence*. This was the origin of the serious
misunderstandings — now resolved, we believe — that had arisen
between Stravinsky and this younger generation. Stravinsky regarded
history neither as conscience nor master, but as his property and his
instrument. He saw the whole course of history as available to him, and
he criss-crossed it with abandon and delight, sometimes at the risk of
losing his power of conviction. Why did he do this? In order to put the
clock back? To support an imagination suddenly paralysed after the
Sacre? No: rather to rediscover beyond but also at the very heart of the
complex constellations of musical history, perpetually recurring down
the ages, certain active *constants*. To reach down through this whole
subsoil to the roots of his own musical invention and to a tradition
conceived as living and experienced as necessary. And finally to look
for complex and repeated answers to his own constant and unwavering demands in the world of the sacred, of the archetype and of *style*.
We shall be returning to these fundamental questions throughout the
book.

However, there is *Le Sacre du printemps*, a work certainly 'committed'
to the historical process, and a small number of other 'revolutionary'
masterpieces; and finally, after forty years in the desert as a creative
artist, there is the encounter with Webern which proved his 'salva-
tion'. Are we perhaps to see Stravinsky as first 'making' contemporary
history like the rest, but soon abandoning it, only to catch it in flight
again by the grace of his 'conversion' to serialism?

This fallacious theory is at last being abandoned, involving as it did the total condemnation of three-quarters of Stravinsky's output as 'erroneous' and the recognition as 'correct' of only those works that belong to the composer's 'positive' periods. It was a theory of a generation of composers dominated by the preoccupations of their own decade; and indeed what other standards can a composer apply to any important music but those that he applies to his own? Thus Pierre Boulez's[1] remarkable rhythmic analysis of the *Sacre* made across a single musical dimension tells us less about the *Sacre* than about the problems of rhythm which were a burning issue for Boulez at the time. In the same way Henri Pousseur's[2] equally interesting study of *Agon*, twenty years later, reflects — in the mirror of a work in which tonality and twelve-tone series appear together — the search for a wider serial perspective in which these two hitherto mutually exclusive concepts could be combined: an ambition which was never in the composer's mind when he wrote *Agon*. Seen in this light Stravinsky's music has a *continual modernity*, a power of metamorphosis in each successive generation of composers, whose own works constantly reveal a multiplicity of new facets of Stravinsky's. Surely speaking *of* his work means in the first place speaking *to* it.

Are their different conceptions of history, language and form, that separated the younger generation from Stravinsky, or reduced their points of contact to a number of individual works or linguistic elements, of less significance now?

The situation of music today is fluctuating. We have long outgrown the exclusive puritan discipline to which a considerable number of composers voluntarily submitted; and the common grammar based on Schoenberg and Webern has even been questioned, in some quarters, in its basic assumptions (atonality). Music now enjoys multiplicity, with widely differing languages juxtaposed within a single work, and draws on an inventory of ideas and techniques which is unsurpassed in richness. Nothing is obligatory, nothing is banned; and the laws once thought to be unbreakable have disappeared (and with them the security that they gave). Composers are free to prospect not only the present and the future but also the past, which was until recently forbidden territory. Does this mean a regression, a débâcle? Are composers excavating history for the stratum of poetry which suddenly petered out, once serialism had had its day? No, certainly not. What they are trying to discover are the permanent forces that underlie *all* music and thus highlight their own music's specific qualities.

Does that mean that the paths of today's musicians and of Stravinsky cross and touch each other in the dizzy historical perspective that we now enjoy? It certainly means that we are now able to chart more exactly the specific characteristics of both, and thus to judge Stravinsky better. It means that only now are we able to grasp the true significance of Stravinsky's work *as a whole* — something that has not hitherto been possible, as we can see from the fact that for almost fifty years there has been no significant study of the subject in France or — apart from E. W. White — in Europe.* To attempt such a synthesis, though certainly difficult, is now urgent, and one of the aims of this book.

*

Le Sacre du printemps, one of Stravinsky's most glorious masterpieces, is considered one of the most famous of all twentieth-century compositions, and one which shattered the history of modern music. But what role did it actually play? What were its origins? What was its effect on the musical language of Stravinsky's contemporaries and successors, and indeed on his own musical idiom?

If we examine the course of European music since *Le Sacre*, it is astonishing to see how absolutely alone the work stands and to note the absence of any subsequent 'fallout' after the explosion. Was the 'bomb' of 29th May 1913 too powerful for his contemporaries? As far as the public went, it hit only the elegant first-night audience of the 'Ballets russes'. Musicians soon recovered from the momentary shock and went on with their own different concerns. Which of the composers of the twentieth century really applied to his own music any of the new ideas of form or the extraordinary rhythmic innovations introduced by Stravinsky? None. Debussy rejected them — he was shattered† by the rhetoric of a work so remote from his own; but did he nonetheless grasp its potential significance, since he defended himself so violently? 'A savage's music with every modern comfort' — is the comment of someone instinctively springing to his own defence; but it also reveals admiration for its workmanship. Be that as it may, nothing in Debussy's own music suggests the shock made by the *Sacre*: he was to go his own way, which would have its own enduring future and lead to a far-reaching reform of the rhythms of modern musical language. But

*The extent of this gap can be judged by the continuing pertinence and perspicacity of a number of books such as those by Boris de Schloezer (1929) and André Schaeffner (1931) in France, and more recent articles by Pierre Souvtchinsky and particularly by André Souris (written before 1970 and published in 1976). The two books published before the Second World War are in fact much more original and up-to-date than those by Robert Siohan (1959) and Michel Philippot (1965).

†Misia Sert,[3] who was sitting next to Debussy at the performance, reports him as saying: 'It is terrifying, I don't understand it.' But was Sert a reliable witness?

this was quite independent of the *Sacre* and indeed alien to its spirit. Neither Ravel nor, still less, Les Six took up the legacy of the work. There may be echoes of the *Sacre* in Varèse (*Hyperprism*) and Bartók (*The Miraculous Mandarin*), but they are very distant and more textual than structural, closer to reminiscence than to syntax. Schoenberg and his disciples were totally mesmerized by the suspension of tonality and only admired from afar this work that might have come from a different planet.

Nearer our own time Messiaen and Boulez have made a profound study of the specifically rhythmic element in the *Sacre*, and Boulez's analysis in particular marks a new departure in the history of musical research. Yet both men's own music is oddly alien to the technique and poetry of the *Sacre*. Their considerable rhythmic innovations, which have influenced three generations, are rooted in Debussy and once again quite independent of Stravinsky, to whom they are actually opposed on a number of fundamental points, such as metrics. Did the *Sacre* indeed affect the course of musical history? The 'revolution' caused by the *Sacre* is in fact a myth, if we understand by revolutionary only those works that profoundly transform the language of later generations, as was the case with Debussy. In this we may echo Stravinsky himself, who seems to have been the only clear-sighted observer of his own music. 'I have been dubbed a revolutionary despite myself,' he says in the *Poetics of Music*. 'The tone of a work such as the *Sacre* may have seemed arrogant, its language raw — because of its novelty: that in no way implies its being revolutionary in the most subversive sense of the word.'

As for the effects of the *Sacre* on Stravinsky's own works, Boris de Schloezer[4] was to observe that, 'Everything that he has written since 1914 is a deep-felt reaction against the *Sacre*'. And in fact block harmonies were replaced by linear writing, harmonic aggregates were thinned out and melodic lines — which were earlier dependent on the chromaticism inherited from an earlier generation (but were already beginning to clarify in *Petrushka*, as we shall see) — were to take on a clearly diatonic character. The lightning rhythmic innovations become absorbed in their background and are reduced to lapidary structures. The orchestral style becomes increasingly transparent to the point of being unrecognizable; its sumptuous features are abandoned, and its 'exotic' resonance, once enjoyed for its own sake, sacrificed in the interests of precise clarity. In fact the very sense of Stravinsky's music seems to be changed.

*

There have been two stereotyped pictures of Stravinsky's career as a composer. The first, now being dropped by musicians but still upheld by the general public and even by a number of critics, shows Stravinsky moving on from 'the revolution of the *Sacre*', to 'the reaction of neo-classicism' and from there to 'the avant-gardism of the serial works'. The second picture, which is no less *facile* and enduring, presents Stravinsky as profoundly and authentically Russian in his early works but later abandoning this allegiance for a 'cosmopolitanism' which some considered a matter for regret and others for congratulation. It is this second picture that I now wish to examine.

Does the national character of a work depend on whether or not it contains national elements in the text, whether quoted literally or used freely? The belief that this is the case became a veritable credo between the two World Wars, the period of 'back to folk-lore' and of militant nationalism; and it is still very common throughout Western Europe, especially in the case of Slavonic and Central European countries, which possess a particularly rich and highly-flavoured folk-music much admired in the West. Stravinsky himself protested violently against this tawdry exoticism, this stereotyped image of Holy Russia manufactured in Paris: what he called, 'Vodka-isba-balalaika-pope-boyar'. The music of Messiaen is influenced by Hindu rhythms and ancient Greek metres and Boulez can hardly be said to use 'national themes'; yet both remain profoundly French composers, although their Frenchness may be more difficult to define and is a matter of general conception and style, and certainly nothing to do with folk-music. In the same way Stravinsky's Russianness is not to be sought in the melodic sources of his early stage works, in which the themes were for the most part entirely original, even though based on popular Russian archetypes (*Petrushka, Les Noces*), oriental (*Firebird*) or archaic (*Sacre*) models, according to the nature of the ballets concerned. Where, then, could it be? In the 'school' from which he sprang as a composer? Let us consider for a moment the position of music in Russia when Stravinsky was studying and composing his first works.

Since Russia's late arrival in the world of 'learned' music, the language used by Russian composers was that of Western Europe. Glinka, who is considered the father of Russian music, combined with an extraordinary grace the popular native tradition and the fashionable Italian style of his day, achieving a delicately balanced 'urban' style that we know not only from his own music but from Tchaikovsky's *Eugene Onegin* and the work in which Stravinsky paid homage to Glinka, namely *Mavra*. This delicate balance had hardly been established before it was challenged by the militant nationalism of the so-called 'mighty handful' or 'the Five' (Borodin, Rimsky, Cui, Balakirev and Mussorgsky) — 'those slavophiles of the populist species' as Stravinsky called them. The fact that their 'national style' was, as Stravinsky said, ready-made and imposed from above meant that it did not belong to the real tradition and could not develop properly, but was soon to founder in academicism; and indeed only Mussorgsky experienced this come-down as a tragedy, and he did not survive it. His own masterpiece, *Boris Godunov*, was to suffer at the hands of the academics, who 'corrected' the so-called clumsiness of his writing under cover of restoring the work to its 'true glory', Rimsky's version being followed by the even more deplorable intervention of Shostakovich.

It was not the crumbs of nationalist and 'folkish' doctrine that the young Stravinsky wanted to pick up from his master Rimsky. What he wanted, and received, was precisely an academic training in the best Western European techniques of musical composition. Stravinsky as a young man naturally deferred to Rimsky, conforming to the hierarchical traditions of Russian Society (with respectful letters, hand-kissing and the like), and Rimsky's authority over his pupil may well have affected the aesthetic presuppositions and the 'colour' of his earliest compositions. We can see this in *Firebird*, where he shows an incredible mastery in his handling of the highly-coloured style of *Le Coq d'or* and *Scheherazade*. There are even reminiscences of this spectacular display of colour in the *Sacre*; but that was its last appearance and it was only after this that Stravinsky's real Russianness found full expression in the deepest roots and features of his musical language. A radical diatonic character, a powerful and varied rhythmic scansion, a firmly-drawn melodic line, clear, bitter harmonies, an assertive brilliance in tone: a 'stripped' style in fact, transparent in texture and with a solid bone-structure — these are the fundamental constants of Russian music, to which should be added an inherited tendency to the hieratic. And these are, in fact, the basic characteristics of Stravinsky's music, which were to remain unchanged even in his serial works. They might be called the composer's 'passport', granting him freedom to cross frontiers, continents, nationalities, styles and epochs. This is the first key to the unity of his whole output.

If Boris de Schloezer was right in saying that the *Sacre* was 'not a beginning but an end, a finality' leaving no trace in the composer's subsequent works, *Les Noces* is an inaugural work in which the definitive characteristics of Stravinsky's aesthetic are already taking shape. It is not simply a matter of the general traits of a language enumerated above: we also find in *Les Noces* the actual foundations of a poetical world and, with that, a new key to the unity of Stravinsky's work.

After the *Sacre*, *Les Noces* represents an almost complete break (though that break had been prefigured in *Petrushka*). Instead of the extravagant musical spectacle there is the hieratic ikon; instead of the splendour and fascination of the orchestra, the asceticism of a rigorously functional ensemble of players, while the bare proceedings of a ritual replace the developments of what was — however well controlled and organized — in fact musical expressionism. But through this drastic reduction, both of quality and quantity, Stravinsky reveals a fundamental attitude to music: for him it belongs to the realm of the *sacral*.

'In his chief works this ritual element replaces the lyrical and the purely entertaining such as we find them in the works of so many other composers. He is probably the only twentieth-century composer in whose music this sacral element is a determining factor. Whether the subject be sacred or profane, Stravinsky's music is always in a profoundly inward and mysterious way the celebration of a sacral rite,' as Pierre Souvtchinsky writes.[5] In the *Sacre* this quality still appears diffuse, sensuous, enveloped in 'a magic resonance', overflowing with sumptuous Bacchanalian poeticism, and masked by a romantically tinged subjectivity. But in *Les Noces* it is overwhelmingly clear, and so it was to remain in the *Symphonies of Wind Instruments*, in *Oedipus Rex* and the *Symphony of Psalms*, right up to the *Mass* and the last serial works, *Threni* and *Requiem Canticles*.

Such an attitude implies a *distancing* of the object, and this will later be achieved by the composer making use of already existing formal and stylistic schemes as mediating networks, interchangeable perhaps but none the less experienced as essential. From this point onward Stravinsky was to banish from his music all deliberate attempts to 'signify' and all imitative imagery: 'non-expressiveness' and 'objectivity' were common, approximate attempts to describe this aesthetic attitude. 'Feeling' is now crystallized in a codified language and in the hieratic symbols of a musical convention in which the individual is transcended, whatever the origin, the grammar, and the technique of a work, and regardless of whether its subject be sacred or profane. And here, I believe, is to be found the second key to the unity of Stravinsky's work: ritual order.

*

The major works following *Les Noces* spring from the same basic attitude, but they belong quite specially to another common denominator of Stravinsky's musical aesthetics, namely the archetype. In these works subject-matter and occasional pretext are transcended, while subjective musical characteristics are reduced to purely structural lines of force, and the works themselves achieve universality through the medium of a convention imposed on both their language and their form.

Renard and *The Soldier's Tale* are the first works in this field and they were succeeded during the following decades by *Apollo Musagetes* and *Agon*, *Mavra* and *The Rake's Progress*, *Oedipus Rex* and *Canticum Sacrum*.

This is true for instance of *Renard*, in which the convention used by Stravinsky — that of the popular story-teller in mediaeval Russia — was totally fantastic because forever lost. But it allowed Stravinsky to make of *Renard* not so much *a* story as *the* archetypal story. In the same way Stravinsky used a more recent and more familiar convention, that of the *opéra bourgeois*, for *Mavra*, an archetypal opéra-bouffe of the 1830s in Russia, guaranteed (as it were) by the explicit patronage of Pushkin and Tchaikovsky. After reinventing village folk-lore in *Les Noces* and dreaming up the cult of mediaeval Russian 'troubadours' in *Renard*, Stravinsky revived in *Mavra* the Italian-style airs and romances sung in the streets and the salons of Moscow and Saint Petersburg. Similarly, *Apollo Musagetes* does not directly introduce an ancient Greek theme in contemporary musical dress, but transposes it through the rhythmic and other stylistic conventions of the French seventeenth century, using the alexandrine for structural purposes and iambics for the basic material. Thus the work is no longer a ballet based on an ancient Greek theme but the very archetype of the mythological ballet of the Grand Siècle. So too with *Oedipus Rex*, which the composer himself called *an archetypal drama*, with its carefully compartmentalized formal prototypes, airs, duets and ensembles, its frozen rhythms, its fossilized action, its impersonal masks and its Latin text. We shall be returning to all these works, which form the links in a single unbroken chain of concepts. Apart from their different languages, styles and conventions, each suited to its individual case, these archetypes provide us with another constant, a further key to the unity of Stravinsky's work and the musical vision from which it derived.

*

If the ethnic, ritual and archetypal criteria in Stravinsky's work can be established quite apart from the categories of form, subject and technique, how are we to approach the stylistic metamorphoses, the linguistic mutations in that work? Those mutations are very real and we must question them, and indeed question ourselves, as to their nature and extent, attempting to establish a more sophisticated typology than the crude categories of 'neo-classical' or 'serial' into which they are often facilely divided. We must also ask ourselves why, at bottom, these mutations occur.

There are not many of Stravinsky's works that are not, in one way or another, related to the universal *corpus* of music. The diversity of origin, epoch and style with which these works are allied is quite as striking as the originality of their conception and vocabulary. As we have seen, *Firebird*, the *Sacre* and *Renard* all belong to an imaginary Russia in which the oriental alternates with pre-history or the Middle Ages; and in the same way *Mavra* belongs to a vanished *bourgeois* Russia in which Glinka's Italianate style combines with Tchaikovsky's romanticism and the gypsy-songs of the streets. If *Pulcinella* is a brilliant stylistic exercise based on borrowed textual material — in fact much more than that — (and thus forms an exception in the stylistic typology of Stravinsky's works) *Oedipus Rex* is related, formally, to the secular oratorio as developed by Handel, and melodically to Italian *bel canto*. *Apollo Musagetes* is generally said to be an evocation of Lully, but its rhythms stem from Racine. *Persephone* is stylistically a hybrid, but one in which it is not difficult to find references to French music, whether it be Debussy, Ravel or Dukas. *Le Baiser de la fée* is quite openly — even textually — a homage to Tchaikovsky, whereas Rossini might be said to stand godfather to *Jeu de cartes*. The *Symphony of Psalms* and the *Mass* are related, though more in spirit than in letter, to both the Renaissance and to Ars Nova, *Ebony Concerto* to jazz, while *Dumbarton Oaks* is strictly modelled on a Brandenburg concerto. *The Rake's Progress* returns to *Così fan tutte*, while in *Agon* we find the most wonderfully stereotyped tonal cadences (particularly in the 'Fanfare' and the long cadences of the 'Interludes') side by side with serial structures, all in a single work. This list is enough to show the speed and the appetite with which Stravinsky criss-crossed the whole of musical history, from the Middle Ages to the present day, abolishing the notion of history as chronology at a single stroke. He was determined to make the whole of history his own, to use it for whatever attracted or inspired him at that moment, whatever the occasion or circumstance, and to use it to create a new work by Stravinsky. But at what level and to what degree is Stravinsky himself effectively present in all these works?

In Stravinsky's works there are, it appears, different kinds of relationships to history and historical forms. In some of them, cultural elements — possibly of his own invention — occur as primary material, which is then freely exploited by the composer's imagination. Instances of this are the *Sacre*, *Les Noces*, *The Soldier's Tale*, *Symphony of Psalms* and the *Mass*. In other works Stravinsky recreates a tradition — and recreates himself within that tradition — basing his music on models, either real or imaginary, which his language adapts, stylizes, updates, or transforms as in *Apollo Musagetes*, *Mavra*, *Oedipus Rex*, *Persephone* and *Canticum Sacrum*. There is also still another type of procedure, quite distinct from those, in which the composer allows his model such a pre-eminent role, such significance and such an overwhelming presence that the two functions are inverted, the model itself shaping, subverting and dictating the idiom of the piece. Notable instances of this are *Dumbarton Oaks*, the *Concerto in D*, the *Violin Concerto*, the *Symphony in C* and to some extent *The Rake's Progress*. These, I think, are the only instances in which it is legitimate to call Stravinsky's an art 'at the second degree', or 'Alexandrine' and to speak of a partial, temporary inhibition of his creative powers. The personal factor will always enter into such judgments, and there are certainly people who admire the *Symphony in C* but reject many others of these works. If such works may appear, generally speaking, unconvincing or even pale, we should remember that historically the 'second rate' among the productions of great composers is a very variable rate indeed — and only composers who have never written 'second-rate' work (all of them did, though not perhaps Mozart — the sole exception ?) should cast the first stone at Stravinsky! It is also a remarkable fact that, although there is in general very little connection between the biographical facts of a composer's life and his work, these 'Alexandrine' pieces do roughly coincide with the exiles, wars and upheavals through which Stravinsky lived. Thus the works that followed the First World War — *Pulcinella* and *Mavra* — distantly anticipate the mood of the *Symphony in C* and *Four Norwegian Moods* that belong to the Second World War. With his usual penetration Stravinsky showed himself aware of this when, observing that at the end of the war the neo-classic schools 'had come to a dead end'; but he took good care to include Schoenberg in the picture.

Having suggested the major outlines of this controversial problem, we can now examine the causes and the aesthetic motivation of Stravinsky's stylistic wanderings.

Chronicle of my Life, unquestionably Stravinsky's most authentic piece of writing, strikes the reader by the confidence which it reveals in a supra-individual formal *order*.

The need for restriction, for deliberately submitting to a style, has its source in the very depths of our nature, and has a bearing not only in matters of art, but in every conscious manifestation of human activity. It is the need for order without which nothing can be

achieved, and upon the disappearance of which everything disinteg-
rates. Now all order demands restraint. But one would be wrong to
regard that as any impediment to liberty. On the contrary, 'style',
restraint, contributes to its development, and only prevents liberty
from degenerating into licence. At the same time, in borrowing a
form already established and consecrated, the creative artist is not in
the least restricting the manifestation of his personality. On the
contrary, it is more detached and stands out better when it moves
within the definite limits of a convention.

This refers to *Oedipus Rex*, but it has a much wider application and
may be said to underlie all Stravinsky's thinking about music, in which
it appears as an unceasing search and a kind of dogma.

What did he in fact mean by 'order' and 'constraint'? He was clearly
not speaking of any arbitrary order, any 'discipline for the sake of
discipline', but of a demand that is as much ethical as aesthetic — for a
style in the collective sense: 'something common to a number of people,
something by which a work belongs to a definite epoch and a definite
country and may even achieve a universal signficance' (Schloezer).
According to Stravinsky it is only by rising above 'the anarchy of
individualism', and by means of a style, that an artist can achieve
'universality in the spiritual order', join his voice to the world-concert
and contribute to its harmony.

It happened that the age in which Stravinsky lived a great part of his
life as an artist — the years between the two world wars — was the
opposite of a stylistic age to which his work could belong. Beethoven
had already destroyed the old stylistic certainties and questioned every
aspect of the musical language that he had inherited. He opened the
way to Romanticism which celebrated the coming of liberty, the
individual and the primacy of the subjective; but also — like an
infinitely sad lament — the loss of a commonly shared language, and
mourning for a lost paradise which romantic artists would try to
recover in the legends of the Middle Ages. Expressionism was
Romanticism's final convulsion and it translated that solitude into
Munch's terrified, frozen scream (the subject of a picture); likewise into
Nolde's tragically grimacing figures and the nightmare music of
Erwartung. Already the tonal foundations of the musical language of this
anguished, tottering world were foundering, but such a world was soon
to discover the unconscious forces by which it was impelled — 'the
plague', as Freud ironically called it. This was the hour before the dawn
of a new era in human consciousness as well as in music, and there was
no longer any common language of expression. Where, at this critical

time, was Stravinsky to find that universality, that supra-individual order that he already sensed as essential to his creating — where but in the forms of the past? 'If an artist is born', as Schloezer says, 'in an exaggeratedly individualistic age in which anyone who wishes to prove his worth is forced to exaggerate his own individuality and violently decry other artists, then only one course is open to him, and that is to revive the forms of the past.' Stravinsky was to spend thirty years of his life in such a situation and was to defend his position, as though it were an ecclesiastical dogma, with such obsessional fidelity that he inspired — or perhaps we should say 'authorized' by his signature — some pages in his *Poetics of Music* so peremptory in tone and so conservative in attitude that they could have been written by Vincent d'Indy. This dogma was to prove the rallying-cry of a host of followers, or epigones, who did not share Stravinsky's deep spiritual need as a creative artist but found in the past a refuge for their inability to cope with the storms that were shaking the musical world of their day. Stravinsky was 'adopted' by them . . . just long enough for him to escape from their clutches and leave them in complete disorder.

For at the age of seventy he was able at last to discover a *contemporary* answer to this indefatigable quest for a style, without prejudice to his effective liberty in relation to history or to his concern with the continuity of tradition. It was to prove a new source of life to his genius, but he was to remain his own master, a solitary figure. Are we to imagine a Stravinsky 'converted' to the idea of historical progress? No; now, more than ten years after his death, we can see that it was not he who went, cap in hand, to history, but history who came to him: that he did not question history — he addressed it.

*

Schoenberg himself regarded the twelve-tone row, which made its first official appearance in the Waltz of his opus 23 (1923), as an instrument of power — 'I have made a discovery which will assure the preponderance of German music for a hundred years'. To the rest of the world, however, and to Stravinsky, this seemed an essentially 'individualistic' act and intolerable. It was not until Webern — whom Stravinsky was later to call 'that cutter of dazzling diamonds' — gave Schoenberg's almost mystical doctrine a much wider bearing, both conceptual and technical, that serialism could form the basis of the common musical language that our century had hitherto so painfully lacked. Since just after the Second World War, it had developed, evolved, and changed, won victories, had obsessions. But although the majority of composers are today questioning its validity, it is impossible to deny that, by the part which it played in the creative work of at least two generations, serialism acquired the supra-personal, universal character of a *style*. That Stravinsky, at seventy, should have recognized in serialism the *modern* answer to his lifelong quest is a measure both of the depth, the persistence and the demanding nature of his stylistic need and of the lucidity and youthfulness of his mind. This linguistic turning-point of the early 1950s, when he initiated the style he was to continue until his death, appears to us today as a natural and logical one. Was it in fact a turning-point or a clean break, a recognition of his aspirations, or a 'conversion'? In changing his style, did Stravinsky deny his own past (and thus encourage us to deny it ourselves)? And did he, in so doing, relax his grasp on the continuity of musical history? And, finally, was Stravinsky in adopting serialism prompted by the same reasons as the composers of the Second Viennese School, reasons that have so importantly evolved in the minds of today's younger generation?

Serialism gains its definition from three fundamental criteria corresponding to the three main phases in its evolution:

1. as a system negating an earlier order regarded as obsolete (tonality), a system in which the positive rules and the formal proscriptions are aimed at excluding privilege or tonal reminiscence of any kind;
2. as the promulgation of a new general grammar based on total chromaticism (in the first place of pitch, and later of durations, intensities etc.);
3. as a new philosophy of music (and not a 'philosophy of new music') based on concepts and working-principles of discontinuity, relativity and plurality.

The theorists of serialism, as so defined, are no longer Leibowitz or Adorno, but the composers themselves — most notably Boulez for relativity and syntactic categorization and Stockhausen for the plurality-in-unity of a new musical continuum. To these two names should be added that of Henri Pousseur, for his expansion of a serial way of thinking into a wide range of particular categories.[6]

Of the original postulates of serialism Stravinsky may be said to have retained *none* — certainly not the negation of the old tonal order, which he regarded as still perfectly valid and to deny which would have been to deny himself. Nor the grammatical postulate based on serial doctrine, for although Stravinsky's musical grammar might be called serial in his last works, it was almost always personal, *varying* from one work to the next, always tending to preserve a markedly diatonic character and observing no proscriptions with regard to repetition or octave doubling, for instance. To any serial *Weltanschauung*, properly speaking — such as younger composers have developed from the consideration of the intimate nature and the implications of their language — Stravinsky remained resolutely opposed, loudly and clearly proclaiming both in his music and in his writings his continued belief in the principles of fixity, polarity and gravitation, of tension and relaxation, which he regarded as fundamental. At the same time he admitted in theory, and demonstrated brilliantly in practice, the co-existence in a single work (in both *Canticum Sacrum* and *Agon*) of two reputedly irreconcilable worlds, the tonal and the serial.

What, then, did Stravinsky see in serialism if he rejected its original hallmarks? A new field of operations, and one particularly well-suited to realizing his own long-standing ideas about style and aesthetics in general, a field that had its own internal order and coherence yet was wide open to speculative possibilities — and finally a network of conditions that invited the elaboration of new *conventions*, both stricter and more up-to-date, if not much more inventive, than those that controlled the *Concerto in D*. We shall be returning to the exterior circumstances, mostly biographical in nature, that brought about this ultimate act of appropriation which enabled Stravinsky to give the works that he wrote after 1952 an unquestionably greater strength and power of conviction 'of the first degree' than anything that he wrote in the 1940s. But, it must be said, not for the sake of a more, or less, orthodox serialism, but because of the possibilities Stravinsky discovered in it that he could adapt to his own purposes. In other words, it was not a case of Stravinsky 'surrendering to serialism' but of his transforming and bending serialism to his own unwavering purpose. And this is a case unique in the history of modern music.

By this single act Stravinsky disconcerted his old epigones by turning his back on them and escaping at the very last moment from being their trustee, while at the same time baffling those of the younger generation who were hostile to his music, by stealing their own arguments. At seventy he could once again afford the luxury of not conforming to his commonly accepted image. But in doing this he was only showing himself more faithful than ever to his stylistic demands.

Here, then, I believe, is the final key to his whole work, the revelation of his unity as a man and the continuity of his career as an artist. When we listen to *Canticum Sacrum* and *Oedipus Rex*, *Les Noces* and *Threni*, *Symphonies of Wind Instruments* and *Requiem Canticles*, it is the conceptual similarities and symmetries of which our ears and our mind should be aware, not the contradictions and the 'breaks' between one manner and another. Despite different grammars and the framework of different, equally strict stylistic conventions, the same ritual ordering of the musical discourse both in the sacred cantata for St Mark and the secular oratorio *Oedipus Rex* celebrates, with the same majesty and 'distancing', in one case the Logos and in the other an immemorial myth. The evangelist and the ancient poet share the same ritual Latin, a language that is both dead and alive. The same is true of *Les Noces* and of *Threni*, both based on a ritual, one belonging to peasant tradition and the other to liturgy. Beyond their differences in syntax — diatonic modal scales in the one and twelve-tone series in the other case — the two works share the repudiation of all expressive gesture and all musical mimicry. Both refuse to interpret or describe: they *demonstrate*. The text of *Les Noces* belongs to oral tradition, that of *Threni* to the Old Testament, but they have a common denominator in ritual (and, as we shall see, almost the same vocal accents and inflections are found in both).

As regards formal organization, both works are characterized by hieratic rhythmic scansions, by closed structures that succeed each other without links, and by harsh antiphonal alternations between solo and choral passages. And as regards style, they share the same aspiration to the supra-individual and the same 'distancing' of the object — whether it be life or death — the music finding support, and then freedom, by virtue of powerful mediating clauses.

Freedom — not only for the composer but *of the work itself*. Stravinsky's music is firmly founded on its ritual, stylistic and archetypal contracts and the hieratic emblems of expression which answer for the wraith of any obligatory 'meaning'; and it is thus freed from the necessity of *being anything more than itself*. This is doubtless what the composer meant when he wrote that all-too-famous sentence in *Chronicle of my Life* — 'Music is by its very essence incapable of expressing anything' — a sentence which has aroused such a mountain of comment that the composer regretted ever having spoken or written anything about his art.

By an apparent paradox it is this strict codification of style, forms and symbols, reduced to petrified 'signs' or even to stereotypes which, in fact, restores to music not only its liberty but its true identity, so that it becomes its own property and not that of the 'speaker'. It may surely then be said also to restore to those who understand it a very intimate and precious share of liberty.

Language, as Roland Barthes observes in his admirable *Leçon*,[7] is power, the subduing of one human being by another 'by the authority of statement and the gregarious nature of repetition'. If this is the case, we may surely conclude that in no other music are these demons governing human expression so well dominated or avoided as in Stravinsky's. We are of course the prey, and doubtless the fascinated, willing prey of these immortal and authoritative masterpieces which — from the days of victorious Romanticism till our own — have been telling us, beyond all possible questioning, what we are and what we should be. To quote Barthes again, liberty is 'not only the ability to remove oneself from the power of another, but also — indeed primarily — the ability not to subject anyone else'.

Only a narrow line divides the creative liberty of the speaker from that of the listener. Only two other twentieth-century composers beside Stravinsky have been able to exorcize the spirit of tyrannical rhetoric from their music: Debussy and Webern. 'Everything in Debussy', says André Souris,[8] 'happens as though the substance of music were self-continuing, both the agent and the product of its own power of connection (liaison), as though nothing external interfered with its mode of being'. In this way music is restored to itself and goes beyond 'assertion', or what Barthes calls the libido dominandi, the passion to dominate. It belongs to the moment and its time is a pure, self-engendering spring, only distinguishable by its flow and, as Boulez says, 'irreversible'.

As for Webern, he worked on the borderlines of silence and on the fringes of a language liberated as much from the weight of its spiritual as of its tonal load. And there, perhaps in the last resort, is where he and Stravinsky join hands. Like Webern, but by a radically different way — by imprisoning the load of assertion within strict formal convention and hieratic emblems — Stravinsky contrived to exorcize the spirit of domination from the language of music, to guarantee its liberty and our own, to disencumber both it and us, to assure us living-space: and to subject nobody. And it may be that it was to this very secret quest that Stravinsky sacrificed the Sacre, the solitary masterpiece that had no progeny.

Webern's silence corresponds to Stravinsky's ritual scansions: two composers of 'sacred' music, obverse and reverse of a single medal and both called to restore music to itself. For their search was identical — Webern pursuing his own path, revealing to music a new space and a new time and giving a single rest the character of eternity; and Stravinsky conceiving his whole work as belonging to the millennium of a perpetual present. Through and beyond this time and this space, past and present, Stravinsky's music stands in its sovereign unity, indefatigably writing and rewriting the very sign, the ideogram: music.

II

Apprenticeship

IGOR FYODOROVICH STRAVINSKY was born on 5 (17) June* 1882 at Oranienbaum, on the Gulf of Finland, where his parents were spending their holidays. They lived in St Petersburg at no. 66 Kryukov Canal, where the composer spent the whole of his youth. His solemn baptism — by total immersion according to the Orthodox rite — took place on 29 June (Old Style)* in the cathedral of Saint Nicholas.

The name Stravinsky comes from that of a small river in Eastern Poland, the Strava, and the family name was originally Soulima-Stravinsky, the Soulima being another river, a tributary of the Vistula. The composer was to give the name of Soulima to his second son. The Soulima-Stravinskys who owned land in this part of Poland dropped the first half of their name when they settled in Russia during the reign of Catherine the Great.

On his mother's side, the composer's great-grandfather, Roman Fourman, was also an ancestor of Diaghilev, who was thus a distant cousin. He enjoyed the title of 'Excellency', though it is not known what his exact functions may have been. His daughter had married Kiril Kholovodsky, a Ukrainian born at Kiev, who became Minister of Agriculture and a member of the Tsar's Council of Thirty. He died of tuberculosis, which was to cause the death of many members of his family including the composer's first wife, her mother, and his eldest daughter. His younger daughter, Milena, and her daughter, as well as the composer himself were all affected by the disease and obliged to spend long periods in sanatoria.

On his father's side, the composer's grandfather, Ignaty Stravinsky, was a Polish Catholic who remained even in advanced old age a great 'ladies' man', thereby causing considerable embarrassment to his son Fyodor. He had married in 1834 Alexandra Ivanovna Skorokhodova, a Russian and Orthodox, and their son Fyodor Ignatievich, born at Chernigov in 1843, was baptized in the Orthodox faith according to the law concerning the children of mixed marriages. Orthodoxy was

*The Julian and Gregorian calendars differed by 12 days up to 1900 and after that by 13. Stravinsky celebrated his birthday on 18 June. The Gregorian calendar was adopted in the USSR after the revolution.

therefore the composer's religion, although he was not a seriously practising believer until he was over forty. Despite composing music for the Catholic rite, he never abandoned his allegiance to the Orthodox Church.

Fyodor Ignatievich Stravinsky was originally destined for a career in the civil service, which, quite apart from its innumerable and sometimes purely nominal powers, was something to which all middle-class families of the day aspired to belong. He therefore embarked on the study of law, as was usual in such cases, when he left the lycée. When, however, it was observed that he had a good bass voice and a 'good ear', he left the university and went in 1869 to the St Petersburg Conservatoire, where he studied singing with the famous Everardi. He completed his musical studies, with brilliant success, after three years, and an engagement at the Kiev Opera was soon followed by a début at the Mariinsky Theatre, St Petersburg on 30 April 1876 in the role of Mephistopheles. He was the first Stravinsky to become a musician. It was during the time he spent in Kiev that he met and married Anna Kirilovna Kholovodsky, the small and rather pretty daughter of the Kiril Grigorevich who had been a member of the Council of Thirty. The children of the marriage were Roman (born in 1874), Yuri (1879), Igor (1882) and Guri (1884).

Fyodor Stravinsky's brilliant career lasted a quarter of a century, and he owed his success not only to the quality of his voice but to his talent as an actor. He sang sixty-six roles all told, which ranged from Leporello to the bass-roles in the works of Verdi and Wagner; his performances in *Boris Godunov* seem to have been particularly admired. He received the order of St Stanislas in 1891 and the renewing of his contract with the Imperial Opera assured him of a constantly rising income.

As a father Fyodor Stravinsky was strict and lacking in warmth. 'The only tenderness he ever showed me was when I was ill,' the composer observed in *Memories and Commentaries*, where he recalls his father's authoritarian manner and his outbursts of uncontrolled temper. 'His death drew us much closer together,' he says sarcastically. His relationship with his elder brothers was equally chilly; he had nothing in common with them and no real affection for them: 'They bored me.' Roman, who studied law, died at the age of twenty-one in 1895, and Yuri, who became an engineer, lost all contact with his musician brother after the revolution and disappeared just before the siege of Leningrad, in 1941. For Guri, on the other hand, Igor had a great affection. Guri was a shrewd and sensitive character, musically gifted and the possessor of a very fine baritone voice, which would certainly have enabled him to make a career as a singer, had he not died in 1917 of scarlet fever which he caught while he was working as a Red Cross auxiliary in Romania.

Igor had no more than a 'dutiful feeling' for his mother, by whom he felt rejected; Anna Stravinsky's relationship with her children was severe and rigid rather than affectionate. It was only after her husband's death that 'she behaved slightly less selfishly and the pleasure she took in torturing me seemed slightly less intense', as the composer wrote in his seventies. All his filial feelings seem to have been transferred to his German governess Bertha ('Bertushka') Essert, who spoke hardly any Russian, so that German, being the language of the nursery, became a second mother-tongue to the composer. I mention this paradoxical fact in view of Stravinsky's aversion to German composers (including Beethoven) that he showed to varying degrees until well advanced in age. Bertha was to have a place in his family for forty years and to bring up his own children until her death at Morges in 1917. 'I wept more tears for her than I was later to weep for my mother.' The nursery, which he shared with Guri and seldom left, was far removed, not only topographically, from Fyodor Stravinsky's studio; only faint echoes from it can have reached the child. Igor's first musical impressions came from the country and its peasants — as we learn from the first page of *Chronicle of my Life*, where the composer tells the story of the dumb peasant who produced a 'suspicious rhythmic sound' with his hand in his armpit, accompanying a song of two repeated notes. Stravinsky also remembers that unforgettable song, a song in octaves or in unison, sung by the village women returning from work and how it reminded him of bees' humming. 'That was the first time that I was aware of myself as a musician,' he wrote in 1935, in *Chronicle*. These words reveal the strength and persistence of those early impressions, though not perhaps the beginning of a real awareness which was to develop only slowly and with difficulty. Like Schumann, Stravinsky at the age of seventeen was more interested in painting and the theatre than in music, though he was already dissatisfied with anything less than perfection. 'I have made a sketch of a sunset,' he tells us, 'and now would like to have the opportunity to see a number of good pictures, so that I can become even more dissatisfied with my own work. Only in such circumstances can I be certain of making progress.'[1]

His childhood summers were spent first at Pechisky, in the Western Ukraine, where his mother's sister Catherine had an estate; but the boy liked neither the place nor his strict, authoritarian aunt. It was there, however, that he met his cousin Catherine Nossenko — daughter of his mother's eldest sister — who was later to become his wife. In about 1890 Catherine's father, Dr Gabriel Nossenko, bought a distillery and a large property at Ustilug in Volhynia, close to the Polish frontier. The house stood among woods, rivers and fields and the climate was declared good for Igor's fragile health. From 1896 onwards he and Guri spent their summers there, the elder brothers preferring Pechisky (where Roman in fact died in 1895). Igor became at once so deeply attached to the Ustilug countryside that soon after his marriage, in 1906, he built a house there himself, 'The Old Farm'.

It is hard to say whether his father's brilliant musical career helped the development of his son's gifts. He was a remote, almost mythical figure to his children, and it may well be that this retarded rather than hastened Igor's awakening to music. When at the age of nine he started piano lessons, it was for conventional reasons rather than with any idea of a future career. In any case he seemed as a child to show no particular bent for music beyond a taste for getting to know it, both by listening and sight-reading. His first teacher was the daughter of a violinist from the Mariinsky Theatre called Snietkov and she was followed by a pupil of Anton Rubinstein called Khashperov, a woman with a great reputation as a teacher.

With her the young Igor studied the classical and romantic repertory, except for the works of Chopin for which she had no use. Her teaching method was strict and she seems, like most piano-teachers of the day, to have aimed primarily at achieving a polished performance. It is an interesting fact that she firmly forbade the use of the pedal, and the composer was later to wonder humorously whether this accounted for the *secco* style of the *Concerto for Piano and Wind*. Under this teacher Stravinsky progressed far enough to perform Mendelssohn's G minor concerto and to distinguish himself sight-reading Rimsky-Korsakov's operas. Improvising, which he began to enjoy, was considered suspect. 'I was often accused of wasting my time instead of devoting it to proper practising.' Stravinsky was always evasive about the harmony lessons with Fyodor Akimenko and the counterpoint lessons with Vassily Kalfaty that he had at this time. Harmony he found desperately dull, in any case, but not counterpoint at which he worked hard on his own, with a textbook to help him.

Until he was fifteen Stravinsky attended the no. 2 gymnasium of Saint Petersburg, and after that, the privately-run Lycée Gurevich. He wore the standard school uniform and regularly missed the early tram (the lycée was thirteen kilometres away from his home) thus involving himself in a considerable expenditure of cab-fares — but the cab journey was so pleasant! Already we can see two deeply-rooted traits

that were never to change — a certain taste for luxury and an extreme
carefulness with money — which was later to become a marked avarice.
This is how he described the journey to Ustilug to his parents when he
was nineteen: 'With all my care and economy . . . the journey cost 26
roubles 45 kopecks; ticket: 8.70; baggage: 1.30, journey by horse: 5
roubles and 70 kopecks (and 20 kopecks for tea), transport of basket
from Kovel to Ustilug: 4 roubles and 50 kopecks (and this was by
private arrangement) . . . . Now the minor expenses: porter 1 rouble
and 60 kopecks; and refreshment at the station 1 rouble and 95
kopecks.'²

Meanwhile, however, his longing for music became more definite
and more urgent. With the key of his father's musical library in his
pocket, he was able to embark on an orgy of score-reading; but the first
great musical shock in his life was a performance at the Imperial Opera
of Glinka's *A Life for the Tsar*, which he already knew from the piano-
score, though it was the first opera he ever saw in the theatre. 'It was
then I heard an orchestra for the first time — and what an orchestra,
Glinka's!' This 'unforgettable' impression was clearly so strong that it
actually erased earlier impressions, for he had in fact already seen
Tchaikovsky's *Sleeping Beauty* at the Mariinsky, had heard an orchestra,
when he was seven or eight, and had declared himself 'enchanted'.

Stravinsky's first musical essays were prudent rather than ambi-
tious. At fifteen he made a piano transcription of a Glazunov quartet,
apparently the first occasion on which he committed music to paper
(1897). With all the candour and spontaneity of youth he showed this to
the composer. 'Although he knew my father, he did not receive me very
kindly and glanced carelessly at my manuscript which he declared
"unmusical", leaving me deeply discouraged.' Was it this experience
that quickly cooled the boy's admiration for symphonic form and for
Glazunov's 'solid style'? All his life Stravinsky was to express nothing
but hatred and contempt for Glazunov, largely provoked no doubt by
Glazunov's hostile and jealous attitude towards him.

The coldness and scepticism that Stravinsky encountered in his own
immediate family and the discouraging attitude of others were to some
degree compensated for by the warm welcome and musical interest of
one of his uncles whom he often visited. Alexander Yelachich's five
children were hostile, arrogant and sarcastic towards Igor and Guri,
who were a little older than them. But Yelachich himself was 'very
kind'. He introduced Igor to the works of Beethoven, and later to
Brahms, Bruckner and Wagner whose music they played in piano duet
transcriptions (all composers, of course, later to be violently rejected by
Stravinsky). The world that he met at the Yelachichs' consisted of civil

servants, well-off landowners, lawyers or magistrates who prided themselves on their liberal ideas, which were then fashionable. It was exactly the same world as that from which 'the Five' had sprung and Stravinsky describes these people with their so-called 'advanced opinions', in *Chronicle*, giving full rein to both his malice and his conservatism:

> The mentality is a familiar one — a perpetual carping at 'tyrannical' government, a compulsory atheism, a bold proclamation of the 'rights of man', a cult of materialistic science and, at the same time, an admiration for Tolstoi's amateurish version of Christianity. This mentality was accompanied by a special taste in the arts and it is not hard to imagine the music that aroused interest and enthusiasm in this circle. Naturalism was inevitably the order of the day, a naturalism carried to the pitch of realistic expression and including as a matter of course popular and national tendencies and the worship of folklore.

After finishing his secondary studies in 1901 Stravinsky enrolled as a student in the faculty of Law at the University of St Petersburg. His father was not sufficiently impressed by his attempts at composition to allow him to take up a musical career and insisted that he follow the same course as he himself had been obliged to take, with a view to obtaining 'a respectable position'. Although this decision was prompted entirely by social convention, it was not wholly unreasonable, Stravinsky at nineteen appearing as no more than an amateur. His theoretical grounding was weak and he had not attended the Conservatoire (had he even expressed a wish to do so?). His few compositions, such as the Glazunov transcription (now lost) and a number of *Andantes* for the piano, showed little originality. Yet despite this he was irresistibly attracted to music, and what had hitherto been a mental conflict now became a certainty to him. The constraint exercised by university life liberated his desire to create — a type of reaction which was often to recur throughout his life. In his constricting student's uniform Stravinsky recognized himself as a composer and acted on it. When his father died of cancer of the throat on 21 November 1902, he had already made up his mind. He even attempted to leave home, saying in a letter to his mother that 'life at no. 66 Kryukov Canal is impossible', but he relented when his mother fell ill a few days later.

Though he remained enrolled at the University for four years, it was with a total indifference. He put in no more than fifty appearances there in all that time. His whole life was now engrossed in music — working at counterpoint by himself and trying to compose, among other things,

a setting of Pushkin's 'Storm-cloud' and a piano *scherzo*, both dated
1902, which have been rediscovered and are now in the Leningrad
State Library. Thanks to a pass which his father had obtained for
him, he spent every evening at rehearsals at the Mariinsky Theatre,
and at concerts, where he heard the great pianists of the new century:
Hofmann, Eugène d'Albert, Sophie Menter, Reisenauer, Anna Les-
chetizky and, among violinists, Auer. The symphony concerts of the
Russian Imperial Music Society were conducted by Napravnik (who
lived in the same house as the Stravinskys) in programmes of the
classical repertory, with an occasional 'contemporary' work of the
second rank thrown in. Napravnik was to remain for Stravinsky the
perfect orchestral conductor — 'Absolute sureness of intention and
strictness in performance . . . a total contempt for any kind of affecta-
tion or exterior "effect" . . . not the smallest concession to the audience . . . a faultless ear and a faultless memory and, as a result,
performances of perfect clarity and objectivity', as he wrote in *Chronicle*. These were the qualities that the composer demanded of all his
performers. The only other institution competing for the attention of
the musical public of St Petersburg was that of the 'Russian Symphony Concerts' founded by the great musical patron and publisher
Mitrofan Belayev, who had 'his own' composers whom he
championed, publishing their works and arranging for their performance. Chief among these were Rimsky and Glazunov, and later
Lyadov, Tcherepnin and other Rimsky pupils — the heirs of 'the
Five', in fact. This group 'soon, and perhaps unconsciously,
developed a new academicism and gradually replaced at the Conservatoire the old academicians who had directed it since its foundation
by Anton Rubinstein'. (*Chronicle*)

   At this time Stravinsky was an admirer of both the music and the
'advanced' ideas of his elders and his contemporaries. 'With the feeble
means at my disposal', he wrote, 'I did my very best to imitate them in
my attempts at composition.' But his critical cast of mind soon broke
his allegiance to 'the Five'. He made a close friend of Ivan Pokrovsky,
eight years his senior, a great lover of music and the arts, with an
enquiring, cultivated mind and very much in touch with the new trends
in the West. Pokrovsky continued the liberation of the young
Stravinsky a stage further by introducing him to French music —
Gounod, Bizet, Delibes and Chabrier. 'I found in them', Stravinsky
wrote, 'a different type of musical writing, different harmonic methods,
different melodic conception, a fresher and freer feeling for form. This
gave rise to doubts, as yet hardly perceptible, with regard to what had
up till then seemed unassailable dogma.' (*Chronicle*)

His encounter with Rimsky, though decisive to his development, was not a revelation of 'new ideas' so much as of a discipline, freely and joyfully accepted thanks to the veneration in which he held the older composer, who was then the unquestioned master among Russian musicians. In him Stravinsky discovered a true father. He had met Rimsky's youngest son, Vladimir, at the university and it was Vladimir who brought about the meeting between the two, Stravinsky taking the first step. In the summer of 1902 he spent some time with his father and mother at Bad Wildungen, and it happened that Rimsky was spending the summer not very far away, at Heidelberg, where his son Andrei was a student at the university. Stravinsky went to Heidelberg on his own account to ask Rimsky's advice. 'I told him of my wish to become a composer and asked what I should do.'

Rimsky was not discouraging, but he was certainly not enthusiastic. Did he sense the reality of Stravinsky's vocation, which was still so uncertain and so unable to find expression? He refused to make any hasty judgment, asked to see more of the young man's work and spoke guardedly and indeed wisely. His advice was to continue studying harmony and counterpoint and not to go to the Conservatoire, where he considered the atmosphere unsuitable. Most important of all, he himself would accept Stravinsky as a private pupil as soon as he knew enough musical theory.

Rimsky's house was in future to be open to this young man who had just lost his father. On the same day every week Rimsky's pupils met there to play and discuss each other's work. But Gima — as he was affectionately called — did not make progress with his 'theoretical studies'. He admitted to being lazy, particularly in anything to do with harmony, and to preferring to read, go to concerts and meet new people — and to work at his solitary counterpoint. Free of strict parental discipline, he now made the discovery of the intellectual and artistic world of St Petersburg. Rimsky's own house was full of young people with varying intellectual interests — painters, writers and scholars — and among them Stepan Mitusov, who was to become a close friend and to write the libretto of *The Nightingale*. Despite his conservatism Rimsky was generous and tolerant in his attitude to these 'young folk' and indeed to 'new' music from the West, as his comment on Debussy showed — 'Better not to listen to Debussy,' he said, 'you might get used to it and end up by liking it.'

These were the years in which Diaghilev appeared on the scene with his avant-garde arts review, *Mir Iskusstva* (The World of Art), which was started in 1889 and brought together all the 'advanced' artists of St Petersburg. Diaghilev also organized a number of important exhibitions of modern art in the years between 1889 and 1903. At the same time three of Stravinsky's friends — Ivan Pokrovsky, A. P. Nurok and W. F. Nouvel — started the 'Evenings of Contemporary Music', which introduced the public to the works of Franck, Dukas, d'Indy, Debussy, Ravel, Strauss, Reger and the young Russian composers of the day. Stravinsky listened to this music, which was entirely new to him as it was to the Russian public, with great interest; but he was critical and guided by his personal tastes, which were never fundamentally to change. Franck's academicism and d'Indy's scholastic (and Wagnerian) mentality were immediately alien to him, while the strong modern note in Debussy struck a deeply sympathetic chord. The most surprising thing about this twenty-year-old, who was not markedly precocious, was his clear-sightedness and his ability to reconcile his tastes and his aims. 'It is not to be supposed that my sympathy for the new trends that I have just described were then strong enough to replace my adoration of the old masters.'

The first public performance of a work by Stravinsky took place in 1905, at one of the 'Evenings of Contemporary Music'. The work was the *Piano Sonata in F sharp minor*, which had already been performed privately, and no doubt 'passed', at Rimsky's, and the pianist was Nicholas Richter. This was in fact the first piece that Stravinsky had written since he started studying with Rimsky, who was at that moment nursing his asthma in the country, where he generously invited the young Igor to spend a fortnight. 'He set me to compose, under his watchful eye, the first movement of a *sonatina* after explaining the principles of a *sonata allegro*. His explanation was wonderfully clear, and I was immediately aware of his great qualities as a teacher. He told me the range and the register of the various instruments of the modern symphony orchestra and explained the first elements of the art of orchestration.' He was in fact to spend the next three years as Rimsky's pupil.

'Rimsky was a tall man, like Berg and Aldous Huxley and, like Huxley, he had weak sight, wearing blue-tinted spectacles, sometimes keeping an extra pair on his forehead, a habit of his I have caught.' (*Memories and Commentaries*) He was meticulous but patient, and combined great knowledge with great lucidity of mind. What in fact did he teach Stravinsky? Certainly instrumentation rather than composition and, *through instrumentation*, the analysis of classical forms. This is an important consideration, if we remember the indissoluble linking of sound-material and form in Stravinsky's mind. Of course the practical application of an organic interdependence of this kind cannot be 'learned', only cultivated. As Rimsky's pupil, he knew from the start what he must look for and what was uniquely his. Did he demand more than that? He was, for the time being, still under the spell of his master and the stylistic conventions of the day, which he was happy to follow. But he was to pass this generous instruction of Rimsky's as it were through a 'filter', retaining the older man's technique but not his aesthetic views. The early years of Stravinsky's career are astonishing for this sense of direction, tentative perhaps but amazingly certain of the aim in view, a gift for discovering — as though guided by radar — what is, or will later become, his own, exclusively personal truth.

Stravinsky spoke a lot about his studies with Rimsky, both in *Chronicle* and in *Memories and Commentaries*, the passages in the earlier (1935) book being clearly not only fresher, but more detailed and more personal than those in the later (1959).

> He adopted the plan of teaching form and orchestration side by side, because in his view the more highly developed musical forms found their fullest expression in the complexity of the orchestra. I worked with him in this way. He would give me some pages of the piano score of a new opera he had just finished, which I was to orchestrate. When I had orchestrated a section, he would show me his own instrumentation of the same passage . . . and I had to explain why my orchestration was different from his. (*Chronicle*)

Eighteen months later Stravinsky began the composition of a symphony which, though written under Rimsky's supervision, seems to have been very influenced not only by Rimsky but also by Glazunov ('robustness of form') and also by Tchaikovsky and . . . Brahms. It was finished in 1906–07 and dedicated to 'my dear master Nicholas Andreevich Rimsky-Korsakov'. The opening 'Allegro moderato' is an exercise in sonata form. The 'Scherzo' is a lively movement which includes a Russian popular song *pochissimo meno mosso* and the 'Finale' contains another, the counting-song 'Tchicher-yacher', which was to appear again, with text, as the third of the *Three Little Songs* (1913). Rimsky insisted on Stravinsky hearing his own work, and had it performed, with the cantata *Faun and Shepherdess* for mezzo soprano and orchestra, which was based on a Pushkin text. The cantata contains three songs — 'Shepherdess', 'Faun' and 'River', and it was accused of the suspect 'Debussyism'. At the performance arranged by Rimsky on 27 April 1907, and conducted by the Imperial Kapellmeister Wahrlich in general's uniform, Rimsky sat by his pupil's side and made comments: 'That is too heavy, you must be careful when you use trombones in the middle register.' 'The only unfavourable comment I received,' says Stravinsky, 'was from Glazunov, who came up to me after the performance and said: "Very pretty, very pretty."' (*Memories and Commentaries*).

Stravinsky's marriage to his cousin Catherine Nossenko took place on 11 (or 24) January 1906 at the village of Novaya Derevnia near St Petersburg. An imperial ukase forbade marriage between first cousins, and it was therefore necessary to find a priest who was not too fussy about family documents. The only people present were the bridegroom's witnesses, Andrei and Vladimir Rimsky-Korsakov. When they returned from the church, Rimsky was waiting for them on the steps and gave his pupil his blessing, holding over him an ikon which he then offered to him as a wedding-present.

The young couple settled first at 66 Kryukov Canal but moved after a year into their own apartment on the Angliisky Prospekt. Their eldest son, Theodore, was born in 1907 and Lyudmila in 1908. Every summer they went to Catherine's father at Ustilug, where they built their own house according to Stravinsky's plans. His big Bechstein was taken to Ustilug, which was to see the birth of many works marking his gradual discovery of his own musical personality. *Pastorale* (1907) was a wordless song for soprano and piano, followed by two *Songs* (1907–08) on texts by Gorodetzky, disapproved of by Rimsky who considered them 'decadent'. *Scherzo fantastique* and *Fireworks* were also written at Ustilug and it was these works that marked a decisive turning-point in Stravinsky's career.

Scherzo fantastique, or *Les Abeilles* (The Bees), was inspired by Maeterlinck's *La Vie des abeilles*, which Stravinsky and his wife read with delight in 1907. Oddly enough this was, in Stravinsky's mind, a piece of real 'programme music', though based of course on a purely musical idea that had occurred to him before he read Maeterlinck's book and was not in any way pictorial. A ballet based on this music, by the choreographer Leo Staats, was given at the Paris Opéra ten years later; it does no more than use this programmatic intention, which is defused by being visualized. Stravinsky forgot his original intention and would hear nothing of any 'story' being attached to the piece. 'A piece of bad literature was printed on the title-page of my score to please my publisher, who thought that a story of this kind would help the sale of the music.' Robert Craft's publishing of an envelope addressed to Stravinsky, with the following note in his hand, was extremely relevant[3] — 'Letter from M. Maeterlinck, and his ridiculous statements concerning the subject of *Les Abeilles*, a classical ballet without subject composed on the music of my *Scherzo fantastique*'. (Stravinsky's irritation was caused primarily by the fear of having to pay a royalty to Maeterlinck — a periodically recurring fear in relation to the composer's many stage works.) Stravinsky might have been feared lost, if only for the time taken to compose a single youthful work, in the wastes of that 'programme music' which he found so profoundly alien, but here we find him reacting violently. . . . Fifty years later he still found that the orchestration of this piece 'sounded', that the music itself was 'light' — and that although it might be slightly indebted to Rimsky's 'Flight of the Bumble Bee', the piece as a whole owed more 'to Mendelssohn via Tchaikovsky than to Rimsky'.

The manuscript had been rapidly read through and approved by Rimsky, but he never heard it performed. At the end of 1907 his health had begun to fail. On the occasion of Rimsky's daughter Nadezhda's engagement to the composer Maximilian Steinberg, Stravinsky told Rimsky of his intention to present them with an orchestral fantasy, *Fireworks*. He finished it in six weeks at Ustilug, but when he sent the score to his old master, the parcel was returned marked 'deceased'.

Both the pupil's natural respect for his master and the sense of hierarchy, so strongly developed in Russia, find expression in the way Stravinsky used to end his letters to Rimsky. 'I bow humbly and send you my heartfelt regards' . . . 'I embrace you in my thoughts, dear Nikolai Andreevich, and send my regards to your family'. 'Devoted and grateful until the grave'. [4] But beneath these deferential formulae we can feel Stravinsky's filial affection and profound gratitude. His grief at learning of Rimsky's death, which was unexpected despite his poor health, is a measure of the attachment that he felt to this real father. He broke off work on the orchestration of *Fireworks* to try to express that grief in a *Chant funèbre*. He was, in fact, to have great difficulty in getting this performed. It was only after numerous requests and much string-pulling that the first performance was given, under Felix Blumenfeld, in the big hall of the Conservatoire on 13 February 1909. Both score and parts were immediately lost and the work survived only in the composer's memory. 'It was a procession of all the solo instruments of the orchestra, each placing a wreath — in the form of a melody — on the composer's grave, against a deep background of tremolo murmurings simulating the vibrations of bass voices singing in chorus.' (*Chronicle*)

Fireworks was finished at Ustilug in 1908. Written for a large orchestra, with an important percussion part, it is both more tense rhythmically and altogether more original than *Scherzo fantastique*, which it matches in spectacular instrumentation. It is in fact a dazzling résumé of the young Stravinsky's stylistic and technical powers, a summing-up of his skill as a craftsman. Although slightly conventional the work remains even today a model of the way in which the resources of a large orchestra can be used in order to achieve a brilliant sonority and it still constitutes a 'test' of the quality of an orchestra, if not of a conductor. 'Something improvisatory and trivial, something irregular but also astonishingly confident removes any hint of the old master's academic prescriptions from this homage to Rimsky-Korsakov,' says André Schaeffner.[5] 'Except for some rippling flute passages the sound-picture of the piece is as uninterruptedly aggressive as a continuous volley.' The piece was given its first performance on 6 February 1909 in one of a series of concerts founded by Alexander Siloti — a great piano pupil of Liszt's, a great conductor and patron of music. These concerts, and those later organized by Koussevitzky, carried on the work begun by the 'Evenings of Contemporary Music', which in fact continued until 1911, though with reduced funds. The evening of 6 February 1909 was to be a decisive one for Stravinsky's future, for among the audience was a unique figure — Diaghilev.

III

With the 'Ballets russes'

DIAGHILEV WAS A man of altogether exceptional aims and ambitions, a *grand seigneur* in manner, physical appearance and dress, a passionate and jealous homosexual, a gambler always ready to take big risks, ludicrously superstitious, both generous and envious, capricious but obstinate, deeply cultured but anti-intellectual — and above all else gifted with a prophetic vision of the future of an artist or a work, an almost infallible instinct of their chances of success. His name is still linked with the modernity of the opening years of the twentieth century. 'He had a wonderful flair,' Stravinsky wrote, 'a marvellous faculty for seizing at a glance the novelty and freshness of an idea, surrendering himself to it without pausing to reason it out. I do not mean to imply that he was at all lacking in reasoning power. On the contrary, his reasoning powers were unerring, and he had a most rational mind; and though he frequently made mistakes or acted foolishly it was because he was carried away by passion and temperament, the two forces which were predominant in him.' (*Chronicle*)

His journal *Mir Iskusstva* was a landmark and formed a world of its own in the cultural life of Russia at the opening of the new century, and when it went bankrupt Diaghilev, though still spurred on by the passion for exhibiting and enchanting which was his own form of creation, felt that he had had enough of the intellectual and artistic circles of St Petersburg, with their sterile quarrels in which academicism was always in the end victorious. He therefore decided to conquer Paris. He began by organizing in 1906 an exhibition of Russian art at the Grand Palais, following this the next year with five concerts of Russian music at the Opéra, with Chaliapin, Rachmaninov and Nikisch. The year after (1908), he turned to opera and put on the first performance in France of *Boris Godunov* (in Rimsky's version) with Chaliapin in the title role and with magnificent sets brought from Russia. His efforts were crowned with success, and what first stirred only the curiosity of the Parisian public — hard to please but easy to sway — soon became 'the rage'. At the beginning of 1909 he turned to ballet, putting on *Les Sylphides* complete, Borodin's *Polovtsian Dances* and a composite piece entitled *Le Festin de Cléopâtre*. A number of the Chopin pieces for *Les Sylphides* were orchestrated by Glazunov, Lyadov and Tcherepnin; and Diaghilev, who had been impressed by the brilliant orchestration of the *Scherzo fantastique* and *Fireworks* at the Siloti Concerts, had no hesitation in commissioning the young Stravinsky to orchestrate the A flat major *Nocturne* and the E flat major *Valse brillante*, which form the finale of *Les Sylphides*. The work was quickly finished, and while Diaghilev and his company — led by Pavlova, Karsavina and Nijinsky — embarked on their triumphal journey to the Théâtre du Châtelet, Stravinsky retired quietly to his summer-quarters at Ustilug and continued working on *The Nightingale*. The libretto for this opera, based on a story by Hans Andersen, was by the composer's friend Stepan Mitusov, with a number of suggestions of Stravinsky's own. Shortly before his death Rimsky had seen and approved the first sketches.

Returning in triumph from Paris, Diaghilev feverishly set about preparing the new season of his young company, later to become the 'Compagnie des Ballets russes'. He meant to put on three more ballets, with choreography by Fokine: Schumann's *Carnaval*, Rimsky's *Scheherazade* and a new work based on the Russian legend of the Firebird. Liadov was sounded as a possible composer of the music but refused: he was a slow and meticulous worker and would need a year to finish such a task. Diaghilev therefore handed the commission to Stravinsky — and we can imagine the mixed feelings of delight and apprehension with which the twenty-seven-year-old composer received Diaghilev's telegram. Having once made up his mind to accept, Stravinsky withdrew with Andrei Rimsky-Korsakov to the family property of Lzy to plan the work. No sooner had he arrived than he set to work at full tilt. 'All that winter,' he says in *Chronicle*, 'I worked hard, and this meant being in continual contact with Diaghilev and his collaborators. Fokine worked on the choreography of each number as I sent them to him. I was always at the company's rehearsals and the day used to finish with Diaghilev, Nijinsky (who was not in fact dancing in this ballet) and me sitting down to a large dinner washed down with a good claret.'

From now on Stravinsky was present at all the gatherings of the 'general staff' of the 'Ballets russes': the first musician to join Fokine, the painters Bakst and Benois and the producer Grigoriev. Although still at the beginning of his career, he already made himself felt by his natural sense of the theatre as well as his general culture and his lively imagination. Benois, with whom Stravinsky felt in deep accord on artistic matters, leaves us in no doubt.

Apart from music, one of the links between us was Stravinsky's passion for the theatre and his interest in the plastic arts. Unlike most musicians, who are generally quite uninterested in anything except music, Stravinsky was deeply concerned with painting, architecture and sculpture. Although he had no expert knowledge in any of these, we always valued discussing them with him because he 'reacted' so strongly to everything that concerned us most deeply. In those days he was a charming and willing 'pupil', avid for precise information and always anxious to increase his own knowledge. But the most delightful thing about him was his undogmatic attitude.[1]

When Stravinsky arrived in Paris, at the end of May 1910, for the last rehearsals of *Firebird*, it was a triumph from the very beginning. There, on the huge stage of the Opéra, he had an overall view of the whole of Fokine's choreography, and although he had some reservations — finding Fokine's contrasting of feminine gentleness and masculine violence exaggerated — musically he felt confirmed in his ideas and absolutely sure of himself. 'Take a good look at him,' Diaghilev said. 'He is a man on the threshold of fame.'

Firebird had its first performance on 25 June 1910 at the Paris Opéra and was conducted — marvellously, according to Stravinsky himself — by Gabriel Pierné. Golovin was responsible for the sets and the costumes (except those of the Princess and the Firebird, which were designed by Léon Bakst). Karsavina danced the title role and the work received a fantastic ovation. The next morning Stravinsky was famous.

*

When Stravinsky made his appearance on the musical scene, there were three parties in Russian music, each with its own aesthetic. First the academic, or eclectic, party headed by Glazunov and the Conservatoire, and then that of 'the Five', characterized by a fairly conventional nationalism and a prudent 'modernism', influenced by Wagner among other composers. The third, which was closer to the first than to the second, but more authentic because it acknowledged its Russian roots and boasted of a specifically Russian kind of classicism, was Tchaikovsky's party — Tchaikovsky considered as the direct heir of Glinka *via* 'Europe', particularly Italy. In following Stravinsky's development it is useful to bear in mind this somewhat oversimplified alignment of tendencies, on all of which he was to draw for his own purposes, and all of whom he was to outstrip.

His youthful works obviously fall into the first category: they reveal an unrivalled talent for orchestration, if no outstanding artistic personality. With *Firebird* the picture suddenly changes: Stravinsky achieves his own power of expression and a style that was never again to

be nondescript, and he becomes fully aware of national affinities that
will be further explored and defined. *Firebird* itself belongs, of course, to
the second stylistic category — that of the inheritance of 'the Five', but
only for a brief moment in his career. In fact it was on Rimsky's death,
which left him alone and free, that Stravinsky seemed willing to
continue the style of his old master, giving it a maximum efficacy and
also enriching it with sonorities quite foreign to Rimsky: they echoed
Debussy most, though still to a limited degree and on the harmonic side
only. As we shall see, Stravinsky had no sooner assimilated his master's
style than he abandoned it, and the *Sacre*, where its last traces are to be
found, was in fact its death-blow.

Firebird began as an idea of Diaghilev's before Fokine provided it
with a plot, and Stravinsky made a masterpiece out of it. It is a happy
instance of a work developed by a team, at those very meetings of
Diaghilev's 'general staff' already mentioned. Stravinsky appears to
have been kept up-to-date with the smallest details of the choreography, following every stage minutely in his score. Is this tantamount
to admitting that his music — which is perfectly tailored to the dancers'
requirements and powerfully 'pictorial' in character — cannot be
separated from the stage and the plot? The universal popularity of the
work in the concert hall is enough to prove the contrary — that the
composer had here, in fact, at the outset of his career, performed the
miracle of creating a work which is both functional and autonomous,
where indeed the two aspects mutually reinforce each other.

It was a well-proven principle of classical ballet, that the plot should
bring two different worlds and three main characters face to face; and
so it is in *Firebird*. The evil world of the magician Kashchei and the good
world of the Firebird confront the hero prince, Ivan Tsarevich, who
triumphs over the forces of evil with the help of the Firebird. The plot is
revealed by simply listing the nineteen carefully elaborated 'numbers'
which form the ballet.

1. Introduction
2. *Scene One*: Kashchei's gardens
3. Appearance of the Firebird pursued by Ivan Tsarevich
4. Dance of the Firebird
5. Ivan Tsarevich captures the Firebird
6. Pleading of the Firebird
7. Appearance of the thirteen Princesses under Kashchei's spell
8. The Princesses play with the golden apples (Scherzo)
9. Sudden appearance of Ivan Tsarevich

10. The Princesses' *khorovod*, or round dance
11. Daybreak
12. Magic carillon; appearance of Kashchei's guardian-monsters, who capture Ivan Tsarevich
13. Arrival of Kashchei the Immortal; his dialogue with Ivan Tsarevich for whom the Princesses plead
14. Appearance of the Firebird
15. Dance of Kashchei's attendants under the spell of the Firebird
16. 'Dance infernale' of Kashchei and his subjects
17. Lullaby (the Firebird)
18. Death of Kashchei — darkness
19. *Scene Two*: crumbling of Kashchei's palace and lifting of spells; the stone warriors return to life; general rejoicing.

There is nothing 'revolutionary' in the sumptuous and bewitching musical language of *Firebird*; that is probably the reason for its immediate success with the public. Harmonically it may even seem unenterprising when compared with Wagner and Debussy, both fashionable at this date. One of the most effective features of the score, if not the most original one, is the contrast between the 'evil' world symbolized by chromaticism and the 'good' symbolized by the diatonic. We find the same contrast in Rimsky's *Le Coq d'Or* and even earlier in *Parsifal*. The orientalisms in the score (the Lullaby, for instance) also come from Rimsky; and although Stravinsky was to be implacably hostile to all such 'orientalizing' later in his career, it can hardly be held against a young composer (with Rimsky's *Sadko* and *Tsar Saltan* already engrained in his mind) who is asked to evoke *the very idea* of a legendary Russia. Diatonic elements derived directly from traditional sources (such as the *khorovod* or the big final theme, which recalls Glinka's 'Slava!' chorus and Mussorgsky's 'Great Gate of Kiev') were taken from nos. 2 and 79 of Rimsky's *Hundred folk-songs*.

As a kind of melodic and harmonic middle term between the diatonic, the chromatic and the 'oriental', Stravinsky uses an interval that colours the whole piece — the augmented fourth or tritone, which enables him to include all three elements, to unite them, or even to emphasize or neutralize their tonal functions just as he wishes. There is a simple and effective instance of this principle at the opening of the

Ex. 1

work, where the melodic thirds (alternating major and minor) assume 'ambiguous' harmonic identities in the context of the tritone.

Melodically, harmonically and thematically *Firebird*, although Stravinsky's first completely personal work, is nevertheless paradoxically an end rather than a beginning. (The *Sacre* holds in this respect a particular position, as we shall see later.) It is in the rhythmic field that Stravinsky here gives evidence of immediately individual and strikingly effective ideas: Kashchei's 'Dance infernale' for example, is an experimental prototype of certain great rhythmic developments in the *Sacre*. There were of course the models of Borodin's 'great wild dances' by no means distant since the 'Ballets russes' were performing the *Polovtsian Dances* with Fokine's choreography. But Stravinsky was already exhibiting his ability to make dissymmetrical use of a number of opposed (but still simple) 'rhythmic characters', oppositions capable of producing a quite extraordinary musical energy. Moreover he knew not only how to produce, but also how to conserve this energy, by a strict economic strategy that ensures its constant renewal by all the parameters in succession — intensity, mass and, above all, timbre (as we shall be seeing soon).

The 'motor element' in the 'Danse infernale' is the systematic opposition of two rhythmic elements, one syncopated and the other coinciding with the basic metre of the piece. Not that Stravinsky could claim to be the discoverer of syncopation as a dynamic element! But, as André Schaeffner has said, 'he uses it with a quite individual violence, consciously and systematically'. What gives this music its strength is in fact Stravinsky's personal use of this principle. These are the three constituent elements:

Ex. 2

A forms the syncopated rhythmic base (composed of two analogous elements, one veering to the tonic and the other to the diminished fifth degree of the scale); B is a 'strong' melodic-rhythmic structure composed of a variable number of quavers: and Z is an isolated rhythmic explosion — a big *fff* chord falling, at different intervals, like a chopper and cutting the whole into sections of unequal size. It works in the following way (the numbers indicating how many times the same element is repeated):

A 3 B 1 /Z/   A 2 /Z/   A 1 B 1 /Z/   B 2 /Z/   etc.

This shows the contradictory behaviour of the pair A–B in his first period, and its aperiodic scansion brought about by Z (most commentators present this pattern as consisting of equal periods of four bars each, neglecting to account for Z, and thus violating the very principle of the whole scheme). As shown above, A tends to shrink progressively (A3 — A2 — A1) in relation to B, which becomes increasingly important (B1 — B1 — B2), while Z remains invariable. In the second period, which is just as simple to analyse, the anchor-points of the pattern are multiplied; the different parameters — harmonic and chronometric density, overall intensities, mass and particularly timbre are so many factors of rhythmic efficacity, all increasing the power of the system in the listener's perception.

If timbre is an overall 'decorative' element in *Firebird*, the factor of magic 'climates of sound', it achieves a definitely functional role in the 'Danse infernale' — that of *rhythmic lector* and, formally speaking, that of *information-regulator*. This means that differences of timbre both individualize, modify, contrast and renew the aspect of the rhythmic cells, and that the various instrumental stages in the course of the work constitute so many new occasions on which the play of differences is made perceptible in a way that is always fresh and novel.

The 'Danse infernale' is a model of strategic progression, continually revealing the interferences, modifications and relayings between the different parameters, with a single end in view — that of maintaining at its maximum the listener's awareness of the dynamism of the music. Stravinsky's manipulation of *difference* is most judicious: even parametric inversions and the contrasts, for example, of 'negative' intensity (sudden *pianissimos*) constitute 'minus-sign' events quite as effective as those of increasing progression.

All the great composers have no doubt instinctively applied this principle of parametric compensation, used with spectacular results by Beethoven from his early quartets onward.[2] Even so Stravinsky here uses it with such an effective and efficiently accomplished art and builds up a flawless, unceasing progression from beginning to end, one that literally transports the listener to a state of paroxysm. This is certainly one of the chief reasons of the work's brilliant success.

In its original form *Firebird* lasts forty-five minutes and demands a very large orchestra (fourfold woodwinds). Stravinsky himself made a number of suites and arrangements, the best known of which are the following:

1911 Suite for large orchestra, consisting of five 'numbers' and ending with the 'Danse infernale'

1919 Suite with double woodwind, ending with the Grand Finale — prepared at Morges

1945 *Suite de ballet*, consisting of ten numbers and lasting almost half an hour — prepared in the United States

Stravinsky made arrangements for violin and piano in 1929 and 1933. Mention should also be made of 'Summer Moon', a slow fox-trot based on the theme of the Princesses' *khorovod*, lyrics by John Klenner ('Summer moon, you bring the end of my love story . . .' in an arrangement by Lou Singer).

Firebird was not only an immediate success with the public; it also won Stravinsky the admiration of the artists present at the first performance, chief among them Debussy, who congratulated him warmly on the stage of the Opéra. Early admirers also included Ravel, Manuel de Falla, Florent Schmitt and Satie. During that same summer (1910) Stravinsky met Puccini and Casella, Sarah Bernhardt, Proust, Giraudoux and Claudel. He and his wife, who was expecting her second child, spent the summer at La Baule, and there he wrote settings of two Verlaine poems, 'Un grand sommeil noir' and 'La lune blanche', both for baritone and intended for his brother Guri, who, however, never sang them in public. The family left for Switzerland in September, and on 25 September their son Sviatoslav-Soulima was born in a Lausanne clinic.

In the meantime Diaghilev had determined to commission a new work from Stravinsky. On his way back from Venice, where he had been spending his holidays with Nijinsky, he called on Stravinsky in Lausanne, who told him about 'a kind of Konzertstück' for piano and orchestra, the first movement of which is already finished.

In composing the music I had in my mind a distinct picture of a puppet, suddenly endowed with life and exhausting the patience of the orchestra with diabolical cascades of arpeggios. The orchestra in turn retaliates with menacing trumpet blasts. The outcome is a terrific noise which reaches its climax and ends in the sorrowful and querulous collapse of the poor puppet. Having finished this bizarre piece, I struggled for hours, walking beside Lake Geneva, to find a title that would express the character of my music, and consequently the personality of this creature.

One day I leaped for joy. I had indeed found my title — Petrushka! The immortal and unhappy hero of every fairground in every country. (*Chronicle*)

Are we to consider this a 'programme'? Assuredly not, since Stravinsky supplies a formal procedure, however sketchy, running through (not to say governing) all his puppet's misadventures. This time it was no longer a question of providing a story with 'musical illustrations', still less of 'interpreting' or 'translating' sentiments. It was a matter of determining the behaviour of a musical form in order to deduce from it a series of stage archetypes.

One question we may well wish to ask ourselves before we go any further is how it came about that a composer who was by nature, and on his own showing, hostile to all 'figurative' and 'expressive' music should have shown a predilection for the ballet, in which 'expression' may be stylized, but a plot, a content, a narration is nonetheless quite definitely 'figured'. Did he, like Wagner, feel the need of some significant 'support' to release his musical thought? Was he in some way caught up in the machinery of the 'Ballets russes' and of his own success in the theatre? He may well not have been indifferent to any of these factors, but we may suggest that the first of them — the 'significant support' — was the least important to him, except *a contrario*. In fact any stage plot, of whatever kind, seems to have allowed him in some way to 'purge' his music of the narrative, rational and psychological elements and to entrust the plot to the stage-action, supported very clearly, though very schematically by often purely musical — in the case of ballet, rhythmical — means. Apart, then, from these structural anchor-points — which are themselves powerful unifying factors — the music remains entirely autonomous, with its own validity and its own vitality. The narrative element in these works, from a purely musical point of view, is an added plus. Such are the conditions that enabled Stravinsky to achieve in all his stage (as also in his liturgical) works that miraculous balance between the functional and the autonomous, the 'figurative' and the 'abstract', which links them in spirit with the great theatrical and religious forms of the Renaissance.

As he listened to Stravinsky describing his *Petrushka*, Diaghilev saw in a flash that a stage development of the idea could, and should, make a superb ballet. Together they planned the setting — 'butter-week' in St Petersburg, with its crowds of loafers, the magician, the marionette-theatre and its three puppets who escape to live their own 'drama' — Petrushka, the Ballerina and the Moor. It was Diaghilev's idea to get Alexandre Benois to plan the scenario jointly with Stravinsky. The painter was at first unforthcoming, having had a quarrel with Diaghilev about money, but eventually felt unable to resist the suggestion. Stravinsky had meanwhile completed the music of the first two scenes while spending the winter at Beaulieu-sur-mer with his family. At the end of December 1910 he paid a short visit to St Petersburg to show his score to Fokine and Benois, who declared themselves 'enchanted'. He did not then realize that he would not see his native city again for another fifty years; at that moment it seemed to him, as a 'young Parisian', very provincial.

The collaboration continued by correspondence after Stravinsky's return to Beaulieu, until Benois travelled to Monte Carlo the following spring (1911) to meet Diaghilev and Stravinsky. What was Benois' effective contribution to *Petrushka*? Certainly enough for him to be regarded by SACEM* as legally joint-author of the libretto and thus authorized to claim one-sixth of the rights, even on concert perform-ances of the music. Stravinsky did everything in his power to alter this arrangement, but he was unsuccessful; and his resentments being always long and bitter, particularly where money matters were concerned, he eventually came to avoid Benois until the year 1929, when a further quarrel made the break between the two men final.

The scenario of *Petrushka* is not so much a narrative as a succession of pictures. The synopsis printed at the beginning of the score seems primarily visual. The 'drama' — or rather its archetype — consists in the evolution of these pictures, and the characters which appear in them, in a ruthless, inexorable manner that has nothing realistic, still less anything romantic about it.

It is a sunny winter day in Admiralty Square in St Petersburg about the year 1830. Among the crowd there are decent citizens, drunkards, children, street-musicians and fair-dancers. The puppet-master opens his theatre and we see Petrushka, the Ballerina and the Moor who, under the spell of their master's flute, come to life and, to the amazement of the spectators, leave the little theatre and mingle with the crowd.

Petrushka has fallen in love with the Ballerina, who rejects his

*The French society of composers, authors and publishers, which takes care of royalties.

advances and sets out to seduce the Moor, a rich figure in his oriental garments, lying on his divan and playing with a coconut. Petrushka is mad with jealousy and interrupts their love-scene only to be thrown out by the Moor. At the height of the fair (Nurses' Dance, Coachmen's Dance, the Bear-Leader, Two Gypsies etc.) Petrushka reappears pursued by the Moor who, despite the Ballerina's efforts to restrain him, kills Petrushka with his scimitar. As night falls, it begins to snow, Petrushka dies surrounded by the motley crowd. But he was no more than a puppet, and at the end his soul — his ghost — appears on the roof of the little theatre, cocking a snook at the audience.

The music of *Petrushka* also resembles a succession of pictures, not unlike 'collages', with its bands of crude, heavily contrasted colours and its 'objets trouvés'. The texture of the music is strongly diatonic and marked by sudden changes like magic-lantern slides; and into this weave Stravinsky inserts the well-known song 'Elle avait une jamb' de bois', two of Lanner's waltzes and a large number of Russian folk-songs some of which he had used before (e.g. the first theme of the 'Nurses', a song for dancing taken from Rimsky's collection and used by Balakirev as long ago as 1858). If we compare this with Stravinsky's music hitherto, the whole conception is astonishingly novel — a complete break with the past and a radical option for the future.

What are the differences of language and *tone* that make *Petrushka* a key-work in Stravinsky's development?

The more one listens to *Petrushka*, the stranger becomes its position between *Firebird* and the *Sacre*, from both of which it differs fundament-ally, as we shall see. It marks the end of those links with neo-romanticism that we found in *Firebird* with its glittering harmony, its magic-sounding, almost neo-Wagnerian orchestra, its oriental-style melodies and in fact its expressionism — all of which were to reappear, oddly enough in the *Sacre* and then to vanish for ever from Stravinsky's music.

Harmonically speaking, Stravinsky bade farewell to chromaticism with *Petrushka* and became essentially diatonic, as he was to remain — paradoxically — even in his serial works. Chromaticism appears in only one brief episode — the 'Tour de passe-passe' (juggling-trick) that was such a favourite of Debussy's. There chromaticism and whole-tone scales are combined in an extremely subtle passage, where tonality is reduced to no more than a hint, then violently asserted a moment later. As far as melody goes, it is in *Petrushka* that the indelible traits of Stravinsky's language appear and establish themselves: precise out-lines, terse expression, bareness and even, according to Schaeffner, 'the stiffness of *organum*'. Here too we find for the first time Stravinsky's characteristic *space* — neither specifically harmonic nor truly polyphonic, but alternating between the two, with moments of antiphony (borrowed from Russian folksong) and still more of heterophony. This means the interplay of closely similar lines, more or less synchronized, skilfully interwoven or deliberately separated, reflections and mirror (or distorting-mirror) images, sporadic parallelisms and relations of dependence (rather than of that interdependence which is the essence of counterpoint). At most we may say that the 'space' of *Petrushka* resembles a façade rather than a structure in depth, an Italian-style theatre in which the front of the stage is occupied by an often breathless succession of linear (more rarely harmonic) figures which are presented in an astonishing — and illusory — perspective, thanks to the depth of the stage (or orchestra), the slips being used like reflecting-mirrors. The real locus of this perspective is timbre, not the *trompe l'oeil* polyphony; only this timbre is no longer 'magic', as in *Firebird*, but functional. In the image of Mozart, and in opposition to Wagner, the Romantics, Rimsky and *Firebird*, Boris de Schloezer comments, Stravinsky 'sees the different groups of instruments in terms of melodic ideas and harmonic systems which must be made as effective as possible'.

Rhythm is a primordial element in *Petrushka*, although still very dependent on harmony and melody, freeing itself occasionally and with amazing success in 'Tour de passe-passe', where melody and harmony are no longer in command. The use of variable metres, as in *Firebird*, is here systematically developed, causing constant surprises by shifts of tempo or accent. One of Stravinsky's methods is to superimpose different 'strata of durations', while still retaining the link with the instrumental 'polymelodies' (though without yet forming the spectacular polyrhythmic *structures* of the *Sacre*). The tie with popular rhythm is strong whether in straight quotation or in violent distortion. If rhythm in *Petrushka* is generally speaking isochronous, its metres and accentuations affecting asymmetrical periods, and if it depends on harmony rather than polyphony, its function appears obviously and most effectively in the field of *form*, in the juxtaposition of strongly characterized rhythmic and tempo sequences. This reveals how well-suited such music is to the ballet where compartmentalized, contrasted and forcefully articulated structures are of vital importance.

With chromaticism temporarily dispensed with (though it was to reappear in the *Sacre* and *The Nightingale*), the function of harmony in *Petrushka* is on the one hand the powerful assertion of tonality, on the other the violent colouring of a given aggregate by causing 'disturbances' in its sound spectrum. (To most people this recalls Picasso, but to me, it recalls Matisse.) Building new colours is essentially the purpose of the famous 'polytonalities' in *Petrushka*, and in particular in Petrushka's own theme:

Ex. 3

There has been much discussion of this passage, in which C major and F sharp major are superimposed on each other, distilling a 'dissonance' as bitter and pungent as angostura. Was it this 'paradoxical' savour that the composer intended by his crude disposition of tonalities? That was certainly part of his purpose, since this is not a case of real polytonality. Such samples (for they *are* samples, not linguistic principles) do not lead the tonalities concerned towards any real development (as Milhaud was to do) but simply present them as indissociable phenomena; furthermore, they remain merely episodic in character. Michel Philippot curtly reduces the harmony of *Petrushka* to polytonality,[3] but I prefer the phenomenological attitude of André Schaeffner: 'Perhaps this chord [the C and F sharp major] has no real *explanation* and must be accepted as an irreducible unit of sonority.' And indeed the ear actually hears harmonic phenomena of this kind as timbres. This is exactly what Schaeffner is implying. It is even possible to suppose that the justification of everything in Stravinsky's music that appears to be polytonal, or pseudo-polytonal, all disturbances of the harmonic spectrum, lies in its actual *sound*, acting on the specific colour of the structure.

The most important characteristic of *Petrushka*, and the most significant for Stravinsky's future, is the total absence of that 'psychological' element so noticeable in *Firebird*. The music seems not to interpret the drama or the characters but to coincide, as it were, with the theatrical element, to make a kind of ideogram: it does not 'live' the story so much as represent it at a distance through coded signs. With *Petrushka* Stravinsky definitely abandons all illusion of musical realism and even goes so far as to make deliberate use of conventional 'realistic' elements as a sort of alphabet of musical-dramatic action, very similar to that used by choreographers, with which it harmonizes perfectly. The listener faced with this network of music and spectacle, simultaneously frozen and bubbling with life, supple and rigid, is free to give way to his own imagination, emotions and dreams.

Petrushka marks the end of Romanticism: music henceforward is not to be concerned with miming emotions. Stravinsky said that for him the real Petrushka is the ghost which appears on the roof, the other only a puppet, and when the ghost cocks a snook at the audience, it is indeed Stravinsky who is cocking a snook at music 'charged with meaning' and at the very post-Wagnerianism of which he will henceforth be a sworn enemy.

This new, fresh air that music, thanks to Debussy and Stravinsky, breathed at the opening of the century was to be tainted in the years between the wars, but Paris and soon all Europe welcomed it with delight — until concussed by a new shock.

There are several versions of *Petrushka*, the best known being the 'revised version of 1947' for a slightly reduced orchestra (triple woodwinds). It comprises a number of substantial changes in the orchestration and appears to have been intended for the concert-hall rather than for the stage. A careful comparison of the two versions has been published by the Soviet conductor Rozhdestvensky.[4] In the absence of a distinct 'concert suite', various cuts authorized by the composer make it possible to adapt the score according to circumstances in the concert-hall.

In 1921 at the request of Artur Rubinstein (and for a fee of five thousand francs) the composer made a piano transcription of *Petrushka* which includes 'Danse russe', 'La Chambre de Petrouchka' and 'La Semaine grasse'. The approach to the keyboard in this transcription is primarily vertical — percussive and involving wide leaps — and the work is universally regarded as one of the masterpieces of modern virtuoso writing for the instrument.

The first performance of *Petrushka* was at the Théâtre du Châtelet on 13 June 1911. The conductor was Pierre Monteux and the work was a triumphal success, to which Nijinsky's amazing performance in the title role, Karsavina's Ballerina, Benois's sets and Fokine's choreography all contributed. It is impossible to exaggerate the importance of the active role played by the composer in the *stage presentation* of the work, which finally confirmed his professional status as a man of the theatre. His comments on the performance were laconic. He 'liked' the sound of the orchestra and the success of the work gave him 'absolute confidence in his ear', this at a time when he was starting a big new composition. Back at Ustilug he was already at work.

*

During those three years, 1911, 1912 and 1913, three visionary composers were creating the very idea of modernity by which the new century was to live. It was as though music, on the eve of a murderous world war, was opting for its survival and its future by taking the form of three masterpieces. And by a strange coincidence the authors of those three works — Le Sacre du printemps, Jeux and Pierrot Lunaire — all in fact met during those three years, even if the meetings were no more than fleeting and established the uniqueness of each, if not his actual antagonism toward the others.

Before we go on to Stravinsky's magnum opus, let us first consider for a moment the composer whose light hand traced the course of a new musical era, fluid and elusive as water — Debussy; and then that other solitary, working in secret to give the final blow to the already toppling edifice of tonality — Schoenberg. Even while Stravinsky was forging the telluric rhythms of 'Augures printaniers', echoes of these crossroad encounters on the threshold of the new century could be perceived in two rarely heard, and, as it were secret, compositions, as we shall see.

'I was seeing a lot of Debussy at that time,' Stravinsky wrote in Chronicle, 'and I was deeply touched by the sympathy that he showed both for me and for my music.' This rather distant tone gives no hint of the real and profound admiration that he felt for Debussy's music and which Debussy in his turn, though more generously, reciprocated. The two were made to understand and respect each other, though this mutual recognition may seem something of a paradox in view of their diametrically opposed conceptions of musical time — Debussy's being entirely fluid, transcribed in 'absolute' time-values, whereas Stravinsky's obeyed a pulsation implicit from the very outset and always present however subservient, distorted or stretched. Debussy's time — and especially in Jeux which is contemporary with the Sacre — overflows the metre, which it subverts and eventually denies, despising the 'four-square' and filling every instant with infinitely differentiated durations dependent exclusively on their immediate, concrete relationships with each other. Stravinsky's time, on the other hand, as affirmed in Petrushka and even now being further explored in the Sacre, acts as accomplice to the metre, which it uses to make its rhythmic content clear, whether these be with or against the basic metre. The 'bar-line' pulsates, vibrates and leaps, engendering an irresistible dynamic force. . . . Yet over and above these different conceptions of duration

Stravinsky and Debussy were still united in their awareness and acknowledgement of rhythm as the most important parameter of their music.

Furthermore they shared a common horror of 'schools', of 'messages' and composer-thinkers. Both had felt the influence of Wagner and both had shaken it off before long, finding his world, in which there are no smiles, uninhabitable — their own worlds being peopled with joy. They also shared a ferocious, irreverent, penetrating and biting sense of humour, an extreme reserve — especially about their private lives — and a taste for refined, luxurious ways of living.

The 'summit meeting' between the two artists took place on 9 June 1912 at the house of Louis Laloy, who has left a wonderful account of the occasion, which he still remembered in 1928.[5]

> On a bright spring afternoon in 1913 [sic] I was strolling with Debussy in my garden at Bellevue, waiting for Strawinsky.* As soon as he caught sight of us, Strawinsky ran open-armed to embrace Debussy who glanced at me over his shoulder, both amused and touched. Strawinsky had brought with him the four-hand piano transcription of his new work, Le Sacre du printemps and Debussy agreed to play the secondo part on my Pleyel — which I still have. Strawinsky asked if he could take off his collar, and glaring through his spectacles, with his nose almost touching the keyboard and occasionally humming some part that did not appear in the piano-score, he engaged in the torrent of sound the soft, agile hands of his partner, who followed without blinking and seemed to make nothing of the difficulties. When they had finished, it was no longer a question of embraces or even of compliments. We were dumbfounded, thunderstruck as though by a hurricane from the remote past, which had seized our lives by the roots.

*

Zvezdoliki or Le Roi des étoiles (the meaning of the Russian word is 'star-faced'), one of Stravinsky's strangest and most seldom performed works, is dedicated to Debussy and dates from 1911–12. It is written for male chorus and very large orchestra (fourfold woodwind and eight horns). Balmont's text has a mystical, symbolical character such as might well have appealed to Scriabin. How such a text could appeal to Stravinsky is a puzzle, particularly after the blinding daylight and the humour of Petrushka. Equally puzzling is the musical language of the

---

*This is Laloy's spelling, used by the composer himself up to the time when he settled in the USA, when he changed to 'Stravinsky' for reasons of pronunciation.

work, which has nothing to do with *Petrushka* and only distantly foretells the *Sacre* in certain harmonic procedures which in fact recall Debussy.

The harmony of *Zvezdoliki* is 'cumulative' — the composer piles up the sequences of triads which form the foundation — with sevenths, ninths, thirteenths, making great use of simultaneous major and minor thirds, often giving the voices and the instruments chords that are more or less related, or more or less alien to each other. The final chord of the piece is a good instance.

Ex. 4

Properly speaking, the harmonic functions are relatively weak: we are moving away from the hyper-tonics which we find in other works, and even from the sense of weight and attraction. Once again the harmony is here a matter of *sonority*, and these additive-cumulative chords are like 'mutation-stops', as though the work were conceived for a gigantic organ. Writing chords means writing timbres before even writing any harmonic functions: and this is what first Debussy, and following him Stravinsky, were acutely aware of doing during these early years of the present century. This formed a still further link between them, another aspect of their half secret yet profound kinship.

The strangest thing of all about *Zvezdoliki* is its asymmetrical form, built up by imbalances and consisting of large slabs of timbres and masses, huge forces apparently ludicrously out of proportion to the length of the work, which seems to come to an end almost before it has begun. It is in fact said to last six minutes. Musically it seems to be over in a moment, leaving the listener in a state of frustrated desire and painful suspense.

Zvezdoliki did not have its first performance until 1939 when it was given, thanks to Paul Collaer, at Brussels, conducted by Franz André. The occasion was the purchase by the Brussels Conservatoire of a copy of the score in a public sale. Darius Milhaud was present at the performance and wrote in the *Revue Musicale* (1939) that '*Le Roi des étoiles* is a window on to a fantastic fairy world'. Debussy acknowledged his reception of the score thus: 'The music of *Le Roi des étoiles* remains extraordinary . . . it is probably "the harmony of the eternal spheres" of which Plato speaks (don't ask me where!). And I cannot see any possibility of a performance of this cantata for "worlds" except on Sirius or Aldebaran! On our more modest planet, a performance would leave us as stupid as a pancake. . . .'

*

These were crucial years during which the masterpieces of twentieth-century music seemed hurrying to be born, and it looked as though it were a historical necessity for the solitary protagonists to meet and acknowledge each other's existence, however much their idioms might differ. While Debussy was writing *Jeux* and Stravinsky the *Sacre*, in December 1912 Schoenberg was giving the first performance of his *Pierrot Lunaire* in Berlin. Stravinsky was present at one of these, as though at a secret rendezvous with history.

Stravinsky went to Berlin via Bayreuth, which he had visited that same summer (1912) at Diaghilev's suggestion, as though before meeting Schoenberg he should become fully aware of his dislike of post-romantic German aesthetic ideas by studying them, as it were, at their very source. (This aversion was shared by Debussy, who was later to exaggerate it to the point of becoming a rabid nationalist.) Stravinsky found the atmosphere of Bayreuth 'depressing', the theatre 'like a crematorium'; and if, as he says in *Chronicle*, 'Wagner's music is too remote from me today', what he found most repellent was 'the unconscious mimicking of a sacred rite' in this whole 'Bayreuth comedy, with its ludicrous protocol'. His allergy to Wagner's music was, if possible, to grow as time went on. What, then, was his attitude to Schoenberg after their meeting in Berlin?

This meeting between two major figures of the new century was, as we have already said, symbolic; but it was also a real confrontation. Stravinsky's hearing of *Pierrot* in the Choralionsaal at midday on 8 December 1912 (he kept the ticket sent him by Schoenberg) was more important to him than he suggests in *Chronicle*. Aesthetically speaking, he says laconically, this was a 'return to the outdated Beardsley cult' and technically an 'unquestionable instrumental success'. But writing to Karatygin[6] five days after the performance, he said: in '*Pierrot Lunaire* the whole unusual stamp of [Schoenberg's] creative genius comes to light at its most intensive.' And two months later, in a *Daily Mail* interview: 'The Viennese are barbarians. They chased Schoenberg away to Berlin. Now Schoenberg is one of the greatest creative spirits of our day. . . .'

Of the actual performance Stravinsky remembered that 'the audience was quiet and that . . . I wanted Frau Zehme [the soloist in the first performances] to be quiet too, so that I could hear the music'. According to Eduard Steuermann, who was the pianist on this occasion and is quoted by Stravinsky, the two composers met several times in Berlin, most notably at a dinner at Schoenberg's, where Berg and Webern were also present; although, as Stravinsky was to observe in *Dialogues*: 'Alas, I have no recollection of this, my First and Last Supper with the hypostatic trinity of twentieth-century music.' And so, too, fifty years after that Berlin meeting:

> The real wealth of *Pierrot* — sound and substance, for *Pierrot* is the solar plexus as well as the mind of early twentieth-century music — was beyond me, as it was beyond us all at that time, and when Boulez wrote that I had understood it 'd'une façon impressioniste', he was not being kind but correct. (*Dialogues and a Diary*)

The two composers remained on good terms for a time (Schoenberg sat next to Stravinsky at a performance of *Petrushka* during this same visit) and there was an exchange of letters between them in 1919, when Schoenberg expressed a wish to include some chamber pieces by Stravinsky in the programmes of his Society for Private Performances in Vienna. And there ended the contact between the two, a contact that was at that time not only symbolical but real in spite of their different aesthetic outlooks, their incompatible temperaments and official declarations of variable authenticity. The evidence lies in one of Stravinsky's little masterpieces, the *Three Japanese Lyrics*, written at exactly the time of his visit to Berlin, sketches for which are to be found among sketches for the *Sacre* in a notebook that we shall be discussing later. The piano version of the first of these three pieces, 'Akahito', is dated 19 October, the instrumental version 29 December, both 1912. 'Mazatsumi' is dated '18–21 December', and 'Tsaraiuki' 22 January 1913. These datings are not without importance, as they show that the chamber-group to accompany the soprano voice — two flutes, two clarinets, piano, two violins, one viola and one violoncello — was decided hardly more than a few days after Stravinsky's Berlin hearing of *Pierrot Lunaire*, in which the instrumental group consists of flute, clarinet, bass clarinet, piano, violin or viola and violoncello. The *Three Japanese Lyrics* were inspired by the reading of a small anthology in which only the authors' names are given — hence the titles of the three pieces. 'The impression that I had of these poems was strikingly similar to those I received from Japanese prints, in which the graphic solution of various problems of volume and perspective suggested the search for something analogous in music.'

This was how they were originally conceived, and these three *haiku* are certainly 'pure Stravinsky'; but they all — and particularly nos. 2 and 3 — show the profound influence of *Pierrot*, the music going to the very extreme limit of tonality. The instruments, closely resembling those employed in *Pierrot*, do indeed emphasize the polyphonic character of the music; but Stravinsky's handling of them is more subtle and delicate than Schoenberg's.

Stravinsky found difficulty in admitting the impression made on him by *Pierrot* (though it is plain from these three *haiku*) and he was not very generous in doing so; but it was not in fact so much genuine influence as the fascination of a technical challenge. Behind the sevenths and ninths in the polyphonic web of 'Mazatsumi' and 'Tsaraiuki', the aesthetic of these three pieces, the 'specific gravity' of the musical discourse — which is light, transparent and before all else 'distanced' — are at the opposite pole to Schoenberg's sombre, bitter, sarcastic rhetoric.

The strangest, at first sight, but certainly the most important aspect of the whole affair is the fact that Stravinsky's aesthetic as it were *traverses* Schoenberg's to meet that of Webern, whose works were of course wholly unknown to Stravinsky at this time. The kinship between Stravinsky and Webern, as it were over the 'corpse of the father' (Schoenberg being fated, as we know, repeatedly to 'die'), and beyond any chronological conception of history, can be sensed in the *Klangfarbenmelodie* (melody of timbres) of 'Tsaraiuki'. Boulez, writing of the *Three Japanese Lyrics*, speaks of this 'new sensitivity in their elliptical concision', something that Webern had already discovered. It will reappear in a number of the short pieces that Stravinsky wrote about this time, as we shall see.

'Thus, in relation to Schoenberg', as Boulez continues, 'Stravinsky, though using a useless vocabulary, an inconsequential morphology, a syntax that is virtually null and void, still seems [in the *Three Japanese Lyrics*] to have achieved poetry of overwhelming beauty'.*

We should remember that the instrumental ensemble used in *Pierrot* also tempted Ravel when he wrote the *Trois Poèmes de Mallarmé* (1913), although he had never heard Schoenberg's work but only the — no doubt eloquent — account of it given by Stravinsky on his return from Berlin.

There is a letter to Madame Casella, written by Ravel from Clarens and dated April 1913, in which he proposes the following programme for a concert of the Société de Musique Indépendante:

*How, then, may we ask, can this strange synergy of three nullities, according to Boulez, produce 'overwhelming beauty'?

1. Schoenberg — *Pierrot Lunaire*
2. Stravinsky — *Mélodies japonaises*
3. Ravel — *Deux Poésies de Stéphane Mallarmé*

It seems like a dream. . . . The concert was given on 14 January 1914, but without *Pierrot Lunaire*.

IV

Le Sacre du printemps

GENESIS AND THEME

THE *Sacre* BEGAN as a premonitory vision that appeared to Stravinsky at St Petersburg in 1910, when he was still working on *Firebird*. He tells the story in his memoirs:

> One day I had a fleeting vision which came to me as a complete surprise, my mind at the moment being full of other things. I saw in my imagination a solemn pagan rite — sage elders, seated in a circle, watched a young girl dance herself to death. They were sacrificing her to propitiate the god of spring. Such was the theme of *Le Sacre du printemps*. (*Chronicle*)

When Diaghilev was told about it in Paris, he was enthusiastically in favour of a stage-work on this theme. As we know, the realization of the plan was held up by Stravinsky's work on *Petrushka*, *Two Balmont Poems* and *Zvezdoliki*. Nicholas Roerich was not only a very talented painter who had done the sets for the 'Ballets russes' *Polovtsian Dances*; he was also an archaeologist and an authority on everything to do with the ancient Slavs. Diaghilev decided that Stravinsky and he should be jointly responsible for the scenario of the *Sacre*, and Roerich in fact proved a very valuable collaborator, although — as on many other occasions — Stravinsky was later to minimize his part in the undertaking. The two of them had agreed on the main outlines of the work by the summer of 1910, when the composer wrote from La Baule telling his collaborator that he was already working on the score. It was not, however, until July 1911 that the final form of the plot was decided upon. Roerich was then at Talachkino, near Smolensk, staying on an estate lent him by Princess Tenichev, and Stravinsky joined him there, arriving by goods train in a truck that he shared with a bull. The scenario of the *Sacre* was worked out in a few days, including the titles of the various dances and of the work itself.

On his return journey Stravinsky met Diaghilev at Karlsbad (Karlový Váry) and received a formal commission for the work. In November of that year Stravinsky was to receive from Diaghilev, in

Paris, the sum of 479 francs 80 (!) on account of fees the total amount of which we do not know.

In the meanwhile Stravinsky, who had already outlined the 'Introduction' and 'Augures printaniers', left Ustilug for the Lake of Geneva where he settled with his family in the pension 'Les Tilleuls' at Clarens. He continued to work there without a break on the *Sacre* which was planned for the 1912 season of the 'Ballets russes'. It appears that the first part of the work was finished by Christmas 1911, but rehearsals were not started on the date planned, owing to delays caused by the preparation of *L'Après-midi d'un faune*, for which Nijinsky — who was to be choreographer of the *Sacre* as well — had demanded a hundred and twenty rehearsals. The two new ballets in the 1912 season, therefore, were Debussy's and Ravel's (*Daphnis et Chloé*) both of which Stravinsky enjoyed, having gone to Paris specially to see them. The scandal over the *Faune*, is well known. Nijinsky, in the title role, deeply shocked the audience in the boxes by a gesture, with the scarf left behind by the Nymph, suggestive of sexual penetration. According to Stravinsky (*Memories and Commentaries*, p. 36), this was 'entirely Diaghilev's idea', as indeed was everything aimed at emphasizing Nijinsky's virility.

The composer, thereupon, repeatedly returned to his work on the *Sacre* in between journeys to Ustilug, Switzerland, Paris, London, Vienna and Berlin, where Diaghilev kept inviting him to share in the triumphal progress of *Firebird* and *Petrushka*. Stravinsky who, as usual, composed the work more or less straight through from beginning to end, with only a few exceptions, completed 'Glorification de l'élue' in the spring of 1912. He spent the summer at Ustilug and then returned to Clarens, where he stayed at the Hôtel Châtelard, having hired a piano, and set to work on the second part of the *Sacre*. He completed the 'Danse sacrale' on 17 November 1912. 'I remember the day well, as I was suffering from a raging toothache, which I then went to have treated in Vevey.' (*Expositions and Developments*). The final version of the score bears the date 8 March 1913.

Stravinsky always insisted that there was no 'plot' in the *Sacre*. 'My new ballet, *Le Couronnement du printemps*,[1] has no plot. It is a series of ceremonies from ancient Russia.' And right at the beginning, in 1910[2]: '*Vesna Sviashchennaya* is a musical-choreographic work . . . it represents pagan Russia and is unified by a single idea — the mystery and great surge of the creative power of spring. The piece has no plot. . . .' Stravinsky was right to insist, for a distinction must be made between plot, or story, and choreographic theme. Usually the story presents a 'programme' by means of a narrative, and implies its stage representation, whereas the 'theme' plays an essentially structural part, its 'content' being of secondary importance, or at least reduced to a few basic ideas — as indeed in the case of the *Sacre*.

There exist a number of different versions of the theme of the *Sacre*, all of them short. I will mention three. The first of these is in Stravinsky's own hand and is dated 1910 by Craft, though it seems difficult to suppose that it is previous to the work done by Stravinsky and Roerich at Talachkino in 1911, so close is it to the final version and to the titles of the individual dances. The following is a more or less literal translation from the Russian:[3]

First Part: The Kissing of the Earth
The spring celebration. It takes place in the hills. The pipers pipe and the young men tell fortunes. The old woman enters. She knows the mystery of nature and how to predict the future. Young girls with painted faces come in from the river in single file. They dance the spring dance. Games start. The spring Khorovod. The people divide into two groups opposing each other. The holy procession of the very wise, very old man interrupts the spring games, which come to a stop. The people pause trembling before the great action. The old man blesses the spring earth. The kissing of the Earth. The people dance passionately on the earth, sanctifying it and becoming one with it.

Second Part: The Great Sacrifice
The maidens carry on secret games, forming circles. One of them is the promised sacrifice. The lot will fall to the one who is twice caught in the closed circle. The maidens exalt the chosen victim in a martial dance. Ancestors are invoked. The Chosen Victim is entrusted to the Old Sage. In their presence she performs the great sacred dance — The Great Sacrifice.

The second version worth quoting here, in as much as it is very little known, is the one that Roerich sent to Diaghilev in a letter of spring 1912:[4]

I. *The Kiss of the Earth*
Yarilo begins his adoration of the earth
The earth starts to bloom — a golden blooming
Divination with twigs
The people dance for joy
They pick flowers and bow to the red sun
The oldest and wisest is led to kiss the rich soil
The people stamp on the earth with great gladness

II. *The Great Sacrifice*

Day and night the stones are always in the hills. The maidens hold secret games there. They glorify the victim. They call the oldest and wisest as witness to the victim. They give the victim to the beautiful Yarilo.

The third version is the one that appeared in the programme at the first performance on 29 May 1913 — not apparently signed, but very clearly marked by the 'symbolism' which was the literary fashion of the day.

Scene 1: The Adoration of the Earth

Spring. The earth is covered with flowers. The earth is covered with grass. A great joy reigns over the earth. The men abandon themselves to dancing and question the future according to the rites. The Ancestor of all the sages himself takes part in the glorification of Spring. He is brought in to be united with the abounding and magnificent earth. Each man stamps the earth in ecstasy.

Scene 2: The Sacrifice

After the day, after midnight. On the hills are the sacred stones. The girls play mythical games and seek the great way. The one who has been chosen to be delivered to the gods is exalted and acclaimed. The Ancestors are invoked as venerable witnesses. And the wise ancestors of man watch the sacrifice. It is thus that the sacrifice is made to Yarilo, the magnificent one, the flaming one.

First Performance

Rehearsals of the *Sacre* began in Berlin at the end of 1912, after endless postponements, and gathered pace as the company moved between Vienna, London and Monte Carlo. Stravinsky violently interrupted one of the first rehearsals by dismissing the German pianist and taking his place at the piano, adopting a tempo twice as fast and almost beyond the physical ability of the dancers, roaring and stamping. He watched Nijinsky with great care, though not unbrokenly, as he had repeatedly to return to Clarens to finish orchestrating the work (March 1913) and after that to work on the orchestration of Mussorgsky's *Khovanshchina*. Important parts of this work had been left unfinished (other than by Rimsky-Korsakov) and now Diaghilev wanted to stage it. This work of completion was a considerable undertaking which

Stravinsky suggested sharing with Ravel, who spent March and April with him at Clarens. (This was the occasion on which Stravinsky showed Ravel the score of his *Three Japanese Lyrics* and 'described' to him *Pierrot Lunaire*, which he had just heard in Berlin.)

The company of the 'Ballets russes' had been chosen to inaugurate the new Théâtre des Champs Elysées built by the Perret brothers in the Avenue Montaigne. The company arrived in Paris at the beginning of May but was joined by Stravinsky only on 13 May. *Jeux*, which Diaghilev had commissioned from Debussy for this same inauguration, had its first performance on 15 May and was greeted with general indifference. The first stage rehearsal of the *Sacre* in the Théâtre des Champs Elysées took place on 18 May. There were to be very few full rehearsals of the work with the orchestra (26 and 27 May). Stravinsky had already made certain modifications suggested by Monteux in letters, and concerning purely orchestral sonorities; but he seems to have interfered in neither the musical interpretation nor the choreography, which he was later violently to attack. The dress rehearsal on the 28th was attended by Debussy, Ravel and all the Paris press; it took place in an atmosphere of complete calm and gave not the slightest hint of the stormy reception of the work the next day.

That famous evening of 29 May 1913 has been fully, no doubt too fully, described. The 'scandal' of the *Sacre* is a favourite subject with musical journalists and even today remains a symbol of the confrontation between conservatives and avant-garde, ancients and moderns, revolutionaries and reactionaries. But was it really a case of revolution? Have we not been misled by the 'scandal'?

There was undoubtedly an element of provocation, Diaghilev had distributed a number of seats just behind the dress-circle (and very near the boxes) among 'young people' who were instructed to applaud the work at all costs. This was a fatal error, putting a match to the ammunition-dump in fact. . . . It is nonetheless true that the 'sound and fury' to which the first performance of the *Sacre* has been reduced by historians could only have occurred within an *established* — a well established — *relationship*: its occasion, if not its cause, was Stravinsky's very success with a public which had hitherto perfectly accepted him. The violent reaction of that public to the *Sacre* was due to the disturbance of their listening habits by elements in the musical language which were certainly unfamiliar, even brutal, but were still intelligible and judgeable enough to be rejected. Once that stage is passed (as it was not passed on this occasion) and a language becomes totally incomprehensible, nothing happens — as in the case of

Webern, whose music never caused a true scandal, because its novelty was *beyond* the judging-power of the public.

Of course the social background of the audience played an important part (the dress rehearsal, where the audience consisted of professionals, had been perfectly calm) and Cocteau's descriptions in *Le Coq et l'Arlequin* are too well known to quote. We can imagine the potential musical receptivity of the 'fancy' audience at a Paris first night in 1913. Their rejection of the music, however vociferous, could have no possible *historical* importance, being purely social, local, superficial — and momentary. Part of it was due, as we shall see, to the choreography; and not least to the chain reaction set off by the first audible disturbances which started counter-protests. The dancers were soon unable to hear the music or even the shouts of the choreographer, desperately trying to substitute his own voice for the cues in the music. . . .

Stravinsky, who was sitting at no. 111 in the fourth row of the stalls, left his seat as soon as the protests began and went backstage. He gives the following account in *Chronicle*:

I have refrained from describing the scandal which it evoked; that has already been too much discussed. The complexity of my score had demanded a great number of rehearsals, which Monteux had conducted with his usual skill and attention. As for the actual performance, I am not in a position to judge, as I left the auditorium at the first bars of the prelude, which had at once evoked derisive laughter. I was disgusted. These demonstrations, at first isolated, soon became general, provoking counter-demonstrations, and very quickly developed into a terrific uproar. During the whole perform-ance I was at Nijinsky's side in the wings. He was standing on a chair, screaming 'sixteen, seventeen, eighteen' — they had their own method of counting to keep time. Naturally the poor dancers could hear nothing by reason of the row in the auditorium and the sound of their own dance-steps. I had to hold Nijinsky by his clothes for he was furious and ready to dash on to the stage at any moment and create a scandal. Diaghilev kept ordering the electricians to turn the lights on or off, hoping in that way to put a stop to the noise. That is all I can remember about that first performance. Oddly enough at the dress-rehearsal, to which we had, as usual, invited a number of actors, painters, musicians, writers and the most cultured representatives of society, everything had gone off peacefully and I was very far from expecting such an outburst.

Everyone knows Cocteau's story of how, after this turbulent scene, he, Stravinsky, Diaghilev and Nijinsky took a cab to the Bois de Boulogne at two o'clock in the morning, Diaghilev weeping quietly and muttering Pushkin. The composer never confirmed this rather romantic account that appeared in *Le Coq et l'Arlequin*. His own account of how the evening ended is laconic. 'We were excited, furious, disgusted and . . . happy.' According to Stravinsky, Diaghilev's only comment was: 'Exactly what I wanted.'

Three days later Stravinsky ate some oysters — in a month without an 'r' in it — and went down (was it the oysters?) with a bad attack of typhoid immediately afterwards, spending six weeks in a nursing-home in Neuilly, where his mother came to look after him. Meanwhile in the theatre world *Khovanshchina*, in the joint orchestration of Stravinsky and Ravel, was a triumph at the Théâtre des Champs Elysées, and in the social world Madame Debussy telephoned Madame Stravinsky to offer her the use of her motor-car. . . .

CHOREOGRAPHY

According to Stravinsky himself it was Nijinsky's choreography which was largely responsible for this 'setback'.

> His ignorance of the most elementary notions of music was flagrant. The poor boy knew nothing of music: he could neither read it nor play an instrument, and his reactions to music were expressed in banal phrases or the repetition of what he had heard others say. As one was unable to discover any individual impressions, one began to doubt whether he had any. These lacunae were so serious that his plastic vision, often of great beauty, could not compensate for them. My apprehensions can be readily understood . . . I discovered that I should achieve nothing until I had taught him the very rudiments of music: values (semibreve, minim, crotchet, quaver etc), bars, rhythm, tempo and so on. He had the greatest difficulty in remembering any of this. Nor was that all. When, in listening to music, he contemplated movements, it was always necessary to remind him that he must make them accord with the tempo, its divisions and values. It was an exasperating task, and we advanced at a snail's pace. It was all the more trying because Nijinsky complicated and encumbered his dances beyond all reason, thus creating difficulties for the dancers which it was sometimes impossible to overcome. This was due as much to his lack of experience as to the complexity of a task with which he was unfamiliar. (*Chronicle*)

Stravinsky's attempts to make the young choreographer understand the musical structure of the work are confirmed, as we shall see, by a valuable document. We may, however, question the justice of the severe judgments expressed in *Chronicle*. Not only did the composer approve Nijinsky's work 'on the spot', but a few days after the first performance, on 4 June 1913, he declared to Henri Postel du Mas in *Gil Blas*: 'They are wrong. Nijinsky is an admirable artist capable of revolutionizing the art of ballet. He is not only a superb dancer, but he is capable of creating something new. His contribution to the *Le Sacre du printemps* was very important.'

Nijinsky fell into disgrace with Diaghilev by marrying, as he did in September 1913. (Stravinsky was to observe later that 'it was difficult to imagine the strength of Diaghilev's sexual prejudices'.) In a letter to Benois written in October of the same year, Stravinsky defended Nijinsky saying: 'As far as I am concerned, the hope of seeing anything valuable done in the choreographic line has been cancelled for a long time.'[5]

How then are we to imagine the choreography of the *Sacre*? To be honest, we know very little about it, since neither Cocteau nor the French critics give a precise account. The little that Cocteau said was later corroborated by Stravinsky: 'The fault of the choreography lay in the parallelism between the music and the dancing, the absence of interplay, of any "counterpoint" between the two.' Or in Stravinsky's words: 'This textual identity between choreography and music seems in fact to have been a basic fault in Nijinsky's whole conception.' On the other hand Stravinsky's idea of building 'a series of extremely simple rhythmic movements executed by great blocks of dancers and having an immediate effect on an audience', this 'counterpoint of masses', seems to have been well realized by Nijinsky. The only fairly detailed description was given by the *Times* critic writing about the first London performance of the *Sacre* — at which the composer was unable to be present owing to his illness:

First we have purely ritual movements of a primitive kind, such as leaping on the earth and looking towards the sun; then imitative or realistic gestures, seen when all the dancers shiver with terror at the entry of the old seer; and lastly movements of a purely emotional value, neither ritual nor imitative. . . . What is really of chief interest in the dancing is the employment of rhythmical counterpoint in the mass for group movements. . . . But the most remarkable of all is to be found at the close of the first scene, where figures in scarlet run wildly round the stage in a great circle, while the shifting masses within are ceaselessly splitting up into tiny groups revolving on eccentric axes. . . .[6]

These short statements suggest that Nijinsky's ideas do not seem to have been as 'aberrant' as has often been assumed, and that at least in general outline they fell in with Stravinsky's own ('large counterpointing of masses'). They also show the points in which Stravinsky's reservations were justified — namely his complaint that Nijinsky's choreography reduced the dancing to a duplication, or imitation, of the music. We must not forget that in any case that choreography was formally approved by the composer who had come from Lugano to Venice in the summer of 1912, and gone to Berlin in November, to explain his music to Nijinsky and to help him with the work. This collaboration, though often interrupted and certainly not without its stormy moments, had continued right up to February 1913 (in London). The evidence on the whole subject has been set out by Vera Stravinsky and Robert Craft in their book, where it appears under the heading, 'Stravinsky, Nijinsky, Dalcroze and the *Sacre*'.

ELEMENTS OF A CORPUS

The huge *corpus* of the *Sacre* comprises, in addition to orchestral scores and the corresponding 'clean' manuscripts, a number of other documents among which some of the most interesting are the *Sketches* and the *Piano reduction for four hands* which the composer made and gave to Misia Sert in 1913, buying back the manuscript at a London sale in 1967. The reduction was published in 1913 and not reprinted for a long time. The composer's own working-score is covered with notes on the choreography for Nijinsky, and this was probably the score used by Stravinsky and Debussy on the occasion of their piano duet performance of the *Sacre* at Louis Laloy's. It was certainly the copy meant for the rehearsals with the dancers. Stravinsky's notes are in Russian and were later deciphered by Robert Craft with the composer's help and published, in 1969, as an appendix to his study of the *Sketches* (see below). They reveal on the one hand the primary part played by the composer in organizing the actual *spectacle* and on the other the constructive — not conflicting — nature of his work with Nijinsky in making explicit the work's musical structure, something of which Stravinsky later spoke as a despairing task. These can in any case contribute to a revaluation of Nijinsky's contribution to the *Sacre* as choreographer.

The second and far away the most important document is the book of *Sketches* for the *Sacre*. This belonged to the Paris collector, André Meyer, who died some years ago, and was published in facsimile by Boosey & Hawkes in 1969 at Pierre Souvtchinsky's suggestion, with a preface by François Lesure and a study by Robert Craft.

The publication of this valuable collection, the original material of which was authenticated by Stravinsky when he visited André Meyer in 1963, was a major event in the history of modern musicology. We can in fact watch a masterpiece appearing piecemeal, one flash following another almost in the order in which it appeared finally, and often orchestrated in the same way. This spectacular process might possibly seem natural enough to the historian but does not cease to amaze and intrigue the musician. What in fact was the position, and the exact function of these fragments, so elaborate in their diversity and for the most part so *perfect*, in the growth of this enormous work?

Once we start enquiring the exact moment at which they appeared we immediately come up against a contradiction in the purely material sphere. Was it not strange that this superb, blank exercise-book should have been bought (according to the composer's account in 1963) at a stationers in Varese, on Lago Maggiore in the company of Maurice Ravel, who is said to have bought one of the same kind 'doubtless during the winter of 1911–1912', according to François Lesure? The two composers did indeed make an expedition to Lago Maggiore, but it was in late March or early April, 1913, when Ravel and Stravinsky were at the Hôtel des Crêtes in Clarens, working on the orchestration of Mussorgsky's *Khovanshchina*. The *Sacre* was of course completely finished by then. There seem to be two possible explanations. Either the notebook was indeed bought in 1913 — which would mean that the *Sketches* were made . . . after the definitive version of the score: or Stravinsky's memory played him false in 1963, which is very possible in the case of a man of eighty. Clearly this second hypothesis is the rationally acceptable one, since in the other case François Lesure's logical dating of the manuscript 'as probably 1911–1912' would be mistaken, whereas according to the second hypothesis it would be correct, the musicologist instinctively correcting Stravinsky's very probable mistake about the date at which the notebook was bought.

Even though there is no question of when the *Sacre* was written (1911–1912), the *Sketches* are no less intriguing and worrying to the musician who studies them, by reason of their *nature*. Why do they contain so few tentative passages, so few regrets, so few scratchings-out? How do they come to be so 'finished'? Why are they, in other cases, so fragmentary (one, two or three very polished structures comprising a few bars of one dance, followed by the same of another etc.)? How can such a complex work be built up from fragments which are for the most part so minute *and* so perfect? Why are these sketches so vague in the matter of rhythmic processes as those, particularly, of the 'Danse sacrale', where Stravinsky seems more concerned with harmony and

orchestration than with rhythm? The speculative rhythms seem either
to have been already 'obvious' to his mind or else to have 'come
naturally' from his pen. . . . In this matter there are very few indications of 'basic' rhythms, of developments of rhythmic cells or of formal
organization. Was there another set of sketches for the *Sacre* in
existence, which was more tentative and less perfect? It is tempting to
suppose so, as it is hard to imagine Stravinsky composing the *Sacre* —
at the piano! — from this single document. The function of this
notebook, therefore, seems more ambiguous than that of a 'working'
set of composition-sketches such as the elaboration of any work of this
complexity would seem necessarily to suppose: we are tempted to
regard the existing set as a 'log-book' of the composition of the *Sacre*
rather than as actually instrumental in that composition.

Many details in the notebook look as if the contents were a
recording of structures already worked out and in some cases even
finished — and this would in a way contradict the whole idea and
function of a 'sketch'. If we feel bound to reject, however sadly, the
Borges-like hypothesis of a notebook drawn up *after the event* (i.e.
imagining Stravinsky to be capable of such a trick, either as a gift to
dazzle Diaghilev, or for some other reason), we cannot exclude the
idea of a kind of *repertory* of critical points in the score, transcribed
before, during and indeed even after the definitive version of the work.
There is in any case no question of Stravinsky having the complete
structure 'in his head' before writing it down: that, we know, was not
at all the way he composed, which was by repeated trial and error and
always in connection with the actual sonorities, which he spent hours
trying out at the piano.

The sketches of the 'Introduction', which are missing, would
assuredly throw more light on this document. Yet although the
Sketches alone do not, in my opinion, provide a faithful account of 'the
genesis of a masterpiece' so much as an inventory (exquisitely calli-
graphed with four different-coloured inks) of its different structures at
different stages of their development, it is impossible to deny their
interest. Quite apart from the musicological interest, the beauty of
Stravinsky's handwriting, and its perfect legibility, make the document not only easy, but delightful to study. But how such a masterpiece was in fact created remains a mystery.

AESTHETICS

As we have said, the *Sacre* occupies a unique position both among
Stravinsky's works and in twentieth-century music.

Petrushka already represented a break with the world of *Firebird*, which was linked to the Russia of Rimsky, with its chromaticisms and constant modulations. If this break was definitely confirmed, both as regards harmony and instrumentation, by the works that Stravinsky wrote after 1915, the *Sacre* marks a moment of suspense, a pause in the composer's evolution, a summing-up of the past in certain respects and a vision of the future in others.

The whole 'bewitching' harmonic poetics of Romanticism is consumed in a sort of sacrificial fire in the *Sacre*. But it is already being interpreted, orientated in a new direction toward the forming of *sound-blocks* which, though retaining — and sometimes even exaggerating — certain primary harmonic functions, are given a value of their own. The criteria of traditional harmonic analysis are only applicable, as it were, *pro memoria*: that is to say, they can easily reveal the constitutents of these sound-aggregates and their functions: but to what purpose? To the analytical eye these aggregates may be transparent enough, but to the ear they have a strangely opaque consistency, like irreducible entities that cannot be resolved into simple harmonic components. Thus the *Sacre* necessitates a new approach, no longer analytical (according to traditional harmonic criteria) but phenomenological. We shall see, for instance, that there are five or six different conventional interpretations of the repeated chord in 'Augures printaniers', all equally plausible though mutually contradictory and all equally useless. The only musically realistic attitude to this chord is to regard it specifically, as a sonority valid in its own right. It is this co-existence, which in itself implies a mutation in our harmonic ideas, that is one of the unique features of the *Sacre*, and it cannot be reduced to any kind of linear evolution.

The *Sacre* is equally ambiguous instrumentally, containing as it does the last echoes of the magical sonorities of *Firebird*. Debussy was certainly no stranger to this idea of self-sufficient sonorities, the synthesis of extremely refined harmonic structures and instrumental alloys. As Boris de Schloezer wrote in 1919, 'In the *Sacre* the composer temporarily re-establishes timbre as a self-sufficient element . . . again handling the orchestra not as an ensemble of different elements, the sole justification of whose co-operation is the structure of the composer's thought, but as a single, multi-registered instrument open to exploitation in order to obtain specific, independent effects.' This analysis is of course applicable to only one aspect of the question and only very approximately. The instrumental writing in the *Sacre* appears to us today as much more 'functional' than it seemed in the past. This is particularly true of the 'Introduction', where it is indissolubly and organically linked to the counterpoint, and of 'Augures printaniers', for instance, where timbre assumes the role of specific and active parameter just like the other elements of the musical language as we shall be seeing later.

The rhythmic aspect of the *Sacre*, the workings of which have been so brilliantly set forth by Boulez, has been more discussed than any other; and it is in fact the most novel and the most spectacular, as well as historically the most disconcerting, feature of the work; for it is through this aspect that the work appears in all its splendour as a totally isolated phenomenon without precedent and without successor.

Where, in fact, do the rhythmic innovations in the *Sacre* come from? There is no answer to this question if we consider the history of music as a straight line. To discover rhythmic invention comparable in power to Stravinsky's we have to go back to Ars Nova and to the Renaissance. The only nineteenth-century composer capable of similarly bold rhythmic ideas was Beethoven, timidly followed by the German Romantics. Chopin and Liszt were bolder innovators, drawing their rhythmic sensibility from national traditions which were, through them, to enrich Western European music; but it is not until Debussy who was, like Stravinsky, a solitary figure, that we can speak of a modern rhythmic invention. In the introductory chapter I tried to show how groundless are the much repeated assertions that this 'bomb', the *Sacre*, had changed the course of musical history. Both in Paris and elsewhere the work remained without any echo, regarded by composers with either suspicion or admiration, but always at a distance. The vague echoes of the *Sacre* that are to be found in the works of Bartók, Milhaud and Varèse remain purely textual, without any real effect on structure, a handful of reminiscences or 'objets trouvés' with no influence in any case on the actual *language*. In the same way the works written after the last war show no influence of the *Sacre* whether the composers be post-Webernians or passionate followers of Stravinsky.

What, then, constitutes the real 'scandal' of this work — is it the stormy reception that it received from a first night ballet-audience in May 1913, or the fact that it stands alone in musical history?

FORMAL, REAL AND PROBLEMATIC UNITY

As far as form is concerned, the *Sacre* is a discontinuous, compartmentalized work. The works which precede and follow it in Stravinsky's output, *Petrushka* and *Les Noces*, are more continuous thematically, 'stronger' in formal organization (even though very little indebted to already existing formal schemes), whereas the *Sacre* defies — at least at the 'topographical' level — all traditional ideas of organic unity. There are not many similarities, reminiscences or repetitions in the music and virtually no developments or recapitulations. As André Schaeffner puts it:

These themes are not linked in any way except by a vague and subtle assonance resting on the excessive use of the interval of the fourth, the narrow span of fifths, fourths, even thirds within which they for the most part lie, their very simple articulation suggesting that they may be borrowings from Russian folksong. The whole work grows only by additions from outside, by total and continuous renewal, perpetually abandoning the rhythmic-harmonic material on which it seized for a moment so ferociously.

There are of course occasional thematic elements, like the *khorovod* of the 'Augures printaniers', which reappears in both 'Cercles mystérieux' and in 'Jeu du rapt'. These are exceptions, however, and do not invalidate Stravinsky's rule which is to give each piece in the *Sacre* its own thematic material and 'burn it up' completely on the spot. How, then, does Stravinsky achieve that astonishing unity of which the listener is immediately aware? The answer, I think, is: by means of general technical principles underlying all the music in the work, such as the elaboration of rhythmic cells and their asymmetrical variations, systems of superimposed harmonic aggregates, strongly polarized modal and tonal melody, the dialectic of concurrent rhythmic principles in several numbers, the principle of melodic and/or rhythmic *ostinato* (elements to which we shall be returning). It may seem paradoxical, but we believe it legitimate to add to these general 'objective' unifying factors a number of 'negative' constants, such as the total and astonishing absence of the rhythmic figure 'dotted quaver, semiquaver' fundamental to the rhythms of Romanticism and the post-romantic age.

The unity of the *Sacre* is, therefore, to be sought neither in existing or traceable formal schemes nor in any theory of formal organization, but in persistent characteristics of style and technique that, as it were, *impregnate* the multifacetted and heterogeneous elements of the work. The listener has therefore a task to perform, which is fundamental — a rewarding activity inseparable from all musical listening worthy of the name, but which in the case of the *Sacre*, is one of the main unifying agents, inasmuch as the score exhibits this unity only in a problematic form. Instead of explicit or conventional formal schemes the score provides the listener with the material necessary (though not in itself sufficient) for a creative participation of this kind.

The discontinuity of the *Sacre* contradicts those 'objective formal guarantees' that are so reassuring to composers — the formal schemes, whether ancient or modern, acknowledged or unacknowledged, concealed or manifest, which cannot in fact guarantee but only circumscribe the field of a virtual unity.

Is this tantamount to saying that the *Sacre* has no general structural system to underpin the listener's formative activity? Certainly not. Apart from the principle of contrast and complementarity — day and night, male and female — that governs the 'Introductions' to both parts of the work (the spring awakening of nature and the moonlit nocturne), it is possible to distinguish in the overall form three major structural categories on which to base an active listening to the music. The first is that of the *khorovods* (from *khor* = a choral song and *vodit'* = to lead). These are essentially melodic, mostly feminine and generally modal, as we find them in 'Rondes printanières' and 'Cercles mystérieux'. Here Stravinsky gives full rein to his imagination, inventing melodies that powerfully evoke his idea of ancient Russia. (It should be remembered that he borrowed very seldom from existing Russian folk-song. An exception is the bassoon theme in the 'Introduction', which is derived from a Lithuanian, not Russian, melody that appears as no. 157 in Zhuzhkevich's collection of folk-songs.)[7]

Dances form the second category — 'savage' dances for men or women such as the 'Glorification de l'élue', 'Danse de la terre', 'Danse sacrale', 'Jeu du rapt' and 'Jeux des cités rivales'. These are dominated by discontinuous and asymmetrical rhythms; and Stravinsky also introduces a number of other elements drawn from existing popular music, but transformed to the point of being unrecognizable.

The third category is that of *processions*, such as the 'Cortège du sage' and 'Invocation des ancêtres'. In these the metre is regular and the tempo slow but they may contain as many as ten 'rhythmic strata' piled on each other.

If we study the *distribution* throughout the score of these three categories, we shall be astonished by the concordances that are revealed, and recognize this as one of the factors in our perception of the formal unity of the work. This distribution follows the pattern set out below, in which K = *khorovod*, D = dance and P = procession. (Ex. 5)

This grand 'rhythm of forms', applicable in both parts of the work reveals the symmetrical disposition of the three categories, and concerns not only the music (all parameters without exception) but also the choreography — and thus the totality of the work in all its aspects, its overall formal structure.

Ex. 5

I–Introduction	Augures	Rapt	Rondes	Cités	Cortège du sage	Adoration	Danse de la terre

```
                   ┌─────────────────────────────────────────────────┐
                   │                       ┌───────────┐             │
        D       D       K         D         P           P             D
                                  └─────────────────────────────────┘
```

II–Introduction			Cercles	Glorification	Evocation	Action rituelle	Danse sacrale

```
                   ┌─────────────────────────────────────────────────┐
                   │                       ┌───────────┐             │
                K         D         P           P                     D
                   └─────────────────────────────────────────────────┘
```

TEMPORAL CATEGORIES

There are essentially two categories of time in the *Sacre*: 'fluid' and 'striated', to borrow a clear and simple distinction of Pierre Boulez'. (These categories are generally confined to durations and accents but may be theoretically extendable to other parameters of the sound continuum, and even to harmony,* in order to broaden the meaning of our concept of rhythm.)

Fluid time is not marked in advance by a regular pulsation, either explicit or implied. It knows virtually nothing of any references outside its immediate manifestation, and is measured in 'absolute' values. It is the time that we find in a number of early works, either unbarred or with bar-lines serving as no more than guide-points. It is the time that we find in electro-acoustic music and — basically — in Debussy and (on closer examination) in Wagner; and in most serial music. We also find it in the 'Introduction' of the *Sacre* — though 'fluid time' is rare in Stravinsky.

Striated time, on the other hand, implies an *a priori* periodicity which marks its passing by pulsations, or regular striation. It is the most familiar variety of musical time, that of the classics, though not necessarily that of pre-classical works. It predominates in the *Sacre*, from 'Augures printaniers' to 'Danse sacrale', where in conjunction

*Fluid (or chromatic?) harmony of Tallis or Gesualdo, of Spanish composers of the Renaissance or Sigismondo of India, of Wagner and Debussy: not reducible to primordial cadence; 'striated' (diatonic?) harmony of Mozart and Haydn, and also Beethoven, put into question by the Romantics, and reasserted by Stravinsky in *Petrushka*, then from *Les Noces* onwards, simplified by 'the Six', jazz. . . .

with another overall chronological system, which is also variable — that of metre — it initiates a dialectic of incredible power.

ANALYTICAL GUIDELINES

Exhaustive analysis of a composition is seldom necessary, and is generally impossible; nor is this the place for it. It may, on the other hand, be of use to examine significant aspects of some of the pieces which compose the *Sacre*, and in the first instance the 'Introduction' and 'Augures printaniers'. (The analysis of these two pieces can only be made in technical terms, and readers not familiar with these, yet puzzled by the problems of the *Sacre*, may nevertheless find some interest in reading what follows. Specialists will do well to arm themselves with a score; the analysis published by Boulez in *Relevés d'apprenti* under the title 'Stravinsky demeure' is also a helpful document for studying the rhythmic aspect of the work.)

Economy is an exemplary feature of the 'Introduction', and it is seen in every parameter — pitches, durations, intensities, registers, timbre, density (both chronometric and polyphonic), mass, all indissolubly linked to each other. The symbolic meaning of this procedure is clear: it is the ideogram of a coming to birth, the spring awakening of nature, the gradual passage from darkness to light. This however is something too general, too obvious, too elementary and familiar from existing comments on the work to need emphasizing here.

The 'Introduction' opens with the well-known bassoon solo which owes its poignancy and nostalgic character to its melody as well as the 'strangled' sound of this instrument in its 'unusual' high register. The ingenuity with which Stravinsky varies and develops the cells of this theme is fantastic. Boulez has underlined the rhythmic aspect, but this cannot in fact be separated from the melodic; and a general diagram of these first seventeen bars will reveal this, inasmuch as it enables the student to group similar and dissimilar elements in the material and to compare them, thus penetrating the essential nature of Stravinsky's way of working. (Such a diagram recalls the 'semiological' approach, already 'classical' in music. Its model is Lévi-Strauss's well-known structural analysis of myth, but its use here does not imply any semiological intention or conclusion.) Essentially it consists here in regrouping for comparison thematic elements that are related ('vertically'), as we find them presented, articulated and arranged

Ex. 6

in musical time ('horizontally'): generative melodico-rhythmic cells, phrasing, caesuras, repetitions, 'cell-rhythms'.

The 'Introduction' may be divided for analytical purposes into a certain number of 'sequences' (four 'phases' according to Boulez) which may themselves be subdivided into parts or phrases, and then into cells with a thematic function — principal and accessory, transitional and/or timbre-forming ('formants'). The diagram already speaks for itself, but our concern will be with demonstrating the functioning of the 'emergent' thematic cells which play a leading part in the actual development.

This paradigm (which is nothing other than the actual score) can be read, or scanned, line by line, from left to right and from top to bottom of the page. In the vertical columns we find elements *of the same type* — thus in columns *a* and *b* the related motifs and their variations; in column *x* the 'secondary' parts whose essential function is to act as 'formants' of timbres (both by their style of writing and by the instrument to which each is entrusted); and in column *y* a cell with a function that is transitional and ambiguous. The first large sequence consists of thirteen bars and takes up most of the diagram, it can be divided 'horizontally' into five parts or phrases (I–V), each containing an unequal number (four at most) of cells. In phrase I, lines 1, 2, 3 and 4 follow the course of the initial motif in the bassoon.

(1) statement
(2) rhythmic variation grouped in 2 × 3 notes
(3) melodic elision into *a* and transitional cell *y* (Boulez regards this as a contrary-symmetrical grouping of 3 × 2 notes); but in view of the later positions of these elements, which are still transitional and 'marginal', we prefer to consider the two quavers D and A with appoggiatura, as an autonomous cell (*y*)
(4) rhythmic variations in faster note values (quintuplet), with its conclusive function on the tonic.

The section is written in the A-mode (with some notes either defective or altered) and oscillates between a fourth above, and a fourth below its tonic, i.e. between the dominant below and the subdominant above. The fact that this latter is reached only in cell 3*y* tells in favour of regarding this cell as an exception. The C sharp of the horn in the second bar introduces a bold tonal ambiguity (not seen in the diagram).

In the second phrase, the 'pressure' of variation increases, making itself felt in (1) on both the melodic and the rhythmic plane ('triplet within the triplet', as pointed out by Boulez) and on the polyphonic/

sonorous plane, by the intrusion of the formants x and xi (whose function will be systematized later, in the second major sequence). This phrase, more complex thanks to the high index of its variation and its 'consequence' x and xi on the planes of timbre and polyphony, consists, as we can see, of no more than a single cell 1.

The third phrase is a defective repetition of the first: cell 2 is in fact lacking, a strange dissymetrical procedure in which the composer refrains from actually recapitulating a figure that could be considered redundant. (Repetition is a double-edged tool which may either function in a dynamic, 'informative' way by activating the memory or, in another context, may be redundant and neutralizing in effect.) This third phrase is joined by a fourth (linked by the tonic) which, by means of arithmetical values of analogous duration (oddly unobserved by Boulez), introduces an entirely new melodic element, IVb, which acquires the function of an anticipated response. To be observed are its new pole of fixation (D sharp), its discursive articulation, its symmetrical play with upbeats and endings round the main accent (D sharp) and finally its concluding variation, $b1$. The fifth and final phrase opens with the 'mainspring' y, here given a role that is not transitional but introductory and strongly marked; this initial major sequence is concluded by the first motif in its hasty rhythmic variant-form (V = I, 4a). We now leave the diagram, which cannot in any case deal with a polyphonic texture. The second major sequence (Boulez's 'phase 2') is built on motif b, already introduced by anticipation in IV. 'Formants x and xi and their chromatic variants, rising and falling, play a transitional part which will 'surface again' at figure ④ in the score, by means of the small (D) clarinet, while the second oboe introduces a new rhythmic motif. At ⑤ the first oboe, and at ⑥ cor anglais and alto flute, constitute new sound-groups with a rhythmic model based on two quavers/quaver triplet (which has already characterized the first sequence); endings bring demultiplications of note-values. There is an astonishing passage of seven bars just before ⑦ — consisting entirely of timbre-formants, based on cells x and xi (see diagram above), an acoustic monochrome without strong melodic or rhythmic features.

The superimposition of new motifs at ⑦ and the re-use of materials in an evolving polyphonic context lead first, at ⑨, to the introduction of two new leading motifs strongly emphasized (oboe, clarinet in D) of contrasting durations, and of formants whose extremely accelerated note-values 'pulverize' the musical material. (Ex. 7)

Are we to follow Boulez and draw the frontier of a 'third phase' at this

Ex. 7

point? It is the differential index in the matter of *timbre*, which is very high here, that seems to be the chief justification for doing so. A climax in the fantastic multiplication of 'rhythmic-melodic partials' is reached at ⑾. Once again we are called upon to hear this texture as a polyphony of 'formants' i.e. as an organized texture of rhythms structuring the timbre, rather than as a polyphony of 'parts'.

The sudden break at ⑿, and the bassoon's return to the opening phrase (in a different form, denser, and with the cells telescoped) introduces the threefold statement of the rhythm and harmonic outline of the following number — 'Augures printaniers' — with the isochronous pulse characteristic of the 'striated' time of the piece.

'Augures printaniers' seems to pose a different problem to each successive generation. For commentators of the Twenties and Thirties (Schaeffner and Schloezer) it was the toughness of the underlying harmony, whereas for Messiaen and Boulez it was simply the rhythmic aspect. Interesting though our predecessors' attitudes may be, what we today find particularly striking in this piece is its general economy founded on *difference*, which governs its development and conveys its information by parametric relays, all done with incomparable skill. This is the aspect that we should like to discuss further.

The harmonic aspect of 'Augures printaniers' may be reduced essentially to what Stravinsky called 'the *tolchok*-chord' — the 'impulse' or 'motor-chord' (see *Sketches*). This is the predominating element on the first page of the famous notebook, where it appears on the fourth line,* complete with its harmony and its specific rhythm — followed immediately by the horizontal projection of the chord as it appears in the final score:

*There is much discussion of whether Stravinsky started with the micro-elements at the top of the page or by this central structure which appears practically complete (on two staves) in the sketches.

Ex. 8 (Sketches)

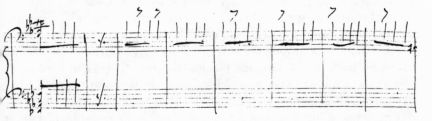

Of the five, six or seven different 'explanations' of this famous chord none is wrong, none entirely right. . . . The first, and most traditional, explains it as a tonal chord of F flat major on which is superimposed its three lower appoggiaturas (E flat, G, B flat) and an 'added' D flat; the inverse being equally conceivable — a tonal chord of E flat major with, below, its three upper appoggiaturas (F flat, A flat, C flat), the lower appoggiatura of the tonic (D flat) forming the added seventh of the fundamental chord (in the view of Schaeffner, who thinks the interpretation of this as a dominant seventh is wrong). According to a third explanation this D flat is an added seventh without any direct harmonic implication, unless we consider the chord E flat, G, B flat, D flat as the dominant seventh of a notional (or rather mythical) A flat which is never stated or even suggested. According to a fourth or fifth theory, commonly held, this chord is polytonal and consists of a simultaneous F flat major and E flat major. A sixth theory has recourse to 'shifting' — the mere mechanical displacement by a semitone of one of the fundamental chords in order to obtain a 'dissonance' — an harmonic tension. Still another explanation, and one which takes into account the fact that Stravinsky was known to compose at the piano, points to the natural position of the hands on the keyboard, left and right respectively falling more or less 'instinctively' on the F flat major of the white notes and the E flat major of the black. . . . There is no point in pursuing such hypotheses or in forming others about the 'historical' origin of the chord: what we are faced with is an overall sound-phenomenon — a *complex sound*, however simple in theory. Whatever its origin or behaviour, this chord must now be considered as an indissoluble unit of sound, and perceived as such for its individual *quality*. In the last resort therefore it is a question of timbre — and we can picture Stravinsky searching lovingly for it at the keyboard: this 'appetite for sound', as he called it, is very much present.

This chord is repeated some two hundred and eighty times in purely qualitative relationship either to itself (in different forms and dispositions, instrumentations and massings) or with other chords sometimes even more radically hostile to 'harmonic' analysis — vertical constructions totally chromatic by nature (seconds, sevenths, ninths) at ⑮ or, in the next bar, entirely abstract constructions of six notes, either superimposed fifths or, before ⑱, fourths. 'Functional harmony', in fact, takes second place to the idea of *blocks*, in the *Sacre*.

The rhythmic structures attaching to such blocks are expressed in 'Augures' not in terms of different durations, as in the 'Introduction', but in terms of intensities or accents on isochronic durations (regular quavers or their multiples), in fact in terms of densities, masses and timbres. This association, this perpetual transformation of all musical parameters under the category of rhythm, in fact imposes (though is this not true of all music?) a generalized idea of rhythm as the point at which all the relations that structure the phenomenon of music converge.

The first 'rhythmic model' provides a convincing example of this (see Ex. 8). Here the rhythms of intensity produced by the accents of the strings are reinforced by the mass-rhythm of eight horns and the *timbre*-rhythm of their brass sonorities, in all its singularity, its qualitative difference in relation to the context.

The structure of this 8-bar rhythmic model is asymmetrical in accentuation, and this asymmetry gives the passage its specific character, just as it owes its dynamism — its brutal violence — to the dialectic established between implicit strong beats and explicitly shifted accents. Boulez's analysis of this model as consisting of four times two (4 × 2) bars throws light on some further characteristics: two 'preparatory' unaccented bars, two consecutive bars one of which is strongly syncopated, finally 2 × 2 internally symmetrical bars (syncope — strong beat/strong beat — syncope). This approach, which is in any case descriptive rather than analytical, seems rather reductive, although it provides a correct summary of the passage; for this is surely a typical instance in which the structure is only singular in so far as its future behaviour is concerned. On the other hand a comparison of this model with one of its later avatars (⑲) tells more in favour of Boulez's analysis; although, here as elsewhere, it deliberately ignores the *melodic* aspect of the new version of the model, which also determines its rhythm, as is generally the case with unaccented structures. These do indeed have their own, implicit, accentuation which is quite as striking as that of structures that are explicitly accented. . . . But we must not anticipate.

The first rhythmic model is followed immediately by a second (at ⑭) more neutral in character: all the parameters concerned in the rhythmic play are here 'blocked' — in fact intensities, timbres and masses do not vary or produce any differences. On the other hand a parameter that took no part in the first model here assumes, almost on its own, the role of generator. This is pitch, which executes a regular pendular movement that appears on the general rhythmic plane as a slight accentuation of the first and the third quaver in the bar. This accentuation is both quantitative (the D flat and E flat are higher than the other notes and therefore stand out) and qualitative: they are the seventh and the 'tonic' of E flat in the upper harmonic constituent of the chord. This is something that favours — though only in this one instance — a local polytonal interpretation of the chord in which, to be precise, three tonalities are superimposed — E flat in the cor anglais, C major in the bassoons, C major/E major in the cellos. We shall see the new models that Stravinsky further deduces, and the functions that he assigns to the two initial models.

The next stage presents us with another aspect of the initial model and a still stricter application of his principle of asymmetry, shifting a single bar within the model and thus ruining any attempt to establish a symmetrical two-bar scheme.

Two other characteristics are worth noticing. On the one hand the dimensions of the repeated chord structure here exceed the original eight bars and spread to ten. On the other hand we find after the fifth bar a new model, very brightly coloured (high and very high woodwinds, and then solo trumpet) and presenting a symmetrical structure within the remaining five bars allotted to it:

Ex. 9

The same is true of the following structure, in more differentiated note-values, built on the chord of superimposed fifths mentioned earlier.

Meanwhile the initial rhythmic model has changed its note-values (sextuplets in the violas), while harmonically we are presented with the superimposition of the two tonalities of E flat and C major.

The exact repetition of the initial model (strings and horns) announces the appearance of a new melodic-rhythmic model, entrusted to the four bassoons, described in the *Sketches* as *dikaya popevka* — savage chant: the very first page presents it in a curious form, disguised by speed (semiquavers) and high pitch:

Ex. 10

This model will provide a pattern of imitations in which the parts are layered and orchestrated so as to produce the clearest possible polyphonic outline. Rhythm is expressed here as much by the various accentuations as by the important points in the melody (climax and close) — these last taking over sole responsibility for the rhythm in the second part of the structure. The augmentation of the polyphonic density is interrupted — and this is typical of the *Sacre* — by a brutal descent to the deep bass and a pause, that we shall be discussing in a moment. This is the end of the first part of 'Augures' — a part in which fundamental rhythmic models are *exposed*, grafted as they are on to a relentless isochronous pulsation. The second part is concerned with the general *progress* of information, brought to a climax by a technique of parametric relays and by constant shifting of the location of difference — a perfect example of Stravinsky's skilful manipulation of space-time.

Silence — a double cut in the bass — a pause — a terrific unleashing of energy in the highest register! After this triple impact, the effect of which is the more violent because it is concerned with differences that are both unexpected and of maximum intensity, there comes the absolute minimum: a murmur of harmonic-rhythmic 'streaks' which are both familiar and regular. In this way, by a very characteristic clean break, Stravinsky 'effaces' the information that has been gradually accumulating (and is already on the way to becoming redundant?) and provides himself with a fresh space-time, a 'zero point', at which we hear only the *pianissimo* pulsing of the cor anglais accompanied by two timbre-'formants'. This pulsation, emphasized at first on its first and third half-beats, is gradually filled out by a systematic embroidery of semiquavers which provides harmonic components comparable to those at the outset; and then by a succession of string-entries, 'formants' of trills that increase the mass and intensify the colours of the music. The rhythmic diminution which then appears in the first violins takes over from the repeated chords and is followed immediately by a new melodic-rhythmic model and its augmented versions.

This model allows the symmetrical model of Ex. 9 to return for a time; it then reappears in the alto flute alone, followed by the two other flutes, while the basic pulsation of the music continues to be amplified by the addition of successive instrumental groups: masses and intensities are augmented with increasing effect. The next relay of information takes the form of a new theme, stated mezzo-piano: economical in intensity but extravagant in timbre, with its four trumpets. This is the simple, songlike theme of the *khorovod*, one of the few themes to which Stravinsky returns later (in 'Rondes printanières').

Ex. 11

The previous models are kept in play, 'orbiting' round the *khorovod* and its trilling counter-subject, while the orchestral volume continues to grow — a double crescendo of mass and intensity. At 30 comes another break — intensity, mass and timbre all suddenly reduced to a minimum, with only the strings' rhythmic murmur in the background. This new cut, or 'negative mass' (so to say), itself creates a powerful difference, and represents another way of restoring yet again, and without any loss, that 'virgin' quality of space-time, in order to enhance the spectacular progression of the final section.

Faster 'formants', brilliant orchestral colours (two piccolos, and *flatterzunge* gradually extending to all the woodwinds) — it is the triumph of the melodic model of 14 at extreme pitches. Marked rhythmically by the return of the basic cell of 'Augures', the model reaches a paroxysm of excitement and spills over into the frenzied ternary pulsations of the next piece, 'Jeu du rapt'.

*

If 'Augures' shows an obsession with regular metre and shifting accents, 'Jeu du rapt' (abduction-game) is marked by an irregular metre that carves its own rhythmic 'slices'. Strong points sometimes coincide with the accents (explicit or implicit) given by the first beat of the bar, and sometimes contradict them; on occasion the two principles unite. Such is the case of the symmetrical, non-retrogradable figure *a*, with its central accent on the strong beat, superimposed on another rhythmic wave *b*, in which the accents shift automatically every four quavers within a basic 9/8:

Ex. 12

This small 'conflict-machine' contains a highly explosive charge.

Rhythmically the most spectacular passage is at 46 , where we see a rhythmic *development* brought about by the dialectical opposing of two elements perpetually evolving in relation to each other, all within a variable metre. Boulez's analysis of this 'opposition between a simple rhythm and a rhythmic structure' is particularly clear, setting out both the opposition and the mobility of the opposing forces. (Ex. 13)

The numbers subdividing B (B2, B3, B4, B6) refer to the number of basic units (quavers) in B. (We can see how the simple rhythm B progressively 'pursues' the rhythmic structure A, which visibly 'shrinks' beneath the attacks of B. These become increasingly frequent and determined, until A is finally 'devoured' and B establishes total control over the structure.) We have already discovered an analogous procedure in the 'Danse infernale' of *Firebird*.

This kind of rhythmic dialectic, structuring a development, can be seen again in the next piece, 'Rondes printanières'. At 54 the whole orchestra comes to a violent halt followed by two piercing explosions in the flutes alone, introducing a simple rhythm developed by the whole orchestra and, in the strings, a rhythmic structure, dominated by the interval of the fourth.

The transference of rhythmic procedures from one piece to another

contributes to the organic unity of the work. But 'Rondes printanières'
also establishes more far-reaching *thematic* links, as in the case of the
khorovod from 'Augures', which only reaches its full expansion at 53,
where it appears in the full orchestra.

Ex. 13

(After P. Boulez)

There are new aspects of Stravinsky's rhythmic invention in 'Jeux de
cités rivales' and 'Cortège du sage'. The first of these, which is entirely
in 'striated' time with a single rhythmic unit — the quaver — is
concerned with irregular metres and the dialectic between deliberate
accents and the frequently changing bar-line, just as later we shall find,
once again, the vertical accent of the B type opposed to the 'horizontal'
rhythmic structure of the A type, as already demonstrated in 'Jeux du
rapt'. These formal procedures are perfectly consistent with the general
form of the work. As for 'Cortège du sage', it is metrically unvarying but

provides opportunities for a fantastic polyrhythmy which is organically
linked with timbre, each instrumental group (and even each individual
instrument) following its own specific rhythms. This can be seen in Ex.
14. Observe

> — the rhythm of the flutes, independent of the bar-line, and then of
>   the piccolo (a crotchet — three crotchets)
> — the oboes' semiquavers and crotchets
> — the clarinets' groups of two quavers
> — the bassoons' appoggiaturas
> — the accentuated binary rhythm of the double-bassoon
> — the totally independent behaviour of the horns (in 3 and 5
>   crotchets)
> — the rhythmic identity between the piccolo trumpet and the
>   piccolo clarinet, on intervals of augmented fourths
> — the internal counterpoint in the trumpets
> — the trombones' 'negative' rhythm in relation to the 'positive'
>   rhythm of the piccolo
> — the rhythm of the four tubas which announce the 'Sage's trumpet
>   theme', its nucleus consisting of two intervals of a minor and a
>   major second, which move independently of the metre
> — the sextuplets, accentuated in 2 × 3, of the timpani
> — the crotchet 'duolets' of the bass drum (sound-rest)
> — the inverted 'duolets' of the tamtam (rest-sound)
> — the 'quartolets' of the guero, or rasp
> — and finally the strings' rhythmic figures (four different varieties)

It is interesting to compare this page with Stockhausen's *Gruppen*
(1958). Stravinsky's intentions here are of course different from those of
Stockhausen, which were motivated by a speculative theory —
establishing a 'rhythm of formants' on the hypothesis of a structural
interdependence between rhythm and timbre, using three orchestras to
form three temporal layers spatially distinct. Ex. 14 does suggest that
Stravinsky may have been searching — intuitively — for something of
the same kind. He appears in any case to have achieved a similar *result*,
since the listener is aware not so much of polyrhythms as such, but
rather of their effect on timbre. Here in fact we have a new kind of
musical spectrum composed of 'partials' that vibrate in rhythmically
differentiated ways; a metaphor, in the field of durations (what
Stockhausen calls 'macro-time'), of the periodic vibrations of frequen-
cies (belonging to micro-time).[8]
The 'Danse de la terre' is preceded by the famous unreal chord of

Ex. 14

'Adoration de la terre' (in Russian, the 'Kissing' of the earth) — a vertical spectrum consisting entirely of harmonics. The Dance itself exploits the rhythmic antagonism that we have already analysed in the 'Jeu du rapt'. The unity of the *Sacre* becomes increasingly clear, supported by the perpetual presence of a logically consistent system of rhythmic development. But the procedure is here taken over by more complex elements. Instead of a horizontal rhythmic structure *alternating* with regular vertical impacts, these two opposed elements are here combined simultaneously. We have the same phenomenon of one element invading another, which gradually wilts away, and of inversions of one element in relation to another. Other elements belonging to type A — a melodic-rhythmic system of triplets and another of semiquavers — come upon the scene (analysed in great detail by Boulez) and, after the familiar break in intensity and mass, are solely responsible for the terrific crescendo. The end of this piece, which completes Part 1 of the *Sacre*, is crowned by a return to the shock-chords on the rhythmic pedal of its opening. It is worth observing that the general melodic line of the C and D major chords, with augmented fourths added, derives oddly enough from a popular tune noted down by Stravinsky in the *Sketches* and not kept (in order to recognize its identity the pace must be mentally slowed down). The Russian heading means 'Dance of the earth'.

Ex. 15

*

Much has been said about the 'chromaticism' of the 'Introduction' to Part 2; but this chromaticism does not concern the thematic material of either this or, as we shall see, of 'Cercles mystérieux' which follows immediately, any more than it undermines the tonal harmonic functions of the music: it is essentially a matter of the harmonic disposition of the actual timbre. 'Chromaticism', in fact, should be understood here in its etymological meaning of *colour*. If the chromatic inheritance of Rimsky, as we saw it in *Firebird*, can still be said to be present here, it is only as a distant poetic memory. It appears in the orchestral 'backgrounds' in which instrumental blocks of harmony are 'protracted' by conjoint chromatic steps.

In opposition to the chromatic surface of this 'Introduction', the thematic material is basically diatonic, with its predominant fourths and major seconds. Its sources are twofold.

In the case of the wonderful *khorovod* at 83, with its nocturnal and feminine atmosphere, and its corollary theme (five bars after 93 — 'Cercles') the generating element was another popular tune which though not used as such by Stravinsky, provided the intervals and the rhythm for both the 'Introduction' and 'Cercles'. This is the melody which appears twice in *Sketches* (on page 50 and page 53) and is identified as coming from Rimsky's collection with the name *Utushka* ('little duck'). Here, first, is the hidden source of the two *khorovod* themes and then the themes themselves:

Ex. 16

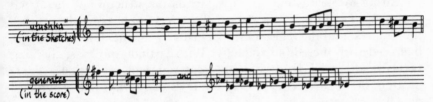

These examples speak for themselves. Note the predominance of the interval of the fourth in the original tune and how Stravinsky distributes it in his two themes.

The second theme in the 'Introduction' appears just before 85 and again at 86 in the delicate counterpoint of the two muted trumpets. It originates in 'Cortège du sage', and appears in this very form at 83, in the cellos (discontinuous rhythmic values of 3, 6, 4 and 2 crotchets),

Ex. 17

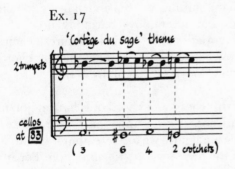

before its inversion in the two-trumpet counterpoint; the two seconds (major and minor) which give the theme its character, thus establish a further thematic 'bridge' in the *Sacre*.

The archetypal succession of *khorovod* — dance — procession continues to govern the pieces which now follow. 'Glorification de l'élue', which appears in *Sketches* as 'Danse sauvage', is one of the peaks of the *Sacre* thanks to its rhythmic power and originality. No summary of this piece can do it justice: if, for instance, we say that it is ternary in form (ABA), we immediately obliterate the dissymmetrical character of its rhythms, which are directly related to its form. 'Thus it is rhythm that determines the architecture of this "Glorification de l'élue" quite as much as — perhaps even more than — the musical layout, which in any case remains static in spite of the different instrumental dispositions.'(Boulez)

A purely rhythmic approach to this piece gives little idea of the complexities that analysis can reveal, the 'instrumental dispositions' appearing to play as important a part as the structure of the actual durations. The formal articulation of the piece appears in the masses, the timbres, and the registers — particularly the masses — which are balanced with incredible audacity. With virtually no bass, shooting skyward and marked by discontinuous sonorous projections, 'Glorification de l'élue' seems to defy the laws of gravity, like a pyramid dancing on its apex.

'Evocation' and 'Action rituelle des ancêtres' belong to the category of *procession* and are characterized in the one case by metric discontinuity governing a vertical rhythm, and in the other by metric continuity with a great variety of rhythm within the polyphonic texture. Both are relatively stable stages between the 'decentralized' rhythm of 'Glorification' and the 'Danse sacrale' which follows. The latter furnishes, as it were by itself, a summary of all the chief aspects of the work: continuity/discontinuity, horizontal rhythm/vertical rhythm, stable metre/shifting metre, and harmonic constants. Like 'Augures', 'Danse sacrale' employs harmony precisely in order to generate the differentiations between structures, each of which is dominated by its own specific chord. The opening chord is certainly bitonal in origin; but do we ever actually *hear* a chord as bitonal, let alone polytonal?

We can analyse this chord as a chord of E flat (major/minor) and D major with a seventh added in the upper parts (see A, Ex. 18). But if we examine this simple amalgam, we discover that it has another function in the harmony of the *Sacre* — a *unifying* function. For it resembles in structure the 'Augures' chord (see Ex. 8), and in both we have the semitone 'shift' and the added seventh, thus providing a harmonic link between the first and the last pieces in the work.

Just as the harmony, whatever its origin, is not the 'vertical sum' of its constituent parts but a new, irreducible block, neither can the form of 'Danse sacrale' be reduced to a 'horizontal' (or linear) scheme of successive stages. If we say that 'Danse sacrale' is a rondo, 'we do no more than affirm the strictest, but also the most summary truth' (Boulez). Each of these parts proceeds, in fact, from a different rhythmic principle, the whole amounting to a recapitulation of the rhythmic procedures of the *Sacre*, though raised to the highest power of speculation — and effect.

The first part of 'Danse sacrale' is articulated in aperiodic rhythmic cells. Apart from their varying durations and changing metres, it is the complex relations between masses, timbres and intensities, quite as much as the harmonies, that structure this ensemble of discontinuous impacts. Three elements are distinguishable, which we will call A, B and C. In A, which consists of two cells divided between high and low, a weak mass and a strong, the contrasting harmonic densities are not identical if the first of them is a D in the bass, a D (less clear) in the timpani, or a rest visible at the beginning of B, Ex. 18; and if the chord of the second cell is spread or close (the double embroidery of the D forming, in this instance, a small 'cluster'):

Ex. 18

The second element B, which is linked to its predecessor harmonically, consists of a 'silent upbeat' (a paradox that appears justified in the circumstances), an accent and an ending — the accent itself being sometimes missing. It too is very dependent on the metre, on the varieties of attack, masses, registers and timbres (off-beat rhythm, *staccato-tenuto*, high-low, brass-strings-woodwinds-percussion all in shifting combinations) that differentiate the structure each time.

Apart from responding to these same parametric criteria of

differentiation, the third element C consists of three types of cells and has a specific harmonic and rhythmic structure of its own; its behaviour is cadential in character and we shall, therefore, not be surprised to find it in the *coda* of the work, where its third cell — a rising one — plays an important part.

These three elements, in their different alternations and concrete rhythmic structures, make up the 'refrain' of 'Danse sacrale' and immediately identify it beyond all doubt. The clarity of its musical constituents ensures its impact on the listener: in fact everything in this highly speculative process 'comes off' musically. It is well worth consulting Boulez's detailed diagrams for an alternative scanning of both this first 'refrain' and its later appearances and transformations. (See Boulez, 'Stravinsky demeure', pp. 128–135).

In the first 'couplet' of 'Danse sacrale' we again meet one of the familiar procedures of the *Sacre*, the dialectical confrontation of two rhythmic structures, one of which consists of vertical impacts (M), the other of a chromatically descending horizontal figure (N). The first of these obeys the principle of the constant distributive variation of the semiquavers of its cells; the other shows very delicate variations of pitch-repetition and polyphonic 'overlapping' of timbres.

Ex. 19

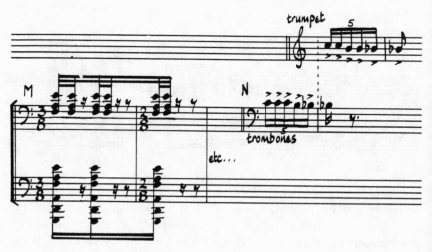

At the outset these elements are arranged respectively in 'background' and 'figures', the timbre and intensity of N (trombones and trumpets *ff*) standing out against the pulsation of M (strings, low woodwinds and horns). Even so we shall observe M evolving during the course of the piece, doubling its rhythm by shortening durations and increasing intensity thus eventually (as we have observed on another occasion) threatening, if not actually 'devouring', the element N, despite N's increased aggressiveness.

The refrain is repeated a semitone lower; in *Sketches* Stravinsky makes a note to 'transpose the whole into C sharp major', referring to the 'D major' original. On the other hand the rhythmic structure and the proportions are identical.

The second 'couplet' presents an entirely different rhythmic structure. It rests on an *ostinato* composed of the following pitches, rhythms and timbres:

Ex. 20

A glance at Ex. 23 will show the importance attached to this in *Sketches* (green ink for the pitches and rhythms, red for a number of possible instrumentations). Observe the use of timpani as precisely pitched 'melodic' instruments and the two leaps of a major seventh and a minor ninth, absolute chromatic intervals that violently contradict the diatonic theme announced first by the horns and then by the high strings. This theme displays — and will display even more markedly in its later developments — a direct relationship with the popular theme quoted in connection with 'Danse de la terre' (see Ex. 15).

Ex. 21

Ex. 21 reveals a still further unifying link between, in this instance, the final pieces of the two parts of the *Sacre*. (Nor is this all; in another sketch we find the theme of the 'Sage' as well! It is true that this does not appear in the definitive version, but it still proves the composer's wish to create 'objective' unifying links.)

Stravinsky abandoned the insistent repetition of the D (top line of same sketch) in its original regular form, but it appears in much more subtle rhythmic forms in the final score. The D is 'frozen' into longer, asymmetrical note-values, above the pulsating *ostinato* shown in Ex. 20.

Ex. 22

The quavers of the diatonic theme *x* in Ex. 21 will become crotchets when the clarity of the instrumental counterpoint makes this necessary. But Stravinsky will not hesitate to go back to the repeated D of *Sketches* and even to exaggerate these repetitions for expressive, 'orgiastic' purposes, as it seems.

The 'rondo' flies into fragments; the 'second refrain' is no more than a 7-bar enclave in the 'second couplet' making possible a regrouping of note-values, the repeated notes becoming aperiodic groupings of 3–4–2–3 at the end of the couplet.

The orchestral mass and the intensity both increase greatly: the coda starts with a *fff* accent. It is built on transformations of the initial elements A, B and C; contains two parts; and acts as a kind of powerfully transfigured 'third refrain'. Essentially the first part uses A and B, with an element announcing C — five descending semiquavers — appearing twice to prepare the second part. This, according to Boulez, will only make use of C which, as we approach the end, continues to gather note-values to itself: starting with the five original semiquavers Boulez enumerates successive groupings of C_5, C_6, C_7, C_8 and even periods of C_{14} in which 'module 5' can nevertheless be identified. On the other hand this final passage may just as well be considered as based on a new cell of two and three semiquavers, preceded by an upbeat of which the constant characteristic — it proves gradually to be clearly deliberate — is its *upward motion*:

Ex. 23

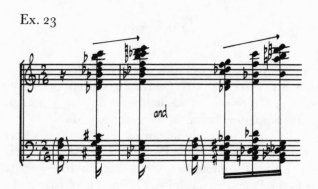

The conflict of intensities-masses-registers-timbres reaches a paroxysm in the three final bars where, as in 'Augures' and 'Rondes', the orchestral *tutti* gives way to the solitary *pianissimo* scale-passage of the flutes alone. Against the orchestra at full strength and the dynamic marking *fff*, Stravinsky suddenly sets a minimum mass, intensity and timbre in the topmost register: a 'negative' accent once again conveying a powerful difference. A correspondingly violent contrast is produced by the explosion of intensity that follows, the sudden descent to the depths of brass, basses and percussion, 'positive mass' and unmistakable in its effectiveness.

Thus the axe falls, and with it ends *Le Sacre du printemps*.

V

Critical Years

THE FIRST LONDON performance of the *Sacre* took place on 11 July 1913 while Stravinsky was recovering from typhoid in his Neuilly nursing-home. The reception was neither enthusiastic nor hostile, most of the polite applause being apparently for Marie Piltz, who was dazzling as l'Elue. It was only in April 1914 that the work was to have another, concert performance in Paris, at the Casino de Paris, and this was a triumph for the composer, whom his admirers carried on their shoulders to the Place de la Trinité. The 'bomb' of 1913 had no sequel, in fact. . . .

Out of the clinic, Stravinsky returned to Ustilug to convalesce. Still weak, he could only return to the three small songs that he had begun in 1906 and now dedicated to his children, *Souvenirs de mon enfance*: 'The little magpie', 'The crow' and 'Tchicher-yacher', for voice and piano, finished at Clarens in November 1913 and later orchestrated (1930). But he had already decided that he would set about composing a major work, and this was the opera *The Nightingale*, commissioned by the Moscow Free Theatre for a sum of 10,000 roubles, with the prospect of a performance during the following year.

The Nightingale, 'lyrical tale in three acts', with a libretto based on Hans Andersen by Stepan Mitusov, had in fact been begun in 1908; and just before his death Rimsky had 'approved' some of the music of Act 1 at a piano hearing. The original commission and subsequent success of *Firebird*, followed by *Petrushka* and the *Sacre* had distracted the composer's attention from this project which now suddenly gained a new interest for him thanks to the timely commission from the Free Theatre. The immediate problem was how to achieve unity of style: for his music had undergone great changes between 1908–09 and 1913–14.

Stravinsky's first solution was to persuade the theatre to accept Act 1 as a complete work in itself, and when the theatre rejected this idea and he was obliged to make a choice, he persuaded himself that, given the paucity of action, Act 1 could be considered as a kind of prologue, which would justify its style being different from that of the rest of the opera. Having made up his mind, Stravinsky completed Act 2 at Clarens and Act 3, in 1914, at Leysin where his wife was in a sanatorium with tuberculosis. Their fourth child, Maria-Milena, was born here.

In the meantime the Moscow Free Theatre went bankrupt and Diaghilev turned up, as though by a miracle, at Leysin, in January 1914, with the suggestion that the opera should be given to the 'Ballets russes' in Paris and in London. Stravinsky seems to have agreed to this without demanding any additional fee. . . .

Act 1 of *The Nightingale* opens with an introduction which, it has often been pointed out, recalls both Debussy ('Nuages') and, by the chains of alternating thirds and fifths, Mussorgsky. Stravinsky was later to write: 'Though I knew he [Debussy] would have liked the Mussorgsky-Debussy beginning, he probably would have said about that, too, "young man, I do it better".' (*Memories and Commentaries*)

Stravinsky remembered writing in the diary that he kept between 1906 and 1910 and left in his safe in Russia: 'Why should I follow Debussy so closely when the real creator of this operatic style was Mussorgsky?'

Over the limpid harmonies of the 'Introduction' rises an elegiac melody followed by the song of the Fisherman down by the water — and nothing could be less like Debussy or more Russian than this fresh melodic line with its simple, swaying rhythm. The Fisherman, a child of nature and rather out of place in this imaginary China, is waiting for the Nightingale, whose song we soon hear, at first as an instrumental 'improvisation' in G flat major, and then as a vocalise, delicate and tender. Stravinsky is by no means trying to evoke a 'real-life' nightingale here but its stylized archetypal song, or rather the *musical idea* of a nightingale's song, in the style of the *romances* in Russian operas written under French influence. . . . The Court of China itself is archetypal, deliberately showy in fact, with its conventional pentatonic music and sham characters — 'musical-box' automata and little else. . . . The bird follows them to the palace, invited to charm the Emperor.

In Act 2 (since we must follow Stravinsky and call each of the three scenes of the work an 'act', although the whole opera lasts less than an hour) we encounter the composer's new dazzling orchestral palette acquired with the *Sacre*. Here in fact we have the link between the *Sacre* and *The Nightingale* — the wealth of the orchestra with its novel and fascinating sonorities, designed to create an atmosphere of mystery. The other 'novelties' are to be found equally in *Petrushka* — the occasional instances of bitonality, the powerful harmonic polarities and the bold melodic outlines. As for the *rhythmic* reminiscences of the *Sacre*, they are already becoming blurred: the triple polyrhythm in the 'Marche chinoise' and a number of changing metres such as the following are no more than survivals:

Ex. 24

The dramatic action of the piece does not really begin until the middle of Act 2, and it takes the form of a 'musical competition', the confrontation of two poetic principles — the creative freedom represented by the Nightingale and the 'soulless', mechanical principle represented by the artificial Nightingale, a Japanese 'import' presented to the Emperor, whose fancy it has taken:

Ex. 25

The real nightingale does not wait for the Emperor's decision but flies away.

Act 3 is the real centre of gravity of the work, the intrusion of fear and death providing the necessary theatrical interest. In the 'Marche des spectres' the good and the evil deeds of the Emperor appear at his deathbed. A very simple melody, impressively entrusted to bassoons and deep brass, is taken up by the chorus and announced *fortissimo* by the horns, recalling the dramatic colours of the *Sacre*:

Ex. 26

The scene derives its musical and dramatic power from the contrast between this archaic tune and the redeeming song of the returning Nightingale. The world to which this contrast belongs is once again that of popular *epos*, both Russian and universal, revolving round the two inseparable forces of Eros and Thanatos, the song of love and the song of death. And it is here, where the musical language is stripped of conventional *chinoiseries*, that the song of the bird, as it fights for life, is most moving and most irresistibly beautiful.

In this context the 'Bonjour à tous!' that marks the Emperor's recovery and the 'happy ending', sounds less convincing than the final return of the Fisherman's song on which the curtain falls.

The Nightingale was put on in a hurry, but very charmingly, and given by the 'Ballets russes' at the Paris Opéra on 26 May 1914 under Pierre Monteux. As Stravinsky was to say later: 'Scenically, thanks to Alexandre Benois, who designed the costumes and the sets, it was the most beautiful of all my early Diaghilev works.' (*Memories and Commentaries*)

In accordance with a principle of Diaghilev's, the singers — and especially the Nightingale (coloratura soprano) — were placed in the pit and 'dubbed' by dancers on the stage. The musicians who attended this first night seem to have been enthusiastic, though Debussy, of whose opinion Stravinsky was nervous, seems not to have reacted.

A symphonic suite, *Chant du rossignol* was composed at Morges in 1917 for the 'Ballets russes', who could only give the work in 1920 at the Paris Opéra with sets by Matisse. This suite consisted of a new 'montage' of the music of Acts 2 and 3 with important cuts and transformations. The dazzling orchestral writing was possibly Stravinsky's final farewell to the world of the *Sacre*, from which this splendid work is in other respects very far removed.

*

Immediately after the production of *The Nightingale* Stravinsky went back to Switzerland, settling in a chalet at Salvan, in the Valais, where he worked at *Pribaoutki* and the *Three Pieces for string quartet*, which he dedicated to Ernest Ansermet. On 2 April of this same year Ansermet conducted the composer's youthful *Symphony* at Montreux, inviting him to conduct some of the rehearsals, a new experience which turned out to be a kind of 'dress rehearsal' for his career as a conductor. He and Ansermet met earlier at Clarens, where they were neighbours, but from now on they became close friends. Ansermet was already indefatigable in propagating Stravinsky's music, and was to continue to be so, as the composer willingly acknowledged, until, in 1929, a spectacular quarrel over Ansermet's cuts in *Jeu de cartes* more or less ended their friendship.

Hardly a month before war was declared, Stravinsky paid a short visit to Ustilug and Kiev — his last visit to his native country until fifty years later, when he returned as an American citizen and as an interpreter of his own music. He brought back with him from Kiev P. Kirievsky's *Recueil de chants populaires*, a basic work on Russian folklore, like Afanasyev's. As the war spread, Stravinsky — dimly aware of being finally exiled — plunged into the study of these texts, in which he was to find inspiration for almost all the works of the immediate future. His imagination was already fired, and he was selecting, sorting and preparing texts for what were to become *Les Noces, Renard, Pribaoutki, Berceuses du chat* and the *Quatre Chants paysans russes*, or 'Saucers'. As for Diaghilev, his astute mind was busy with plans for the 'Ballets russes' to tour in North America, undismayed by the fact that the company was at the moment scattered to the four winds. He reserved to himself the right to present *Les Noces*, which was already beginning to take shape, and dreamed of a spectacular 'super-Russian' *Liturgy*, complete with ikons, vestments etc. — a project that offended Stravinsky's convictions in more ways than one. He refused to lend his hand to a stage-parody of the Orthodox Mass (having found fault with Wagner for doing precisely that with Parsifal). Diaghilev, moreover, seems to have wanted to get the two works for the price of one (*Les Noces*) — something strictly forbidden by Stravinsky's ethical code in money matters.

As war continued to rage, his stay in Switzerland, originally a temporary one, depending on Catherine Stravinsky's health, became permanent, and the composer settled with his family in the villa 'La Pervenche' at Clarens, where he was Ansermet's tenant. Stravinsky was to spend almost six years in Switzerland, which he loved and where he found refuge and security if not material resources. The war had robbed him of his publishers and of a large proportion of his royalties. The Editions Russes de Musique being in difficulties, Stravinsky tentatively approached Ricordi's through Alfredo Casella. Was it, as Casella later maintained, Stravinsky's 'excessive' demands that 'scared' Tito Ricordi? However that may be, his refusal meant that the famous Milan publishing-house missed one of the great contracts of the century. . . .

He was perpetually on the move but the rhythm of his travelling became progressively slower. In London for the first English performance of *The Nightingale* he was fascinated by the sound-patterns of the bells of St Paul's, which he jotted down as his taxi passed the cathedral.

In Florence he spent a fortnight as the guest of a depressed Diaghilev, whom he was in any case to meet soon afterwards in Rome at the Italian première of *Petrushka*. In London, and again in Rome, he met Prokofiev, who was also looking for a publisher. For Diaghilev Stravinsky had in his suitcase the *Three Easy Pieces* for piano duet, the 'March' dedicated to Casella, the 'Valse' dedicated to Satie and the 'Polka' dedicated to Diaghilev himself, whom he had imagined as 'a ring-master in tail coat and top hat, cracking his whip and giving orders to his eques-triennes'. (*Chronicle*)

Meanwhile Stravinsky's wife's health had made it necessary to move from Clarens to Château-d'Oex. He found a room with a piano where he could work, but it was so cold that 'the piano strings succumbed' (*Chronicle*). 'For two days I tried to work there in overcoat, fur cap and snow-boots, with a rug over my knees', but he had to give it up. It was in these conditions that he began the sketches for *Les Noces*. . . .

In the late spring of 1915 Stravinsky settled at Morges (where there is now a Quai Igor-Stravinsky) and there he was to remain for the next five years. Not far away, at Lausanne, there was a group of 'Ballets russes' artists clustered, as it were for protection, round their tutelary god Diaghilev. The composer would arrive by bicycle, in plus-fours, and there he would find Massine, the painters Bakst, Larionov and Goncharova and Ansermet, who was to become the company's permanent conductor.

It was through Ansermet that Stravinsky met C. F. Ramuz, over a glass of the light Swiss wine. In his memoirs Ramuz recalls with admirable candour this first meeting and his subsequent friendship with the composer, honestly trying to identify their two personalities:

I could see at once, for instance, that you, Stravinsky, like me, liked bread when it was good and wine when it was good, and bread and wine together, one for the other, one by the other . . . I got to know you in and by the kind of pleasure I saw you take in things, the 'humble things', as the saying goes, and certainly the most basic. We first came to understand each other through a certain kind, a certain quality of delight experienced by one's whole being. As you know, I love the body, because I cannot really separate it from the soul; I love especially the wonderful unity there is in their total sharing of any activity, when abstract and concrete are mutually reconciled, and explain and throw light on each other.

Stravinsky may have loved 'humble things', but everything leads us to believe that he and Ramuz were linked by their differences rather than their similarities. Ramuz was essentially an idyllic personality, whereas Stravinsky was essentially caustic and sceptical. The fact remains that there was a strong common interest linking this Protestant peasant, the son of Vaudois vinedressers, to this Orthodox townsman, who had been brought up in the atmosphere of the Russian Imperial theatres and come to maturity in the cosmopolitan West. It was an interest in the popular poetry which was one of Stravinsky's main concerns during these war years and of which Ramuz was to become the diligent, modest and imaginative translator.

The works composed during these Morges years were all restricted in scale and length but of great interest. They were namely the *Three Pieces for string quartet*, *Pribaoutki*, and *Berceuses du chat*, composed before *Renard* and during the long and difficult birth of *Les Noces*.

The *Three Pieces for string quartet* were written in April (Leysin) and July (Salvan), and they are dedicated to the composer's new friend Ansermet, who arranged for them to be commissioned *a posteriori* by the Flonzaley Quartet. (It was always one of Stravinsky's principles — and a very sensible one — to write what he wanted and then to get it commissioned.) In this short work we find the chromaticisms of *The Nightingale* refined, and harmonically Stravinsky goes pretty far, especially in the second piece in which the chromaticism is almost complete:

Ex.27

Each of these *Three Pieces* seems to illustrate in a different way how Stravinsky set about absorbing and transforming procedures taken from the *Sacre* into his language. Variable metre and shifted accents (first piece), compartmentalized and contrasted structures with changing tempi (second piece), will evolve in the third piece towards a 'vertical' style that looks forward to the chorale in the *Symphonies of Wind Instruments*. There the wealth of rhythms will be at first sight masked, swamped — but all the more effective. Within the space of a few bars no less than eight real duration-values occur between dotted minim and crotchet. What makes this third piece a small masterpiece is the grouping of these values in structures that are both static (slowness of tempo) and dynamic (durations, accents, variable metres) and their actual *presentation* in time. . . . Objectively speaking, these pieces have nothing in common with Webern's except their brevity. Syntax (tonal in the one and atonal in the other), repetition (essential to Stravinsky and banned by Webern), musical character (vertical in the one and horizontal in the other) are all different; yet paradoxically the only place for these *Three Pieces* in the *living* history of music is by the side of Webern's op. 5 and op. 9. Both are instances of entirely new models of the perception of musical time, of extremely concentrated and refined temporal phenomenologies, both in their different ways *setting* — as a jeweller 'sets' — the individual moment, which is unique and irrevocable for Webern and resounds in the memory for Stravinsky. Apart from their differences, which we today find it easy to discount, these two, Stravinsky and Webern — who did not even know of each other's existence at the time — seem to have been the only composers during these remarkable years to have penetrated, in works that last no more than a few moments, to the heart of time.

Pribaoutki is generally translated 'chansons plaisantes'. But a literal translation is difficult, 'Sayings', Stravinsky suggested to Romain Rolland. 'A very old kind of popular poetry consisting of a succession of words with virtually no meaning but linked by visual or musical associations.'[1] Stravinsky's explanation of the word also reveals what attracted him, as a musician, to a text quite apart from its meaning — the pure play of words and phonemes. Setting these fragments to music made him also aware of something of primary importance for his work — namely the fact that in Russian popular poetry the word-accents of the spoken language have no validity when the verses are sung. The composer is therefore *organically* free to do what he likes with the word, shifting accents to suit the needs of the music alone.

Pribaoutki was composed at Salvan and Clarens between June and September 1914 but did not have its first performance until 1919, when it was performed in Paris at the Salle Gaveau. As in the *Three Japanese Lyrics*, the instruments used in *Pribaoutki* are very much the same as those of *Pierrot Lunaire* — flute, oboe (also cor anglais), clarinet, bassoon, violin, viola, cello and double bass accompanying a *man*'s voice, if Stravinsky's wishes are to be obeyed, which is very rare with this work.

Most of the texts come from Afanasyev's collections. The titles are 'Kornilo' (probably a peasant name) translated as 'L'Oncle Armand' by Ramuz for some reason; 'Natashka' ('Le Four'); 'Le Colonel'; and 'Le Vieux et le lièvre' (The old man and the hare). The vocal line is diatonic, the instrumental accompaniment much more chromatic, with polytonal and even atonal phrases.

Bartók, pondering in 1920 on the compatibility of folk-based music and atonality with reference to *Pribaoutki*, came to the conclusion that there was little point in analysing the work from this point of view; Stravinsky was so unfailingly successful in endowing every sound with powers of attraction. In this instance it was, of course, no more than pseudo-atonality, or 'strongly polarized atonality' (if such a paradox is permissible). This was a common characteristic of Stravinsky's language at this time, present in the *Pieces for string quartet*, very clear in the *Japanese Lyrics*, still vaguely surviving here and there and later to be resurrected in such serial (or partially serial) works as *Canticum Sacrum*, where it is a constituent element of the language. It was a problem much discussed by the previous generation and already remote. Deciding how open Stravinsky was to an occasional atonalism, and how important such moments were in his whole pre-serial output, is much less important than identifying a number of formal procedures which such questions have overshadowed. In this sense 'Le Vieux et le lièvre' in *Pribaoutki* and the last of the *Three Pieces for string quartet* seem to be 'temporal models', exceptional for the alternation of their compart-mentalized structures and their *tempi*, and above all for the incredibly subtle differentiation of timbres (this being perhaps the most impor-tant, 'informed' parameter of the former work). It is not so much the alternate exploration of tonal uncertainty and affirmations of polarity that lies at the heart of the 'dramatic' perception of the piece as the dialectic of contrast and repetition. In fact the obsessive repetition of the 'refrain' — which conjures up vague pictures of desolate wastes — is the real pole of attraction in this piece, if not of the whole work. Each time it returns it seems to overwhelm both time and memory, and to convey the impression of some tragic spell associated with that precise moment.

Berceuses du chat was written in 1915–1916 (Clarens, Château-d'Oex, Morges) for contralto voice and three clarinets (piccolo, normal in A and bass). Here again Stravinsky re-invents popular, diatonic thematic material, with moving polarities and steeped in an 'extra-tonal' harmony. (Ex. 28)

The clarinet writing is wonderfully skilful, often exploiting unusual registers (the low register of the piccolo and the high register of the bass clarinet); it is a pure joy to the ear, particularly the second piece (entitled 'Intérieur' by Ramuz, 'Cat on the stove' in the Russian original) and the third, 'Dodo', a lullaby, where the bass clarinet is

Ex. 28

replaced by the A clarinet in the bottom register. The last piece, 'Ce qu'il a, le chat' is a small *perpetuum mobile* which owes its flavour to a deliberate dissymmetry — the 4-bar couplet with a 3-bar 'answer' (one bar being extended by half a note-value).

*

Les Noces represents both the final outcome and the synthesis of these important works, the blossoming of their idiom in a large overall form. It is a key-work in the Stravinsky canon, essential to the understanding of his later development. With the smaller satellite works described above, *Les Noces* is the most complete expression of what is to be, beneath all his different styles, Stravinsky's present and future attitude to music. Although it was not finished until 1917 or finally orchestrated until 1923, two-thirds of the music was already in existence by 1915, and we must therefore discuss it now. It was so novel coming after the *Sacre* that to postpone that discussion until the date of the work's completion would be to fail to recognize its historical importance.

Les Noces has a complex and discontinuous history. The idea of it was already in Stravinsky's mind in 1914, when he was finishing *The Nightingale* in London and it continued to haunt him at Clarens and Château d'Oex — a work based on the texts of peasant rituals that he found in Kirievsky's famous collection, and adapted. Among these was an important series of marriage-songs. According to Stravinsky himself: 'Kirievsky had asked Pushkin to send him his collection of folk-verse and Pushkin sent him some verses with a note reading: "Some of these are my own verses; can you tell the difference?"' (*Conversations*)

Stravinsky therefore liked to think that the text of *Les Noces* might have included some lines of Pushkin's. Ramuz was entrusted with the French translation.

The working-score (not yet orchestrated) of the two first scenes was finished by the spring of 1915, the rest being completed by 4 April 1917. It was these first two scenes that Stravinsky bicycled from Morges to Lausanne to show to Diaghilev, who was moved literally to tears by the ritual character of the music.

The composer's initial idea of using a gigantic orchestra of 150 was abandoned after sixty-eight bars. The score sketched in 1917 still demanded considerable forces — voices, brass (including two hunting-horns associated with the Bridegroom), piano, two harps, harmonium, cymbalom, harpsichord, percussion and a number of strings. Although this too was abandoned, it already reveals the percussion — in the wide sense of instruments either struck or employing hammers — growing in importance. At the time when he was engaged on *Renard* and *The Soldier's Tale* he made another attempt:

> I next sought for a solution in a smaller *ensemble*. I began a score which required massed polyphonic effects: a mechanical piano and electrically driven harmonium, an *ensemble* of percussion instruments and two Hungarian cymbalums. But there I was baulked by a fresh obstacle, namely, the great difficulty for the conductor of synch-ronising the parts executed by instrumentalists and singers with those rendered by the mechanical players. I was thus compelled to abandon this idea also, although I had already orchestrated the two first scenes that way, work which had demanded a great deal of strength and patience, but which was all pure loss. (*Chronicle*)

Stravinsky then decided to wait until external circumstances forced him to find a solution, always his favourite stimulus to composition: 'I kept putting it off in the hope that it would come of itself when the definite fixing of a date for the first performance should make it imperative. And that, in fact, is what happened.'

The moment *Les Noces* was billed for June 1923 in the 'Ballets russes' schedule, he discovered the final solution to this problem of instrumentation that had so puzzled him:

> I saw clearly that the sustained, *soufflé* (or breath-produced) elements in my work would be best supported by an ensemble consisting exclusively of percussion instruments. I thus found my solution in the form of an orchestra comprising pianos, kettle-drums, bells and xylophones — all of which give precisely pitched notes —

and drums of different qualities and pitches, that are not precisely pitched. (*Chronicle*)

In this way the orchestration of the work went ahead quickly at Biarritz as the winter of 1923 came to an end, and it was finished at Monaco on 6 April. Today, after more than half a century of unparalleled researches in the instrumental field, particularly percussion, the orchestration of *Les Noces* still seems absolutely original and unique in character — and also perfectly suited to its object.

As we said before, *Les Noces* was a turning-point in Stravinsky's artistic development, a key-work that reveals the fundamental characteristics of his music. These have already been discussed in the opening chapter and we have to return to them before observing them within the framework of Russian folk-melody and folk-rhythm.

There was an element of renunciation in Stravinsky's deserting the rich, spectacular orchestration of the *Sacre* and *The Nightingale* for the world of *Les Noces* and the works that followed it. The renunciation was more than simply aesthetic; it was public and personal. In the name of his own individual conception of art and the aesthetic creed by which he was to be guided for the rest of his life, Stravinsky renounced the stylistic pomps and vanities of his major ballets and adopted a much austerer manner, much more intellectually controlled and stripped of all deliberate effectiveness and seductiveness. In doing this he ran the risk of alienating the sensation-hungry public of the 'Ballets russes', *his* public, whom he had hitherto kept well supplied. Miraculously enough, this new austerity did not alienate his public but actually increased his hold over them, so profoundly does this music — strong in its own undisguised strength — touch the very roots of our being.

The austerity of *Les Noces* is not simply a matter of the means it employs, though there is significance in the long journey from an orchestra of 150 to the eventual ensemble. More important is the character of the musical thought itself, which is stripped of all figurative suggestion, all effect, all 'magic' and becomes as hard as a rock.

We have spoken at length about the *ritual* character of Stravinsky's works, both secular and sacred. How does this apply to the text or the music of *Les Noces*?

The text, which is a delight to those who understand the original Russian, is the composer's own 'montage' of ritual sayings connected with marriage. The chief characters and their actions are completely depersonalized. This is not simply a 'village wedding', with bride, bridegroom and mother but a ritual that grips and directs a number of personified symbols, grinding them inexorably down. If there can be said to be any 'action' in these four *tableaux vivants* — four *moments* of a rite — it unfolds in three main directions. The *lament* is here a funeral chant (and in many respects the Russian marriage-ceremony is in fact a funeral rite): what is being buried is the Bride's virginity, symbolized in the first tableau by the 'Lock of hair'. The *invocation* of the propitious divinities follows, serving to canalize the male generative power by means of the rite and its successive symbols. Finally the *laughter* of the community exorcizes the dark forces of sexuality, purifies the leading actors in the drama and softens the heart of the Divinity. It also introduces an element of voyeurism in the form of winks, salacious comments and exclamations to excite the couple. This is for the most part done by the chorus, which resembles that of the Greek drama both in its hieratic character and in its alternate roles of spectator and actor.

It is the music which determines the deep meaning of the subject, not vice-versa; and the music never simply 'illustrates' the text, which would not exist alone and is in any case organically linked to music in all popular art. Musical forms (whether overall, fragmentary or small-scale) 'select', use and explode the text in order to recreate it as an entirely new musical entity. In the same way music determines the stage-spectacle. In Stravinsky's words, the object of *Les Noces* is 'to present rather than to describe'. Music and the stage 'display' a ritual action in the same way as the priest in Russian processions 'displays' an ikon to the crowd, using a rigid distancing ceremonial and avoiding everything that smacks of familiarity or complaisance. There is nothing realistic in this ceremonial, in which Stravinsky characteristically dissociates the roles of singers and dancers, though in fact no roles are actually 'attributed': each voice can present any of the character-symbols. The dancers wear their stage-costumes, the conductor and players — on stage, in Stravinsky's original conception — the dress-clothes which are the vestments of their profession. They are all taking part in a rite.

It is also music that actually propels the action, like some inexorable machine: in fact music may be said to *be* the action, the 'subject' of the work being static and the fragments of text so many successive 'moments' brought to life and rhythmical existence by the music. The most spectacular instance of music propelling the action is to be found in the final tableau, where it is in fact music that creates the religious and erotic ecstasy which compels the couple to move towards the marriage-bed, giving this 'handful of village songs' (as Robert Siohan amusingly calls them) the dimension of a sacrificial action closed by the tolling of a funeral bell.

Les Noces is neither specifically horizontal nor specifically vertical music, but constructed of both lines and blocks. Its most characteristic feature is heterophony, which belongs to both polyphony and homophony, since the melodic idea is presented in perspective, superimposing, varying and multiplying its own images.

Rhythm is based on an obsessive isochronous pulsation, a 'striated' time supermodulated by the changing metres and punctuated by asymmetrical accents of intensity, mass, register or timbre. The *melodic material* is diatonic and confined by the modal-tonal scale-system and the span of each of the voices concerned, but rich in depth and composed of highly differentiated layers. The melody is entirely Stravinsky's own, but modelled on that of archetypal folk-song, the songs *representing* popular Russian ritual wedding-chants, though with no actual quotation. *Harmonically* each structure, whether vertical or horizontal, is characterized by a fundamental polarity within the tonal/modal system. What Boulez calls, rather disapprovingly, *l'hyperdegré* i.e. the superactivated pole of harmonic attraction, is felt here in all its primitive strength, as violently as in the *Sacre* and perhaps even more effectively. The defining intervals of this harmonic material are the octave, the fifth and the fourth, both in the space/depth of the melody and the vertical configurations (chords). Thirds function as accessory denominators of modality/tonality, seconds occur chiefly horizontally, while augmented fourths and sevenths (mostly minor) emphasize the crystalline hardness of the harmony and exclude any hint of blandness. The same purpose is served by the bitonal or polytonal/modal interrelationships between the chords which, when superimposed, go so far as to constitute opaque blocks. Like blocks of granite, these do indeed reveal under the microscope their origins and components, but their dissociative approach is not in this case of much interest, having no bearing on the inseparable entities of what is actually the *musical reality perceived*.

Timbre in *Les Noces* is no longer 'painting in sound', evocation, atmosphere. It is on the one hand factor and *lector* of the rhythm and on the other hand it forms one term of a contrast: percussive and instantaneous as opposed to linear, to the continuity of the singing voice. Any evocative power it may possess is purely incidental; the idea of bells as sacral instruments is here extended to a whole repertory of instruments — pianos, metals, skins and wood — but not to the 'picturesque' or the 'descriptive'. It is a *musical instrument*, well suited to the general ritual character and to the purely practical task of rhythmic scansion. Its immediately and specifically symbolical significance does not appear until the end of the work.

The first part of *Les Noces* consists of three tableaux, the second part is occupied by the fourth of these. The opening tableau is entitled *La Chevelure* (or *La Tresse* — there is no need to insist on the sexual symbolism of hair, though it is of central importance in this case). From the very outset we encounter the 'dissymmetrical symmetries' of the alternations between solo and chorus, the 'antiphonal' principle proper to the convention here adopted by the composer. The following shows the pattern:

Ex. 29

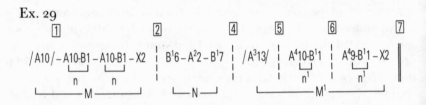

A is the solo soprano, B the chorus; the large figures show the number of bars, and those framed ☐ the numbers in the score. X denotes a special scansion in the solo part, acting as a pivot. n and n^1 show the organic relationships between preceding-following and/or solo-chorus (*raspev* in Russian). M and M^1 are the major periods which include the above 'couples', and N represents a new element, which is central and subject to the same antiphonal principle of *raspev*, though with terms reversed (chorus-solo-chorus).

The rhythmic abstract of A10 shows, slightly magnified, the analogous 'warped' symmetrics in the internal distribution of time:

$$2\left(\frac{3}{8}\right) + \frac{2}{8} + \frac{3}{8} + \frac{2}{8} + 2\left(\frac{3}{8}\right) + \frac{2}{8} + 2\left(\frac{3}{8}\right)$$

If it could take into account not only durations and accents but registers, timbres (phonemes and instruments) and masses, an analysis of the interior relationships between these periods — whose purely topographical aspect is already significant — would mean a progressive approach to the concrete rhythmic reality (and would of course occupy a complete book by itself). . . .

Thematically this first syntagmatic chain reveals at a glance a relationship — in fact an identity — between melodic and rhythmic structure. The soprano's initial melody A returns twice as A13 and A10 and then in the coda as A9. The new element N is characterized by the murmuring of the chorus within the span of two minor seconds, by an ascending/descending melodic break defined by the interval of a third (minor/major/minor) and the return of the murmuring (B^{1}7). Finally the two spectacular insertions by chorus and soloist marked X (actually B^{1}X^2) employ the fall of a minor second to a minor ninth:

Ex. 30

At ⑨ in the score a new chorus appears, identified by its stable binary metre (2/4). This is the chorus of the 'consoling women':

Ex. 31

Here the defining interval is the third, both horizontal and vertical — a 'gentler' interval contrasting with the 'harsh' seconds and augmented octaves that defined the first piece. This example also demonstrates the organic function of the phoneme (i.e. of the timbre in the rhythm), as in the case of the word *klich* (see the transcription of the Russian text and its literal equivalent). This same example also shows the considerable 'softening' of timbre — and therefore of rhythmic information — operated here by the French translation. Although Ramuz tried to remain as faithful as possible to both the sense of the text and the demands of musical accentuation, and his translation was approved by Stravinsky, *Les Noces* should always be performed in the original Russian in order to avoid serious phonetic deformations directly involving rhythmic perception.

After these short analytical notes on the opening of the work we should mention the dialogue between the Bride and her Mother, who invokes the Blessed Virgin (the parts taken respectively by solo soprano and . . . tenor!). This is an instance of imaginary Russian plainsong (homony), in the Dorian mode:

Ex. 32

* (Most pure mother)

Ramuz here makes the mistake of putting a syllable on almost every note, while the composer sets the Russian text in the vocalise-style of Russian plainsong — which is the specific character of the passage.

If both the voices employed and the theme (virginity) give the first tableau a feminine character, Stravinsky's handling of the second is essentially masculine, with its male voices and a crescendo mounting to *fortissimo*. There is less singing and more murmuring, with contrasted vocal 'couples', high-pitched exclamations in parodic vein. The opening continues the text of the first tableau ('Mother most pure') but proceeds by isomorphic harmonic blocks defined by the interval of a third and sung by men's voices *mezza voce*, interrupted by high-pitched tenor and bass exclamations. A second couple is formed by the soloists, mezzo soprano and bass (alternately representing the bride's parents) and soprano and then bass, in close altercation. The music builds up to the climactic *fff* chord of the four pianos at 44 , after which a third 'vocal couple' appears, soloists and chorus alternating antiphonally with contrasting intensities (*pp-ff*), registers (high-low) and masses. This is the invitation to the Virgin to attend the wedding with all the saints of the household. A new contrast, archaic in character, is introduced when the Bridegroom requests a blessing, the Bridegroom being represented *both* by the bass and a *basso profundo* from the chorus. (Ex. 33)

The actual blessing of the Bridegroom by his parents is punctuated by the chorus' shouts of 'Hoi!' and the block-chords of the pianos. 'The swan's feather has fallen — just so does the Bridegroom fall on his knees before his parents' (and in the same way the flower of virginity will fall). The tableau ends with the invocation of the saints — Mikita (not Nikita!), Luke, Cosmas and Damian — and an allusion to the couple's first child. This comes in an implacable crescendo which is a synthesis of all the musical material, presented in a blinding light.

The third tableau is the shortest (147 bars) and is again feminine in

Ex. 33

*(Bless me, father and mother)

character. It is the departure (or 'leading away') of the Bride and employs some material from the earlier tableaux, particularly the first — the chorus of 'consoling women' combined, for instance, with the archaic plainsong element. It reaches its climax at the chorus's leap of a minor seventh and their held cry on 'ou':

Ex. 34

The predominant idea here is the girl's sacrifice, as in the *Sacre*, but what a difference between the two situations in conception and musical treatment! The violent expressionism of the *Sacre* is here replaced by the spare, hard, implacable presenting of an incantation.

The end of the third tableau is static, recalling the earlier lament of the Mother. As the stage empties, the music is reduced to the obsessive repetition of the 'remains' of the Mother's lament, on a falling semitone.

The second part of *Les Noces*, consisting simply of the fourth tableau, is entitled in Russian 'The Beautiful Table', or 'The Red Table', which has much more character than Ramuz's 'Repas de Noces' (Wedding Feast). For this is in fact a ritual meal, as it were, on the body of the sacrificial victim: it culminates in drunkenness and erotic tension, the consummation of the marriage and the tolling of the funeral bell which seals the identity of love and death.

Musically the tableau is built of 'chains', or thematic episodes which flow into each other, occasionally overlapping. Boris de Schloezer, among other commentators, discovers sonata-form here; but if we are to look for any association with traditional forms — which is not the case — the rondo would seem more relevant.

Stravinsky's working of the monotonous chants (the untranslatable Russian *popevki*), is brilliantly skilful and is seen essentially in the linear field, both polymelodic and polyrhythmic. Two converging principles govern the vocal-instrumental ensemble, that of progression and that of parametric 'fanning out', in the sense of increasingly violent contrasts — between registers, choral and orchestral masses, and particularly between the timbres of men's and women's voices, colours, pianos and percussion, all in incredibly varied positions and combinations. In the dynamics there are no 'expressive' crescendos and decrescendos (just as there are no accelerations or decelerations in the tempo). The music moves from one dynamic plane, or platform, to the next and these dynamic planes are skilfully graded, the mass employed serving as 'multiplicator' of the intensity. Stravinsky's characteristic principle of rigorous economy governs the relationships between these parameters. His method, as we saw in the *Sacre*, is that of 'parametric relays' which preserve the fresh quality of the information by constant changing of vector elements within an ingenious dialectic of repetition and variation. From this fundamental point of view *Les Noces* seems to me one of the most accomplished temporal models in twentieth-century music.

Red is the colour of this final tableau. 'One strawberry has joined another' say the chorus (*a*) and in every stage of heterophony we hear the answer, both an outcry and a lullaby, and both erotic (*p*) — 'hai, lyuli, lyuli, lyuli'. A further theme is added by the bass solo singing falsetto (*q*), and a symbolically syncopated rhythm ('the lost ring'!) which is to be one of the motor rhythms of the development, starts up:

Ex. 35

Ramuz: A   per - du -   l'an - neau   do - ré

(has lost the golden ring)

After the chorus's wild cry of 'hoi' and their purely syllabic, meaningless incantations, an important new theme (*b*) is contrasted with (*a*). This is the theme of the goose ('Flying, flying a goose, flying, flying, a grey one, hoi!') and this will act as a pivot or refrain.

A kind of intermezzo, or character scene follows, without a break, and using the picturesque thematic material of first the Bridegroom's father and then the Bride's mother, against the rapid syllabic pulsations of the chorus of men and women. 'Sow the flax and the hemp' (men). 'We are telling you, Nastasiushka' (women) and finally 'You just make her work'. 'Love her like your own soul, shake her like a plum-tree'. The theme of the goose (*B*) returns in a different form, and from it emerges another theme, which is both musically and symbolically important. This is the theme of the swan (*C*), characterized by relays of fourths within the initial interval of the minor seventh.

Ex. 36

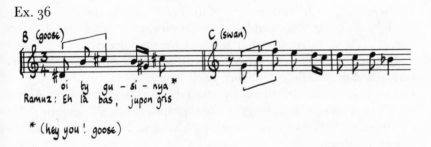

A small (28 bars) *ballade* on this theme is now introduced by the women's voices, both marine and maternal in symbolism, 'I too, was on the blue — on the sea, Lyuli, lyuli on the sea, on the lake.'

The light now shifts gradually on to the couple, and the song of the swan, with its attendant heterophonies, is joined without any transition to that of the Bride, which is musically of primary importance, though still only faintly heard (*y*):

Ex. 37

This is the only authentic *popevka* in the work — all the rest of the 'popular' material is of Stravinsky's own invention, or re-creation. In any case this is not a peasant-, but a factory-song, a work-song in fact. It will become the song of the bed, the song that shepherds the Bride and Bridegroom to their destiny; and we immediately hear the words 'I want to sleep!' (*z*) — this in its turn will become the theme of the bell and is in fact simply the motif of the lost ring, without the syncopation:

Ex. 38

* (I want to sleep – me and you)

This, however, is the beginning of a new preliminary ritual episode, the 'warming of the bed' by two of the onlookers. Musically it may be thought of as a 'second couplet' — a complex series of 105 bars forming a kind of thematic recapitulation before the final period.

This has already been introduced *mezza voce* (*y*: see Ex. 37, original form) and gradually establishes itself as the dominant theme (y^1, y^2 etc.) above the initial themes (especially *a* and its corollary *p*) and finally explodes in all its glory in the sopranos (Ex. 37, final form). The factory-song becomes an invocation of Eros, so high-pitched that it is almost a scream. . . .

The following diagram shows the complex form of the movement:

$$(a + \frac{a}{p} + \frac{a}{q} + /x/ + b + \frac{b}{a} + \frac{e}{b+a} + b \rightarrow c + \frac{c}{c^1}) + (y + y^1 + z + a + \frac{y^2}{a} + y^3 + \frac{y^4}{a}$$

$$+ z + \frac{z}{a} + a + y^5 + y^6) + (z^1 + \frac{z^1}{a^2} + q^1 + /x^1/ + p^1 + z^3 + y^7 + z^1 + z^2)$$

It is clear from the above that there is no question of sonata- or rondo-form here. What we have is an *evolving* form in which the opening themes (*a*, *b* and *c*) are gradually superseded by those that follow (*y* and *z*), the syncopated theme *x* both forming a point of reference and generating *z*; *y* evolves in its own way, rising in the Dorian mode to an erotic frenzy which is both irrepressible and icy, and reaching its climax in y^7, with the final high B. Finally *z*, which grew out of the original *x* syncopation, will become the maternal theme of cradle-rocking and then the funeral bell. . . . And so, as the noise and excitement of an orgiastic celebration gradually die down, the symbol-characters are left alone to face their destiny, guided both by their own instincts and by the irresistible rite celebrated in participation with the community.

The *Coda*, where the final theme also stands alone, introduces — both agonisingly close and light-years away — the bell which is the reminder of both death and birth.

The sonority devised by Stravinsky for this passage is a unique alloy in the history of music. It is produced by the chords of the four pianos and the vibrations of a bell and two crotals, and the sound hangs in what might well be called eternity, gradually invaded by silence.

*

When Stravinsky brought tears to Diaghilev's eyes by playing him the first two tableaux of *Les Noces*, in the spring of 1915, the great impresario was planning the company's American tour. Stravinsky did not succeed in getting himself included on the tour in order to conduct his works at the 'Met.', as he hoped. The company left Bordeaux without him on 1 January 1916. Shortly before leaving, Diaghilev had given two brilliant gala performances in aid of the Red Cross, one in Geneva and one in Paris, and raised 400,000 francs. For Stravinsky these concerts were a *rite de passage* — his first successful experience as a conductor, with *Firebird*, Ansermet being in charge of the rest of the programme.

After Diaghilev's departure, Stravinsky found a host of friends in wartime Paris, and among them the Princesse de Polignac (Winnaretta Singer), an old friend and a highly cultivated woman — a painter, a pianist and an intelligent patron of the arts. As long ago as 1912 she had offered the composer a fee of 3,000 francs for a chamber work, but it was only now that the details of the nature of the piece were discussed between them. They decided on a musico-theatrical work, to be performed at the Princess's house 'after the end of the war'. This was the origin of *Renard*, a work on whose general musical and dramatic outlines the composer had already pondered at Château-d'Oex, quite independently of any commission. . . . Now he put *Les Noces* aside, having completed (but not orchestrated) the first two tableaux, and set to work on the new piece.

The 'Ballets russes' enjoyed a triumph in the United States, crowned by the presence of Nijinsky in the *Spectre de la Rose* and *Petrushka*. (Although excluded, Nijinsky was called on at the last moment to join the company.) Meanwhile Diaghilev had come to an arrangement with the Teatro Real in Madrid, and it was to Spain that the company returned in mid-May. To Diaghilev's delight they were joined by Stravinsky, and the success of *Firebird* in Madrid was such that Stravinsky was presented personally to King Alfonso and to both the queens. He was not greatly impressed by Iberian folklore or Iberian cooking (though enthusiastic about the bull-ring music and the *paso dobles* played by the *bandas*). The religious feeling and the mysticism of the works of art that he saw in Toledo and in the Escorial made a deep impression on him, and he discovered an essential similarity between the Catholic fervour of Spain and the Russian religious spirit.

Back in Switzerland Stravinsky worked every day with Ramuz on the texts of *Pribaoutki, Berceuses du chat* and *Renard,* translating the Russian texts literally and then explaining the demands of the tonic accents and the musical rhythm. At the same time, as a pendant to the three earlier piano pieces, he wrote the *Five Easy Pieces* for piano duet, 'Andante', 'Napolitana', 'Española' (a souvenir of his stay in Madrid), 'Balalaika', and 'Galop' — light-hearted pieces, musically-speaking easy and destined later to form two orchestral *Suites,* which became world famous.

Like Ramuz, Stravinsky was at first enthusiastic about the so-called February Revolution in Russia (1917) and spoke of returning to Russia, though both men were soon disillusioned. Diaghilev, although a convinced monarchist, also reacted to the events in Russia, but as a man of the theatre; he decided to alter the end of *Firebird* and to present the Tsarevich not with the sceptre and the crown but . . . a red flag. This new 'version' was short-lived, encountering as it did the unanimous disapproval of both his personal friends and faithful followers. Immediately after the February Revolution Diaghilev settled in Rome, and with him Massine, Bakst, Cocteau, Ansermet and the painters Balla and Picasso. The Red Cross Charity Gala at the Teatro Constanzi — with Futurist sets by Balla and *Firebird* and *Fireworks* conducted by Stravinsky — was to open, in accordance with wartime practice, with the national anthem. The Tsar having just abdicated, it was impossible to play 'Bozhe tsarya khrani' (God save the Tsar) and Stravinsky therefore orchestrated the well-known 'Song of the Volga boatmen', at Diaghilev's suggestion, dictating the score to Ansermet in the course of a single night.

It was during this stay in Rome that Stravinsky met Picasso, who was working with Cocteau on the sets for *Parade.* They took to each other at once. Both anti-Romantic, both constructors of forms, both *demon-strators,* they seemed made to understand one another. The element in which they both worked was reality — a reality *reinvented* from its own structure and its own concrete materials, whether sonorous or pictorial. This reality was for each of them both a source of inspiration and an object of speculation. For both were speculators, speculators but not theorists; they left others to do the talking, to keep up the endless commentary on their stylistic metamorphoses. They have often been compared — and not without reason — to two Proteuses, though what they in fact have in common is that they are Protean only in appearance. . . . If there were different 'periods' in the work of both, these were temporary and, sooner or later, outlived, revealing *constants* rather than deep changes. Just as Cézanne and Monet now exist 'outside' Impressionism and Mallarmé exists 'outside' Symbolism, it is chiefly for the historians that Picasso is 'Cubist' or 'Neo-classical' — and the same is to be true, as we shall see, of Stravinsky.

Were the first portrait-sketches that Picasso made of Stravinsky in Rome really so strange to contemporaries? There is the well-known story of one of these sketches being seized upon by the Swiss military authorities at the Italian frontier, in Chiasso. 'That is not a portrait. It is a plan!' Looking at the amazing *likeness* of the composer that Picasso captured in these sketches, we may well wonder today at the mental aberration of contemporaries, and by no means Swiss frontier-officials only!

In May 1917, with the war still raging, and Stravinsky back in Switzerland working on *Renard*, the 'Ballets russes' in Paris gave the first performance of *Parade*, which brought together Cocteau, Satie, Picasso and Massine.

Stravinsky had met Satie at Debussy's house. 'I took to him at once,' he says in *Chronicle*. 'He was a sly one, astute and intelligently malicious.' Did Stravinsky appreciate the neutral quality of Satie's music, its refusal of all subjectivism and detachment from all 'expression'? He only liked 'certain pages' of *Parade*, in any case, and *Parade* is in fact more valuable as a manifesto than as a work of art in its own right. According to Richard Buckle,[2] 'Cocteau wanted the work to reveal the mysterious, eternal element in everyday life. Picasso thought it a rather bitter and slightly vulgar entertainment, something that the Cubists would have expressed by a guitar or a coffee-pot on a newspaper. Satie had written "present day" tunes, satirical dances that were typically French without being Debussy-like. Diaghilev had wanted to prove that the "Ballets russes" could make a new start. In a way each of them had succeeded.' But *Parade* was no more than a moment in history, and the scandal that it created at the Théâtre des Champs Elysées was a very Parisian one and doubtless much exaggerated. The generation that looked to Satie, that of Les Six, took *Parade* as a point of reference. Today the work is remembered for the aesthetic gesture that it represented rather than as a *spectacle* — the exact opposite of *Renard*.

*

Renard, 'histoire burlesque chantée et jouée', was completed at Morges in 1916–1917 and is one of the masterpieces of this period. It was composed piecemeal, beginning with the end and working back at intervals to the opening. The texts come from Afanasyev's collection and are in some cases considerably modified — a clever 'montage' of which Stravinsky, as author, was justly proud. The choice of this tale might not, legally, entitle him to royalties, but it already constituted a preliminary creative act; his claim to regard *Renard* as his literary property was amply justified by the work of adaptation, linking, and the functional alterations to the music, all of which reveal an amazing gift both as narrator and as man of the theatre.

As in Chaucer's *Canterbury Tales* and the *Roman de Renart*, the old Russian tale of the Fox and the Cock is based on incidents in the eternal debate between the good and the bad, the naïve and the sophisticated, the deceiver and the deceived. Slyness wins, but not for long. The Fox may twice catch the Cock and end by killing him (which he asked for), but providence — in the shape of his friends the Cat and the Goat — intervenes and punishes the culprit — and 'si l'histoire vous a plu, payez-moi c'qui m'est dû', the final words of Ramuz's version.

The *Sacre* makes virtually no reference to the Russian popular musical vein beyond the ingenious elaboration of a few archaic melodic elements, but with *Les Noces* and *Renard* it is quite different; both are powerful developments of explicitly archetypal popular customs and sayings, although their basic folklore material is entirely remodelled. There is, however, a clear distinction between the two, for whereas in *Les Noces* Stravinsky recreates both religious and secular aspects of a ritual that was still practised, *Renard* is based on an art that is lost and forgotten except for a few faint traces in Dal's collection (according to B. Asafiev[3]). This was the free, purely oral (and the therefore ephemeral) art of the Russian minstrels, or *skomoroshi* — itinerant singers, jugglers, mounte- banks and buffoons, authors of satirical, even political rhymes, condem- ned of course by the Church but popular, public witnesses, chroniclers and interpreters of village life and its feudal background. It was the laughter and mockery of the *skomoroshi* that canalized and exorcized the protest of one of the most bitterly oppressed peoples in history, serving them as both *catharsis* and defence, a condition of survival. The troubadours of Western Europe were entirely different, with their refinement and their whole theme of *amour courtois*; and they are well documented: we know their instruments, their movements, their chronology, their written poetry and music. Russia has nothing to compare with this, but in return possesses something that has no parallel in Western Europe — a live tradition of popular song, powerful and in daily use right up to the beginning of the twentieth century and the Revolution. It is on this tradition that Stravinsky drew for the musical and poetic figures, the melodies and the rhythms of *Les Noces* and there that he rooted the 'histoire burlesque chantée et jouée' of his *Renard*. But it was thanks to Stravinsky's musical genius rather than to any ethno-musicological hypotheses (which he neither could nor would put forward) that *Renard* — having undergone a 'sea-change' in his hands — transcends its original archetypal setting of symbolic tale 'with animals' and becomes *the* Russian folk-tale acted and sung on trestles, something approaching an archetype within an archetype.

The music of *Renard* is as clarified and as concentrated as Stravinsky could make it, with every note and every figure performing its own precise and indispensable function. The *skomoroshi* were clowns and acrobats as well as *chansonniers*, and Stravinsky included this circus element in his theatrical design for the piece. The essential features of circus are absolute precision and the absence of all personal emotion, anything 'vague'. These are the constant characteristics of all Stravinsky's work and especially his ballets, in which they reflect the incessant movement and the unstable balance of the dancers' bodies. In *Renard*, as elsewhere, the balancing-tricks are performed by the irregular metres, the displacing of accents, and the instrumental virtuosity which is released in this setting. The opening, for instance, seems to have a binary rhythm but in fact oscillates between binary and ternary in an extremely ingenious way:

Ex. 39

In the same way the acrobatic metres of the Cock who has fallen into the trap set by Renard follows this pattern:

$$\left(\frac{3+4}{8} + \frac{4+3}{8}\right) 2 + \frac{3}{4} + \frac{7}{8} + \frac{5}{8} + \frac{6}{8} + \frac{2}{4} + \left(\frac{3}{8} + \frac{3}{8} + \frac{2}{8}\right) \text{ etc.} \dots$$

The melos of *Renard* is diatonic-modal and derived basically from a system of fifths and fourths touching on two neighbouring tonics. The range of the voice parts is very small, with occasional surprise-leaps extending even to two octaves (in falsetto). The instrumental range, on the other hand, is very wide, particularly in the part of the cymbalom, which is the most important instrument in the score and plays a kind of umpire-role. Stravinsky was introduced to the cymbalom by a Hungarian player, Aladar Racz, whom he heard in a Geneva restaurant. He fell in love with the light, percussive sonority of the instrument and immediately bought one and learned to play it.

Timbre is very important in *Renard* and is linked to rhythm by organic relations of accentual identity or opposition. Apart from the cymbalom and other percussion instruments the rest of the orchestra is normal, with one of each instrument excepting horns, of which there are two. There are four solo singers, two tenors and two basses, neither of course, associated with any 'role' and each in turn representing different characters in the story. They are generally placed in the orchestral pit, while the stage is occupied by mimes in costume. (The performance put on by Boulez and Jean-Louis Barrault at one of the Domaine Musical concerts in the Théâtre Marigny was an unforgettable experience.)

The opening and closing March to which the actors come on to the stage (and later leave it) is followed by the first two phases of the piece. These comprise the dialogues (repeated) between the Cock and the Fox (parade, seduction, *salto mortale*, capture and rescue by the Cat and the Goat). The third phase is occupied by the 'epilogue' — the punishment of the culprit by the other animals. At a breakneck speed, and still accelerating, the various characters (which are vocally interchangeable), deliver themselves of their syllabic 'saws', their *pribaoutki* and *skoropogovorki* (lit. fast wisecracks) which become increasingly meaningless. They are interrupted by onomatopoeic words such as *tyuk-tyuk* (*pizzicato* guzli) or *syom-syom-peressiom* translated as 'Zoum-Zoum-Patazoum' and 'oral' onomatopoeics all to do with eating, munching blinis, pirozhki and shchi. The following shows the literal translation with Ramuz's version below:

Oh toi Renardette Renardine	Foxy, little Foxy
Soeur sans vice et sans péché	Guileless, innocent little sister
Comme chez notre petit père	As at home with daddy
On y beurre les p'tits blinis	They butter the little pancakes
Ainsi on t'attend en visite.	So they are waiting for your visit.
Aïe Aïe Aïe Mèr' Renard très charit-	Eh, mother fox, so charitable, so
able, très vénérable	venerable,
Viens chez papa et tu verras là-bas	Come to papa's and you'll see
Chez papa comment on te soign'ra	How well they'll look after you there
Tu verras comme c'est servi	How good the food is
C'n'est pas comme ici	Not like here
Y a du beurre sur la table.	There's butter on the table.

Is it the texts that 'create' their own rhythm and melody? Certainly not. They may 'inform' the primary musical material, but it is only the better to be dominated by the musical structures by which they are freely ployed and deployed. This kind of osmosis, in which music is always the deciding factor, enables Stravinsky to achieve a perfect synthesis of words and music, in which there can be no question of either element claiming pre-eminence or priority.

Renard was not performed at the Princesse de Polignac's house in the Avenue Henri Martin, but only in May 1922 at the Paris Opéra. Diaghilev, who was extremely jealous of anything arranged without him, was annoyed with Stravinsky for having 'discussed' *Renard* with the Princesse de Polignac, but his interest in the work proved stronger than his annoyance and they came to terms. The work was given under the aegis of the 'Ballets russes', with choreography by Bronislava Nijinska (who also danced the title-role) and sets and costumes by Larionov. The composer considered this 'one of the most satisfying' productions though ill-suited to the vast spaces of the Opéra and ill-matched by the rest of the programme.

Stravinsky sold the manuscript of *Renard* to Princess Violette Murat in 1917.

*

The *Trois Histoires pour enfants*, for voice and piano, based on popular texts, were also written at this time, between 1915 and 1917, at Morges in fact. They comprise the well-known 'Tilim-Bom', 'Les Oies et les cygnes' (Geese and swans) and the 'Chanson de l'ours' (Song of the Bear). They are 'Webernian' in length, the three together not lasting more than a few minutes; and they contain unexpected piano effects and some 'dissonant' harmonies (ninths in the second song). 'Tilim-Bom' imitates bells and has been much arranged — for orchestra (1923), for flute, harp and guitar (with 'Les Oies et les cygnes' in *Quatre Chants*, where the other two pieces come from *Quatre Chants russes* — see below). The 'Chanson de l'ours' is the story of the bear who had a paw cut off by a woodman, made himself another of birchwood ('grince, grince, patt' de bouleau') and came back and ate the woodman and his wife. . . . The fifth (A flat – E flat) is an *ostinato* imitating the bear's bandy-legged walk.

The *Quatre Chants paysans russes*, also called *Soucoupes* (saucers) are not to be confused with either the *Quatre Chants* or the *Quatre Chants russes*. They were composed in 1914 (at Salvan) and between 1916–1917 (at Morges), for women's voices unaccompanied, and transcribed forty years later with an accompaniment of four horns. 'Saucers' refers to an old Russian way of fortune-telling — holding saucers smoked in a candle-flame by three fingers and interpreting the fingerprints. Stravinsky found his texts for these songs in Afanasyev's collection — 'Near the church at Chigissakh', 'Ovsen' (an old Slavonic sun-god), 'The Pike' and 'Monsieur Ventru' (Mr Pot Belly), the last piece (1915) closely resembling *Les Noces* in style. These songs follow the principle of *raspev* (antiphony), a solo voice (or the chorus in unison) alternating with the harmonies of the chorus. In 1953, when Stravinsky added the four-horn accompaniment, he was writing *Agon*, (in which the fanfare is perhaps recalled by the transcription). However, the brass adds nothing important to the *a cappella* version, which is perfect as it stands.

*

The masterpiece among all these small vocal works was written slightly later, in 1918–1919. Both in poetic range and in musical workmanship the *Quatre Chants russes* is the most visionary and unusual of the series. *Les Noces* had already been composed (though not as yet orchestrated) and these songs reflect the composer's experience of a large musical form: they are a kind of 'miniature frescos' in the literal sense, however contradictory this expression may seem.

The title of the first in Ramuz's translation is 'Canard' (the duck). It is a rondo remarkable for the severity of its rhythms and the logic of its melodic development, in which intervals open like a fan — seconds becoming minor, then major thirds, fourths, fifths and so on. This transforms the archaic-sounding folk-tune, which is not simply stylized but 'transposed' into a modern musical language.

The second, 'Chanson pour compter' (counting song), is a quick *pribaoutka*, with the piano *ostinato* taking the lead through a maze of changing rhythms, harsh seconds and ninths, ending with a sudden high-pitched shout.

The third song, 'Le Moineau est assis' (The sparrow is perched) bears in Russian the subtitle 'saucer' and consists of six alternating couplets and refrains. It is very 'choral' in character and since there is in fact no chorus, the responses to the soloist are made by the piano. The piece ends majestically with a 'gloria' consisting of multiple rhythmic variants — there are at least twelve on the two syllables of the Russian word *slava* (glory).

The fourth is entitled 'Sektantskaya' — translated by Ramuz as *chant dissident*, but the reference is religious, not political and 'Sectarian song' best reproduces Stravinsky's meaning. It dates from 1919 and stands apart from the other songs by the melancholy and poetic nature of its melody. This character has been explained by the loneliness and despair of the composer, cut off by the Revolution from all contact with his native land. The disposition of intervals in the melodic material recalls Bartók's 'reversed seconds', and these diatonic and chromatic seconds in contrary motion give the melody an extremely hard, bitter character, conjuring up the storm of snow and wind of which the text speaks. The Russian words of the opening are very important for their timbre:

Ex. 40

The punctuation of the vocal line by the piano is at first very modest, but there is a sudden eruption of violent 'groups' which cut across the text. Towards the end the song — and the intermediary rhythmic values — expands a little and the melody achieves a kind of muted blossoming. . . .

As has already been said, the *Quatre Chants* for voice, flute, harp and guitar include 'Tilim-Bom' and 'Les Oies et les cygnes' from *Trois Histoires pour enfants* and 'Ronde' and 'Chant dissident' from the *Quatre Chants russes*, whose instrumental version was made in 1953–1954.

Berceuse is a very short piece for voice and piano, written to a French text prepared by Ramuz from a Russian text of the composer's. It was written at Morges on 10 December 1917 and dedicated 'A ma fillette'; and it is one of the few works written at this time that had not until recently been either published or 'arranged'.

Between 1914–1918 Stravinsky also transcribed for large orchestra his *Three Pieces for string quartet*, adding a short *étude* in the Spanish style (written originally for pianola) and calling the whole *Quatre Etudes pour orchestre*. He gave the individual pieces titles — 'Danse', 'Eccentric', 'Cantique' and 'Madrid' — and the work is a showpiece for both orchestra and conductor, frequently performed.

When he returned from Rome via Chiasso, Stravinsky had a cruel shock in the sudden death on 28 April 1917 of his old German governess Bertha Essert ('Bertushka').

> She was an old friend, who had entered my parents' service before I was born and had looked after me in my earliest days, a friend to whom I was deeply attached and whom I loved like a second mother.

This tragic note in *Chronicle* is absolutely convincing and reveals the 're-direction' of his love for the mother who never returned his affection. He had hardly recovered from this shock when he learned of his brother Guri's death (3 August) on the Rumanian front — the only brother he had ever loved and with whom he could really talk.

Stravinsky had originally greeted the October Revolution with enthusiasm, telegraphing to his family in St Petersburg: 'Toutes mes pensées avec vous dans ces inoubliables jours de bonheur [que] traverse notre chère Russie libérée' (All my thoughts with you in these unforgettable days of happiness through which our beloved liberated Russia is passing). But this enthusiasm, proclaimed at a distance, was to be short-lived, and Stravinsky's voluntary exile would very soon become exile for ever. Is 'Chant dissident' in fact an echo of the feelings of a Russian in those circumstances, a man who had reached the 'point of no return'? Stravinsky was always to remain very guarded about any connection between his life and his music, and it is not hard to understand the reason: if there is indeed a link between them, it is never where one would expect to find it.

In addition to the effects of these successive bereavements on his morale, Stravinsky's material situation gave him much cause for anxiety, war and revolution having cut off all remaining support from Russia. With a sick wife and four children he was in real need. To deal with this situation he joined with his friends Ramuz and Ansermet, and an interior decorator named Auberjonois, in a plan to create a 'pocket theatre' piece, small enough to be mobile and suitable 'for even the smallest localities'. Even so the most modest undertaking needs capital behind it, and it was only after numerous refusals of help — 'not always polite but always categorical', as Stravinsky recorded — that Werner Reinhart, of Winterthur, came forward with the necessary money. Reinhart was a warm-hearted man, a great financier and extremely cultivated. He was a lover of both music — playing the clarinet and bass clarinet — and painting, his family collection of pictures being now one of the finest museum-foundations in Europe. He started his career as a patron by financing what was to be *Histoire du soldat* — The Soldier's Tale.

*

The subject of the new work was taken once again from Afanasyev's collection. Since the spring of 1917 Stravinsky had been attracted to the cycle of stories connected with the enforced recruiting for the Russo-Turkish war under Nicholas I and the so-called 'rekrutskya' songs — the laments of women who were being forcibly robbed of sons and sweethearts. There is no trace of these actual historical events in *The Soldier's Tale* — which is in fact a kind of miniature *Faust* — except the chief character, a soldier on leave. In his memoirs Stravinsky mentions two Afanasyev stories — one in which the Soldier first makes the Devil drunk on vodka and then gives him shot to eat, telling him that it is caviar; and the other of a deserter who has a violin (his soul) which he is tricked by the Devil into surrendering. Ramuz's imagination was fired by these stories and he soon began to sketch a 'libretto'. As usual, Stravinsky considered himself as joint author of the work, and Ramuz and he agreed to tone down the Russian character of the original and so give the story a universal application, thus increasing the similarity to the old Faust-story. Georges and Ludmilla Pitoëff, who were at that time living in Geneva, were consulted on the stage presentation of the work and eventually danced the roles of the Devil and the Princess.

As we have seen, the instrumental demands of *The Soldier's Tale* were deliberately restricted to an ensemble of seven players which included representatives of all the 'families' of the orchestra — strings (violin and double-bass), woodwind (clarinet and bassoon), brass (cornet and trombone) and a very elaborate percussion section. Writing of this work later, Stravinsky insisted on:

> the interest afforded to the spectator by being able to see these instrumentalists. I have always had a horror of listening to music with my eyes shut, with nothing for them to do. The sight of the gestures and movements of the various parts of the body producing the music is fundamentally necessary if it is to be grasped in all its fulness. . . . These ideas induced me to have my little orchestra well in evidence when planning *The Soldier's Tale*. It was to be on one side of the stage, and a small dais for the reader on the other. This arrangement established the connection between the three elements of the piece which by their close co-operation were to form a unity: in the centre, the stage and the actors; on one side of them the music, and on the other, the reader. (*Chronicle*)

The Soldier's Tale was not performed until 28 September 1918 — only a few weeks before the war ended — in the municipal theatre at Lausanne, with sets and costumes by René Auberjonois, Ansermet conducting, with the assistance of the Pitoëffs and three students from

Lausanne University: Elie Gagnebin as the Narrator, Gabriel Rosset as the Soldier and Jean Villard-Gilles as the Devil. A few weeks before the first performance Stravinsky had thought of dancing the 'Danse triomphale du Diable' himself, but for some unknown reason gave up the idea.

Although designed so as to be mobile, the work never got on the road or reached 'even the smallest localities', Spanish flu having broken out and numbered among its victims players, actors, members of the public and Stravinsky himself (though it lasted only a week in his case). In the meantime the war had come to an end. . . .

Despite its apparent simplicity *The Soldier's Tale* is one of Stravinsky's most mysterious masterpieces. There is nothing 'striking' about it — no Russian folklore, no brilliant instrumental effects and no spectacular innovations but a minimal instrumental ensemble and minimal stage requirements (in any case optional). It is a work of pure music, a matter of musical relationships and proportions and of variations on these, with no care for gesture or effect. The material is simple, even commonplace, but 'structured to the second degree', having undergone often imperceptible *distortions* to which it owes its uniquely fresh quality. *The Soldier's Tale* is an archetypal fable beyond all doubt, but it is also an archetype of music itself. All these constructions, these melodies, these rhythms and even the apparently most trivial — though in fact the most incredibly refined — phrase (like that of the cornet in the 'Marche royale', for instance) *represent music*, are the original outline, the sign manual, the very ideogram of music.

The work consists of six scenes and two intermezzos preceded, like *Renard*, by an introductory march.

The 'Marche du soldat' immediately establishes the character, the subject and the material of the work by means of an elementary rhythmic double sign — the strong and the weak on the one hand and the dotted quaver/semiquaver on the other (*a*). This is typical of Stravinsky: remove the symbol and short-circuit the so-called 'significant' musical image by means of the elementary conventional form of this image itself. One-two! The movement is made, the game has started. The material is set out at once, with no fuss and nothing but the bare essentials.

Ex. 41

First come the conventional figures of type *b* in the cornet, then the thematic statement *c*, in which the bar-line begins to crackle and to jump, 'setting off' the rhythm. All we need here, while the narration is going on, is a small development *e*, and then the final explosion, the 'grand *tutti*' (*f*) of the six instruments strongly supported by the percussion.

'The curtain rises. The music (percussion) continues. The scene shows a river-bank. Enter the Soldier. He tunes his violin,' as Stravinsky notes in the score.

Ex. 42

Have we not here an *ideogram* of all instinctive music-making, of all
fiddling and all fiddlers? And at the same time no pretensions to
'significance' in this figure which makes fun of the 'image' by stylising
it. Harmony (thirds), rhythm presenting them in couples, bar-lines that
grate, crack and jump, *tiré* and *spiccato* bowing, caterwauling 'violin
thirds' — all against the background of the double-bass *ostinato*. It is a
musical scene very characteristic of Stravinsky but one in which
Adorno would not feel at home.*

From thirds to sixths, from *spiccato* to *legato*, the violin continues on its
own archetypal way though, as the Soldier observes — 'on voit que
c'est du bon marché, il faut tout le temps l'accorder' — it was cheap
enough to begin with, like the player! Now, however, as the Devil comes
on the scene, he is given a 'generating theme' that we shall meet again
later. From now on music and speaker alternate and frame successive
tableaux vivants without the music ever losing its complete autonomy. In
fact the 'pastoral' scene that comes next, with the music of scene 3
(derived from scene 1) and the shadow of Part 2 (derived from the
opening March) constitute a perfectly self-contained miniature
symphony.

It is hardly necessary to recall here the story of *The Soldier's Tale*.
Having made his pact with the Devil, the Soldier, another Faust, sets
out to cure the King's daughter. The 'Marche royale' starts with the
trombone and is ornamented by the cornet, with its famous:

Ex. 43

It is not just the 'tune' of this phrase, but also (one would like to say:
especially) its ornamental quintuplets and its delightful vulgarity of
sound that are really its 'thematic' elements, the subject of the piece
and a *locus classicus* of Stravinsky's musical humour — look at the loving
care he expends on varying this archetypal dance-hall ornamentation,
extending it or cutting it down to a triplet, and adding the clarinet

*In the second part of his *Philosophy of the New Music* (entitled 'Stravinsky or the
Restoration') Adorno devotes a chapter to *The Soldier's Tale*, with sub-titles such as
'Infantilism', 'Depersonalization', 'Hebephrenia' and 'Catatony'. . . . both the *Sacre*
and *Renard* come in for much the same sort of treatment. Adorno makes a passionate
defence of Schoenberg as the paragon of modernity; but was it appropriate, in order to
reinforce this defence, to choose Stravinsky as the 'negative' term in an essentially
dualistic view of musical history?

which he requires to play in the purest 'sheet-music' style. And then we have clarinet and violin sharing an ingeniously vulgar 'couplet':

Ex. 44

all set in a strict, symmetrical scheme.

The 'Petit Concert' in scene 4 forms, with the 'Trois danses' of scene 5, the central and more elaborate part of the work. All the material that has been used hitherto is brought together and worked over with dazzling skill. The form of the first part is asymmetrical, with clarinet, cornet and violin unfolding the first 28-bar sequence in a transparent polyphony; the main part, which passes from one instrument to the other, is based on one of the themes of 'The Stream' (see below, Ex. 52). The second part is à chromatic episode (8 bars) and the third (17 bars) serves both as abbreviated recapitulation and transition. The short central part is based on a theme that Stravinsky heard in a dream (he dreamt of a young gypsy, fiddling to amuse her child and using the 'full length of the bow', while the child clapped its hands in delight):

Ex. 45

This gives rise to a long series of heterophonies in different instruments; and then come two 'couplets' derived from the 'Introduction', motifs *d* and *c* in Ex. 41. In this way all the material stated at the opening is gradually 'burnt up'. The first of these couplets is a good example of Stravinsky's polyrhythmic technique. (Ex. 46)

This passage, judiciously quoted by Eric Walter White, has also been remarkably analysed by André Souris,[4] who traces five rhythmic species here, four of which (binary and ternary) remain unchanged, while the fifth is rhythmically independent and constantly varies (clarinet and trombone).

Ex. 46

Next come 'Trois danses: Tango, Valse et Ragtime'. These too are all archetypes, especially the tango, which was then the rage all over Europe and a great favourite with Stravinsky, who used it in a number of small works. It opens like this (violin and percussion):

Ex. 47

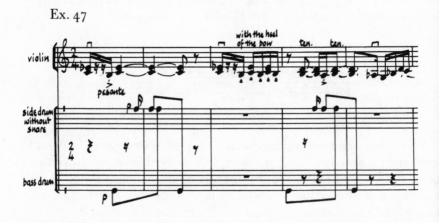

The waltz is pure fiddle music, the sort of thing that used to be played by street musicians, and the typical ternary accompaniment is caricatured, with the violinist even playing both melody and accompaniment.

Ex. 48

The 'Ragtime' is a virtuoso piece, especially for the violin which plays the leading role in these three dances — since it symbolizes the chief character, who is here dancing with the Princess, miraculously restored to health by music. The 'Petit Concert' and these 'Trois danses' might be said to correspond to a 'symphonic suite', in which the first 'movement' is based on careful thematic elaboration and the 'Trois danses' correspond to an *andante* ('Tango'), *scherzo* ('Valse') and finale ('Ragtime'). Such a ground-plan is clearly no more than an approximate simplification, and yet it reveals the overall form of the work, in which the first part is taken up with the setting out of the material and the second has a 'symphonic' and dramatic importance that gives it a central character. The 'Danse du diable' that follows leans heavily on the thematic material of the opening and seems to be initiating a kind of finale. The discomfiture and sham death of the Devil makes what appears to be a dénouement, with the exhausted Devil stretched on the ground and dragged off the stage by the Soldier and the Princess. They fall into each other's arms to the accompaniment of the 'Petit Choral', in four parts with string tremolo accompaniment — still another archetype (obviously comic) this time of the Protestant chorale, with its correct two cadences, 'broken' at the dominant of D major and 'perfect' at the tonic of . . . E minor, thus cocking a snook at academic propriety.

The 'Couplet du diable' is an essentially rhythmic transition-piece with strictly synchronized recitation and counterpointed by fragments of the opening March. This leads to the 'Grand Choral', asymmetrically constructed now in seven periods of 4–5–5–2–4–5–4 bars respectively. These periods are separated by pauses which are used by the Narrator, whose voice is the voice of Destiny now leading the Soldier to go 'beyond the bounds' and enter the Devil's sphere of influence. There he will leave his soul — his violin — and in the 'Marche triomphale du diable' this fatal exchange takes the form of a marvellous musical 'voyage'. The violin grows gradually fainter, literally fading away and finally disappearing, as the percussion becomes more and more insistent and is eventually the only sound left, cold and indifferent. We have here in fact a *Klangfarbenmelodie* consisting of four timbres (two snare-drums, side drum and bass drum), and these determine not only the actual durations but also the (asymmetrical) distribution of rhythms within the changing metre. Look, for example, at the bottom line of the following example and the part played by the bass drum (both register and tone-quality) if you wish to grasp Stravinsky's principle in this final passage:

Ex. 49

Despite the internal rhythmic activity in these final bars, the end of *The Soldier's Tale* is frozen into immobility; stripped of everything, the music continues inexorably to end in the void. As at the end of *Les Noces*: solitary and soulless. The place of the soul is taken by Fate, there marked by a bell and here by the funeral drums.

*

To thank Werner Reinhardt for his financial assistance with the first production of *The Soldier's Tale*, Stravinsky wrote for him in 1919 the *Three Pieces for solo clarinet*, the manuscript of which is now at the Rychenberg Foundation in Winterthur. Deprived of the vertical dimension (chords), and with nothing but the clarinet's own different tone-colours to exploit, Stravinsky here makes even greater play with the relationship between melody and rhythm, each inseparably forming the other. The combination of concentration, or density, with economy of means is worthy of Webern.

The first piece recalls the songs written between 1913 and 1915. It is a long meditative sequence for the A clarinet, darker-coloured and more sombre in character than the B flat. Play with repetition/ variation of asymmetrical cells constitutes a sort of 'macro-rhythm' in the listener's mind, a wonderful effect, and the feeling of tonality is lost even more completely in the final phrase than in the rest of the piece:

Ex. 50

There are no bar-lines in the second piece, but Stravinsky insists on the importance of the player's breaths which mark the punctuation of the music. The piece is in fact purely rhythmic, very complex and structured by pitches, durations, accents and phrasing. Harmonically speaking it is quite atonal, though constantly lent a semblance of tonality by temporary 'poles of fixation'.

The last piece is for the B flat clarinet, which is more agile and 'sharper-flavoured' than the A. It moves fast and is a fiendish display of shifted accents and changing metres in a material consisting of short cells, the whole being confined to the high register of the instrument with its rather 'coarse' quality of tone. These three pieces are both a challenge to the analyst (who could devote a hundred pages to their rhythmic aspect alone) and a pure delight to the listener. By comparison *Piano Rag Music*, 'bearing in mind Artur Rubinstein's agile, strong and skilful fingers' seems rather faded now, though still witty and vivacious. Stravinsky said that what he liked most about it was the fact that 'each rhythmic episode in it was dictated by the actual fingers', and that is precisely what now seems its least interesting feature.

During the rehearsals of *The Soldier's Tale* before the Lausanne performance, Stravinsky wrote, in great haste, his *Ragtime* for nine instruments, percussion and cimbalom. Is *Ragtime* jazz? According to the composer it was 'a portrait of jazz' — that is to say, another archetype, acid and biting in sound and containing a virtuoso cimbalom part. As he finished the orchestration of this piece on the morning of 11 November 1918 Stravinsky could hear the French guns over the frontier announcing the armistice.

With the war over, Stravinsky soon realized that the Treaty of Brest-Litovsk meant the final destruction of the last bridges connecting him with Russia. It was a difficult winter. He took a long time to recover from Spanish flu and did not feel able to face a large-scale composition, preparing instead a second *Firebird* suite for smaller orchestra (60 players). Meeting Diaghilev the next spring in Paris, he tried to tell him about *The Soldier's Tale* and its success, but Diaghilev was his usual jealous and exclusive self and refused even to talk of a work that had been composed with any performers in mind but those of his 'Ballets russes'. For both temperamental and professional reasons Stravinsky refused to accept Diaghilev's overbearing possessiveness, and therein lay the seeds of their final rupture. The immediate form taken by the ill-feeling between them was a rather sordid lawsuit about unpaid author's royalties, with Ansermet and Misia Sert acting as mediators and much argument not only about money owing in royalties but about 'human' grievances, including the emotional blackmail and threats, so typical of Diaghilev. Of course it all ended, as usual, with a reconciliation, with sighs of resignation — and a new 'brilliant idea' of Diaghilev's. . . . A performance of *The Soldier's Tale* by members of the 'Ballets russes' was eventually arranged in the reception-rooms of the Hôtel Crillon, where Diaghilev was staying. A plan to make a ballet out of *Chant du rossignol*, which Diaghilev had commissioned from Stravinsky after the opera, attracted the composer because it would mean working with Massine and Matisse, who was to do the sets and costumes. But he refused on the ground that *Chant du rossignol* was a concert piece, static in character with highly wrought textures, and therefore ill-suited to choreographic treatment (although in fact there was a performance, which proved extremely successful).

Diaghilev's next 'brilliant idea' was far better calculated to bring the erring sheep back to the fold of the 'Ballets russes'. He had been very impressed by the recent success of a ballet based on Domenico Scarlatti, *The Good-humoured Ladies*, which had been given in Rome and Naples, with sets by Picasso. What Diaghilev had in mind was something similar, to be based on fragments of Pergolesi's music which had lately been unearthed in Italian conservatoires and London libraries.

> There was a very considerable amount of material, which Diaghilev showed to me, urging that I should seek my inspiration in it and compose the music for a ballet the subject of which was to be taken from a collection containing various versions of the amorous adventures of Pulcinella.
>
> I have always been enchanted by Pergolesi's Neapolitan music, so entirely of the people and yet so exotic in its Spanish character. The proposal that I should work with Picasso, who was to do the scenery and costumes and whose art was particularly near and dear to me, recollections of our walks together and the impressions of Naples we had shared, the great pleasure I had experienced from Massine's choreography in *The Good-humoured Ladies* — all this combined to overcome my reluctance. For it was a delicate task to breathe new life into scattered fragments and to create a whole from the isolated pages of a musician for whom I felt a special liking and tenderness.
> (*Chronicle*)

The whole idea was explained to Stravinsky one spring afternoon in Place de la Concorde, and knowing nothing of Pergolesi beyond the *Stabat Mater* and *La Serva Padrona*, he found it at first disconcerting. But his 'special liking' and 'tenderness' for the eighteenth century in general, and its stylistic conventions in particular, were quite genuine. However, it was now that the temptation to use the musical history of the past as a stylistic resource for the present formed and strengthened in Stravinsky's mind. *Pulcinella* is certainly not a 'neo-classical' but a truly 'classical' work, being composed — or rather 're-composed' — entirely of already existing pieces. It was, however, the prelude to a long period of work which it did in some degree reveal to the awareness of a Stravinsky already orientated in that direction.

*

Pulcinella: 'music by Pergolesi, arranged and orchestrated by Igor Stravinsky' — so runs the title of the work created during 1919, the last to be written at Morges. But is the music really by Pergolesi? According to the calculations of Professor H. Hucke, Pergolesi is responsible for only ten of the twenty-one fragments used, the rest being the work of Gallo, Chelleri, Parisotti. . . . If these revelations are in fact true, we learn nothing more important than the fact that, inasmuch as the composers of one age and one country share a stylistic convention, this convention may blend to the point of confusion fragments dispersed under the name of a single author. And was it not precisely this longing for a common style — a style so 'shared' as to be virtually anonymous — that fascinated Stravinsky?

The story of *Pulcinella* comes from a seventeenth-century Neapolitan manuscript and is a classic tale of love under different disguises. All the girls love Pulcinella, and therefore their lovers decide to disguise themselves as him and to put him to death. Pulcinella exchanges clothes with his friend Furbo, who then pretends to die and is resuscitated by his 'double'. All the lovers end by marrying. The story is in itself quite unimportant, a code rather than a story, an archetype rather than an anecdote. As such it can be superimposed on others of the same kind and merely illustrates Stravinsky's regular preference for certain structural types of theatrical plot, to which *Petrushka* and *The Rake's Progress* as well as *Pulcinella* also belong.

The forces that Stravinsky employs in *Pulcinella* reflect a quite clear intention: a reduced orchestra with no clarinets, and strings divided into *concertino* and *ripieno*, in fact a solo quintet contrasting with the main body. The three soloists (soprano, tenor and bass) form part of the orchestra and are placed in the pit, quite independent of the characters on the stage. The different numbers of the work are very carefully chosen and elaborated so as to form an entity strictly articulated by tempo, density, rhythmic character, dynamics and tonality. But all

these elements, though related to each other in extremely subtle
degrees of contrast, seem as though 'supermodulated' by tone-colour,
which is the essential dimension of the work. With its limited orchestral
resources and pre-determined melodic material there is not a great deal
of scope in *Pulcinella*, but what inventive, unexpected and highly-
flavoured instrumental combinations! Apart from some transposing,
the upper parts and the harmonic bass of the original music are left
unchanged, but the harmonies are recomposed and *layered* in accordance with a very Stravinskian conception of the placing and ordering of
the components of any chord. Inversions, emphasizing what are
conventionally secondary elements, etc., serve as distorting mirrors or
rainbow prisms, creating a musical perspective in which the very small
is often brought to the fore and what is fundamental placed in the
background. Every detail in this dazzling score makes its point,
whether it is the violin we recognize from *The Soldier's Tale*, the bassoon
staccatos, the exposed horns or the rich brass–string contrasts. . . . The
oboe is the most-favoured instrument in *Pulcinella*, whether it be in the
famous 'Serenata', in the 'Gavotte' and its first variation, or in the
second, in which it answers a trio of soloists (flute, bassoon, horn). This
kaleidoscopic use of the orchestra is Stravinsky's sign-manual,
revealing his paradoxical and profoundly original mastery of a pre-
determined material; but it shocked Diaghilev who, it seems, would
have preferred a simple, elegant orchestration in the eighteenth-
century style. The composer, however, insisted on pursuing his own
musical alchemy, resulting in a complete transubstantiation of the
original material; and in the event this was the chief reason of the great
success of the work.

Picasso also roused Diaghilev's wrath by suggesting sets and
costumes not of the *commedia dell'arte* but of the Offenbach type,
including half-masks with enormous whiskers. When the enraged
Diaghilev threw these first sketches on the floor, Picasso was deeply
offended, but then relented and produced the maquette of a small
eighteenth-century Italian theatre with chandeliers, boxes etc. in
which the *commedia dell'arte* appeared as a theatre within a theatre. In
the end only one Picasso set was used — a superb one, apparently,
showing a moonlit Naples street looking on to the bay, with Vesuvius
smoking in the background.

Massine had been completely misled by having only fragments of the
piano-score to work on; and, as these arrived from Morges, he did not
realize that Stravinsky did not have a large symphony orchestra in
mind, but only a modest orchestra of thirty-three players.

In spite of this stormy atmosphere and misunderstandings further exacerbated by Diaghilev, Stravinsky seems greatly to have enjoyed the many rehearsals that he attended. *Pulcinella* had its first performance on 15 May 1920 at the Paris Opéra, with Ansermet conducting, Massine in the title-role and Karsavina as Pimpinella. The public was enthusiastic, but most of the critics complained of the 'sacrilege' committed on Pergolesi, a really idiotic criticism that many people took very seriously. The famous party given the next day by the Persian prince Firouz (who appears as Prince Mirza in Radiguet's *Le Bal du Comte d'Orgel*) helped both authors and cast to forget this slight contretemps. It was typical of the 'roaring twenties' which were just beginning. Here is Jean Hugo's account[5] of the party given in the Paris suburbs at the house of a certain Amouretti, a former convict:

> Beside Stravinsky, Picasso and his wife, Diaghilev and Massine, there were Misia and Sert, Princess Eugène Murat [Princesse d'Austerlitz in Radiguet], Lucien Daudet, Jean Cocteau, Auric, Poulenc and Radiguet who immortalised the evening. Prince Firouz [Mirza in Radiguet] was a magnificent host. A lot of champagne was drunk. Stravinsky got drunk and went up to the bedrooms, collected pillows, bolsters and mattresses and threw them down from the balcony, starting a pillow-fight between the guests. . . . The party ended at 3 a.m.

Pulcinella was a major turning-point in both the life and the art of Stravinsky. In 1920 he finally moved from Switzerland to France and opted for the West rather than Russia. As an artist he remained faithful to his fundamental beliefs but from now on he gave them different *supports*, the first (and for a long time to come the most important) being the classical one. He was later to describe the part played by *Pulcinella* in his evolution in the following terms (in *Expositions and Developments*):

> *Pulcinella* was my discovery of the past, the epiphany through which the whole of my late work became possible. It was a backward look, of course — the first of many love-affairs in that direction — but it was a look in the mirror, too.

VI

Between the Wars 1

'As, WITH THE return of peace, life resumed its activities in the whole of Europe, particularly in France, I realized that I could no longer remain in the involuntary isolation to which the war had confined me. I therefore resolved to take my lares and penates to France where, at the moment, the pulse of the world was throbbing most strongly,' writes Stravinsky in *Chronicle of my Life*. In fact the choice had not been so clear-cut and the composer had considered settling in Rome, even getting Malipiero to book a definite apartment, though this fell through. The close ties which he had formed with Paris, where he had had his great successes and where there was a great burst of creative activity, finally proved too strong to resist, and the first step was taken when the composer took his family to Brittany for the summer of 1920. There he completed his last tribute to the Pays de Vaud — the *Concertino for string quartet*, composed at the request of the leader of the Flonzaley Quartet of Geneva, Alfred Pochon. The *Concertino* is a kind of *sonata-allegro* with a markedly dominating part for the first violin. At the first performance in New York, in September 1920, neither performers nor audience seem quite to have understood the work; and it was little played until 1952, when the composer transcribed it for an ensemble of twelve instruments, ten woodwind and brass and two *obbligato* parts for violin and cello, the violin part remaining very close to the original. This transcription is a good example of Stravinsky's orchestral taste for delicate instrumental flavours and unusual alloys.

One of Stravinsky's greatest works, *Symphonies of Wind Instruments*, was begun and partly written at Carantec. It was finished at Garches on 20 November 1920.

'Garches 214', a telephone number that appears in Stravinsky's diary,[1] was the number of Gabrielle Chanel's house, where Stravinsky and his family took refuge on their return from Brittany. It was a short visit for Catherine Stravinsky and the children, however, as Chanel soon became the composer's mistress. The affair remained a secret for a long time until Paul Morand made it public property.[2] The two had probably met through Misia Sert, who was at the centre of all the intrigues in the social and the artistic worlds in Paris. Chanel's generosity was no less than her beauty and intelligence: horrified by Diaghilev's more or less empty coffers, she decided to support financially the 1920 revival of the *Sacre*, giving Diaghilev the enormous sum of 300,000 francs on the strict condition that no one should be told. . . . Of the course of her affair with Stravinsky we know little except that it was short-lived. In any case she kept Stravinsky at Garches until the spring of 1921, while he installed his family near Biarritz for the 'good Atlantic air'.

When the *Sacre* was revived at the Théâtre des Champs Elysées on 15 December 1920, the choreography was no longer that of Nijinsky, who was by then in a mental home. Not only would it have been impossible to reconstitute his original choreography in sufficient detail, but to do so would have been to revive unpleasant memories of the stormy première and also, no doubt, the jealousy and resentment that Diaghilev felt for Nijinsky. The new choreography by Massine was simpler and more austere, based on Byzantine mosaics with even a hint of Cubism. Although Stravinsky accepted it when submitted to him by Massine, he was later to express some reserves about it being 'rather forced and artificial' owing to its bittiness. He did, however, acknowledge the 'unquestionable talent' both of the young choreographer and of Lydia Sokolova, who danced 'l'Elue'. Chanel further contributed to this production by having all the costumes made in her own ateliers.

After installing his family near Biarritz, Stravinsky joined the 'Ballets russes' in Spain, where he conducted *Petrushka* in the presence of King Alfonso XIII. He spent Holy Week and Easter of 1921 at Seville with Diaghilev.

> Throughout those seven days we mingled with the crowds. It is astonishing that these fêtes, half-pagan, half-Christian, and consecrated by time, have lost nothing of their freshness and vitality — notwithstanding the travel agencies and all the guides who are beyond price but have to be paid, and notwithstanding, moreover, the particular kind of publicity which has been their fate. (*Chronicle*)

Who else was there? Did Stravinsky ask Chanel to go with him, as Morand makes Chanel say? This is a difficult question to answer as a careful comparison of dates seems to suggest that, at the time of the Spanish visit, Stravinsky had already started another — very fleeting — affair, with Génia Nikitina (who danced with the 'Chauves-Souris' under the name of Katinka), also known as Geneviève Via and called by Stravinsky, on the back of a photograph showing the two of them at a bull-fight in Bayonne, 'la cantatrice aux yeux verts' (the singer with green eyes). However that may be, it was in this very Parisian milieu dominated by Chanel and Misia Sert, and in the euphoric atmosphere of successful love-affairs (which he was very good at concealing) that Stravinsky, with his accustomed imperturbability, was to complete at Garches one of his most serious and fervently unworldly works.

*

Symphonies of Wind Instruments began with the final chorale, which Stravinsky wrote in Brittany on 20 June 1920 at the suggestion of Henri Prunières, editor of the *Revue musicale*. The piano version was published in December 1920 in a supplement to the *Revue musicale* entitled 'Le Tombeau de Claude Debussy', containing some ten short pieces by different composers.

Much has already been said of the close friendship between Stravinsky and Debussy — a friendship of mutual respect and admiration, although not without its resentments or attempts to 'score', particularly on Debussy's part.

Stravinsky felt Debussy's death deeply.

> I grieved not only at the loss of one whose great friendship had been marked with unfailing kindness towards myself and my work, but at the passing of an artist who, in spite of maturity, and health already hopelessly undermined, had still been able to retain his creative powers to the full, and whose musical genius had been in no way impaired throughout the whole period of his activity. (*Chronicle*)

The mutual respect and admiration of these two unusually clear-thinking artists did not imply an identity of aesthetic ideas:

> It is clear that his aesthetic, and that of his period, could not now stimulate my appetite or provide food for my musical thought, though that in no wise prevents me from recognizing his outstanding personality or from drawing a distinction between him and his numerous satellites. . .

> While composing my *Symphonies* I naturally had in mind the man to whom I wished to dedicate them. I used to wonder what impression my music would have made on him, and what his reactions would have been. I had a distinct feeling that he would have been rather disconcerted, as he was, I remember, by my *Roi des étoiles*, also dedicated to him, when we played it together as a duet for one pianoforte[?] . . . According to my idea, the homage which I

intended to pay to the memory of the great musician ought not to be
inspired by his musical thought; on the contrary, I desired rather to
express myself in a language which should be essentially my own.
(*Chronicle*)

That language is, once again, the language of ritual; and it was the
most personal tribute that Stravinsky had to offer, to dedicate to the
memory of Debussy — 'an austere ceremony unfolding in short
litanies'. What the death of the French composer and the loss of a
personal friend inspired in Stravinsky was not the direct expression of a
feeling of grief, the mimicking in music of lamentation, but a lofty
discourse and forms that ritualize and transpose that feeling: a
dispassionate chorale and hieratic instrumental litanies. Seen in this
light, all the writing in the *Symphonies* follows this conception logically,
not simply by its character, its austere melodies and their heterophonic
treatment but also by its colour, the bitter and violent tone-colours
saved from any sentimental connotation by the absence of the violins
from the instrumental ensemble.

Symphonies of Wind Instruments is astonishingly novel and complex in
form. It is all of a piece in its unfolding, following a system of anchor-
points, prefigurations, developments and reminiscences of a game with
'before', 'after' and 'now' in a way that has no parallel in modern music
except, perhaps, in Boulez's *Le Marteau sans maître*. As with Boulez, the
principal element of differentiation here is *tempo*, each formal section
establishing three interrelated basic metronomic speeds, which are for
a crotchet 72, 108 and 144, the second being half as fast again as the first
and the third double the speed of the first. (We shall call these tempi I,
II and III.)

It is not easy to find one's way about in a structure such as this, one
that cannot be reduced to a neat symmetry or to any classical, pre-
existing scheme. The first marker is in fact *tempo* in its three categories
which correspond to three types, three definite 'regions' of the work, as
is shown by the diagram below:*

First note the persistent presence (and the asymmetrical returns) of
S, which is the primary element of the piece, its actual origin — the
chorale in memory of Debussy. Reduced to representative specimens
of its two fundamental aspects, harmonic (S^1) and harmonic/melodic
(S^2), it is linked to the structure of 'refrain' A and its numerous
transformations, each time that it returns. Tempo I is reserved for
these two structures. A and S complement each other in that they
form a pair of opposites, and also by the fact that A will gradually

*See also Eric Walter White, *op. cit.*, p. 294.

Ex. 51

'shrink' and its role be taken over by S, which becomes increasingly important.

A-S, therefore, constitutes a clear axis running through the whole work at the basic tempo. A, however, has a quite important property as refrain-structure and unifying agent — possessing not only the harmony (simplified) of S but, at least schematically, the melodic germ of M and the rhythmic structure of P, as we shall see later. This means that A is neither a 'theme' nor a 'part' of the work but rather its synthetic structure or, better still, its 'genetic programme'.

Integrated into this evolving spiral are two stages of a *melodic* character, M and N, and these are in tempo II, the intermediate tempo, in accordance with their tranquil and fluid manner of utterance. Stravinsky here employs a heterophony between the two voices, one of which is a modified version of the other. M^1 and M^2 are 'neutral' melodic fragments constructed of three and five notes respectively in a varying metre of extraordinary subtlety. N^1 and N^2, on the other hand, are more strongly characterized, another heterophonic pair with an additional heterophony of M clinching the interdependence of these two melodic groups, already linked by their tempo (II). Finally, P is a *rhythmic* stage and this is in tempo III, the fastest and therefore the best suited to this kind of development.

These three stages, which correspond to the three tempi, are linked, fused/defused and anchored by a close working of the transitional or preparatory cells x, y and z. x is a rapidly swaying cell introducing (or 'fusing' indeed) tempo III and stage P, which it announced as early as ③ in the score. We shall only meet x again at the end, in the intensified preparation of P, where this cell will prove to be the generator of the rhythm, and therefore the dominant character, of P. y is a descending melodic-polyphonic cell, sometimes final (as at its first appearance) and sometimes initial. Finally z, staccato and in double ternary rhythm, is only found inserted in the 'melodic' part, in tempo II, for the sake of contrast.

The final *temporal* distribution of stages S, x and P is most remarkable. S is exposed from the outset and continues to assert its presence, appearing as a 'motto' during this last part, twice stated before the actual chorale itself. Here in fact we find two moments which, on the analogy of *Le Marteau sans maître*, might be called 'Before chorale, I' and 'Before chorale, II'. Meanwhile P, secretly prepared by cell x, is both pre-echoed by what might be called 'Pre-P' and recapitulated in an abbreviated 'Post-P' (see Diagram). In this way future, present and past are telescoped in musical time — that is to say in the form — in an entirely novel and extremely effective manner.

Also worth noting are such ternary or binary structural symmetries as

$$A - S^1 \; S^2 - A + x$$

at the opening, followed by

$$S^1 - S^2 - S^1 + y$$

or

$$y' - A^2 S^2 S^3 - y''$$

(linear pseudo-symmetries) or again

$$y' - A^3 A^4 - y''$$

and, in the macro-structure,

$$M^1 - M^2 \cdots^7 \cdots M^2 - M^1$$

(mirror pseudo-symmetry), not to mention formal equivalents such as 'Before P — P — after P' or the evolving formal series 'Before S, I' — 'Before S, II' — S.

Finally we should observe the total absence of all textural repetitions in this score which nonetheless imprints itself on the memory and lives by the dialectic of known/unknown, the reappearances of the 'known' resulting from the constant metamorphosis, or what Michel Butor would call 'la modification', in which memory plays an important part.

Stravinsky called *Symphonies of Wind Instruments* a hieratic discourse, austere and ritual in character, but this discourse is by no means disincarnate or abstract, since it is entirely anchored in its own specific sonorous material, that material being itself in a state of constant metamorphosis. The specific sound appears here both as a *reader* of the form, sealing the singularity of each stage, and — last but not least — as a constant delight to the ear. Unlike the 'magic' rainbow orchestra of the *Sacre*, the orchestral palette used in *Symphonies* is hard, rough and alternately luminous and sombre. The harmony moves in granite blocks, the melody in scalpel-strokes and the rhythm in electric discharges. . . . At this point our discussion enters the realm of metaphor or, in other words, leaves us on the threshold of what cannot be put into words.

*

Also from the Garches period come the eight easy pieces for piano known as *Les Cinq doigts* (the five fingers), finished in February 1921. Once the fingers of the 'young' pianist have been placed on the keyboard, his hand does not change its position, this being indicated at the beginning of each piece:

Ex. 52

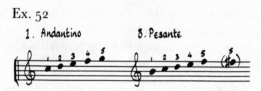

The tempo of each piece provides the title: 1. *Andantino*, 2. *Allegro*, 3. *Allegretto*, 4. *Larghetto*, 5. *Moderato*, 6. *Lento*, 7. *Vivo*, 8. *Pesante*. In no. 4, the *Larghetto*, we discover the 6/8 *alla siciliana* music of the 'Serenata' in *Pulcinella*. In no. 1 a remote Russian flavour combines with a reminiscence of Debussy's *Etudes*; no. 2 vaguely recalls the cornet in *The Soldier's Tale* (Royal March); no. 4 leans on *Pulcinella* as we have said; in no. 6 there is a distant, nostalgic memory of *Pribaoutki* ('Le Vieux et le lièvre') and no. 8 is a tango which plays with piling up different tonalities.

Les Cinq doigts is another step towards so-called 'neo-classicism'. Echoes of the past become more frequent, the modal writing is reduced to major and minor and the restless alternations of the bar-line begin to settle down: we find ourselves in the classical-tonal world, with stable metres.

Many years later, in 1961, Stravinsky was to orchestrate *Les Cinq doigts* for an ensemble of fifteen players, slightly altering the order, the tempo and some of the details of the pieces. He dedicated them, as *Eight Instrumental Miniatures*, to his Los Angeles friend Lawrence Morton, one of the organizers of the Monday Evening Concerts, which corresponded to the 'Domaine musical' concerts in Paris.

*

In June 1921 there was a performance at the Théâtre des Champs Elysées of Cocteau's *Les Mariés de la Tour Eiffel* (The Eiffel Tower Wedding) with music by 'les Six',[4] a group of young composers who took Satie as their model and prided themselves on their anti-Wagnerian — and even 'anti-impressionist' — views. Diaghilev had nothing to do with this work or the typically Parisian scandal that it caused. He did however attend the performance, carefully picking out for his own future 'use' the best composers of the group and commissioning ballets from them: *Les Fâcheux* (Auric), *Les Biches* (Poulenc) and *Le Train bleu* (Milhaud).

All these 'young men' — who are affectionately recalled in Georges Auric's memoirs[5] — were passionate admirers of Stravinsky, although their aesthetic ideas were consciously 'simpler' than his, but at the same time (as expounded by their spokesman Cocteau), more literary. Stravinsky appreciated their admiration and on several occasions spoke favourably of them, though holding himself slightly aloof, as we can see from a letter that he wrote to Auric on 17 November 1922:

> In Paris I saw Satie and Poulenc several times. The latter has written two sonatas. One for horn, trumpet and trombone and the other for clarinet and bassoon, both very well written and significant, I think, in the sense that he gets rid of the 'modern prejudices' you speak of. I very much liked the music of these two sonatas, very fresh music which reveals Poulenc's originality more clearly than any of his other compositions. In addition to that, this music is very, very French. . . .

The summer of 1921 saw two triumphs of the *Sacre* in London — one in concert-performance and the other at Covent Garden, where it had had a rather lukewarm reception some years earlier. On this occasion Stravinsky stayed a considerable time in London, where he attended the first performance of *Symphonies of Wind Instruments*, included rather at the last moment in one of Koussevitzky's concerts. According to the composer the result was 'a débâcle':

> I fully anticipated that the *cantilènes* of clarinets and flutes, frequently taking up again their liturgical dialogue and softly chanting it, did not offer sufficient attraction to a public which had so recently shown me their enthusiasm for the 'revolutionary' *Sacre du printemps*. This music is not meant 'to please' an audience or to rouse its passion. (*Chronicle*)

The placing of the work in the programme, immediately after the brilliant *Coq d'or* marches, may have been damaging, and the distance of the players from the conductor and the public seems also to have played a part — something that would be unthinkable today when orchestras have become accustomed to the different groupings demanded by contemporary works. During his London visit Stravinsky was also commissioned by Diaghilev to orchestrate and adapt Tchaikovsky's *Sleeping Beauty*, the only available score of which contained serious gaps, the missing numbers appearing only in the piano score. Stravinsky was delighted to orchestrate these numbers and to compose the necessary bridges between them:

> It was a real joy to me to take part in this creation, not only for love of Tchaikovsky but also because of my profound admiration for classical ballet, which in its very essence, by the beauty of its

ordonnance and the aristocratic austerity of its forms, so closely corresponds with my conception of art. For here, in classical dancing, I see the triumph of studied conception over vagueness, of the rule over the arbitrary, of order over hazard. I am thus brought face to face with the eternal conflict in art between the Apollonian and Dionysian principles. The latter assumes ecstasy to be the final goal — that is to say, the losing of oneself — whereas art demands above all the full consciousness of the artist. There can therefore be no doubt as to my choice between the two. And if I appreciate so highly the value of classical ballet, it is not simply a matter of taste on my part, but because I see exactly in it the perfect expression of the Apollonian principle. (*Chronicle*)

While he was working on the orchestration of *Sleeping Beauty* in London, Stravinsky and Diaghilev discussed an opera symbolically dedicated to the memory of Tchaikovsky, Glinka and Pushkin: *Mavra*.

*

Historically speaking, *Mavra* is the most controversial of all Stravinsky's works. It may not mar the profound unity of his *oeuvre*, but it marks a turning-point. From *Mavra* onwards Stravinsky seems to have consciously looked to art itself for inspiration, to have made already existing works, or styles, the point of departure for his own, thereby preserving the constants of his language and his aesthetic — the approach to the archetypal, the distancing of the sacral and, most important of all, the search for a stylistic framework, a search to which history and its products certainly furnish many clear and different answers.

What in fact is the difference between *Mavra* and Stravinsky's previous works? Whereas *Les Noces*, *Pribaoutki* and *Renard* are founded on the characteristics (not the actual products) of Russian *folk*-music, as 'invented' by Stravinsky, *Mavra* is based on Russian *art* music and recreates the 'town style' of Glinka's and Pushkin's day, something consisting of popular elements and fashionable Italian features, remodelled by entirely 'European' stylistic techniques. In the nineteenth century the language used in Moscow and St Petersburg drawing-rooms was French, and this half-Russian, half-French jargon was — in a certain social stratum — one of the languages of the Russia of those days, just as 'authentic' as 'vodka-isba-balalaika' and other 'racy' flavours that so irritated Stravinsky by their facile picturesqueness.

Whenever the question of Russian music arose, Stravinsky never failed to point to its double aspect: 'town' and 'country' (folk); 'impure' and 'pure'. By 'town' what Stravinsky meant in essence was Glinka and Tchaikovsky, as opposed to the nationalist 'Five':

> Was not the difference between this mentality [that of Glinka and Tchaikovsky] and the mentality of the 'Five', which had so rapidly become academic and concentrated in the Belaieff circle under the domination of Rimsky-Korsakov and Glazunov, that the former was, as it were, cosmopolitan, whereas the latter was purely nationalist? The national element occupies a prominent place with Pushkin as well as with Glinka and Tchaikovsky. But with them it flows spontaneously from their very nature, whereas with the others the nationalistic tendency was a doctrinaire catechism which they wished to impose. (*Chronicle*)

Stravinsky considered, on the other hand, that Tchaikovsky and Dargomyzhsky were the true descendants of Glinka, the heirs of musical Russia inasmuch as they, unlike the 'Five', achieved a would-be universal style by creating a synthesis between the popular element and Western musical principles, a true assimilation of the two, which was from now onwards to be Stravinsky's own aim.

Mavra is based on Pushkin's verse-tale *The Little House at Kolomna* adapted by Boris Kochno.

> On the musical plane this poem of Pushkin's led me straight to Glinka and Tchaikovsky, and I resolutely took up my position beside them. I thus clearly defined my tastes and predilections, my opposition to the contrary aesthetic, and assumed once more the good tradition established by these masters. (*Chronicle*)

The libretto of *Mavra* is that of a typical Russian *opera buffa* 'imported from Europe' and acclimatized to Russian conditions: it is totally, guilelessly conventional and the same may be said of the music with which Stravinsky provided it, music that is 'truer' than the models on which it is based — in fact, *yet another archetype*.

The story of *Mavra* is simple. The daughter of the house, Parasha (soprano), is in love with the handsome hussar Vassili (tenor). Air and 'Chanson tzigane', followed by a conversation between Parasha and her mother about the cook's death. Parasha will find a new servant, who is in fact the hussar, dressed as a woman and called Mavra. Quartet for Parasha, her mother, Mavra and a neighbour. Once alone, the lovers sing their grand duo. When Parasha goes, Mavra takes the opportunity to shave. Unexpected return of the mother — amazement, horror. The air sung by Mavra is cut short by his escape through the window . . . *coda.*

The piece contains thirteen 'numbers', quite distinct from each other and linked by passages of dialogue which have the function of recitative but which are not part of the music's structure, the musical line remaining completely autonomous.

The vocal writing is that of the Russo-Italian kind mentioned above, which by no means eschews *bel canto.* Parasha's air has the Russian 'flavour' that we find in Tchaikovsky's songs.

Ex. 53

Drug moy mi – lyí, kras- no sol-nish-ko moyo-
(Darling heart , o you sun of my life)

Observe the strong tonal articulation, the basic diatonic character and the dynamic rhythm obtained by anticipating the tonic accent in a shifting metre. Harmonically *Mavra* is relatively simple, but melodically the use of parallel figures in imitation reveals an essentially 'horizontal' way of thinking without being actually contrapuntal. There are some paradoxical hints of jazz, particularly in the quartet. The orchestra, with its reduced string section, is dominated by the winds — the typical band, in fact, used for serenading beneath a girl's window.

A Russian 'vieux vaudeville' of the 1830s transformed into an *opera buffa,* the women expressing themselves in the lyrical-sentimental style actually in use among the *petits bourgeois* of the day, and the hussar in a swaggering gypsy style, with waltzes, Siciliennes, songs and duets in the Moscow–St Petersburg drawing-room version of Rossini, Bellini and Weber: this is the hotch-potch that Stravinsky appropriated with the skill and flair for detail, which at every turn reveal themselves to a careful scrutiny. A feature of the work that is more noticeable in performance than in reading the score is its monothematicism, everything essential in the music seeming to derive from Parasha's felicitous air quoted in Ex. 53. Equally striking, though in this case to the reader of the score rather than to the listener, are the rhythmic symmetries revealed by the vocal lines. On occasion these almost become what Messiaen has called 'non-retrogradable rhythms' (rhythms, that is to say, which remain identical whichever way they are read):

Ex. 54

Consider also the very elaborate and unusual counterpoint in the famous quartet led by the 'new cook' (melodic material derived from Parasha's song) at the words, 'Feklusha will have worked hard for ten years'.

Yet all these ingenious details were wasted, and *Mavra* was a failure. Why?

Stravinsky — who was very disappointed — partly blames the context in which the new work was given at the Paris Opéra, where the *Sacre* and *Petrushka* were also in the programme and effectually drowned the light, small-scale *Mavra*. Added to that, the public still associated Stravinsky with the *Sacre* scandal and its 'barbaric' flavour. They were therefore disappointed by this change of style and the lightness and transparency of the new work — a universal reaction, in fact, to any composer's change of style. Stravinsky himself seems to have been no more aware of this change than he was in the case of *Les Noces*, which was a genuine break with the luxuriant style of the *Sacre*. The critics, on the other hand, were extremely aware: Boris de Schloezer in the *Nouvelle Revue Française* replying with moderation but a certain amount of discomfort to Vuillermoz's violence, and foreseeing in *Mavra* the beginning of 'second degree' creation, the composer 'at one remove' from his composition.

There was surely another reason for *Mavra*'s failure beside those already mentioned and a decisive one: its paleness as an opera, the neutral character of its theatrical language and the thinness of the story, both cruelly accentuated on the stage. The work remains a stylistic exercise that does not directly grip the listener and can only really interest connoisseurs of Russian music. There was in fact a grain of truth in such smart, or simply silly, comments as '*Mavra* — mavrant'* and 'Excellent! at last something by Stravinsky that we can allow our daughters to listen to!' (reported by Poulenc). The work is in fact ambiguous. On first impact it can be simply a disappointment, but at a deeper level it raises the whole problem of 'grafting' in art and how it is perceived. This was not how it appeared to Stravinsky himself, of

*A French pun: mavrant — navrant (pitiful).

course, since he considered tradition — whether folk or urban, peasant or bourgeois — to be something *permanent*, a possession to be not only preserved but made use of. Yet this is how it could, at best, be understood by the public — as a *cultural* work, one in which culture puts itself on the stage for the delight of the few. No doubt the works written for the concert-hall and the ballets could sometimes invite a (properly speaking) more 'cultural' listening, whereas opera makes use of conventions in order to transcend them and achieve, if only by an illusion, a true 'representation of body and soul'. The principal character in *Mavra* is . . . convention itself. The whole of *Mavra* is, as it were, in quotation-marks, and what is quoted is a vanished style — and in this lies its elegance, its cleverness but also its limitation.

Mavra was begun in the summer of 1921 at Anglet and finished in the spring of 1922 at Biarritz. A preliminary performance was given on 27 May 1922 at the Hôtel Continental in Paris, with just the singers and Stravinsky at the piano. The first performance took place a few days later, on 3 June, at the Opéra, with sets by Survage and Gregor Fitelberg conducting. Despite the high quality of this and later productions (Berlin, Krolloper: 1928; Rome Opera: 1942) *Mavra* never caught on.

After the chilly première there was a reception at the Hotel Majestic, packed with celebrities. Proust (who arrived very late, as he always did) was on Stravinsky's left. 'You admire Beethoven, of course?' 'I hate Beethoven'. 'But, cher Maître, the last sonatas, the last quartets?' 'Worse than the others', grunted Stravinsky, who was in a filthy mood after the tepid reception of his new work. It must be remembered that his admiration for Beethoven's last quartets came very late; these exchanges with Proust may very well be authentic.

*

Stravinsky settled in France in 1921, dividing his time between Paris and Biarritz, where he rented a house for his family in the centre of the town, the Villa des Roches. For three years this was one of his homes, the other being the famous studio in the Maison Pleyel, rue Roche-chouart. He had signed a seven-year contract with Pleyel's for the transcription and 'recording' of all his music on their mechanical piano, the Pleyela.

My interest in the work was twofold. In order to prevent the distortion of my compositions by future interpreters, I had always been anxious to find a means of imposing some restriction on the notorious liberty, especially widespread today, which prevents the public from obtaining a correct idea of the author's intentions. This possibility was now afforded by the rolls of the mechanical piano, and, a little later, by gramophone records.

This means enabled me to determine for the future the relationships of the movements (*tempi*) and the nuances in accordance with my wishes. It is true that this guaranteed nothing, and in the ten years which have since elapsed I have alas! had ample opportunity of seeing how ineffective it has proved in practice. But these transcriptions nevertheless enable me to create a lasting document which should be of service to those executants who would rather know and follow my intentions than stray into irresponsible interpretations of my musical text. (*Chronicle*)

This same obsessional attitude, which was soon to be transferred from the mechanical piano to the gramophone, was also reflected in the arrangement of his work-table, as described by Jean Cocteau in *Le Coq et l'Arlequin*:

There is a terrifying orderliness about Stravinsky — like a surgeon's case of instruments. . . . Seeing Stravinsky at Morges, Leysin or at Pleyel's where he lives when he is in Paris, is like seeing some animal in its carapace. Pianos, drums, metronomes, cymbaloms, stave-pens, American pencil-sharpeners, desks, shallow side-drums, bass drums — they are extensions of the man himself, the pilot's cockpit, the insect's weapons. . . .

Late in the summer of 1922 Stravinsky went to Berlin to meet his mother, whom the Soviet authorities had given permission to emigrate. He had arranged to stay in Berlin a week, but his mother's departure from Russia was repeatedly postponed and he eventually spent two months there. It was post-war Berlin, with inflation and extreme poverty, and as soon as his mother arrived, he left for Biarritz as quickly as possible. There he started work on the *Octet for Wind Instruments*, which was initially a 'sonata' with no definite instrumentation. Composition was held up by work on the final orchestration of *Les Noces*, which Diaghilev had announced in his programme for 1923, and Stravinsky went back to the *Octet* when he was finishing his work on *Les Noces* at Monte Carlo, where the 'Ballets russes' company was staying.

After *Symphonies of Wind Instruments*, and particularly after *Mavra*, neither of them really successful, *Les Noces* was a triumph in Paris. It was given by the 'Ballets russes' at the Théâtre de la Gaîté Lyrique with Ansermet conducting and Georges Auric, Edouard Flament, Hélène

Léon and Marcelle Meyer playing the four pianos. This triumph restored public confidence in Stravinsky.

Les Noces had of course been conceived ten years before; does that mean that the public realized the metamorphosis that had occurred in the composer's style and now declared its preference for his earlier manner? Not really, but there is no doubt that *Les Noces* is very superior to *Mavra* by its lofty style of beauty, its strength and violence and its musical and choreographic accomplishment, quite apart from any change in style — a change that was in any case less visible at the time than it is now.

On 1 July a rich American couple, Gerald and Sarah Murphy, gave a party to celebrate the new work. They were very friendly with the 'Ballets russes' and fanatical admirers of Stravinsky, and the party was given on board the sloop *Le Maréchal Joffre*, which was moored in the Seine by the Chambre des Députés. Stravinsky was the first to arrive, in order to inspect the seating arrangements of the guests, he himself sitting on the right of the Princesse de Polignac. The party included Picasso, Milhaud, Cocteau, Ansermet, Diaghilev, Kochno (now a close collaborator and friend of Diaghilev's), Larionov, Goncharova, Germaine Tailleferre, Marcelle Meyer, Tristan Tzara, Blaise Cendrars. . . . Ansermet and Marcelle Meyer were in charge of the music, at the piano. Cocteau, in the uniform of 'captain' of the sloop, after wandering about with a lantern, suddenly opened a door and shouted 'we're sinking!' There was a laurel-wreath with the words 'Les Noces — Hommage', presented by Ansermet and Kochno. Stravinsky, taking a run, jumped clean through it.

The next month he went to Weimar for a performance of *The Soldier's Tale*, put on by the Bauhaus with Hermann Scherchen conducting. Klee and Kandinsky were in the audience, and so was Busoni who, according to *Chronicle*, 'had always been described to me as an irreconcilable opponent of my music' but was sincerely moved by the piece and told the composer so. 'But don't let's imitate him!' as he wrote to a friend.

These first years in France were a time in which Stravinsky was, consciously or unconsciously, seeking a partner. He was anything but a Don Juan by temperament, and after the short and very discreet affairs with Chanel and Katinka he met the woman who was to become his second wife and his companion for almost half a century. Vera de Bosset, whose father was French by origin, her mother Swedish, was born in 1888 in St Petersburg. Thomas Mann spoke of her 'typically Slavonic beauty' and she certainly behaved like a Slav, though she had hardly a drop of Russian blood. She was first married to a man called Shilling and then, in 1918, to the painter Serge Soudéïkine. She worked in the theatre, she was a gifted painter and costume-designer and did a lot with the 'Ballets russes'. Stravinsky met her with Diaghilev in an Italian bistro in Montmartre and asked her to dinner at Fouquet's. According to Vera Stravinsky herself and to Robert Craft, who have provided us with a meticulous account of the circumstances, the relationship must have started at about this time — 'from 1921 to 1939 a triangle was the geometry underlying Stravinsky's existence'.[6] In fact it was not until 1940, after Catherine Stravinsky's death, that Stravinsky married Vera de Bosset, in the United States.

As early as 1922 Stravinsky seems to have spoken of Vera to his wife (though in exactly what terms we do not know) and the two became acquainted. Did this double life inspire the composer with feelings of guilt and thus give rise to 'a new religiosity that appeared both in his music and his life'?[7] As we have seen, Stravinsky was fundamentally a deeply religious person, although this had not hitherto shown itself in his personal practice or in his choice of musical subjects. About 1925–1926 the religious feeling suddenly asserted itself and was to remain with him for the rest of his life. He told Craft in 1957 that, in order to compose works like *Threni*, he had to 'not only believe in the symbolical sense, but in the person of the Lord, the person of the Devil and the miracles of the Church'.[8] Faith and its dogmas: that attitude is as characteristic of the man as his aesthetic credo was characteristic of the musician: before all else, *form*.

*

The *Octet* was begun in Biarritz at the end of 1922 and finished at the studio in rue Rochechouart on 20 May 1923. It is for flute, clarinet in B flat, two trumpets, two bassoons, and two trombones, one of these being a bass trombone, which was to be a favourite instrument with Stravinsky. The first of its three parts is not a sonata form but a condensed version of that form; and emphasis is quite as much on thematic exchange as on the tonal plan (which gravitates round B flat major), on the system of modulations and the principle of recapitulation. The second movement is a set of variations on a waltz-theme in which the ternary rhythm is contradicted by interpolations in four-time. To ascribe to this movement a definite tonality would be wrong, and would in fact misrepresent the composer's intention, which was to suggest tonality without adopting any single key except episodically. The variations are brilliant, not modelled on any definite style but growing out of the specific sound-quality of the instruments in a series of mutual exchanges. Originally the work had been conceived in the abstract, something very unusual with Stravinsky:

> I began to write this music without knowing what its sound-medium would be — that is to say, what instrumental form it would take. I only decided that point after finishing the first part, when I saw clearly what *ensemble* was demanded by the contrapuntal material, the character and structure of what I had composed. (*Chronicle*)

If the *idea* of counterpoint is one of the main ideas in the *Octet*, what is its reality? Except in the final *fugato* — and really even there — Stravinsky's is primarily a kind of pseudo-counterpoint, a deliberate suggestion of the *very essence* of counterpoint. Like a conjurer, he produces a counterpoint that is 'truer' than the true, making a *trompe-l'oeil* use of space and employing for the most part two voices (if not even a single one, when the second is in fact a heterophonic variation of the first).

Intensity is reduced to 'the dynamic limit which determines the function of the volumes in play', or, as he wrote in 'Some ideas about my *Octet*' in *The Arts* (January 1924): 'I have excluded from this work all nuances between the *forte* and the *piano*; I have left only the *forte* and the *piano*.' The score of the *Octet* shows that this is not strictly true, since there are all kinds of nuances from *fortissimo* to *pianissimo*; but listening to the work shows Stravinsky to be quite right, since the convergencies and the contradictions in his subtle dynamics do in fact constitute a perfect *trompe-l'oeil* effect and give a 'black and white' impression.

Whereas *Petrushka* and *Mavra* make use of pre-existing material — either invented or reinvented, peasant or urban — the *Octet* uses model forms: sonata, variations, *fugato* and, particularly, a *writing* typical of these forms, developed with great virtuosity but without a sufficiently strong hallmark of any period or any style. As André Schaeffner, who writes excellently about all this period, puts it: 'The various elements that the composer collects together in these works are in no way exceptional and they take on a universal, not to say impersonal character.'

This is the *abstraction* of which Stravinsky speaks in his article in *The Arts*:

> This sort of music has no other aim than to be sufficient in itself. In general, I consider that music is only able to solve musical problems; and nothing else, neither the literary nor the picturesque, can be in music of any real interest. The play of the musical elements is the thing (quoted in E. W. White, *Stravinsky*).

With its ageless materials, its abstract scales and arpeggios, its ternary stereotypes (swiftly masked by the superimposition of some binary rhythm) and its deliberately trivial (and suddenly sublime) melodies, the *Octet* may well excite both pleasure and irritation and yet appear like *Mavra* and many other Stravinsky works, a primarily 'intellectual' piece to be listened to at one, or even two removes. But is this in fact so important to us? This is one of those ideograms of Stravinsky's which, when deciphered, has only one sense and that is music — the whole of music and nothing but music.

Koussevitzky was entrusted with the *Octet* for one of his concerts at the Paris Opéra, but on one condition — that it should be conducted by the composer. The same article in *The Arts* contains a clear statement of Stravinsky's ideas on *performance* in general, and its antithesis, *interpretation*, ideas that have never changed.

> I have arrived at this conclusion: when the centre of gravity finds itself in the form considered as the only emotive subject of the composition. When the author puts into it such a force of expression that no other force could be added to it (such as the will or personal predilection of the executant) without being superfluous, then the author can be considered as the only interpreter of his musical sensations, and he who is called the interpreter of his compositions would become their executant. (*Ibid.*)

After this 'official début' as a conductor Stravinsky occupied a privileged position as the performer of his own music, not only for the reason given above but also because to fix a 'standard' interpretation of his music the pianola could produce only fossilized models; and last — but by no means least, as we know in his case — for financial reasons. In fact the fees that he received for large, and therefore time-consuming, commissions were, as he pointed out, comparable to those that famous pianists or conductors earned several times a week or month. Conducting and, on a smaller scale, piano-playing were therefore to become Stravinsky's major source of income for the rest of his life. We shall be returning later to the nature and quality of his gifts as a conductor.

*

At the beginning of 1924 Stravinsky conducted the *Octet*, *Mavra* and the orchestral suite from *Pulcinella* in Brussels and accepted engagements in Barcelona and Madrid. He also composed, at Koussevitzky's request but for his own use, the *Concerto* 'pour piano suivi d'un orchestre d'harmonie'. This would both employ him in his new role as pianist — which he was cultivating with the assistance of Czerny's exercises — and also satisfy the taste for wind instruments revealed in his most recent works. He reserved an exclusive five-year right to the solo part in the *Concerto*, which he finished at Biarritz in April 1924 and played, with Koussevitzky conducting, at the Paris Opéra on 22 May of the same year. After the end of the first movement Stravinsky had a memory-lapse when he saw the reflection of his own fingers on the lid of the instrument. He took a long time carefully wiping his hands with his handkerchief until Koussevitzky whispered the first notes of the second movement; the performance then continued without further incident and was a triumphal success. Stravinsky was to take a long time to get over stage-fright as a soloist, and he was to be greatly helped in this by the Princesse de Polignac, who arranged *avant-premières* of all works in which he was to appear in person, either at her house in Avenue Henri-Martin or in her palazzo in Venice.

The *Concerto* perfectly conforms to the demands of the genre, including a tripartite, sonata-style form, a virtuoso solo part and cadenzas. Bach is very clearly its patron-saint, the harmony is predominantly of the 'wrong bass' description, the pulse of the music unflagging, with displaced accents and variable metres being the basic principle of the work's rhythm. The biting, acid flavour of the orchestral sonorities — no strings except double basses — is quite delectable.

After a rhythmic 'Overture', the 'Allegro' is dominated by a Bach-like figure consisting of two semiquavers and a quaver and reaches its climax in a virtuoso cadenza. The 'Largo', which, as far as melody goes, recalls the *Italian Concerto*, and harmonically a chorale arranged by Busoni, brings back memories of Manuel de Falla; and has an astonishing, hesitant, tortured conclusion. The final 'Toccata' opens with what seems to be a fugal subject, but soon adopts 'vertical' writing for the orchestra, while at the same time highlighting the pianistic skills of the soloist; the *fugato* interlude is a stylistic quotation rather than a genuine contrapuntal development. The double 'Coda' makes great play of displaced accents and barlines that leap, insist, shift or explode.

Musically speaking, the *Concerto* is a complete success. Not only does it meticulously fulfil its contract ('lawyer-like', as Stravinsky says) but it presents itself to the listener sparkling with wit and energy, delighting and revivifying him and charming him by precisely the sense of *success* that it communicates. The Bach references are in this case a true relish, though it was not always to be so. It is definitely not what Proust's Swann would call a 'prrrofound' work; but the past seems here happy to conspire with the present to give a pleasure compounded of cultural awareness and the vitality and immediacy of the actual texture of the music. 'Back to Bach' was to be a slogan during the years between the wars, but only with the epigones. Hitherto Stravinsky's language had been too Russian for anyone to follow, let alone imitate him. But here he is now speaking an 'international' language (though in fact remaining Russian in all essential characteristics) and thus issuing an open invitation to short-lived imitators. 'Back to Bach!' had the authority of the great man and was already the height of fashion. The only person to escape was . . . the great man himself, for whom Bach was an occasional 'prop'. He had the whole history of music at his disposal and he was to make use of it all for his own purposes. And, in his next work, he was already shuffling the cards.

The *Piano Sonata*, commissioned by the Princesse de Polignac, composed in 1924 and played by the composer for the first time at Donaueschingen in July 1925 and later at the I.S.C.M. Festival in Venice, is a kind of Tower of Babel. Each movement is based on a different musical period and arouses different reactions. In his memoirs, Stravinsky refuses to allow that 'Clementi, Haydn and Mozart' were his models or that he followed the stereotyped sonata form associated with them. Schoenberg thought that its inspiration was Bach and made it the object of one of his three *Satires*, as we shall see. Boris de Schloezer saw in it a reference to Mozart or possibly Carl Philip Emmanuel Bach, and others mentioned Scarlatti. Stravinsky himself described the second movement ('Adagietto') in particular as 'Beethoven frisé'* (curly Beethoven). None of this actually defines any 'model', but rather suggests that Stravinsky was once again trying to create an 'archetype', in this case of the classical piece, 'to dream', yet to avoid any definite outline. But in any case, through all this mass of references, Stravinsky was to remain Stravinsky, whether or not we choose to follow him along the trail he is leading us with varying success.

Stravinsky's first great opponent was, of course, Schoenberg. He and his disciples and friends were deeply committed to serialism and found Stravinsky's eclecticism and *passéisme* not only incomprehensible but intolerable. The instinctive incompatibility between the two had long existed, though it had been more or less discreet. The *Sacre* and *Pierrot Lunaire* had overcome the incompatibility of these two 'sacred monsters' and brought about a mutual respect, while young Webern and Berg exchanged enthusiastic letters about Stravinsky's big early works.

*Obviously true as far as the ornamental writing and the phrasing are concerned.

The break came after the Venice festival at which Stravinsky played the *Sonata* and Schoenberg conducted his *Serenade*. Did they hear each other's works on that occasion? They certainly avoided a meeting, and on his return from Venice Schoenberg wrote the *Three Satires*, one of which — a double canon — is 'dedicated' to Stravinsky:

> Who's that coming along?
> Why, it's little Modernsky!
> He's got himself a pigtail,
> which looks very pretty!
> What *real* false hair!
> What a wig,
> Just (as little Modernsky imagines)
> Just like Papa Bach.

At this stage of Stravinsky's development, his music was not so much 'blameworthy' for its stylistic prejudices as unequal in actual quality. The *Sonata* may well be said to fail in the attempt to be 'archetypal' and to be only half-convincing, with its rather blunt play of melodies and rhythms, which reveal *procedures* rather than real originality and invention; but the same cannot be said of his next work, the *Serenade en la* (Serenade in A) (1925). Here eclecticism goes from Scarlatti to Debussy; the music follows a tonal, or rather 'polar' convention, centred round A; and each of the four movements is designed to play for roughly the same time as one side of a '78' gramophone record. In spite of this it has an astonishing stream of invention that fascinates the listener. The initial 'Hymn' has a generous, majestic quality and contains original harmonies of a severe beauty. The most remarkable of the four movements is certainly the 'Romanza', which is as free and loosely constructed as an improvisation. 'Rondoletto' is a characteristic two-part invention in a simplified counterpoint; and the final 'Cadenza' has chains of parallel chords in 'whole tone' progression like Debussy, and exploiting the colouristic aspect of the piano. Each of these four pieces ends with harmonics of the note A, like a kind of luminous halo, a tenuous link but sufficient to hold these strange, fragile little 'musical objects' together.

In the autumn of 1924 Stravinsky left Biarritz, whose winds and waves he found 'trying for the nerves', and settled with his family in Nice at Mont Boron, where he finished the *Sonata*. He then set out on a tour that took him to Warsaw, Prague and Leipzig, playing his *Concerto* with Furtwängler in Berlin, with Mengelberg in Amsterdam and with Ansermet at Lausanne. This was a brilliant opening of a career on which he was to be fully launched by his first three-month tour of the USA for which he left on 27 December 1924. He conducted the New York Philharmonic on 8, 9, 10 January (1925). Boston, Philadelphia, Cleveland, Chicago, Detroit and Cincinnati followed — all major orchestras with famous conductors, who accompanied his performances of *Concerto*. One of the most important concerts of this tour was in fact one of the least spectacular — 'an evening of chamber music with Igor Stravinsky' given at the Aeolian Hall, New York, on 25 January 1925. The programme consisted of the *Octet*, *Ragtime* and *Renard* conducted by the composer, who also accompanied Greta Torpadie in nine songs. The critic Paul Rosenfeld has left an eye-witness account of a rehearsal with Stravinsky:

> He came rapidly on to the stage from the wings, a metallic insect, all swathed in hat, spectacles, muffler, overcoat, spats and walking stick, and accompanied by three or four secretarial or managerial personages. The man was an electric shock. In a minute business was upon the entire assemblage. There was a sound of peremptory orders . . . never a doubt as to exactly what he wanted and the means to arrive at his end! A kind of interest radiated from him to the musicians, who began entering into the spirit of the animal comedy (*Renard*). . . . He commenced singing the words in Russian, even danced a little up on the conductor's stand in his pink sweater. . . .

In his interview with Rosenfeld, it was Stravinsky who did the questioning.

> 'Suppose you went out and narrowly escaped being run over by a trolley-bus — would you experience some emotion?'
> 'I suppose so, Mr Stravinsky.'
> 'So should I. But if I went out and narrowly escaped being run over by a trolley-bus, I would not immediately rush for some music-paper and try to make something out of the emotion I had just felt. . . .'9

Pleased with his success in the United States and having satisfied himself of the 'public understanding' of his music in America and the 'serious interest of the Americans in music in general' (*Chronicle*), he was still glad to return to Europe. His American tour had made him a lot of money and when, after a series of concerts in Barcelona, he returned to Nice it was with a car and a chauffeur — described in a letter to Ramuz as 'very nice, very expensive [. . . .] I bathe each morning in the sea, then compose regularly, then in the afternoon do my correspondence and practise the piano (in order not to lose the technique that I acquired last year).''[10]

The chauffeur, however, was soon dismissed as the composer obtained his own driving licence at the end of 1925 and joined the Automobile Club of Nice-Côte d'Azur, of which he remained a member for several years. He had a Hotchkiss in 1926 and a Citroën in 1927. The first time he drove the Citroën he was had up for parking on the wrong side, opposite Hermes', where he had gone to buy a tie — after which he drove in low gear (unwittingly of course) to Saint Germain- en-Laye and burned out the motor. . . . In 1926 he gave Vera Soudéïkine a Renault and later his own midnight-blue Peugeot.[11] (At Hollywood in his seventies he was to have, among other cars, two big black Lincolns, driven mostly by his wife and occasionally by his assistants.)

In the summer of 1925 Stravinsky drove his Renault to Venice to play his *Sonata* at the Biennale, for a fee of 500 dollars. Just before he left Nice he had an infected finger which made him anxious about his ability to play, and the day before he left he spent a long time in a church, praying. At the concert he made a short preliminary apology on the platform and then took off the bandage — to find his finger 'miraculously healed'. This was exactly the time when he became extremely pious, and his wife even more so. The *Pater Noster* for unaccompanied mixed chorus, written in 1924, was the first of Stravinsky's works with an explicitly religious theme, and it may be regarded as a profession of faith.

On his way home from Venice in September 1925 he stopped at Genoa, where he bought a life of Saint Francis of Assisi, which he read the same night.

It is common knowledge that the familiar speech of the saint was Italian, but that on solemn occasions, such as prayer, he used French (or perhaps Provençal, his mother's language). I have always considered that a special language, and not that of current converse, was required for subjects touching on the sublime. That is why I was trying to discover what language would be most appropriate for my projected work, and why I finally selected Latin. The choice had the great advantage of giving me a medium not dead, but turned to stone and so monumentalised as to have become immune from all risk of vulgarisation. (*Chronicle*)

This account of his first thoughts about the work which was to become *Oedipus Rex* shows that they were primarily about language.

*

Back in Nice Stravinsky thought further about writing a work based on some classical myth and decided to ask Jean Cocteau's help with the text, having been struck by Cocteau's adaptation of Sophocles' *Antigone*. Together they chose the myth of Oedipus. In *Chronicle* Stravinsky is loud in his praises of Cocteau, but it was very different thirty years later when, in *Dialogues and a Diary*, he was to be extremely severe — in fact mercilessly spiteful — on the subject of his collaborator. While the work was in preparation, Stravinsky seems to have told Cocteau exactly what he wanted, which was not a drama of action but a 'still life' transcribed in a deliberately conventional libretto with arias, duets etc. According to *Dialogues* Cocteau's first idea was a 'music drama' and Stravinsky made him rewrite the libretto twice before a final editing. Once complete, the text was given to Jean Daniélou (the future cardinal) for translation into Latin.

> What a joy it is to compose music to a language of convention, almost of ritual, the very nature of which imposes a lofty dignity. One no longer feels dominated by the phrase, the literal meaning of the words. Cast in an immutable mould which adequately expresses their value, they do not require any further commentary. The text thus becomes purely phonetic material for the composer. He can dissect it at will and concentrate all his attention on its primary constituent elements — that is to say, on the syllable. Was not this method of treating the text that of the old masters i.e. of this austere style? This, too, has for centuries been the Church's attitude towards music, and has prevented it from falling into sentimentalism and consequently into individualism. (*Chronicle*)

This is one of the key-texts essential to anyone wishing to see Stravinsky's whole *oeuvre* in the right perspective. Here we find that demand for the 'sacral' and that search for linguistic universality (a point we have already dwelt on), and also the reprobation of their opposite, sentimentality and — even more reprehensible — 'individualism'. Here too is that nostalgia for the past, the 'old masters of the austere style', that same mistrust of the romantic ego and the same desire to find a place in music's universal concert, even perhaps at the price of anonymity. In the course of this quest the only abiding-place for him was convention, the 'immutable mould', and the effect of this on language seemed to him liberating. For convention both frees the music from any connotation, or subjection to feeling, and also rids words themselves of their meaning in the musical text, restoring them as 'pure phonetic material' to the composer.

The following passage is even more revealing:

Just as the Latin, no longer being a language in everyday use, imposed a certain style on me, so the language of the music itself imposed a certain convention which would be able to keep it within strict bounds and prevent it from overstepping them and wandering into byways, in accordance with those whims of the author which are so often perilous. I had subjected myself to this restraint when I selected a form of language bearing the tradition of ages, a language which may be called homologous. (*Chronicle*)

The visual realization of the work presented itself to Stravinsky's imagination at the same time as the music: a petrified stage-picture parallel to 'the freezing of the drama in the music'. (*Dialogues*) A motionless chorus with soloists who address themselves directly to the audience and not to each other, all wearing masks, which are essentially depersonalizing and ritual in character. The emphasis is thus not on the destiny of the individual but on Destiny acting upon him:

> My audience is not indifferent to the fate of people, but I think it far more concerned with the personality of fate and the delineation of it which can be achieved uniquely in music. (*Dialogues and a Diary*)

He set to work as soon as he received the first pages of the Latin text, at the beginning of 1926. According to André Schaeffner[12] Stravinsky kept an exact account of the progress of the work:

> On 11 January [...] he wrote under the word 'Serva' an initial chord and its ternary rhythm; the next day brings the opening of Oedipus' solo, and the 13th and 14th the whole of the opening chorus. After an interruption he embarks on Creon's air (April), Tiresias' oracle (August), Jocasta's air (October), the duet for Jocasta and Oedipus (completed on 16 November) and the final chorus (mid-March, 1927). At 4 a.m. on 10 May Stravinsky finished orchestrating what was one of his most important works, twenty days before its first public performance in oratorio form.

There was no time to lose, since Stravinsky and Cocteau had agreed that the work was to celebrate Diaghilev's twenty years as head of the 'Ballets russes'. It had been meant to be kept secret, but this was clearly impossible; nor was Diaghilev's reception very friendly — he spoke of the work as 'a very *macabre* present'. *Oedipus Rex* was given in concert form, without sets or costumes, for reasons of economy, and met with the lack of success predicted by the man for whom it was intended — but to whom it is not dedicated, the printed score carrying no dedication at all, only the name of Stravinsky — and, in smaller letters, that of Cocteau as 'co-author', not 'author'(!) of the libretto.

Reading Stravinsky's ideas about *Oedipus Rex*, which he wrote down in 1935, is a help in understanding the work's three perspectives: sacral, archetypal and stylistic — though we might imagine it to be bare, arid and reduced simply to the essential structure. This would be quite mistaken, however: *Oedipus Rex* is a composite work, which, unlike many of Stravinsky's works of this period, does not refer to any single historical style or period but to a whole number, ranging from Handel to Verdi and from the Middle Ages to Meyerbeer. Everything about the score suggests that here Stravinsky was literally acting out his dream of universalism, as though he wished to embrace the entire history of music — hence, no doubt, the ambiguous character of the work; for the often almost grotesque insistence on the *detail* of these different styles weakens rather than reinforces its archetypal power. Hence, too, the irritation that various passages may cause by their deliberately banal academicism which is prolonged, repeated and insisted on as though to force the listener to wallow in it; hence also the impression of grandeur which, despite a number of exaggerations, is inseparable from this unique work.

The harmonic key to this strange hybrid is to be found in the first three bars of the introduction, like the motto on a medallion. It consists of three simple pitch-relationships, more or less cadential in character:

Ex. 55

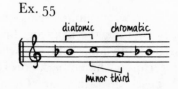

The minor third, which is central here, appears as the basic interval of the work and, viewed in the abstract, as an emblem of its strongly tonal, minor mode character. Its concrete, functional reality appears (bar 4) in the indefatigable bass *ostinato* accompanying the chorus.

Ex. 56

This is obviously not the place for a detailed musical analysis of *Oedipus Rex*, but rather for an explanation of how the network of archetypal forms is constructed, how it appears under many different guises and how these are unified in a system of close tonal relationships.

One of the most important and original features of *Oedipus Rex* is that the *characters* of the drama are represented by the different musical styles and archetypes. The work is a veritable Tower of Babel, everyone speaking his own language but understanding his neighbour, unlike the legend.

Look at Creon, the representative of bombastic classicism in its belated and most corrupt form, a Meyerbeerian archetype. After the chorus' 'Vale, Creo' — one of the errors in the Latin of the text ('Ave, Creo!')* — Creon's deliberately academic commonplaces are further emphasized by the E flat clarinet, which doubles the melodic line at three octaves' distance. What could be more 'intellectual', not to say perverse, than that?

Ex. 57

Tiresias, on the other hand, is an 'authentic' classic; his solemnity is not pompous and the references in his music are 'serious'. This is the world of Mozart's Commendatore:

Ex. 58

The Messenger represents the style of the church modes, but his line is doubled in the deep bass by the double-bassoon and adorned with deliberately stereotyped little counterpoints *à la* Bach:

*The 'phonetic' spelling of the Latin text — which is most irritating — is that found in the score (see the vocal examples).

Ex. 59

The Shepherd is naturally given a 'pastoral' 6/8 and a clearly chromatic line, with a cor anglais drone:

Ex. 60

Jocasta is given conventional operatic forms on a grand Verdian scale — arias in several episodes, recitatives, *da capos* etc. in a brilliant vocal style which is itself a stereotype.

The dramatic recitative at the beginning of Act 2 is one of the most successful Verdian episodes, but the parody — not to say caricature — of Verdian bravura reaches its climax with the famous 'Oracula, oracula', which the listener is forced to accept in all its perverseness — if he can still bear it. . . .

Ex. 61

Observe the totally conventional and deliberately repeated chords in the orchestral accompaniment.

Oedipus himself is a musical chameleon who appropriates every style, from oratorio recitative to *bel canto* vocalizing, alternating between the diatonic and the chromatic, according to the dramatic context and the 'sentiments' to which he is charged with giving conventional expression. The chromaticism of the Oedipus–Jocasta duet is an archetypal model of fear:

Ex. 62

The chief interest of Oedipus and Jocasta as a musical pair — and indeed of the other characters — lies in the generalizing power of clichés as such, the way in which they crystallize within the framework of a secular oratorio all the consecrated formulae of theatrical expression common to opera in every age. . . . The only fact that makes this expressive *repertory* tolerable — and even fascinating to follow — is the fact that it is *frozen*. Unlike the other characters, all static except Oedipus, the ever-present chorus changes and evolves. Supplication (the plague at Thebes), acclamation, surprise, amazement, sympathy (in the literal sense) for the chief actors in the drama — all these are expressed by the chorus, sometimes as actor in the drama and sometimes as spectator; and it employs everything from homophony and heterophony to polyphony, from the style of Handel to late Romantic neo-academicism or the Russian choral conventions of *Boris Godunov* (though the actual archetype of these comes from Glinka):

Ex. 63

The orchestra of *Oedipus Rex* is something of a *tour de force* in that it is almost exclusively vertical without ever being flat. In fact it often reminds one of a huge brass-band and it is most characteristic of Stravinsky where it is reduced in scale and at its most delicate, as in the passage between the departure of the Shepherd and the Messenger and the quiet exchanges between lower strings and woodwind before the revelation of Oedipus' secret. Such passages as these, where Stravinsky is not writing for the whole orchestra, contain the most successful clichés, light and ironical touches such as the solo horn's 'Alberti basses', for example. Jocasta's fanfare after Oedipus' 'Lux facta est' is a perfect success in the timeless style of the theatre:

Ex. 64

The part of the Narrator was conceived by Cocteau, to be taken by himself. His last appearance, in the production of 1952 ('L'Oeuvre du xxᵉ siècle') will never be forgotten by those who saw it, nor will the sets and masks that he designed for it, particularly the monstrously beautiful mask, crowned with tears of blood, worn by Oedipus.*

Stravinsky seems never to have wholly approved of the idea of the Narrator, although it corresponded with his idea of presenting fixed ('frozen') moments of the drama rather than a dramatic action. If he allowed it at the time, thirty years later we find him wholly condemning it in *Dialogues and a Diary*:

*It was made of ping-pong balls dipped in red ink and mounted on a crown of barbed wire encircling Oedipus' enormous head.

I detest the speaker device. . . . The line 'And now you will hear the famous monologue, "The divine Jocasta is dead", is intolerable snobbery. Famous to whom? As to the final '*On t'aimait*', it is the most offensive phrase of all, for it is a journalist's caption and a blot of sentimentality wholly alien to the manner of the work.

The overall unity of *Oedipus Rex* is to be found in its tonal plan, in the establishment of clear, strict harmonic relationships between the formal sequences, as shown below.

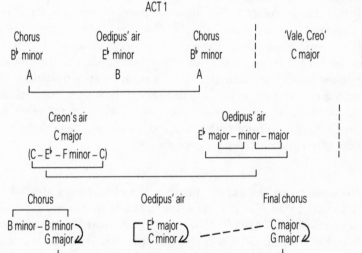

Observe the clear predominance of minor keys, especially B flat minor, and above all the matching of close, relative or homonymous (major/minor) tonalities, as indicated.

How has *Oedipus Rex* worn? Let us leave the final word to Stravinsky–Craft in *Dialogues*:

The music? I love it, all of it, even the Messenger's fanfares, which remind me of the now badly tarnished trumpets of early 20th-Century-Fox. Neo-classicism? A husk of style? Cultured pearls? Well, which of us today is not a highly conditioned oyster? I know that the *Oedipus* music is valued at about zero by present progressive-evolutionary standards but I think it may last awhile in spite of that.

And last it does, in fact, by its petrifaction — Stravinsky's casting of it in an archetypal mould which seems to be indestructible and makes fun of history.

There was an *avant-première* of *Oedipus Rex* at the Princesse de Polignac's a few days before the first public performance, which was on 30 May 1927 at the Théâtre Sarah-Bernhardt. The work had little success and the audience, according to Stravinsky, was 'barely polite'. A static work performed with neither sets nor costumes may well have suffered from being given with *Firebird* and all its musical and visual splendours. Stravinsky contributed indirectly to the expenses of the staging by handing to Diaghilev the 12,000 francs paid him by the Princesse de Polignac for the *avant-première*, but despite this and the economical performance *Oedipus Rex* was taken off after three nights. Klemperer gave what appears to have been a magnificent performance of the work — though with 'ghastly' sets — in Berlin the following year, but the work had difficulty in making its way, no doubt owing to its ambiguous nature — half-opera and half-oratorio, dramatic in essence but deliberately static in presentation. Today, on the other hand, it is precisely this ambiguity that attracts producers, though the piece is still very often given in concert performance.

*

No sooner was *Oedipus Rex* finished than Stravinsky started work on a new ballet that was to consecrate his taste for the stylistic convention of classicism, *Apollo Musagetes*. This was a commission from Elisabeth Sprague Coolidge, for performance in the Library of Congress in Washington — 'a work of thirty minutes duration (a condition I satisfied with the exactitude of a film composer) employing an instrumentation appropriate to a small hall'. (*Dialogues and a Diary*)

As on every occasion when Stravinsky worked for anyone else, (and despite the fact that after the Washington performance the score was to be his, without payment) Diaghilev was furious:

'This American woman is completely deaf.'
'She may be deaf, but she pays.'
'You never think of anything but money.'

The 'money' in this case was 'only' 1,000 dollars.

The subject of *Apollo Musagetes* followed naturally on *Oedipus Rex*, as did the music in which the composer pursued his 'supranational' style, and the choreography, which was in the purest classical tradition, that of the *ballet blanc*:

. . . in which to my mind the very essence of this art reveals itself. I

found that the absence of many-coloured effects and of all super-
fluities produced a wonderful freshness. This inspired me to write
music of an analogous character. It seemed to me that diatonic
composition was the most appropriate for this purpose, and the
austerity of its style determined what my instrumental *ensemble* must
be. I at once set aside the ordinary orchestra because of its
heterogeneity, with groups of strings, wood and brass, the effects of
which have really been too much exploited of late, and I chose
strings. (*Chronicle*)

In this way the composition of the whole ballet seems to have issued
from a simultaneous musical and visual conception. The same was
true, we may remember, of both *Petrushka* and the *Sacre*, but here the
choice is even more explicit, and the work derives its intelligence and
grace from the coherence of its conception, a rigorous specification that
brought together subject, music and choreography in a harmoniously
balanced unity.

As Stravinsky has said, 'the Muses do not instruct Apollo' in this
ballet; 'as a god he is already a master and beyond instruction'. He is
omniscient and perfect and he consecrates the Muses' arts by investing
them with their respective attributes and leading them in the final
'Apotheosis' to Mount Parnassus. The Prologue represents the birth of
Apollo.

According to the legend, 'Leto was with child and, feeling the
moment of birth at hand, threw her arms about a palm tree and knelt
on the tender green turf, and the earth smiled beneath her, and the
child sprang forth to the light. Goddesses washed him with limpid
water, gave him for swaddling clothes a white veil of fine tissue, and
bound it with a golden girdle'. (*Chronicle*)

This prologue forms the first scene of the ballet.
The Muses are reduced to three — Calliope, Polyhymnia and
(finally) Terpsichore — Poetry, Mime and Dance, the last occupying
the place of honour. Each Muse is given her own musical and
choreographic variation in the traditional scheme of 'pas d'action',
'variations', 'pas de deux', 'coda', 'apotheosis'.

Yet, as Stravinsky tells us in *Dialogues and a Diary*, 'the real subject of
Apollo is versification', that is to say, the versification of Racine. Its
structural principle is the alexandrine and its fundamental rhythm —
that of the iambic. Stravinsky is paying homage to seventeenth-century
French poetry and this introduces additional, visual allegories. Speaking of Bauchant's sets and Chanel's costumes for the first performance,
he says that 'the chariot, the three horses and the sun-disc (the Coda)

were the emblems of the Roi Soleil'. Apart from these hidden, if not secret allegories there are no musical redundancies, no fable and above all no . . . ancient Greece, except nominally. Once again, thanks to a secondary convention — in this case that of seventeenth-century France — the work approaches the archetype: while appearing to be a ballet on a subject borrowed from antiquity, *Apollo* becomes *the* mythological ballet of the Grand Siècle.

    Apollo is written for strings, with an additional cello group. The six parts are very carefully proportioned; Stravinsky in fact gave Klemperer exact figures — 8, 8, 6, 4, 4, 4 — for the Berlin production. A string orchestra is particularly well-suited for melodic thinking, and there is no doubt that the melodic, diatonic, linear, even occasionally polyphonic element is the conveyor of that feeling of tenderness which is characteristic of *Apollo* and touches the listener quite apart from the austerity and 'whiteness' of the writing. It is the rhythm, though — and essentially the construction of the durations — that supports the elegant, airy architecture of the work. Just as the rhythm in *Oedipus* remains, whatever one may say, 'passive', so in *Apollo* it is of prime importance. The key-cell opens the gates of the whole rhythmic structure, and it is what Messiaen calls 'non-retrogradable' i.e. the same whichever way it is read, with the iambic as generating element, and its reverse the trochee. Let us see with what exemplary rigour it proliferates and changes shape in the course of the work:

Ex. 66

[Musical notation examples a. through w.]

We find this basic figure (a) at the opening of the Prologue, which it permeates, unobtrusively diminishing and multiplying (b) its short value, then asserting itself by augmentation, in its iambic form (c), at the moment of Apollo's birth, before appearing in its inverted form (d): the final minim is here subdivided into its equivalent in quavers (e).

The answer accentuates the diminished form (f), still coming to rest on the minim. The 'Variation d'Apollon' following the second scene is based on forms that are varied, linked, inverted, metrically varied (g, h, i), while the 'Pas d'action' presents a new, ternary, form (j) contrasting with the binary elements, the end consisting of a very extended form in the solo violin (k).

The 'Variation de Calliope' introduces the alexandrine, which is also based on an iambic cell (l); and here Stravinsky also introduces a motto taken, not, as we should expect, from Racine, but from Boileau:

> Que toujours de vos vers le sens coupant les mots
> Suspende l'hémistiche et marque le repos.

In the 'Variation de Polymnie' the cell is inverted and gives rise to flexible rhythmic variations (m), whereas Terpsichore's variations are more delicate (n, o, p, q). The rhythmic materials in the 'Seconde variation d'Apollon' are stronger, more 'virile' in character (r).

In the 'Pas de deux' the short values are even further reduced (s) and these are the most delicate and the most ingenious of all the variations.

The Coda is based on the simple ternary variation (t) and then the 'negative' rhythm (u) (where a note is replaced by an equivalent rest), before dissolving into ornamentation and successions of syncopations. In the final 'Apotheosis' we find the most extreme forms of rhythmic variation which accentuate differences by augmenting long values and diminishing short (v), eventually arriving at the most complex figure (w), derived from the 'Pas d'action' in which all the long values are lengthened accordingly, in what may perhaps be called an 'apotheosis' of rhythmic variation of the iambic.

Apollo Musagetes had its first performance in Washington on 27 April 1928 with Adolphe Bohm's choreography, and was immediately put on by the 'Ballets russes' at the Théâtre Sarah-Bernhardt (12 June 1928) with the young Serge Lifar dancing Apollo. Balanchine's choreography was so felicitous and so perfect in every way that it has been used all over the world and is still used today by Balanchine's own company, the New York City Ballet.

As an apprentice choreographer, Balanchine had already done some of the dances in *Pulcinella*, but it was *Apollo* that made his reputation. This was also the beginning of an unclouded fifty years of friendship

and collaboration between him and Stravinsky, who shared aesthetic
ideas to an extent that is most unusual for any composer and
choreographer — though it should be remembered that Balanchine
had received a professional musical education.

What in fact the two men shared was a taste for classicism in musical
and choreographic forms, which they had rediscovered in all its purity
Stravinsky was to insist on this formal aspect repeatedly (we have
already talked at length about this in regard to his insistence on style)
While he was still working on *Apollo*, he published the following
statement in an article (in French) in *The Dominant* in December 1927.

There is much talk nowadays of a reversion to classicism, and works
believed to have been composed under the influence of so-called
classical models are labelled neo-classic.

It is difficult for me to say whether this classification is correct or
not. With works that are worthy of attention, and have been written
under the obvious influence of the past, does not the matter consist
rather in a quest that probes deeper than a mere imitation of the so
called classical idiom? I fear that the bulk of the public, and also the
critics, are content with recording superficial impressions created by
the use of certain technical devices which were current in so-called
classical music.

The use of such devices is insufficient to constitute the real neo
classicism, for classicism itself was characterized, not just by its
technical processes which, then as now, were modified from one
period to the next, but rather by its constructive values.

The mere 'thing' — a theme or a rhythm in music, for instance —
is not in itself sufficient to satisfy an artist in the creation of a work
The components of the material must come into a reciprocal
relation, which in music, as in all art, is called form. All the great
works of art were imbued with this quality of interrelation between
constituent parts, interrelation of the building material. And this
interrelation was the one stable element, all that lay apart from it
being unintelligibly individual — that is to say, in music, an ultra
musical element. Classical music — true classical music — claimed
musical form as its basic substance; and this substance, as I have
shown, could never be ultra-musical. If those who label as neo
classic the works belonging to the latest tendency in music mean by
that label that they detect in them a wholesome return to this formal
idea, the only basis of music, well and good. But I should like to
know, in each particular instance, whether they are not mistaken. By
that I mean that it is a task of enormous difficulty, and one in which

therefore serious criticism can show its worth, to achieve immunity from misleading appearances which almost inevitably lead to incorrect deductions (quoted in E. W. White, *Stravinsky*).

Stravinsky spent the summer of 1927 with his family at Echarvines on the Lac d'Annecy. While he was finishing *Apollo* in Nice later in the year, he was approached by the Maison Pleyel — one of whose studios in old rue Rochechouart he had used — with a request to take part in the opening of their new concert-hall in Rue du Faubourg-St-Honoré. The two concerts given to celebrate this event early in 1928 were both memorable, and Stravinsky conducted the *Sacre* at each, a really testing experience since it meant knowing and mastering the rhythmic difficulties of the work *as a performer*.

Orchestrating *Apollo* was not too demanding a task and it left Stravinsky time to pursue his career as a performer — conducting *Oedipus Rex* in Amsterdam, London and Paris, the *Sacre* in Barcelona and *The Nightingale* in Rome, among other engagements. Back in Paris in May he found himself with another studio in the new Pleyel building and on 19 May he played his *Concerto* in the big hall, with Bruno Walter conducting. '[With him] . . . I was quite free from anxiety over the rhythmically dangerous passages which are a stumbling-block to so many conductors' (*Chronicle*). On 12 June he conducted the first performance of *Apollo* at the Théâtre Sarah-Bernhardt and the twelve succeeding performances, as well as the London première on 25 June. All was now prepared for his next work, *Le Baiser de la fée*.

*

Towards the end of 1927 Ida Rubinstein, wishing to start a new ballet company, approached Stravinsky's publishers about rights in *Apollo*. As the European rights had been given to Diaghilev, she proposed commissioning something new from Stravinsky and suggested a 'Homage to Tchaikovsky'. The fee offered was 7,500 dollars.

My well-known fondness for this composer, and, still more, the fact that November, the time fixed for the performance, would mark the thirty-fifth anniversary of his death, induced me to accept the offer. It would give me an opportunity of paying my heartfelt homage to Tchaikovsky's wonderful talent . . .

. . . Free to choose both the subject and the scenario of the ballet . . . I turned to a great poet with a gentle, sensitive soul whose imaginative mind was wonderfully akin to that of the musician. I refer to Hans Christian Andersen, with whom in this respect

Tchaikovsky had so much in common.... [I chose] *The Ice Maiden* ... and worked out the story on the following lines. A fairy imprints her magic kiss on a child at birth and parts it from its mother. Twenty years later, when the youth has attained the very zenith of his good fortune, she repeats the fatal kiss and carries him off to live in supreme happiness with her ever afterwards.... Although I gave full liberty to painter and choreographer in the staging of my composition, my innermost desire was that it should be presented in classical form, after the manner of *Apollo*. I pictured all the fantastic roles as danced in white ballet-skirts, and the rustic scenes as taking place in a Swiss landscape, with some of the performers dressed in the manner of early tourists and mingling with the friendly villagers. (*Chronicle*)

In later productions it was the classical style that predominated — and it is so much the best.

In *Pulcinella*, Stravinsky had already produced virtuoso writing in a style based on a pre-existent work. But whereas he knew little of Pergolesi, discovery and appropriation being in this case simultaneous, Tchaikovsky was a very different matter. This was music with which he was not just familiar but deeply in love; and it aroused his 'musical appetite' to such a degree that he passed from virtuoso juggling with Tchaikovsky's material to a complete identification of himself with the spirit of his great predecessor, and a fascination which found expression in a great outburst of creative activity. In 1934 he was to make a symphonic suite (*Divertimento*) from this work, but in the original score the actual Tchaikovsky music (*Humoresque* op. 10, *Nocturne* op. 19, *Danses russes* op. 40 no. 10, *Valses* op. 50 nos. 1 and 4 etc. and a number of songs) stands side by side with plenty of 'Stravinsky, after Tchaikovsky'. As in *Pulcinella*, the whole piece was recomposed in depth to give it a completely homogeneous appearance — a music, to use André Schaeffner's affectionate description, 'gradually descending upon mankind like Mozart's or Tchaikovsky's'.

Where, you may well ask, is 'the real Stravinsky' in such a case? and the answer is: *everywhere*, not only in passages where he is working 'in' a style but even in those where he is making the actual materials of this style his own. His power of identification, his personality and the hallmark of his music are so strong that in the last resort the actual origin of the object appropriated seems forgotten. 'Impure', as it were genetically, this Stravinsky is 'pure Stravinsky' in its concrete structure. Are we really to sacrifice to some nebulous (and often dubious) concept of original purity an essential part of Stravinsky's output, and to censure him for the multiple sources of his inspiration? Anyone has a perfect right to find fault with individual works and Stravinsky's 'French' period undoubtedly contains some that are open to criticisms. One can hate *Le Baiser de la fée*, find *Danses concertantes* boring and tell *Persephone* to go to hell (as of course she does) — these are matters of personal taste, a question of simply refusing to join in Stravinsky's game. But likes and dislikes apart, we should really ask ourselves the meaning of 'purity' in art and what, in a wider context, is the value of any censorship exercised in its name.

The production of the work by Ida Rubinstein's company at the Paris Opéra (27 April 1928) with Bronislava Nijinska's choreography, seems not to have been a happy one, and it 'left Stravinsky cold'. Diaghilev's furious account of it to Lifar suggests its *kitsch* character, even if we allow for Diaghilev's prejudice:

> What went on on the stage is simply indescribable. All I need to tell you is that the first scene shows the Swiss mountains, the second a Swiss village festival, with Swiss national dances; the third a Swiss mill and the fourth is back in the mountains. . . .

The spitefulness of this account was to be fatal to the friendship between Diaghilev and Stravinsky.

It may be said that Stravinsky's successive acts of 'treachery' with *Apollo* and *Le Baiser* had perhaps made the rupture inevitable. Their first result was to provoke in Diaghilev that instinctive desire to cut. We are talking here of cuts that Diaghilev liked to make in every score submitted to him, with the sole exception of Stravinsky's. Now, however, he transgressed this unwritten law and insisted on cutting the 'Variation de Calliope' in *Apollo*, finding it 'too long'. The composer could only protect his score by conducting it himself or by issuing summonses by registered post. Relations between the two rapidly deteriorated and the only occasion on which they met during the winter of 1928–29 was at the revival of *Renard* by the 'Ballets russes' with a new choreography by Lifar. The atmosphere at this last encounter was poisoned by Stravinsky's explicit preference for the original choreography of the work. On 23 February 1929 Diaghilev with the young Igor Markevich and Stravinsky with Vera Soudéïkine were on the London train, but they did not speak to each other and avoided meeting: the break was complete. In August, when Stravinsky was at Echarvines working on his *Capriccio* for piano and orchestra, Diaghilev died in Venice. Boris Kochno and Lifar were with him. There was no question of his 'dying alone in an hotel like a tramp' as Ansermet has said —

Misia Sert was with him to the end, having arrived on the Duke o
Westminster's yacht, the *Flying Cloud* (the Duke being the lover o
her friend Chanel). Misia's age and the experience of a lifetime devoted
to the art of others brought her very close to Diaghilev; and she gives a
touching account of his last hours at the Grand Hôtel des Bains on the
Lido and of the ferocious hatred between Kochno and Lifar, who
hurled themselves at each other, biting and grappling 'like two
infuriated dogs, fighting over the dead body of their master'.[1]
Diaghilev's funeral was almost clandestine, the exact opposite o
Stravinsky's in 1971, which was marked by all the pomp and solemnity
reserved for an honorary Venetian citizen, though both followed the
same route to the cemetery on San Michele.

Stravinsky felt Diaghilev's death deeply and was overcome with a
sense of guilt:

> Diaghilev was diabetic, but he was not saved by insulin because he
> was frightened of injections and preferred taking the risks attendant
> on the disease. I do not know the medical explanation of his death
> but what I do know is that his death was a great blow to me, and all
> the greater because I had quarrelled with him over *Baiser de la fée*
> (mounted by Ida Rubinstein and bitterly criticised by him) and we
> had not been reconciled when he died. (*Memories and Commentaries*)

VII

Between the Wars 2

DIAGHILEV'S DEATH MEANT the end of the 'Ballets russes', and thus an end for the moment to Stravinsky's work for the stage. His career as performer, on the other hand, was at its height towards the end of the 1920s. He conducted the Nouvel Orchestre Philharmonique de Paris, which Ansermet had founded, and played his *Concerto*, *Sonata* and *Serenade* as well as working on the new *Capriccio*. It was at this time that he transferred his interest from piano rolls to the gramophone. Recording his works became, in fact, something of an obsession with him from now on, his exclusive contract with Columbia making it possible for him 'to express all my intentions with real precision' for the edification of all present and future interpreters of his works. He dedicates four pages of *Chronicle* to praising the gramophone, and to deploring the fact that few orchestral conductors availed themselves of these recordings in order to learn exactly what he had in mind. Nevertheless it appeared to him that the radio and the gramophone record — 'those redoubtable triumphs of modern science' — made it possible to listen to music without the listener making that 'active effort' needed in order to understand any art. Gramophone records could never, he believed, be anything more than an *Ersatz* — a substitute for listening to a live performance — though they were invaluable as a document for consultation. (This, we should remember, was written in 1935.)

Capriccio for piano and orchestra, finished in November 1929, was given its first performance by the Orchestre Symphonique de Paris, with Ansermet conducting and the composer playing the solo part. It is a light, amusing piece, eclectic in inspiration and not — whatever the composer may have said — wholly unlike the *Concerto* of 1924, though 'easier' and less original, especially in the matter of harmony. Speaking of *Capriccio* in *Chronicle*, Stravinsky says that while working at this piece he found his thoughts 'dominated by that prince of music, Carl Maria von Weber, whose genius lent itself admirably to this type of music'.

The opening *Presto* starts with an introduction of large chords and continues with irregular rhythmic groupings (3+3+2 or 2+2+3), so often used by Bartók. The piano part makes great use of percussive attack and repeated notes. The *Andante rapsodico* begins by recalling Bach (like the *Concerto*) but then become freely declamatory and almost romantic in character, styles that only a Stravinsky could reconcile. The finale, which was the first movement to be composed, is an *allegro capriccioso* which gave the work its name and is in fact the most attractive movement of the three. It is a kind of *perpetuum mobile* with a hair-raising toccata-like piano part, in which the repeated notes and the refrain immediately recall the 'Pas de deux' from *Le Baiser de la fée* — and Balanchine's choreography, in which the tiny heads and long legs of the girls in the corps de ballet suggest an array of perfectly controlled spinning-tops.

During this winter (1929) Stravinsky received a commission from the Boston Symphony Orchestra and its conductor Serge Koussevitzky for a symphonic work to celebrate the orchestra's fiftieth anniversary in 1930. This perfectly suited Stravinsky, who was in fact anxious to start work on a major project. He gives a precise definition of what he understands as the symphonic domain:

> Symphonic form as bequeathed to us by the nineteenth century held little attraction for me, inasmuch as it had flourished in a period the language and ideas of which were all the more foreign to us because it was the period from which we emerged. As in the case of my sonata, I wanted to create an organic whole without conforming to the various models adopted by custom, but still retaining the periodic order by which the *Symphony* is distinguished from the *Suite*, the latter being simply a succession of pieces varying in character. (*Chronicle*)

How, in fact, was he to avoid the nineteenth-century model of the symphony? He solved this problem by making use of a *material* and a way of *writing* not hitherto associated with the symphony, in order to bring about a renewal of the form.

> My idea was that my symphony should be a work with great contrapuntal development, and for that it was necessary to increase the media at my disposal. I finally decided on a choral and instrumental *ensemble* in which the two elements should be on an equal footing, neither of them outweighing the other. In this instance my viewpoint as to the mutual relationship of the vocal and instrumental sections coincided with that of the masters of contrapuntal music, who also treated them as equals, and neither

reduced the role of the chorus to that of a homophonous chant nor the function of the instrumental ensemble to that of an accompaniment. (*Chronicle*)

By employing a chorus Stravinsky could also give free expression to his religious sense, which was particularly strong at this period of his life; and it was natural that he should turn to the Psalms for his texts, and in particular to Psalm 150, which is the praise of God through Music. Verses from Psalms 38 and 39 made up the rest of the text.

The *Symphony of Psalms* was composed between January and August 1930 at Echarvines and Nice in a state — as the composer was to say later — of 'religious and musical ebullience'. The score bears the inscription: 'This symphony composed to the glory of God is dedicated to the Boston Symphony Orchestra on the occasion of the fiftieth anniversary of its existence.'

In accordance with his principles Stravinsky does not in this work give lyrical 'expression' to his faith, but invents musical religious forms that are in themselves profoundly significant. Ansermet, who conducted the first European performance (Brussels, 13 December 1930) at the same time as Koussevitzky conducted the Boston performance, said that the *Symphony of Psalms* expressed the religious feelings of 'others' — those of an imaginary chorus to which the choir actually performing the work was an *analogon*. In this way Stravinsky may be said to be once again avoiding the subjective and, in E. W. White's striking words, speaking 'through the imagined faith of an anonymous congregation'. This is in fact true of all his religious music, which never says 'I' or 'thou', but always 'we'.

Psalm 150, which is both the starting-point and the heart of the work was chosen quite as much for its universality as for its actual musical subject-matter — also, no doubt, as a protest against the lyrical and sentimental character of many existing settings. The rhythmic theme of this symphonic *allegro* — whose imperious nature oddly recalls the syllabic utterance of the famous 'Oracula, oracula' in *Oedipus Rex* — is systematically shifted within the bar:

Ex. 67

laudate Dominum,   laudate Dominum,   lauda-te Dominum,   laudate Dominum.

The tense rhythmic utterance remains purely instrumental for some time and is answered and countered by a triplet passage in the woodwind and the two pianos. This, the composer tells us, was suggested to him 'by a vision of Elijah's chariot climbing the heavens'. André Souris' remarkable commentary[1] emphasizes both the 'figurative symbolism' and the 'gratuitous' character of this image:

> For if the musical representation of Elijah's chariot is, to say the very least, far removed from anything expressed verbally in Psalm 150, the same must surely be said of the musical elements, and their relationship to the texts, of the other psalms that appear in the work [. . . .] We never find any direct semantic concordance between music and text. Words are not even allowed their proper accentuation but are reduced to pure phonetic material.

The 'literalness' of the symbol is nevertheless surely significant of a more general and specifically Stravinskian conception of 'representation'. 'Never before had I written anything quite so literal as the triplets for horns and piano to suggest the horses and the chariot' (*Dialogues*). What are we to understand by this? That it is precisely that 'literalness' that the least 'figurative' of composers employs in order to avoid falling into the trap of 'meaning' which he had always denounced as being an illusion in the case of music. He, as it were, *empties* the symbol by reducing it to a stereotype, even a cliché, both denouncing and purifying it by pointing his finger at it.

In the *Prologue*, which is based on parts of Psalm 38, there are a number of structural elements familiar from other Stravinsky works. To take a rhythmic example, we have a horizontal figure variable in metre (a, a1) set against a vertical rhythmic impact (b) — a procedure already familiar:

Ex. 68

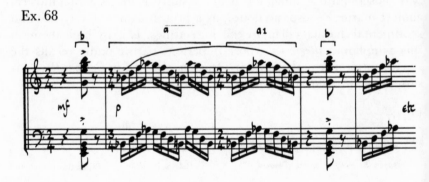

Harmonically (see Ex. 69) there is an obvious concern with unity. A is a broken minor chord with added sixth, derived from a (in Ex. 68), and B is a series of melodic cells dominated by the interval of the third, which plays a constructive part throughout the whole work:

Ex. 69

The instrumental *Fugue* in the second movement encloses the 'defining third' in a major seventh which gives it tension, this seventh being in fact simply the octave transposition of the second third (B-C). The development of this cell by the voices ('double fugue', but as Beethoven might put it, *con alcune licenze*) introduces a pseudo-subject marked by a descending fourth, the whole passage being built up into one of those polyphonic constructions of Stravinsky's that fall into no existing category. As in late Beethoven, in fact, the horizontal writing becomes so rich, its layering so dense, that it virtually dynamites the vertical control; so that the work ceases to belong to what was originally taken to be its formal category and creates its own stylistic 'landscape' — a 'no man's land'.

The *Allegro* with its excited rhythms — the same as that of 'Oracula, oracula' — is followed by Elijah's chariot, superbly orchestrated (real *Technicolor!*); and then we again encounter, at 12 and 20, the breaks in time and in theme of which Stravinsky was so fond. Following this comes the monumental coda on 'Laudate', which André Souris describes as 'a sublime, virtually motionless hymn in which musical time joins eternity'.

Between Echarvines and Nice — where the composer took his daily walk on Mont Boron dressed in a variety of brilliant colours — and the concert tours which perpetually interrupted his composing, his life seemed to be a happy one. By arranging his time-table down to the last detail he was able, to the very end of his life, to reconcile work and pleasure, family life and amorous escapade with Vera Soudéikine, visits to the best restaurants, and to any interesting local 'cultural monument' wherever he happened to be. Despite continual complaints about this or that aspect of his health to anyone who would listen, Stravinsky seems to have been very fit, and an energetic performer in the concert hall. This fitness was maintained by daily exercises and weird diets prescribed by doctors of all descriptions — not only top-ranking specialists in the profession but homeopaths, unfrocked priests or healers. He was never to tire of consulting doctors (sometimes with good reason), a thing in which he took a Proustian delight; and he consumed an enormous quantity of medicaments, often keeping a daily account of his intake with a pleasure that was little short of obsessional.

At the beginning of 1931 Willy Strecker, who was the director of Schott's and a legendary figure in music publishing, persuaded him to write a violin concerto for Samuel Dushkin. Stravinsky was not at first enthusiastic about the idea of writing a virtuoso piece for an instrument which he did not himself play, and only agreed when assured by Strecker that 'Dushkin would place himself entirely at my disposal in order to furnish any technical details which I might require'. (*Chronicle*) The commission came through Blair Fairchild, who was himself a composer and a wealthy patron of music who had adopted Dushkin as his son. The first movement of the concerto was sketched at Nice, but after a number of important concert-trips to London and Paris, Stravinsky decided to leave Mont Boron, where he had spent seven years, and to move to the Château de la Vironnière at Voreppe, in the Isère, where he was to spend the next three years. Dushkin followed Stravinsky in his peregrinations like a shadow, staying first at Antibes and then at Grenoble from where he paid almost daily visits to Voreppe. He was already working on the three first movements while Stravinsky was writing the fourth, the date for the first performance (23 October 1931) being already fixed by the Berliner Rundfunk Orchester, which had secured the rights of the work. It seems that although the soloist gave a brilliant performance, this was not true of the orchestra, which enraged both Hindemith, who was present, and Stravinsky himself, who conducted.

The *Violin Concerto* is more or less inspired by Bach, as is suggested by the titles of the three movements — 'Toccata', 'Aria I and II', 'Capriccio' — and 'in a superficial way' by the 'musical substance' (*Dialogues*). In fact the themes of the work may seem close to Bach; but Stravinsky's use of them is not; for this is an orchestral rather than a polyphonic work, and its specific 'world' is that of tone-colour, *timbre*.

The thematic material is not complicated: it consists of a key-chord (a) and a basic motif (b) (Ex. 70). The chord, which is important in each movement, is more than a harmony: it is a sonority.

Ex. 70

According to Dushkin, Stravinsky wrote this violin chord on the back of a menu in a restaurant and asked him if it were playable. Dushkin at first said 'no', on account of the very wide spacing, but when he tried it on the violin he was amazed not only by its easiness to play but by its sonority, which he found fascinating.

The basic motif (b) is obviously very Bach-like, and it recurs throughout the work, directly inspiring Aria I and appearing in reverse in Aria II. The two middle movements are the most interesting, being very free in form and making extended use of the resources of the violin. Stravinsky gives particular importance to dialogues between the soloist and different instruments in the orchestra, continually changing contexts and colours and the whole 'instrumental topography' of the scene. The writing for the woodwind is particularly brilliant both in the high, but even more in the low register, with the violin ceaselessly passing from one of these extremes to the other. 'Aria II' is a very 'vocal' movement, intensely expressive in character, with the basic motif, inverted, appearing at intervals in the highest register, like a scream. Back to Bach? In fact there is something very Russian in this chant at its moments of paroxysm.

The final 'Capriccio' is linked to Bach by its obsessive rhythm, its passages in diminution and particularly by the *détaché-lié* phrasing which is pure Baroque and handled with great delicacy here. Apart from this, however, the perpetually changing timbre gives the movement its chief character and its dynamic power. Stravinsky nevertheless makes very economical use of this element, which only becomes dominant in the course of the development and triumphs in the coda and the final peroration, where there is a ghostly reference to *The Soldier's Tale*.

In 1941 Balanchine used the score of the *Violin Concerto* for one of his most popular ballets, *Balustrade*, for which Tchelitchev provided the sets.

The *Duo Concertant*, for violin and piano, was composed at Voreppe during the first half of 1932 as a practical *concertante* chamber-work for Dushkin and the composer, who gave the first performance on 28

October 1932 in the big concert-hall of the Berlin Radio. (Stravinsky also made several arrangements for violin and piano of extracts from *Pulcinella* and *Le Baiser de la fée* in order to fill up the programme on their joint tours.) Formally, the *Duo* is closer to the suite than to the symphony, and has this as well as its monothematic character in common with the recent *Concerto*. A concrete need, such as these tours, often prompted Stravinsky to write works governed by two different principles — the one more generally aesthetic and the other, concerning the actual material, strictly musical. Thus the *Duo Concertant* was conceived as a kind of homage to musical versification of the past, and it was closely connected in the composer's mind with his friend Charles-Albert Cingria's book, *Petrarch*: 'Our work had a great deal in common,' he wrote and there was a close affinity between their ideas, summed up in a very Stravinskian way, in *Chronicle*, where he quotes Cingria's own words:

> Lyricism cannot exist without rules, and it is essential that these should be strict. Otherwise there is only a faculty for lyricism, and that exists everywhere. What does not exist everywhere is lyrical expression and composition. To achieve that, apprenticeship to a trade is necessary.

Lyricism such as this, free and rhapsodical, is to be found in the 'Cantilena', 'Eclogue II' and 'Dithyramb' — the other movements bearing the titles 'Eclogue I' and 'Gigue'.

The problem of the musical material to be used was solved in Stravinsky's usual way, by making a virtue of the difficulty itself. Like many other composers of the day, he had not declared his attitude to the vexed question of combining bowed and hammered strings i.e. stringed instruments with the piano. The *Concerto* had made him familiar with the technique of the violin and this enabled him to attack, if not to solve, the difficult question of integrating the two, which he did by *accentuating* the differences between the instruments rather than by levelling them down.

The *Duo Concertant* was played in Danzig, Paris, Munich, London and Winterthur among other places; and in the intervals Stravinsky either played or conducted at Königsberg, Hamburg, Paris, Budapest, Milan, Turin and Rome. Although this concert activity was good for his reputation and his bank balance, it occupied a great deal of Stravinsky's time and energy. He still managed, however, to find time for composition, and at the beginning of 1933 he was approached again by Ida Rubinstein, this time about a work based on a play by André Gide which she wished to stage. The agreements, first between Gide and Stravinsky, and then between Stravinsky and Ida Rubinstein (on the basis of 7,500 dollars, the same fee as for *Le Baiser de la fée*) presented no major problems. These were to arrive later.

*

Persephone is based on an early work of Gide's on the Homeric hymn to Demeter. This had to be rewritten by Gide in order to convert it into 'musical theatre' and thus provide Mme Rubinstein — who was not a professional singer or dancer — with a leading role which would consist of recitation and mime.

Stravinsky had already met Gide in 1910, at Misia Sert's and, in the summer of 1917 — though Stravinsky speaks of it as being 'a few months after the *Sacre*' (in *Memories and Commentaries*) — he was approached with a suggestion that he should write stage-music for Gide's adaptation of *Antony and Cleopatra*, but this came to nothing. Now the two future collaborators exchanged a number of letters and Gide visited Stravinsky at Wiesbaden in February 1933. On this occasion Stravinsky seems to have insisted on the idea of giving the work a ritual, rather than an episodic character. The next day Gide wrote:

> Madame Rubinstein is fascinated by what I have told her about your idea of the work as the celebration of a mystery, thus removing the episodic character that I was at first tempted to give it, which made it into something more like a *divertissement*. I am therefore working along those lines. . . . The subject lies half way between a natural interpretation (the rhythm of the seasons, with the seed dying in the ground to revive during the apparent sleep of winter) and the mystical interpretation according to which Persephone is linked to both ancient Egyptian religious ideas and to Christianity.

The correspondence between the two continued at intervals until 1933 with much discussion of detail and much apparent goodwill on both sides, each ready to adapt his personal ideas to the other's special requirements. Thus we find Gide using his literary authority to turn down a number of Stravinsky's suggestions as alien to the myth, but patiently instructing him in French prosody in reply to a question concerning the poetic use of *encore* and *encor*. Stravinsky, in his turn, asked Gide for supplementary lines for some children's choruses. The correspondence is published in *Memories and Commentaries*.

Whether Gide was shocked by the musical prosody which, in his usual manner, Stravinsky imposed on the text, or whether he was put out by the language used by Stravinsky is not clear. All we know is that on the occasion that he heard this language — at Ida Rubinstein's in

January 1934, when Stravinsky was playing through his music at the piano — Gide's only comment was 'it's curious, most curious' — after which he disappeared as soon as he could.

According to Gide himself it appears that Copeau, who was in charge of the production of *Persephone* and was present on that occasion, said that there could be no question of presenting the work in a realistic setting: it could only be in a single set, either a temple or a church. As we might imagine, Stravinsky seized on this at once, observing enthusiastically: 'It will be like a Mass, and that is what I like about your piece: the action need only be suggested.' Gide tried to protest, pointed to his detailed stage directions, and was so put out that he went to Sicily for a month and managed not to attend rehearsals when he returned.

Stravinsky, puzzled by this coolness, went for support to Valéry, who was an old friend. 'I felt he had understood my views on the tedious subject, of music and words.' And in *Memories and Commentaries*, at the age of almost eighty, he expounded those views (as he had done, in fact, in an article that appeared in *Excelsior* on 29 April 1934, just before the first performance of *Persephone*):

> Words combined with music lose some of the rhythmic and sonorous relationships that obtained when they were words only; or, rather, they exchange these relationships for new ones — for, in fact, a new 'music'. They no doubt *mean* the same things: but they are magical as well as meaningful, and their magic is transformed when they are combined with music.

Gide, on the other hand

> had expected the *Persephone* text to be sung with exactly the same stresses he would use to recite it. He believed my musical purposes should be to imitate or underline the verbal pattern: I would simply have to find pitches for the syllables, since he considered he had already composed the rhythm. The tradition of *poesia per musica* meant nothing to him. And, not understanding that a poet and musician collaborate to produce *one* music, he was only horrified by the discrepancies between my music and his.
> (*Memories and Commentaries*)

Gide was not present at the three performances of *Persephone*, which took place on 30 April, 4 May and 9 May 1934. Shortly afterwards he published his text, with a dedication to Ida Rubinstein, and sent Stravinsky a copy inscribed 'en amicale communion' — to which Stravinsky replied, with characteristic grudgingness, that 'communion' was precisely what did not exist between them, seeing that he, Gide. . . . On the other hand Valéry went to all the performances of *Persephone* and wrote after the first one:

> My dear Stravinsky, I could not get to you Monday evening to tell you of the extraordinary impression the *Persephone* music made on me. I am only a 'profane listener', but the divine *detachment* of your work touched me. It seems to me that what I have sometimes searched for in the ways of poetry, you pursue and link up with in your art. The point is, to attain purity through the will. . . .

If, according to Stravinsky, Gide 'understood little or nothing of all this', it is by no means certain that Stravinsky on his side wholly understood Gide, with his deep knowledge of the theatre and of ancient mythologies, or that he fully grasped Gide's genius as a poet (though he made good use of it as an artist). He even went so far, in a later and less personal text (in *Dialogues and a Diary*), as to say that his 'first recommendation for a *Persephone* revival would be to commission Auden to fit the music with new words' and to turn it into a ballet, with choreography by Balanchine and sets by Tchelitchev.

All that we can conclude from this whole story is that Stravinsky's feelings about *Persephone* were marked by the same reserve that he showed for all 'mixed' musical forms, of which the *melodráma* (the sub-title of *Persephone*) is the most ambiguous of all, not to say the most bastard. 'Sins cannot be undone, only forgiven', as Stravinsky himself was to say of *Persephone* (*Conversations*). It is understandable that the composer tried, by this belated act of contrition, to 'retrieve' his music, to free it from the questionable taste inseparable from its commission for the theatre. For if the *music* of *Persephone* is reputed to be 'boring', and if the composer's ambition to see the work given a place in 'the archives of the day' seems difficult to realize in another form, that music nevertheless awaits discovery, with its disincarnate and rather — perhaps rather excessively — evanescent beauty.

Persephone — 'mélodrame en trois tableaux sur un poème d'André Gide', for *récitante*, tenor, mixed chorus, children's chorus and orchestra — is the third work in what Stravinsky called his 'Greek trilogy', the other two being *Oedipus Rex* and *Apollo Musagetes*. In none of these works was there any question of 'evoking' ancient Greece, which, though something of a literary fashion in France between the wars, is unthinkable in music. Ancient Greece provided a purely formal framework and a subject-matter the greatest virtue of which, in Stravinsky's eyes, lay in its 'distancing', its extra-temporal character. He had discovered the great structural advantage of myths and used them as the basis for a number of important works, for which he devised a would-be equivalent 'classical' musical structure.

The story in Gide's version is both complex and at the same time weak, lacking the bone-structure, the dramatic power and the simplicity that make a good libretto; and it is doubtless this weakness that prevents *Persephone* from being a great stage-work like *Oedipus Rex*. The plot is as follows:

I. Demeter, the goddess of fertility, has entrusted her daughter Persephone to the Nymphs, who sing of the beauties of spring and its flowers. But the high priest, Eumolpus, tells her that the narcissus is not like other flowers. Is this a warning or a suggestion? 'Whoever bends over the flower and inhales its scent sees the unknown world of the Nether Regions.' Persephone disregards the warning, sees the souls of the dead wandering beneath the earth, plucks the narcissus and in so doing seals her fate. 'Thy spring will delight their eternal winter,' sings Eumolpus, as he calls on her to reign over the world of shades.

II. The second scene, 'Persephone in the Nether Regions', is set in the Elysian Fields, between Pluto's palace and the river of Lethe. Persephone lies asleep — 'here she rests and I dare not rouse her' — and wakes to the laments of the Shades, though these 'are not unhappy. Knowing neither hate nor love, pain nor desire, they have no other fate but eternally to renew the gesture of living.' Persephone drinks the water of Lethe, but refuses Pluto's gifts. Mercury tempts her with a pomegranate. 'Where am I? What have I done?' says the *récitante*. 'What has come over me? Support me, sisters! The pomegranate has restored the taste of the earth that I have lost.' As she gazes into the calyx of the narcissus Persephone now sees the earth desolate and her mother searching for her vainly. Eumolpus' song tells us that Demeter has come to the palace of Eleusis and adopted the son of King Seleukos, the child Demophon, who will become Triptolemos and teach men to cultivate the earth; and it is he who will marry Persephone and restore her to the light and the spring of the earth.

III. 'The rebirth of Persephone.' In the temple erected to Demeter the chorus call on Persephone to be born again. Triptolemos removes Demeter's mourning robe. Persephone appears, rejoins her mother and is united to Triptolemos: but she realizes that her fate will in future be linked to the shadow-world:

Yes, I am thine. Take me, I am thy Persephone
But I am also gloomy Pluto's wife below,
And never shall thy embrace, charming Demophon,
Be strong enough to hold me, in despite of love
And a breaking heart, from leaving thee in answer to
The call of destiny. To that dread world of shades,
The world of suffering, I shall go. Think'st thou that such
A love-intoxicated heart can bend its gaze
Over the unhappy gulf of Hades and remain untouched?

Led by Mercury, Persephone returns to the tomb, as Eumolpus and
the chorus sing:

> Spring must be born again,
> The seed consent to die
> In the earth, that in due time
> Harvests may ripen gold.

Persephone is not a short work (45–50 minutes) and its pallid colours
(or shades of white), its relative poverty as a drama, and the fact of its
being a 'mélodrame' have all militated against it. Melodrama is
eminently ephemeral by its very nature, and matters are in this case
made worse by Gide's terribly old-fashioned text, with its endless
accented 'e'-mutes in the choruses. Like a number of pre-Raphaelite
pictures, it will delight the mildly perverse few, like a milky oyster with
the slightly stale taste of summer. The musical themes are restricted in
character, essentially diatonic, and the 'key' harmony — a third within
a fourth — also tends to restrict the vocal span:

Ex.71

Res - te,   reste a - - vec nous,   reste a - vec nous princesse Per- sé-pho-ne
(Stay, stay with us, princess Persephone)

Given the considerable proportions of the work, its rhythmic plan
must be admitted to be elementary, with a rather marked preference for
iambics, particularly in the second scene. If one thinks of *Apollo
Musagetes*, it seems clear that what Stravinsky really had in mind was a
ballet and that it was only the circumstance of the commission that
determined his use of melodrama.

Melodically speaking, there are not many highlights, though what there are have a distinct flavour of their own — the oboe solo, for instance, that accompanies Persephone's progress to the land of shades:

Ex. 72

The choral lullaby entitled 'Sur ce lit elle repose' (On this bed she lies resting) is one of the most touching melodies in the work. 'I composed this *berceuse* for Vera de Bosset in Paris during a heat wave', Stravinsky tells us (*Dialogues and a Diary*).

Ex. 73

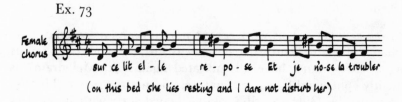

As can be seen, Stravinsky's handling of French prosody was highly personal. There are innumerable instances of this throughout the work and they may well have scandalized Gide, most notably that of the accented feminine word-endings. (Mute 'e' word-endings are normally sounded in French poetry.)

Ex. 74

He himself was delighted with this feature of his setting, in as much as it freed the musical rhythms from any submission to the word, though such liberation must be done with *finesse*, clarity and authority, and within a rhythmic context that justifies it — which is often, but not always, the case in *Persephone*.

It is in the matter of timbre, from which all these elements stem, that

Persephone proved most individual. It has a colour all of its own which words like 'white', 'pale' or 'mother-of-pearl' can only evoke through analogy. Within this basic palette Stravinsky works with an infinite number of nuances. What he has shown elsewhere in violently contrasting or complementary effects he accomplishes here in innumerable gradations of grey and mother-of-pearl.

To ask whether one 'likes' *Persephone* is rather like asking whether one likes' certain symbolist pictures, or oysters late in the season. There is certainly no denying that in order to appreciate *Persephone* a listener must heighten his sensibility to half-tints — something that one is, after all, not always prepared to do. *Persephone* presents challenges which are posed in the setting of any French text, problems that perhaps only Debussy could solve. (But what of the 'petit père' scene in *Pelléas*?) Challenges, charms, limitations, inspired here not so much by Debussy as by Dukas in music and by Maurice Denis in painting; and in poetry — by whom? Why, Gide of course! Quite apart from the agreements and disagreements that we have chronicled between the two men, *Persephone* with its gently archaic vocal lines and its 'white' string-sonorities remains essentially 'Gidian' music; and it was doubtless an act of homage to a French literary ideal still very close to that of the Symbolists in vocabulary, sonority and rhythmic character.

*

It only remained for Stravinsky to give practical expression to his feeling for France by adopting French nationality, and this he did on 10 June 1934. As though bent on integrating himself to the fullest possible extent with French society and the French way of life, he immediately settled in rue du Faubourg-St-Honoré, wrote a book and put his name forward as a candidate for the Académie des Beaux-Arts. The book was the invaluable *Chronique de ma vie*, written with the help of his friend Walter Nouvel and published in two volumes, in 1935 and 1936. As for the Académie, he was persuaded to put forward his name as successor to Paul Dukas by a number of friends, of whom Valéry was one. But in vain, for he obtained no more than 5 votes to Florent Schmitt's 27. . . .

Paradoxically enough, the French public's interest in his music seems to have begun to wane at this time, while Stravinsky himself began to feel a certain sense of detachment from a Europe over which the storm-clouds of a coming catastrophe were beginning to gather. Stravinsky never expressed direct anti-fascist feelings (in fact he dedicated a copy of his *Chronicle* to 'il Duce'), but he was fully aware of the threat posed by the rise of the Nazis in Germany, as can be seen from an earlier letter to Romain Rolland:

It is the highest common interest of all those peoples who still feel the need to breathe the air of their ancient cultures to put themselves on the side of the enemies of the *present* Germany, and to flee for ever the unbearable spirit of *this* colossal, obese, and morally putrefying Germania.

On 27 December 1934 Stravinsky and Dushkin embarked for the United States. Their three-month concert-tour was to bring the composer into much closer contact with America than on his first visit He was to establish a far more solid reputation there, both as composer and performer, and this would bring him a number of important American commissions and — above all, though he was not aware of i — would prepare the way for his second exile immediately before the 1939 war.

In the meantime Stravinsky had already started a new work, the firs movement of which had been sketched in 1931. This was the *Concerto fo two solo pianos*. A concerto without orchestra was something for whicl Stravinsky and Dushkin had experienced a need when faced witl mediocre, defective or extravagantly expensive ensembles, and this wa: the origin of the *Duo Concertant*. Another circumstance was the fact tha Stravinsky's younger son, Sviatoslav-Soulima, was an importan potential partner, having proved himself a brilliant pupil of Nadi: Boulanger and been started on his career as a pianist by his father ir 1933, performing the *Concerto* first in Barcelona and then in Paris. Th *Concerto for two solo pianos* was in fact composed for himself and his son and the score is headed 'This Concerto was performed by myself anc my son Sviatoslav Soulima-Stravinsky for the first time at the Université des Annales in the Salle Gaveau, on 21 November 1935'.

The *Concerto* is a rather '*rive droite*' work — to use a term appropriate to the Parisian circles in which Stravinsky was moving at this time classical in form, though modified by a number of discreet, carefully considered liberties marked by elegance, humour and even some lyrica feeling. This music has often been dismissed as a kind of musical *haut couture*, empty Parisian chatter characteristic of the years between the wars. But in fact it has Stravinsky's verve and reveals at a seconc remove that 'master hand' of his in the highly original structuring of the débris of the classical style. Again, this could not be claimed as : 'prrrofound' work, nor even very original, though why — in the name o what 'historical determinism' — should we find the neo-romanticism o Schoenberg's *Concerto* op. 42 preferable? Is there anything to choose between 'back to classicism' and 'back to romanticism?'

The work has four movements — a 'Sonata Allegro', *con moto*; a slow 'Notturno'; four 'Variazioni' and, without a break, a final 'Prelude and Fugue'.

The first movement is in E minor and sets a percussive opening theme for the piano,

Ex. 75

against a more melodic second subject. The development of the first theme is 'motoric', with much use of repeated, percussive notes. There is even a hint of Prokofiev — though this would have enraged Stravinsky — in the harmony, with its discreet twistings of tonality, and some jazz elements.

Speaking of the second movement in his 15-minute talk on the occasion of the first performance of the work, Stravinsky said:

> when I called it 'Notturno', I was not thinking of such dreamy, formally indeterminate character-pieces as the nocturnes of Field and Chopin, but what the eighteenth century called *Nachtmusik* or, better still, the 'cassations' common at that period. The only difference is that these works were generally in several movements, whereas I have condensed them into one.

The four 'Variazioni' are played without a break. No. 1 has shifting metres, no. 2 is 'orchestral' and violent; the quick chromaticisms of no. 3 recall Rimsky's 'Flight of the Bumble Bee', and no. 4, which is simultaneously binary and ternary, exploits very elaborate rhythmic and harmonic contradictions and is linked to the austere 'Prelude'. The 'Fuga' has a lively, bitingly witty subject, presented with an accompaniment of sextuplets, and makes great use of inversions, breaks and tempo-changes.

Stravinsky often observed that he had no gift for teaching, and in fact he virtually never taught. One of his few experiences in this field was at the Ecole Normale de Musique in Paris, where he took part in Nadia Boulanger's composition course in 1935–1936. Stravinsky would attend once a month to be present, rather than actively assist, at Nadia Boulanger's analyses of his works. The only member of this class to distinguish himself later was Dinu Lipatti who, of course, made no direct use of that experience.

Between April and June 1936 Stravinsky toured Latin America, starting at Buenos Aires, where he conducted several concerts at the Teatro Colon. These included almost all his major works from *Fireworks* and *Apollo Musagetes* to the *Sacre* and *Persephone*, in which his friend Victoria Ocampo was the *récitante*. The *grande dame* of Latin-American letters was Stravinsky's host in Buenos Aires, accompanying him on the second leg of his tour to Rio de Janeiro, where she again took part in a performance of *Persephone*.

At the end of 1936 Stravinsky had a brief affair — revealed by Vera Stravinsky and Robert Craft — with the daughter of the pianist Leopold Godowsky, Dagmar. The fragmentary documents of this episode, which include a complaining letter to the composer, suggest that she was very smitten — and very quickly dismissed: 'You sent me coldly away, without any regard for my feelings, your sole concern being that I should not complicate your life.'

*

When Stravinsky visited the United States for the second time, in 1935, he received a commission for a new ballet from Lincoln Kirstein, the director of the newly-formed American Ballet (later to become the New York City Ballet) and his enlightened patron Edward Warburg. The commission was confirmed and accepted in 1936 and the work was written during the summer and autumn of the same year. *Jeu de cartes*, based on a theme which the composer had worked out with one of his sons' friends named Malaieff, was choreographed by Balanchine and the first performance, conducted by the composer, took place on 29 April 1937 at the New York Metropolitan. The part of the Joker was danced by William Dollar (a name that seemed made for Stravinsky!).

The composer was an inveterate gambler, with a preference for poker. The idea of the ballet seems to have occurred to him one evening in a Paris cab, and he was, as he told the representative of the *Le Jour*, 'so delighted that I stopped the cab and invited the cabby to have a drink with me'.

The plot consists of three 'deals' played out on the green baize of the stage, the game in each deal being complicated by the endless ruses of the treacherous Joker, who thinks himself invincible because he can replace any card in the pack (a notion, however, that horrifies poker-purists like the author of this book). The first deal is concerned with rival sequences or quints; in the second, four queens are set against four aces, the latter formed in fact by the Joker. The third, which is unquestionably the most dramatic, is a contest of three 'flushes'. The Joker seems to be winning with spades, but he is beaten in a royal flush of hearts. Each of the three deals opens with the same solemn 'Introduction' and consists of the traditional choreographic numbers, with minute variations. In the first a 'Pas d'action' and 'Joker's dance' look forward to the future concerto *Dumbarton Oaks* and back to the composer's early *Fireworks*. In the second the 'Marche des coeurs et des piques' (Hearts' and spades' march) is followed by solo variations for the Queens (hearts, diamonds, clubs, spades)* and a 'Pas de quatre'. In the third deal a 'Valse-Menuet' is followed by the 'Combat entre piques et coeurs' (Spades' and Hearts' battle), with a 'danse finale' to celebrate the victory of Hearts.

Jeu de cartes is one of Stravinsky's most eclectic works. There are reminiscences of *Die Fledermaus* and — according to Casella's monograph — references to Jacopo Foroni, an Italian composer who died young in 1858. The waltz in the third deal recalls Ravel's, but 'undramatised'; and in the 'Combat' of the third there is a quotation from Rossini's *Il Barbiere de Siviglia* :

Ex. 76

The orchestration has a freshness, a youthful 'bite' about it, which makes this work a kind of compendium of Stravinsky's 'neo-classical' style. The music seems to be quoting Stravinsky himself even more than Rossini and it is this that will make one like the work . . . eventually.

The Joker who thinks he cannot be beaten and yet is so in the end, is given four lines from La Fontaine's fable of 'The Wolf and the Lamb':

> Il faut faire aux méchants guerre continuelle.
> La paix est fort bonne de soi,
> J'en conviens; mais de quoi sert-elle
> Avec des ennemis sans foi?

(Always be on your guard against the wicked. Peace is excellent in itself, I admit; but what use is it with enemies who are perfidious?)

And so the 'futile and carefree' *Jeu de cartes* becomes a model warning of the fate of Europe, in that year of 1936. . . .

*

*Stravinsky's ideas about poker show a total disregard of the normal precedence of colours in this matter. . . .

The performance of *Jeu de cartes* under Stravinsky concluded the composer's third American tour, which began at Toronto and ended in New York. During it he conducted the New York, Cleveland and San Francisco orchestras and visited Hollywood, where he met Charlie Chaplin (a collaboration between the two, planned in 1935, never came to anything). In Washington Stravinsky stayed with Mr and Mrs Robert Woods Bliss at their property of 'Dumbarton Oaks'. Great musical enthusiasts and patrons, the Blisses commissioned a *concerto grosso* to celebrate the thirtieth anniversary of their marriage, and this was to become the *Concerto in E flat major* known as *Dumbarton Oaks*.

At this point a doctor in New York discovered that Stravinsky had a tubercular lesion in his left lung, and since both his wife and his daughter were already in a sanatorium at Sancellemoz, he was advised to join them on his return to Europe in May. All he did, however, was to settle for the summer in the neighbourhood, renting the Château de Montoux, near Annemasse, where he wrote the first movement of the new concerto, having come to an agreement with the Blisses over the fee (2,500 dollars). The work was to be finished the following March when Stravinsky, not being well enough to conduct the first performance himself, entrusted it to Nadia Boulanger, who was to give an excellent performance at a private party on 8 May 1938.

The *Concerto in E flat major* is for chamber orchestra (single woodwind, two horns and ten strings) and was conceived by Stravinsky — according to André Schaeffner — as 'a little concerto in the style of Bach's Brandenburgs', which could hardly be a more concise or more correct description. It has not only the cut and the proportions of a Bach concerto, but even the specification: a fugal first movement, a second movement (the most delightful of the three) buzzing with short, delicately worked melodies exchanged between the soloists, and a regular *concerto grosso* last movement marked *Con moto*. The movements are linked to each other by string cadenzas, the third culminating in a fugal development of the subject and its exact inversion. The rhythm is square and simple, perfectly Bach-like and — by asymmetrical augmentation — analogous in the first and last movements. The same is true of the phrasing:

Ex. 77

The *Dumbarton Oaks* concerto was the subject of much controversy, René Leibowitz leading the attack and André Schaeffner the defence; but oddly enough the question at issue was not so much the style of the work as the character of its themes. To quote themes is common enough, even commonplace; but to quote a *style* throughout a whole work is much more unusual, more particularly when it is done with such skill. And how wholly delightful this music still sounds to ears accustomed to all the varieties of Expressionism! Once again timbre is the most important element, something that both facilitates the understanding of the polyphonic style and conveys long-forgotten flavours. To prove this *per absurdum* we need only compare the original score with Stravinsky's own transcription for two pianos — a pale, watered-down version, a kind of 'dietetic' Stravinsky, salt-free. . . .

Two further requests reached Stravinsky from the United States, both of which he accepted. The first was another commission from Mrs Bliss, this time for a symphonic work to celebrate the fiftieth anniversary of the Chicago Symphony Orchestra (to become the *Symphony in C*). The second came from Harvard University or, more exactly, from the Committee of the Charles Eliot Norton Chair, the president of which — Edward W. Forbes — wrote inviting Stravinsky to give six public lectures on music. Stravinsky was the first musician to be invited to speak in association with the Charles Eliot Norton Chair, and the contract stipulated that he was to be in residence at either Cambridge or Boston from October 1939 to May 1940; that he should be allowed two months' leave for his concerts; and that he should be allowed to deliver his lectures in French. The total fee for this prestigious assignment was 10,000 dollars.

Meanwhile in Europe there was no mistaking the sombre clouds announcing war. During the autumn of 1938, while Stravinsky was composing his *Symphony in C* for Chicago in his flat in the Faubourg-St-Honoré, came the Munich crisis, and it would be interesting to know whether he foresaw the events of the following winter. In a radio interview with Serge Moreux he spoke of a 'crisis of values', but the context makes it clear that these values were aesthetic and critical and not ethical or political. When he spoke to Moreux of 'the transgression of fundamental laws of human equilibrium' what he had in mind was probably the principle of tonality (and incidentally perhaps Marx and Freud) and not the victories of National Socialism. He was, however, to feel the full force of those victories when his own music was violently attacked at the exhibition of 'Entartete Kunst' (Degenerate Art) held at Düsseldorf in May 1938 — and that in spite of the official protests(!) of the French ambassador in Berlin, M. François-Poncet.

These years of disillusionment with Europe were for Stravinsky primarily years of personal bereavement. The death of his sister-in-law Lyudmila Belyankin in 1937 was followed by that of his elder daughter Lyudmila (Mika) on 30 November 1938 and that of his wife at Sancellemoz on 2 March 1939, both from tuberculosis — and finally, in the same June, of his mother, aged eighty-five. By then Stravinsky, under great strain, was himself at the Sancellemoz sanatorium, which he had entered after his wife's death. It was there that he composed the second movement of the *Symphony in C* and forced himself to work, between March and June, on his Harvard lectures. In this he was helped first by Pierre Souvtchinsky, almost exclusively on the first chapter, and much more importantly by Roland-Manuel, who visited Sancellemoz first in March and then in June. As will be shown in the following chapter, this was by no means a passive collaboration consisting merely of a simple revision or 'putting into shape' of a 'text' by Stravinsky: it was a proper editorial job based on conversations between the two men. Stravinsky, in fact, had never produced more than a few, very short texts, always relying on extremely active interviewers. Robert Craft, who had great experience in this field from the 1950s onward, and the letters that passed between Stravinsky and Roland-Manuel and are quoted by Craft, suggest that the method adopted was 'Stravinsky talking and Roland-Manuel taking notes, which he then wrote up in essay-form ("I have collected my notes and begun actually writing. . . .", letter of 24 March)'.[2] Stravinsky never publicly acknowledged this collaboration, nor did he contradict Daniel Lesur's statement in the *Gazette des Lettres* of 13 April 1946 that the language and the paradoxical style of the lectures recalled those of Roland-Manuel. This version of the facts contradicts the more generally known, but in fact inaccurate, story of an original Russian text drawn up with the help of Souvtchinsky and then translated into French by Roland-Manuel.

The French mobilization in September 1939 surprised Stravinsky at Sancellemoz and he immediately left the sanatorium with Vera Soudéïkine, experienced an air-raid alarm in Paris and embarked at Bordeaux on 25 September on board the *Manhattan* bound for the United States, the country which, though he did not know it, was to be his third 'fatherland'.

VIII

Refuge in Exile

STRAVINSKY ARRIVED IN the United States on 30 September and settled immediately near the Harvard *campus* at Cambridge, Massachusetts. His first lecture was on 18 October. These lectures were first published in French — the language in which they were given, in fact — under the title of *Poétique musicale*, being the first (1945) edition printed without Chapter V, which contained a violent attack on Soviet music. The lectures are generally agreed to contain the quintessence of Stravinsky's ideas, and this is both accurate and at the same time problematical: accurate in that they contain the leitmotifs already familiar from *Chronicle of my life* where they were expressed in a simple and precise way; problematical in that their doctrinaire form and aggressive, authoritarian tone only distantly recall Stravinsky.

Stravinsky was diabolically intelligent, but could he be called an 'intellectual'? He was certainly not a thinker or a theorist (and still less an 'academic', having in fact a deep distrust of universities). His ideas, or rather his convictions, are to be found in his works and emanate from them (not vice-versa). The moment that they were given a doctrinaire form in the dazzlingly elegant French of Roland-Manuel, a zealous and gifted writer, they changed their original character — form determining content (to recall a favourite axiom of Stravinsky's). In this way we find passages in *Poétique musicale* (*Poetics of Music*) where the tone of voice could be Vincent d'Indy's and where certain attitudes of Stravinsky's, which were quite genuine in the first place, are so overemphasized and given such rigid, even reactionary expression that they are often hard to accept.

On the other hand *Poetics of Music* does provide information about Stravinsky's 'practice' — his 'poetics' in fact, and his ideas about inspiration, technique, style and what he conceives as the role of his music. The text, inspired by him (and indeed signed by him) still has a real importance. But it must be read with circumspection, and in the light of his works rather than his words. This, in fact, is the proper attitude to all Stravinsky's writings (except *Chronicle*) none of which were directly written by the composer.

In addition to the Norton lectures, the Harvard contract pledged

Stravinsky to regular meetings with the students of the music department. These consisted partly of informal talks and partly of commenting on students' work — a task that the composer appears to have performed with frankness, though (given his fundamental dislike of teaching) without enthusiasm. These activities left him sufficient time for composition, and the third and penultimate movement of the *Symphony in C* was written at Harvard, the first two movements having been completed in Europe.

There were several series of concerts with the Boston Symphony Orchestra, followed by others at San Francisco and Los Angeles in December. Stravinsky then went to New York to conduct the Philharmonic and, on 13 January 1940, to meet Vera Soudéïkine, who was arriving by boat from Genoa.

Their marriage took place on 9 March in the small town of Bedford, Massachusetts, and was strictly private. When the Norton lectures were over, in May, Stravinsky and his wife went to Los Angeles, where they decided to settle. Steps were taken during the summer to obtain immigrant status for them both, with a view to eventual naturalization, and they then went to Mexico, a visit undertaken for purely administrative reasons, enabling them to 'enter' the United States as part of the quota of Russian immigrants.

They lived first in Beverly Hills and after November 1940 in Hollywood, where the house that they bought, at 1260 North Wetherly Drive, was to be their home for many years.

Why did Stravinsky choose to go to the United States, to relinquish his French nationality and to live in Los Angeles — a town that seemed to European eyes 'at the end of the world'? These were questions which Stravinsky's French friends asked themselves, not without bitterness, as they found themselves faced with the cruelties of the war and the Nazi occupation.

The answer is to be found in a network of related circumstances — the outbreak of war in Europe; the dissolving of family ties by the deaths of his daughter, his wife and his mother in 1939–1940; the invitation to Harvard and the strengthening of his ties with America during his second concert tour; and finally his long-awaited marriage. These were all reasons for avoiding the war and staying in the United States, but stronger than any of them was his instinct to defend himself and his work, and his horror of 'disorder' — which meant in this context, fear of war. The choice of Los Angeles may seem, at first sight, stranger. But Stravinsky remembered having been in better health as regards his lungs after his first visit to the West coast, and the fear of tuberculosis played a decisive part in his choice. That fear was, it seemed to him, to be exorcized by the 'eternal spring' climate of California, in many ways not unlike that of the Côte d'Azur.

Los Angeles, lying between the desert and the ocean, was also at this time the home of Thomas Mann, Schoenberg, Huxley and Werfel — supremely European figures who were to experience there the loneliness of real exile. In *Die Entstehung des Doktor Faustus* Thomas Mann was to say that 'Hollywood during the war had been more cosmopolitan and more intellectually stimulating than Paris or Munich'. Nevertheless, he behaved like a refugee there, and the same was true of Schoenberg, and of Bartók in New York — their position was that of witnesses to their refusal (to come to terms with Hitler's National Socialism). But whereas the position of these men was known to be provisional and consciously political, Stravinsky's felt neither. His attitude was that of a man who had been twice expatriated and of a future American citizen. Countless letters and public statements bear witness to his continuing attachment to Europe and concern with her fate, but the thread of his life had been broken and he was searching for integration. It would certainly be pointless to reproach him for his choice, as some of his European friends were to do in their own extremity, but equally pointless to do as most of his biographers have done, and try to conceal the real break in his life, the egotism of the artist concerned before all else with being able to work in peace — which was in his case the overriding consideration.

Once settled in Beverly Hills, Stravinsky returned to work on the *Symphony in C*, the last movement of which was finished in the summer of 1940. He himself conducted the first performance, given by the Chicago Symphony Orchestra on the fiftieth anniversary of its foundation, 7 November 1940.

*

Symphony in C inspired a number of different comments, written as it was between Europe and America, at the moment when war broke out and when the composer's life was shadowed by the deaths of his nearest and dearest. Many writers have insisted on trying to discover direct echoes of these events in Stravinsky's music, but there are none. If this work can be said to be 'witness' to anything, it is to a void. It may be that it is precisely this 'void' that reflects the worries and bereavements that overwhelmed his mind, and it is quite possible to imagine that in such circumstances the creative powers of any artist might be inhibited or, as it were, distracted. In fact the two 'gaps' in Stravinsky's artistic life — the one marked by *Mavra* and the other by *Symphony in C, Danses concertantes* and *Scènes de ballet* do roughly coincide with the two world

wars and the successive uprootings of the composer's existence. Any
attempts, however, to establish a direct, 'cause and effect' relationship
between exterior events and the music of these works are totally
arbitrary, merely substituting for what is, on any showing, an obscure
and hazy 'reality', an ideal interpretation of our own, in fact our vague
conception of music as containing some kind of 'message'. It can,
nonetheless, be said — in default of anything else — that Stravinsky's
first 'American period' seems to have been a time of relative creative
inhibition, as though the composer had found it necessary to get to the
end of one aesthetic cul-de-sac before discovering a new language and
thereby recovering fresh and solid powers of imagination — in fact his
own, authentic imagination. This crisis, or gap, however, was not
implicit in neo-classicism as such, a language that Stravinsky had been
using for twenty years and in which he had written a number of
masterpieces. The crisis came from the reducing of that language to a
number of formulae, often employed repetitively. *Symphony in C* is, in
fact, evidence of this temporary dead-end in which everything seemed
to come to a halt, contours seem to fade and the musical discourse is
reduced to compulsive repetition.

The elements of objective 'weakness' which analysis can reveal in
Symphony in C may doubtless, in other works and other contexts, appear
as vital brilliant figurations. The fact remains that one has only to *listen to*
this work to observe its weak spots, the poverty of the harmony, the
absence of any bold melodic or rhythmic contouring, and the
conventional character of the whole cut of the music, never relieved by
the smallest challenge or unsymmetrical detail. The opening theme of
the 'Moderato alla breve' is based on the leading-note, the tonic and the
dominant of C major; it develops repetitively:

Ex. 78

Rhythm is reduced to that of the repeating figure, and this — which
in another context might have been charged with meaning or humour

with life in fact — seems here to be no more than an interminably repeated cliché. What could in fact have been a characteristic 'visiting-card' of Stravinsky's, suddenly becomes a nervous tic. . . . The same is true of the 'Larghetto concertante', where the elegant woodwind figures soon become inefficient by being set systematically side by side. Although the third movement has a livelier gait, it never seems to advance, hampered once again by the composer's personal clichés. This is indeed a case of 'Alexandrianism' or 'music at the third remove', since Stravinsky seems to be quoting his own latest style, which itself was quoting. . . .

Nothing changes until the fourth movement, where something suddenly *happens* — the first movement theme returns, to ensure the unity of the work, and is transformed in the bottom register (bassoons), suddenly acquiring significance and strength. The rhythmic figure shown above (Ex. 78) is no longer a nervous tic but a dynamic element, and the harmony regains its old density, suddenly recalling *Symphonies of Wind Instruments* and thus bringing this very disconcerting work to an almost liturgical-sounding conclusion.

It was in this same year (1940) that Stravinsky — as though determined to fox lovers of pernickety annotation — composed a *Tango* for piano (and wordless voice), which he was later to authorize a certain Felix Günther to orchestrate. This was in fact the beginning of his flirtation with entertainment music, a flirtation on which he always kept a very tight hold, as we shall see. The fact remains that the *Tango* is a delectable piece, best known in the piano version, but also orchestrated by the composer himself and transcribed for violin and piano by Dushkin — not just any tango or even a 'good tango' but *the* quintessential tango, another of Stravinsky's 'archetypes'.

Hollywood is synonymous with the cinema, and it was only natural that Stravinsky, who was even more worried than usual about his shaky financial situation, should have had contacts with the 'seventh art'. All of these seem to have come to more or less nothing. The most important, and disastrous, of his experiences with the film world, though it was not his responsibility, was Walt Disney's *Fantasia*, in which the *Sacre* was used for the 'prehistoric' sequence. The Disney Society offered the composer 5,000 dollars for his authorization, kindly warning him at the same time that the *Sacre* would be used whether he accepted their offer or not, as it was a 'Russian' work and as such not protected in the United States. Stravinsky found the result quite deplorable. He was indifferent to Disney's anodyne and imbecile

pterodactyls and diplodocuses devouring each other, but far from
indifferent to the 'arrangement' of his score. Oddly enough, however
he did not make a great fuss about this whole, rather shady transaction
and the '*Fantasia* affair' never really materialized.

Stravinsky's other encounters with the film-world may have been
abortive, but they reveal his astonishing artistic economy, for not
single note of these scores was wasted. The work that he did on a film
about the Norwegian resistance to the Nazis, refused by Hollywood, all
went into *Four Norwegian Moods* (or *Four Norwegian Impressions*), which h
finished in August 1942. These were based on popular Norwegian air
that he discovered in a Los Angeles music-shop. In the same wa
Scherzo à la russe was originally meant for a film with a Russian subject
which was eventually abandoned. The music was first orchestrated fo
Paul Whiteman's Band and then rescored for a large orchestra with
big percussion section, in 1943–44. The piece is in G major and
contains reminiscences of *Petrushka*, not only 'Danse russe' but, subtl
transformed, the famous 'Elle avait une jamb' de bois', as a kind c
symphonic development. 'Scherzo à la russe' is the title of a piano-piec
by Tchaikovsky which Stravinsky had used in *Le Baiser de la fée*. Finall
an idea of Werfel's for a film about St Bernadette never materialized
but gave rise to sketches eventually used in the middle part of *Symphon
in Three Movements*.

Other works prompted by the Hollywood connection include *Circu
Polka*, commissioned by Barnum's Circus for its young star elephan
Modoc, with fifty other elephants and dancers in tutus, and Balanchin
as choreographer. He arranged the whole affair with Stravinsky, b
telephone: 'For what?' asked Stravinsky. 'For elephants.' 'How many?
'A lot.' 'How old?' 'Young.' 'If they're young, I accept. . . .' In fact th
actual polka is very little heard and its middle section is very like th
one that Stravinsky had orchestrated in one of his *Suites* based on th
Easy Pieces for piano, but it is drowned by the triumphant strains c
Schubert's 'Marche militaire'.

Circus Polka should not be thought unworthy, for it is excellen
Stravinsky, nearer to *Petrushka* than to 'neo-classicism'. The shifting
metres (particularly in the first part) rule out the idea of its being a
success with the elephants who — so the specialists tell us — have
preference for pure isochrony. One may even wonder how much th
human audience at Madison Square Gardens appreciated this musi
and whether they grasped what is, to our 'highly educated' ears, th
real charm of the piece, namely its archetypal character as circu
music. However that may be, the *Circus Polka* became hugely popula
and reappeared, as usual, in a number of 'symphonic' versions.

The self-appointed guardians of 'pure' music may well be censorious about these 'concessions' to Hollywood, or at best smile condescendingly. But was there not something to admire, in fact, about Stravinsky's ability to 'take part in the game' in whatever environment he might find himself, and his determination to earn his living by composing instead of soliciting 'subventions' from governments or foundations, as many European composers did? What, in any case, did these 'concessions' entail except the skilful, effective and imaginative adaptation of materials perfectly suited to whatever might be the needs of the individual case? Any *real* concessions were always refused by Stravinsky, sometimes with anger but more often with irony. There was the case, for instance, of a potential Maecenas for *The Rake's Progress*, 'the heir to a chain of grocery stores and a self-styled specialist in "modern art", who would have commissioned *The Rake's Progress* from me, had I agreed to his condition that he should sit in judgment while I played my music to him at the piano' (*Memories and Commentaries*). A rather similar thing was to happen later with *Scènes de ballet*, commissioned by Billy Rose, who telegraphed the composer after the *avant-première*:

YOUR MUSIC GREAT SUCCESS STOP COULD BE SENSATIONAL SUCCESS IF YOU WOULD AUTHORISE ROBERT RUSSELL BENNETT RETOUCH ORCHESTRATION STOP BENNETT ORCHESTRATES EVEN THE WORKS OF COLE PORTER

Stravinsky telegraphed back: SATISFIED WITH GREAT SUCCESS.

Stravinsky's only act of homage to the United States as a nation was his arrangement of 'The Star-spangled Banner' at the time of the Americans entering the war, and it was not well-received. This was undertaken for purely musical reasons, as Stravinsky tells us in *Memories and Commentaries*: 'I was obliged to begin my concerts during the war with the "Star-spangled Banner", the existing arrangements of which seemed to me very poor.' The suggestion would have come from the only pupil he had at the time, Eugene Anderson, to whom he gave more than two hundred lessons for purely financial reasons. The arrangement was made in July 1941, and the manuscript sent to the White House to be auctioned for the war effort — 'but my major seventh in the second strain of the piece, the part patriotic ladies like best, must have embarrassed some high official, for my score was returned with an apology'. In the winter of 1944 he played the piece with the Boston Symphony Orchestra.

Though no one seemed to notice that my arrangement differed from
the standard offering, the next day, just before the second concert, a
Police Commissioner appeared in my dressing-room and informed
me of a Massachusetts law forbidding any 'tampering' with national
property. He said that policemen had already been instructed to
remove my arrangement from the music-stands. I argued that if an
Urtext of 'The Star-spangled Banner' existed, it was certainly
infrequently played in Massachusetts — but to no avail.

*

Hollywood was quite openly interested in using Stravinsky's name
rather than his 'musical substance', but from the beginning he was
approached from other quarters where the interest was in him as a
composer. Thus Werner Janssen's Los Angeles orchestra commissioned a *concertante* chamber work which was composed in 1941–42, first
performed on 8 February 1942 and eventually transferred to the
theatre. The title of this work, *Danses concertantes*, explains its double
nature, but the music is in fact pure ballet. It only remained to entrust
the choreography to Balanchine, who prepared the piece in 1944 for the
'Ballets russes de Monte Carlo', a remote descendant of Diaghilev's
company. The sets were painted by Eugene Berman, who was to be one
of Stravinsky's great friends in Hollywood.

Danses concertantes, for twenty-four players, is one of the works dating
from this period that cause those of Stravinsky's admirers who have no
use for any of his work but the *Sacre* and *Les Noces* to gnash their teeth. In
fact, however, though not a major work, it is well worth rehearing and
re-rating after all these years for, though extremely eclectic, the
bareness and weightlessness of its musical calligraphy anticipates the
composer's serial style. The 'Marche inaugurale' suggests a *concerto
grosso*, a horn passage leading to an extremely effective violin solo; and
the 'Pas d'action' makes use of juxtapositions which may vary in
effectiveness but never fail to surprise. The best things in the work are
to be found in the central 'Variations'. The theme is given a rather
devious definition by the interval of the fifth in its opening statement
changed to an octave in the development of the sound-material. Here
the writing immediately strikes a new note — or at least gives the
listener an idea of the supreme abstraction of a stylistic manner. There
is pure aural delight in the linking of strings and woodwind, the gentle
bowings and the ornaments resembling miniature mounting fireworks.
Then *silence* suddenly finds a place in the score, the tense silence of

suspense which becomes the silence of a break. Next we have a procession of imaginary quotations — of what? from where? — and then abstract passages again, in the shape of wind solos, and finally, to give Balanchine a chance to devise a magnificent conclusion to the sequence, a 6/8 *tempo giusto*, infectious and amusing. The 'Pas de deux' is a *collage* of contrasting episodes, either lyrical or humorous or dazzling; and the listener has the whole scene brought before his eyes, the dance with its multiple emotional excitements and amorous exchanges. The 'Marche inaugurale' returns at the end to remind us that this is a 'neo-classical' work, something that we had almost forgotten.

One of the works originally inspired by a film project is *Ode*, 'chant elégiaque en trois parties' dedicated to the memory of Nathalie Koussevitzky and performed for the first time on 8 October 1943 by the Boston Symphony Orchestra.

The Koussevitzkys were, of course, both publishers and patrons, owners of the Editions Russes de Musique and publishers of most of Stravinsky's works between *Petrushka* and *Persephone*. When his wife died, Serge Koussevitzky set up a foundation named after her which was to commission a considerable number of new works in the near future. *Ode* was one of the first of these. Part of it, 'Eclogue', existed already as the music for a hunting-scene in a film of *Jane Eyre* planned by Orson Welles. Coming in the middle of the work, between 'Eulogie' and 'Epitaphe', this makes a somewhat cynical impression in the context of a posthumous tribute with its four horns, 6/8 hunting-calls and rather *kitsch*-sounding waltz. Stravinsky's answer was that this was a *concert champêtre*, something after Nathalie Koussevitzky's own heart. The outer movements, on the other hand, are haunted by memories of *Symphonies of Wind Instruments* and the final 'Epitaphe', with its beautiful 'white' manner, is incomparably superior to the rest — dignified, distanced, austerely linear and ending with a peroration in the woodwind.

The first performance of *Ode*, which Koussevitzky himself conducted, seems to have been disastrous. The trumpet read his part in C, though it was written in B flat and there were other mistakes due to copyist errors; the work, it seems, was to take a long time to recover from this unfortunate start.

Another *in memoriam* piece, written the following year and entitled *Elégie*, was commissioned by Germain Prévost 'in memory of Alphonse Onnou, founder of the Pro Arte Quartet'. This is a short work for the viola, which can also be played by the violin if transposed up a fifth. The whole piece is played with the mute and is in ternary form, with a middle section designed to give the impression of two-part polyphony. The span of the music is narrow and the melodic line is tranquil and meditative. There is something Russian about this melody and the work itself is a beautiful one, deserving to be heard more often.

The *Sonata* for two pianos was written between September 1943 and February 1944 — the last, worst year of the war for both Europe and the United States, but for Stravinsky a year of astonishing productivity, including the completion of *Scherzo à la russe*, the *Sonata*, the cantata *Babel*, *Scènes de ballet*, *Elégie* and the beginning of the *Mass*.

The three movements of the *Sonata* were composed in the order 3 — 1 — 2, which was rare for Stravinsky, and it had its first performance on 2 August 1944,[1] when Nadia Boulanger and Richard Johnson played it at a college run by Dominican sisters, in Wisconsin. Stravinsky himself played it only once in public — with Nadia Boulanger at Mills College (San Francisco) — but often in private. According to the composer himself, 'the *Sonata* began as a piece for one performer, but was redesigned for two pianos when I saw that four hands were required to voice the four lines clearly' (*Dialogues and a Diary*). It is perhaps one of Stravinsky's most 'neutral' works, and when — as often happens — it appears in the same programme as the *Eight Easy Pieces* for piano duet, composed about 1915, it seems still paler, though it reveals the stylistic link persisting over the gap of thirty years.

Like *Danses concertantes*, the *Sonata* has three movements of which the second — also 'Variations' — is also the most interesting. The opening 'Moderato' is based on F major. A careful listener will gradually recognize the particular *colour* of the music, which vaguely recalls the *gamelan*, and in fact it does not need a very deep knowledge of Balinese music to see that Stravinsky's 'scale' corresponds to a basic Balinese mode, *selisir*, which is characterized by the interval of the major third. This was certainly not in the composer's conscious mind but suggested itself to him as he experimented with embroidering the common chord (possibly with Debussy in mind?). The slow, 'white' theme with which the variations begin is derived from the initial theme, and the unconscious 'Balinese mode' appears plainly in the non-repeated notes of the sequence given below:

Ex. 79

Rather impersonal music, as I said above, that does not insist on the references which it contains — or, perhaps, rather the associations that it stirs, inasmuch as it puts up only a feeble 'resistance' to them — first Debussy, then Satie in the first variation, Prokofiev in the second, Hindemith in the 'Fughetta' of the third, and Satie again in the tranquil harmonies accompanying the modal scale in the fourth variation. In the very short final 'Allegretto' we find ourselves back in the world of the *Easy Pieces*, before 'neo-classicism' had an official existence, let alone a name. . . .

One of Stravinsky's most Hollywoodish commissions during these first years in America was the cantata *Babel*, which he finished in April 1944. The music-publisher Nathaniel Shilkret had the idea of producing a great 'fresco' based on the book of Genesis, with each part entrusted to a different composer, though reserving the 'Creation' for himself. He commissioned a 'Prologue' from Schoenberg, a 'Fall' from Alexandre Tansman, 'Cain and Abel' from Darius Milhaud, a 'Flood' from Castelnuovo-Tedesco, a 'Message' from Ernest Toch and finally 'Babel' from Stravinsky. Other contributions were planned for Bartók, Hindemith, and Prokofiev, but these never materialized. The work was given at Los Angeles in October 1945 under Werner Janssen's direction, but like all works of its kind, it was short-lived, though some of the parts survive as independent pieces. *Babel* is one of these.

Shilkret's actual musical views seem to have been quite clear-cut and they were, needless to say, not Stravinsky's. Shilkret wanted an opposition between the voice of the people — the building and destruction of the tower — and the voice of God, represented by a Narrator. Stravinsky, as an orthodox Christian and a precise theologian, could not admit that God's voice should be represented by a single man. He gave it instead to a male-voice chorus and entrusted the story of the tower to a Narrator.

Like all Stravinsky's works with a sacred subject, *Babel* is a strict work. It comprises a sombre, sumptuous 'Introduction' rich in chromatic intervals but with E as the predominant 'pole'. Linked to this is a second choral section, 'The Voice of God', which ends in a bitonal complex (C and F sharp major). The instrumental *fugato*, closed by a short postlude, contains not only a reminiscence of the 'Allegro' of the *Symphony of Psalms* but also the impatient rhythmic pulsation of the dance — something wholly consonant with the text 'so the Lord scattered them abroad from there upon the face of all the earth'. This was taken from the Authorized Version of the Bible, and it marks the first occasion on which Stravinsky directly set English words, thus embarking on the path which was eventually to lead to the *Cantate* and *The Rake's Progress*.

*

While he was still at work on *Babel*, Stravinsky accepted a further commission, this time for Broadway, from the impresario Billy Rose for his well-known revue, *The Seven Lively Arts*. For 5,000 dollars he had to write a quarter of an hour's ballet to be danced by Alicia Markova and Anton Dolin, with choreography by Dolin. The composition went quickly and was finished in August 1944. There is no plot and the title is *Scènes de ballet*. It was on the occasion of the *avant-première* in Philadelphia that Billy Rose, slightly puzzled by Stravinsky's sonorities no doubt, sent him the famous telegram offering to have the piece re-orchestrated by a 'professional'. This explains the fact that during the long Broadway run of the revue only fragments of Stravinsky's piece were performed. The first genuine performance of the music in the concert-hall was given in the following year by the New York Philharmonic conducted by the composer.

The work is in eleven parts supported on the four 'pillars' of the classical ballet: 'pas d'action', 'pas de deux', 'variations', 'coda'. If we compare this skeleton with its fleshing-out by Stravinsky* we can see that the three 'pantomimes', introduced deliberately, would give the work something of an anecdotal character if they were not, at least in the original conception of the piece, as abstract as the rest. The structure of the ballet was worked out in a single morning by Stravinsky and Dolin, taking *Giselle* as their model (the piece was originally to have been called *L'Etoile* in honour of Markova).² This plan detailed the exact duration of each number, but it was severely mutilated by Billy Rose, whose 'difficulties' with the music may have been the 5/8 rhythms. The definitive choreography of the work was Frederick Ashton's, made for the performance by the Sadler's Wells Ballet at Covent Garden, with Margot Fonteyn, in 1948.

Scènes de ballet seems to the present writer the logical conclusion of a certain genre, one in which the musical structure seems to prefigure, to contain and to prompt a choreographic structure: so that the result is a kind of abstract statement of classical ballet structure itself, yet another archetype. This is the unspoken claim that it makes, thereby assuming the status of an immutable musical model of an equally immutable art and tradition of choreography. Obviously, therefore, *Scènes de ballet* is

*'Introduction', 'Danses' (corps de ballet), 'Variations' (female dancer), 'Pantomime', 'Pas de deux', 'Pantomime', 'Variation 1' (male dancer). 'Variation II' (female dancer), 'Pantomime', 'Danses' (corps de ballet), 'Apothéose'.

not something to be included in a 'potted history' of music, but something to be extracted from or viewed *outside* such a process. Like a dancer on her points, pirouetting within a narrow circle, this music trembles on the borderline of a deliberately *arrested* 'history'; and it is only viewed thus that it reveals its perfect architecture, its extreme intelligence and its wealth of purely sonorous invention. But rather than expect from it what it is not, better avoid it altogether along with similar works by Stravinsky: it is not open to everyone.

The 'Introduction' is based on a rhythm of 4, 6 and 3 initial quavers in which Stravinsky systematically avoids any accent on the strong beat by writing in an irregular metre (5/8): a simple principle of 'syncopation' that had proved its effectiveness from the days of *Firebird* and *Petrushka*. Similarly, at the other end of the work, the organ-like sonorities of 'Apothéose' are not contained by bar-lines, thus avoiding all *tactus*. The 'Pas de deux' in the middle of the work is denounced by the 'purists' for its 'vulgarity':

Ex. 80

It is all there — the A-B-A form, the conventionally trivial triplet accompaniment, the trumpet melody deliberately cornet-like, with horn added. There have been plenty of other examples, but this reaches the sublime . . . the perfect musical cliché of the 'pas de deux' in general, seen in this particular case in the lights of Broadway, a merchandise so immaculately conceived and executed that it is beyond the grasp even of the man who commissioned it. It would be interesting to know how many people realized this. Only one person actually *said* it, as far as we know, and that was Lawrence Morton, that most excellent musician and friend of Stravinsky in Los Angeles:

There is an almost incredibly sentimental trumpet tune. . . . Take away the mark of genius, give it a four-square shape and stick on words by Cole Porter and you have an authentic pop-tune. As it stands, though, it is a celebration of Broadway, a halo for a chorus-girl, a portrait of Mr. Rose as Diaghilev.

Very true. Sensitive souls, however, are advised to abstain. . . .

Scènes de ballet was finished on 23 August 1944, and Stravinsky was just writing the 'Apothéose' when he heard the news of the liberation of Paris. Between the lines of the score Stravinsky jotted jubilantly, in French: 'Paris n'est plus aux Allemands.'

*

The composition of *Symphony in Three Movements* overran the war years. It was begun in 1942, apparently as a piano concerto, finished in 1945 and first performed on 24 February 1946 by the New York Philharmonic conducted by the composer. The work was commonly known as the 'War Symphony' and Stravinsky himself did, in a very evasive way, lend colour to critics' attempts to discover in the music an echo of actual events. His comments were ambiguous: 'It both does and does not express my feelings. . . . Each episode in the Symphony is linked in my imagination with a concrete impression, very often cinematographic, of the war.' Stravinsky is here alluding to films and newsreels — but also, we think, to Werfel's projected film about St Bernadette (he had used, it should be remembered, material from the scene of the apparition of the Virgin when writing the symphony). His last words on the subject are significant: 'The Symphony is not programmatic. Composers combine notes. That is all. How and in what form the things of this world are impressed upon their music is not for them to say' (*Dialogues and a Diary*).

'That is all' — and it is a great deal, for we are considering a masterpiece which makes nonsense of anything tending to reduce it to either a 'programme-work', an example of 'neo-classicism' or even to traditional symphonic form.

The structure of the opening movement has often been classified as a sonata allegro, but never actually analysed as such. . . . Where in fact are its themes and their development, and where is the 'bi-thematic dialectic'? A violent rising introductory passage, marked by timpani, turns out to fulfil no function during the course of the movement, but reappears only at the end — it is a motto repeated *in extremis*. The space in between these two fixed points is occupied by a series of linked but self-contained structures. (Why is Beethoven's name always mentioned in connection with this movement, rather than Debussy's *Jeux*?) These structures are interlinked either by rhythmic 'bridges', by contrasting factors or, paradoxically, by clean breaks. There is a prodigious wealth of ideas, but they are controlled by unifying elements, the most important of which — though not reducible to two contrasting themes — are an arpeggio without its fifth (*a*) and the diatonic oscillation *b*, which is derived directly from the *Sacre*. (Both these elements reappear in the last movement):

Ex. 81

The main dynamic element of the work, which might almost be said paradoxically to replace the bi-thematic principle of the classical sonata-form, is timbre. This Stravinsky uses to emphasize and to illuminate, to seize on ideas, to crush and transform (rather than develop) them, as in a brilliant firework-display. In fact *Symphony in Three Movements* is, from the purely sonorous point of view, Stravinsky's richest score since the *Sacre* (of which we shall have more to say in a moment), the work in which timbre fulfils a primary *motor* (i.e. a modern) function.

The second movement, 'Andante', is a pure balletic delight, with the gentle Italianate *fioriture* of the flute against the delicate pulsation of the strings in D major/minor:

Ex. 82

The plan of the movement might be shown thus:

Ex. 83

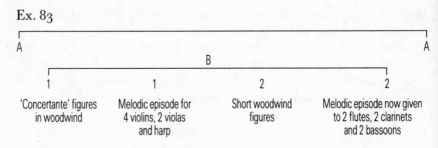

'Intoxicated' by A, the listener is 'distracted' by the multiple charms of B and rescued by the return of A, only — on the return of B — to be 'intoxicated' by C, a variation of A.

An interlude of seven bars brings everything to a halt, there is a moment of hesitation, a moment of tension and we are off — thrown headlong into a finale dedicated to the memory of the *Sacre*. Here the independent structures are very closely juxtaposed, as it were, welded together. First come large chords which contradict each other rhythmically and metrically, regular and irregular, as in the 'Danse de la terre', with the major and minor third of C overlapping each other, as we find throughout the work — chords without the fifth, as employed both vertically and horizontally in the first movement. This is then exploited (as shown in Ex. 15 where the principle used by the composer was analysed in detail with reference to the 'Jeu du rapt') by the confrontation of horizontal rhythmic structures and sharp 'vertical' impacts. A downward transition is halted on the descending semitone and is entrusted alternately to bassoon and piano, rather as in a *Klangfarbenmelodie*. This part leads to a fugal opening, though not of course to a fugue, which ceases the moment it has established its identity — once again Stravinsky is concerned with the 'representation', the 'idea' of a fugue. There follows an episode for the lower instruments, sombre in character, with halved rhythms that irresistibly recall rhythmic figures in the men's dances in the *Sacre*. The Coda is directly inspired by the 'Danse sacrale', lately rewritten by Stravinsky in halved values in order to facilitate performance (though performers continue to prefer the original). What is the relationship between these 're-inspirations' and the score of the *Sacre*? They are certainly of greater importance than the film newsreels to which Stravinsky was referring, since the *Sacre* communicates its own strength and violence to the whole work. *Symphony in three movements* is a wonderful evocation of 'Glorification de l'élue', of 'Danse de la terre' and 'Danse sacrale': it is by no means simply a 'remake' of the *Sacre*, which would be unthinkable, but an original work fertilized by a memory still vivid after thirty years.

*

The moment the *Symphony* was finished, in August 1945, Stravinsky set to work on a completely different piece that Woody Herman had commissioned, *Ebony Concerto* (ebony not referring to the clarinet but to the colour of Africans). He was not quite happy about this, being aware of his lack of jazz experience. His plan was to write a *concerto grosso* in jazz style, with a central *blues* and a clarinet solo part for Woody Herman. After studying this famous orchestra's recordings, he added a horn part and even got a saxophonist to show him fingerings. The work, which went quickly and was finished by 1 December is certainly the best of Stravinsky's jazz-inspired pieces.

Ebony Concerto is, in fact, evidence of the facility with which Stravinsky could pick up both a style and an instrumental technique such as that of the saxophone, trumpets with different mutes or percussion instruments, but even more of his ability to integrate such material in his own musical style. The *Concerto* opens like an 'abstract quotation' of jazz, in a dry and lively manner obviously enjoyed by the composer, and also by his listeners; but it soon establishes connections with the world of *Pribaoutki*. This may seem paradoxical, but the listener is imediately carried back thirty years to the incantation of 'Le Vieux et le lièvre'. The *blues* movement consists of couplets and a refrain called 'Variations', the refrain consisting of a bitter, hovering tune that seems to belong to the Russian steppes rather than the chrome and nickel studios of Hollywood. . . . The trumpets give an anguished answer in the distance and the saxophones take up the refrain again, the rhythm marked by the percussion. One ceases to be aware of the jazz element and hears nothing but highly imaginative instrumental flashes interspersed by short passages for the solo clarinet. What everyone is waiting for is the marvellous return of the refrain in the full band. Is this 'jazz' or the very voice of melancholy — which is, after all, what the *blues* is — whether it be 'ebony' or Russian?

Ebony Concerto was finished in December 1945, and on the 28th of that month Stravinsky and his wife became American citizens. This third, deliberately chosen nationality had no more effect on the composer's profoundly Russian character than his twenty years as a French citizen. He remained just as attached to Russian domestic and religious traditions and rites and, above all, to his native tongue, which he was to speak to the end of his life.

IX

Characters in Search of an Author

LUNCHING AT BEVERLY Hills with Stravinsky on the day of his naturalization, Ralph Hawkes — head of the New York office of Boosey and Hawkes — made him an offer to publish not only all his future works but also everything that he had written between *Petrushka* and *Persephone*, which would mean purchasing them from the original publishers, Editions Russes de Musique. Thanks to this arrangement the composer could now, in 1945, set about the systematic revision of his previous works, with the exception of *Firebird*, which already existed in a third version, and the *Sacre*. He did this in order to ensure the protection of his author's rights, which these works did not at the moment enjoy, but also to improve a number of details and to correct the inevitable misprints (though in this he was not wholly successful). In 1946 he revised *Petrushka* — the '1947 version' for smaller orchestra, already mentioned — and in 1947 the *Symphonies of Wind Instruments*, parts of which he radically rewrote. The following works were only superficially retouched: *Apollo Musagetes* (1947), *Oedipus Rex* and *Symphony of Psalms* (1948), *Pulcinella Suite*, *Divertimento*, *Capriccio* and *Persephone* (1949), *Piano Concerto* and *Le Baiser de la fée* (1950), *Octet* (1952) and *The Nightingale* (1962) whereas the *Balmont Poems* and *Les Cinq doigts* (which were to become *Eight Instrumental Miniatures*) were transcriptions for orchestra.

The first of Stravinsky's works to be performed after his American naturalization was the *Symphony in Three Movements* (24 January 1946).

The first new work *composed* by this new American citizen was also Stravinsky's first commission after settling in the United States, and it came — paradoxically — from Europe.

The *Concerto in D* dates from the first half of 1946. The commission came from Paul Sacher and was meant for his well-known Basle Chamber Orchestra, which gave the first performance on 27 January 1947 in Basle, with Sacher conducting. Though not a major work, the *Concerto* became very well-known thanks not so much to the concerts as to Jerome Robbins, who used the music for one of the best ballets of the post-war years, *The Cage*. How, one wonders, did Robbins find in this rather grey and conventional string piece, enough dramatic substance for twelve minutes of 'the theatre of cruelty'? The plot shows the love-life of the praying mantis, which first castrates and then devours two males of the species, *post coitum*. Both Nora Kaye, who created the part with the New York City Ballet and, some years later, the wraith-like Tanaquil Leclerq — both married in turn to Balanchine — gave unforgettable performances.

The work is in three movements. The opening 'Vivace' oscillates round the tonic D and neighbouring keys, with a simple diatonic theme reminiscent of the Brandenburg Concertos. The short 'Arioso' consists of a melody and accompaniment, rather *kitsch* in character (it is the only time when the praying mantis is allowed a moment of lyrical expansion). The very fast final 'Rondo' is the most effective of the three movements. Based on a tonic pedal (D), it alternates or superimposes impressions on the leading note (C sharp), generator of tension. As one might suppose, this is the climax of the ballet, which is a masterpiece of its kind.

*

An old friend, Nicolas Nabokov, has left a lively account of Stravinsky's Hollywood household at this time, his daily habits and the working routine in his sound-proofed studio.

> His workroom was exactly like his music, and his use of words, in its precision. It was an extraordinary room, perhaps the best organised and best fitted office that I ever saw. In an area of hardly more than ten metres by twelve there were two pianos (one grand and one upright), two tables — an elegant little writing-desk and a draughtsman's table — two glass-fronted bookcases, containing books, music and music-paper, everything arranged alphabetically. Between the two pianos, the bookcases and the tables there were, in addition, a number of smaller tables (one for smokers, with different brands of cigarettes, lighters, cigarette-holders and pipe-cleaners), five or six armchairs and the sofa on which he spent his daily siesta (and on which I saw him next day, lying flat on his back and snoring, quietly and regularly, with a look of contained fury on his face).

Stravinsky showed Nabokov the score of *Orpheus*. He sat at the piano:

> and I stood behind him and watched his small, muscular fingers

running over the keyboard, feeling for the right intervals and the typical Stravinsky melodic leaps. His neck, his head and his whole body marked, by jerks, the ingenious rhythms of each phrase of the music. He grunted, hummed and stopped occasionally to explain something. 'Look at this fugue,' he said as he showed me the epilogue. 'It is developed by two horns, while a trumpet and a violin, in unison, play a long, clear melody, a kind of cantus firmus. Does it not make you think of a mediaeval *vielle*? Listen. . . .'[1]

Although commissioned in the spring of 1946, *Orpheus* was only started after the *Concerto in D* was completed — that is to say, in the autumn of that year. The commission came from Lincoln Kirstein, director of the New York Ballet Society, and it was for Balanchine, who on this occasion collaborated closely with Stravinsky, working out individual scenes and numbers and even a number of choreographic details.

The idea of using the myth of Orpheus was Balanchine's and it immediately appealed to Stravinsky, as one might imagine. The old legend is followed fairly closely in the three scenes, or *tableaux*, and Stravinsky's score gives exact indications of the action, the characters and their different attitudes.

I. 1. *Orpheus laments Eurydice*. He stands motionless, with his back to the audience.
    2. *Air de danse*.
    3. *The Angel of Death and his dance* (at the end Stravinsky puts: the Angel leads Orpheus away to the Infernal Regions).
    4. *Interlude*: the Angel and Orpheus reappear in the darkness of Tartarus.
II. 5. *Pas des Furies* (their violence and their threats).
    6. *Air de danse* (Orpheus).
    7. *Interlude*: the tormented souls in Tartarus stretch out their arms to Orpheus, begging him to continue his singing which brings them consolation.
    8. *Pas d'action*. The Infernal Deities, touched by Orpheus's singing, relent. The Furies surround and blindfold him and then restore Eurydice to him.
    9. *Pas de deux* (Orpheus and Eurydice in front of a gauze drop-curtain). During the final bars Orpheus tears off his blindfold. Eurydice drops dead at his feet.
    10. *Interlude*.

11. *Pas d'action*. The Bacchantes attack Orpheus, seize and dismember him.

III. 12. *Apotheosis of Orpheus*. Apollo appears. He takes the lyre from Orpheus's hands and raises his voice to heaven.

Orpheus is as remarkable for its low colour-scheme as *Symphony in Three Movements* was for its brilliant colouring. The strings predominate and the harp plays an important, sometimes even a melodic, part while the woodwinds are used very sparingly, and mostly as soloists. This deliberate bias regarding sonority, which suited the composer's purpose perfectly, would have put *Orpheus* into the same category as *Apollo Musagetes*, were it not for its melodic poverty, its lack of originality and of inner tension. To be frank, *Orpheus* appears today as one of Stravinsky's least successful works, and before all else as a cliché of clichés — which would matter little if the music had any real animation of its own.

Since accompanied melody predominates in *Orpheus*, the thematic element is important, and Orpheus's own motif appears repeatedly. This is, it must be admitted, one of Stravinsky's least happy inspirations, recalling, as it does, the famous zither tune in Orson Welles's film *The Third Man*:

Ex. 84

violin solo

Oddly enough, the first 'Interlude' contains specimens of what was to be the composer's 'Renaissance-style' serialism in *Canticum Sacrum*, though the return of the diatonic theme, in the 'Pas des Furies', cancels the impression made by this unexpected expedition into the future. Although Stravinsky defended himself against his critics, it must be admitted that the 'Pas des Furies' is quite strongly reminiscent of Czerny, both in the spirit and the letter. The succession of scales, arpeggios and sequences is not even a parody, and at 63 we even find the Stravinsky cliché (used with such ingenuity elsewhere) of the familiar binary accompaniment, which occurs again at 74, both times in C sharp minor.

Orpheus's 'Air de danse' is a 'remake' of Bach, not a 'Bach archetype', and as such difficult to account for. We hear it first in the harp and then on two oboes,

Ex. 85

counterpointing the harp, the oboes and the cor anglais after the intervening 'Interlude'.

The 'Pas d'action' makes use of the initial theme, but then gets bogged down — which is strange for a 'pas d'action' — in neutral figurations which are not, however, without interest. The development of these figurations forms the basis of the 'Pas de deux', which is another slow, colourless movement in the middle of which appears a passage comparable to the much derided trumpet solo in *Scènes de ballet*.

Ex. 86

The best things in *Orpheus* are in the final 'Pas d'action', where there is a change from the rhythmic neutrality which marks the rest of the score.

The final tableau, 'Apothéose d'Orphée', includes the famous *vielle* passage, which is produced by one of Stravinsky's characteristic and both simple and effective instrumental pairings — in this case two violins playing *sul ponticello* in unison with a muted trumpet in B flat:

Ex. 87

The work ends with quiet scale-passages in the harp, representing Orpheus's lyre played by Apollo.

*

'Stravinsky is now in the prime of life and at the height of his powers. What will he write next? What direction will he take, to surprise and delight us? After *Apollo Musagetes* he ought logically to give us a Mass; but is the artist's logic the same as ours?' So ended Boris de Schloezer's study of Stravinsky in 1929. What the 'artist's logic' and a chance commission actually dictated to the composer on that occasion was . . . *Le Baiser de la fée*, and the Mass was not to be written until fifteen years later, in succession to *Orpheus* (which is in fact a kind of pale version of *Apollo*).

Some time in 1942 or 1943 Stravinsky came upon a number of Mozart Masses in a second-hand bookshop in Los Angeles. 'When I played through these rococo-operatic sweets-of-sin I knew I had to write a Mass of my own, but a real one' (*Expositions and Developments*). What Stravinsky meant by this was that his work would be designed to fulfil its proper function and would therefore have to be given a structure which conformed to Catholic liturgy. He was later to remark with some bitterness that his Mass had in fact had a different fate: for in spite of its functional liturgical character the Church frowned upon it. Perhaps the first performance, which took place at La Scala on 27 October 1948 and was conducted by Ansermet, fated the work from the start to concert performance.

The 'Kyrie' and the 'Gloria' were written in 1944, when Stravinsky was seeing a lot of Jacques Maritain and reading Bossuet and Saint Augustine. The rest of the Mass was written in 1947–48. He was to tell Evelyn Waugh:

> My Mass is liturgical and virtually unornamented. Setting the 'Credo' I was simply concerned with adhering to the text, and in a special way. One composes a march to help men to march; and in the same way with my 'Credo' I hope to provide some help with the text. The 'Credo' is the longest of the movements. There is a great deal to believe.

This concise declaration is a key to the Mass and to all Stravinsky's religious music. The composer figures as an intermediary, entirely devoted to serving the *function* of the text and obliged, in some way, to preserve its timeless character. Accordingly all musical 'gesture' is banned from the Mass, which demands a hieratic quality, a bare, 'stripped' style and a syllabic setting of the text not unlike chanting (close to the old tradition).

Everything about the Mass — its ascetic character, the attempt to achieve a timeless language and the instrumentation (two oboes, cor anglais, two bassoons, two trumpets, three trombones and no strings) — places it outside chronological considerations and removes it from the 'neo-classical' category to which it has been said to belong. It is, in fact, quite simply a masterpiece.

The 'Kyrie' closely follows the tripartite form of the liturgical text — 'Kyrie eleison, Christe eleison, Kyrie eleison' — each repeated three times. The choral writing is polyphonic and the instruments 'set' (in the jeweller's sense) rather than accompanying the voices, providing in turn a frame, a foundation, a point of emphasis or illumination, a musical reference.

The 'Gloria' opens with a fanfare that seems to belong to the remotest past, a two-part polyphony. The voices (children and soloists) carry on a dialogue in long singing exercises in conjunct motion, the chorus echoing this hymn of adoration *mezza voce*. This establishes the principle of antiphony between soloists and chorus that dominates the 'Gloria', quite unlike the rich sonorities and massed voices that have been customary in the Church since Baroque times.

The 'Credo' is the central point of the work in every sense — liturgically, musically, chronometrically and topographically. Here the voices seem to be, as it were, marking time, scanning the sacred text syllable by syllable, simply and humbly, their sound never rising above a murmur, except at a few points. The first is at the reference to the Last Judgment, 'Cujus regni non erit finis', where there is a crescendo and a pause, followed immediately by a return to the initial chord and a *mezza-voce* repetition of the chant. The second occurs suddenly, on the word 'ecclesiam', where a dogma is being stated: *poco più forte*, that is, literally and categorically and not in any subtly 'symbolical' or allusive way. But this will now occur quite apart from the textual 'content', as an inherent part of the musical structure: from this point onward the end of each clause of the 'Credo' — whatever its sense — is marked by a sudden increase of intensity. The final 'Amen' is for unaccompanied voices.

It is interesting to compare Stravinsky's 'Credo', which is a perfect model and probably unique in twentieth-century religious music, with its spectacular opposite, the 'Credo' in Beethoven's *Missa Solemnis* which is based, as it seems, on a fundamental conceptual conflict. Beethoven's aim is to 'express' the images and emotions suggested to him by a text which, by definition, owes its power and its quality of permanence simply to its unchanging, hieratic character. Guided by his instinctive assumption of the role of Romantic messenger announcing, in his own person, new ideas, Beethoven overreaches — if he does not actually contradict — his subject and is trapped into the pitfall of theatricalizing the text even more than he does in *Fidelio*. . . . 'The dramatic or descriptive element is given an increasing importance; not only the melodic and rhythmic gait of each phrase, but even the actual form of each section is increasingly determined by the sense of the text', as Jean Chantavoine wrote. 'By dint of trying to give the text the maximum of its potential power of suggestion', as the present writer has said elsewhere,[2] 'and to find a complete equivalent for its imagery in a musical symbol — or rather gesture — Beethoven ends by miming the text rather than transcending it in a musical construction.' As we have seen, Stravinsky's attitude is the exact opposite of Beethoven's.

The symmetrical arrangement of Stravinsky's *Mass* round the central point of the 'Credo' can be seen at the 'Sanctus'. The following scheme will make it clear:

Ex. 88

Kyrie	Gloria	Credo	Sanctus	Agnus Dei
chorus and orchestra	soloists (soprano and alto) and chorus	chorus (syllabic scansion *pp*)	soloists (tenor and bass) and chorus	chorus and orchestra

Whereas the 'Gloria' introduced the antiphonal alternation between the higher-voiced soloists and the whole chorus, the dialogue in the 'Sanctus' is between the lower-voiced soloists and the brass. There is great variety in the writing — heterophony between the strictly graded solo voices; choral homophony alternating with antiphony; four-part polyphony in the 'fugue' at 'Pleni sunt coeli' and then at 'Hosanna', with its repetitions; free polyphony at the 'Benedictus' and finally the homophonic choral and orchestral blocks, which give the end of the *Mass* its organ-like sonority. No commentator seems to have observed the remarkable rhythm of the 'Sanctus' which is hurled at the listener in the first choral entry. (Ex. 89)

A notable feature of the symmetrically-shaped fugal subject is the systematic contrasting of very long and very short note-values, the diminishing of the longest note-values (8–7–6) and the invariability of the generating rhythmic cell. The first 'Sanctus!' of the chorus presents the extremes (1–11) of the rhythmic values concerned.

Ex. 89

In the 'Agnus Dei' chorus and orchestra alternate in a symmetrical antiphonal structure, a perfect example of Stravinsky's wonderful *layering* in which, even more than in his choice of instruments, lies the secret of the unique and inimitable *sonorities* in his music. Here and elsewhere in the *Mass* the antiphonal exchanges and the long drawn-out polyphonies of chorus and orchestra may well recall mediaeval music, but it was not Stravinsky's intention to indulge in any kind of 'temporal exoticism'. André Souris[3] has given a perfect explanation of the origin and the profound rightness of the composer's language in the *Mass*.

> His use of the modes, of chanting, of *melisma* and antiphony have nothing to do with aesthetic theory, and even less with any taste for the 'picturesque'. It was dictated by the symbolic function forming an organic link between these consecrated musical forms and the tradition and perennial character of the Church. Once adopted, at least as 'models', these forms became themselves a source of inspiration to the composer.

*

Not long after the completion of the *Mass*, Stravinsky informed his publisher, Ralph Hawkes, of his decision to write an opera with an English text. He seems to have been meditating a work of this kind ever since his arrival in the United States, and it matured gradually as the English language became more and more deeply rooted in Stravinsky's personality. It is impossible to exaggerate the basic, *sensual* relationship between language and music in Stravinsky's vocal works. There are a mass of writings on the nature and the exact chronology of *The Rake's Progress*, but Stravinsky's own account, written for the first American performance in 1963, is still the clearest in emphasizing the essential points. 'For several years I have nourished the idea of writing an opera in English. By that I mean music conceived in the first place for English prosody and executed in my own way, as I have done in the past with Russian (*The Nightingale, Mavra, Les Noces*), French (*Persephone*) and Latin prosody (*Oedipus Rex, Symphony of Psalms*).'

The subject occurred to Stravinsky during a visit to the Chicago Art Institute in May 1947, when he saw Hogarth's series of prints entitled 'The Rake's Progress', made in 1732-33. These, as Eric Walter White makes clear in his book, are not the original pictures, which now hang in the Sir John Soane Museum in London, and can only be removed from there by Act of Parliament, but contemporary copperplate engravings of the pictures, and thus reversed. The eight engravings, which were much admired from the beginning, have the following titles:

1. *The Heir.* Tom Rakewell inherits from his father; he is pledged to Sarah Young, whom he has already seduced and means to desert.

2. *The Levée.* The Rake is surrounded by dancing-masters, fencing-masters, music-masters and garden experts.

3. *The Orgy.* The Rake, drunk, is seen in the small hours at 'The Rose Tavern', a brothel in Covent Garden.

4. *The Arrest.* The Rake, who has got through his inheritance, is just about to be arrested for debt in St James's Street, when he is saved at the last moment by Sarah Young, who sacrifices her modest savings.

5. *The Marriage.* To restore his fortunes, the Rake marries an elderly lady who is one-eyed but rich. Sarah Young, with Tom's child in her arms, tries to prevent the ceremony.

6. *The Gaming House.* The Rake loses his second fortune at play.

7. *The Prison.* The Rake is in prison for debt. His wife comes to overwhelm him with sarcastic comments. Sarah Young is shown in a faint.

8. *The Mad House.* The Rake has been placed in the asylum at Bedlam, where the faithful Sarah visits him and laments his fate.

Having chosen his subject and decided that he wanted a verse libretto, Stravinsky consulted his friend Aldous Huxley on whom to approach. Huxley immediately suggested W. H. Auden. When Stravinsky approached him through Ralph Hawkes, Auden proved to be free and accepted the invitation to collaborate, with all its conditions. Once this had been arranged Stravinsky himself wrote, on 6 October 1947, inviting Auden to visit him in California, all expenses paid, to decide on the main outlines of the libretto.

Auden arrived in Hollywood on 15 November and was put up on the sofa in the Stravinskys' drawing-room, which was too short for his great height. Part of the 'folklore' of the North Wetherly Drive household was measuring guests' heights, the drawing-room sofa being at this time the only 'accommodation' for passing guests. (These details are amusingly told in Nicolas Nabokov's *Cosmopolite*.)

Early next morning, primed by coffee and whisky(!) we began work on *The Rake's Progress*. Starting with a hero, a heroine and a villain and having decided that these people should be a tenor, a soprano and a bass we proceeded to invent a series of scenes leading up to the final scene in Bedlam, that was already fixed in our minds. We followed Hogarth closely at first and continued until our own story began to assume a different significance. (*Memories and Commentaries*)

The understanding between the two artists was immediate and they made use of the week they had together without losing a moment: Stravinsky had an idea of the style that he wished to use, while Auden had already thought of the possible plot that could be drawn from the Hogarth prints.

We also tried to co-ordinate the plan of action with a provisional plan of musical pieces, arias, ensembles and choruses. Auden kept saying, 'Let's see, now . . . ah, ah, ah . . . let's see . . . ah . . . ah. . . .' and I the equivalent in Russian, but after ten days we had completed an outline which is not radically different from the published libretto.

At the end of 1947 Auden brought in his close friend Chester Kallman as co-librettist. It was not until after Act 1 had been completed that he mentioned it to Stravinsky, who did not say much at first and was annoyed at being faced with a *fait accompli*. In fact, however, he was appreciative of Kallman's contribution and later, when he met him, found the man himself sympathetic.*

The libretto is only distantly related to Hogarth's pictures, their moralizing logic being counterbalanced by the intervention of chance, which is stressed (Tom's inheritance comes not from his father, but from a distant uncle) and by Tom's *acte gratuit* in marrying Baba, the Bearded Woman (who corresponds to the rich one-eyed woman in Hogarth) not for her money but to exercise a so-called 'freedom of choice'. Sarah Young, the 'unmarried mother', is replaced by the chaste Anne Truelove, and the hero's actual innocence — Tom is weak rather than depraved — provides the symmetry between good and evil. But the most important divergence between the libretto and Hogarth, and its true claim to originality, lies in the association with the great Faust-myth. Nick Shadow, Tom's servant and guide (absent from Hogarth's pictures), is no other than the Devil, who plays a part in the dramatic action, which he twists, controls and motivates. In the

*Kallman wrote the second part of Scene 1 and all Scene 3 of Act 1; part of Scene 1 and all Scene 2 of Act 2; and Scene 1 (except for some conversational exchanges) and the card-playing scene in Act 3.

penultimate scene, master and servant, victim and executioner, play cards for the Rake's soul. The thought of Anne saves Tom, but only at the price of his reason. The Devil is thus finally the loser.

The libretto of *The Rake's Progress* is perfect in construction, balance and symmetry, simple but ingenious. It is divided into three acts and three times three scenes, each act following the pattern A-B-A. This uniform ternary principle of organization is traversed by an asymmetrical binary vector — that of *time*, the four seasons from one spring to the next.

ACT 1

Scene 1 : The Trueloves' garden (spring).
Scene 2 : Mother Goose's brothel in London (summer).
Scene 3 : The Trueloves' garden (autumn).

ACT 2

Scene 1 : Tom's antechamber in London (autumn).
Scene 2 : Street in front of the house (autumn, dusk).
Scene 3 : Tom's antechamber (winter morning).

ACT 3

Scene 1 : The same as Act 2 scene 1 (spring afternoon).
Scene 2 : A cemetery (the same night).
Scene 3 : The Bedlam madhouse.

The libretto of *The Rake's Progress* is successful both as poetry and as theatre. The English text — the airs in verse and the dialogues in prose — fulfils all the scheduled demands of a good libretto: clear language, euphonious lines, simple images, lively dialogue, well-defined characters, dramatic surprises, intermezzos, divertissements, a final catastrophe and a moral lesson. If *The Rake's Progress* is flawless as a stage spectacle and needs to be seen in the theatre to be fully appreciated, this is largely due to the libretto. We shall be discussing the music in a moment.

At the same time as the libretto of *The Rake's Progress* was to be handed to him by Auden, who came to Washington especially for the purpose, Stravinsky encountered a young musician of twenty-four, Robert Craft, who was to become assistant, collaborator and *famulus*, and was to remain with him for the rest of his life. Craft had written to the composer a year earlier to ask him for the score of *Symphonies of Wind Instruments*, which was at that time unobtainable, and which Craft wished to conduct in New York. Without hesitation Stravinsky offered him the new version that he had just finished for Boosey & Hawkes, and proposed himself as conductor. In March 1948, therefore, Craft went to Washington to meet the composer and found himself waiting in the hall of the Raleigh Hotel with Auden, who immediately read him part of the text of *The Rake*. Both the Stravinskys then received the two of them in the 'Lily Pons Suite' with generous tooth-glasses of whisky. . . . Craft has left an account of the first offstage impression made on him by Stravinsky's physical appearance. This occurs in the opening pages of the diary that he kept regularly for the more than twenty years he spent with Stravinsky:

> He is physically so extraordinary that nothing less than a full-length statue (not merely a head or a bust) or scaled-to-life-size drawing (the seated portrait by Picasso is misleading) could convey his uniqueness: the pygmy height, short legs, fleshlessness, footballer's shoulders, large hands and wide knuckles, tiny head with recessive frontal lobes, sandy hair (black in photographs), smooth, red neck and high hairline. He is so absorbing to look at in fact that an effort is required to concentrate on what he says. . . . Many of his remarks are so sweeping, absolute, exclusive, as well as so exaggerated and *parti-pris* that the listener is uncertain whether his leg is being pulled. . . .[4]

Stravinsky showed an immediate sympathy for this young man, who did not conceal his admiration and also had a profound knowledge of his music. He was therefore invited by the composer to settle in Hollywood and undertake a number of tasks, the first of these being to sort and catalogue several trunkloads of manuscripts which had just arrived from Paris.*

A more important task with which Stravinsky soon entrusted his new assistant was to help him with the English prosody in *The Rake's Progress*. He had to pronounce and repeat each line of the libretto,

> Stravinsky asking me my opinion on his treatment of the words and phrases; but he used to produce ingenious compromises rather than accept suggestions. . . . He was not excessively concerned with the demands of strong syllables or the tonic accent in English. What did concern him was the possibility of singing the words, placing such a

*This was in preparation for an auction which was to be held at Zurich in 1948. At this, excellent prices were paid for the orchestral score of *Les Noces* (without vocal parts), the piano score of *Apollo Musagetes*, the orchestral score of *Persephone* and the 1947 version of *Petrushka*.

vowel in such a register, the relationship between the word and the timbre of the voice and vice-versa. He paid the most exact attention to these points, despite any assurances that I or others might give him. . . . (*Dix Ans avec Stravinsky*[5])

Making decisions, being obstinate, skirting obstacles, taking advice (either followed or ignored): such was Stravinsky's method of procedure, which was devious and strict at the same time — and which ended in his musical mastery of this libretto written in a language he hardly knew. 'Rather than search for musical forms symbolically expressive of the dramatic content (as in the labyrinthine examples of Alban Berg)', as Stravinsky says, through Craft, in a text dated 'Paris, 1964',

I chose to cast *The Rake* in the mould of an eighteenth-century 'number-opera', one in which the dramatic progress depends on a succession of separate pieces — recitatives and arias, duets, trios, choruses and instrumental interludes. In the earlier scenes the mould is to some extent pre-Gluck, in that it tends to crowd the story into the *secco* recitatives, reserving the arias for the reflective poetry; but then, as the opera warms up, the story is told, enacted, contained almost entirely in song — as distinguished from the so-called speech-song, and Wagner's 'continuous melody' which consists in effect of orchestral commentary enveloping a continuous recitative. (*Themes and Episodes*)

In the same piece Stravinsky asks:

Is it possible for a composer to re-use the past and at the same time move forward? Without bothering about the answer (which is 'yes') this academic question did not worry me while I was composing. . . . On the other hand I ask the listener to suspend judgment, as I did while composing, and to try to discover — difficult though that may be — the real qualities of the opera.

This is a quotation taken from a text written long after the events with which it deals, but it does give a direct answer to the unavoidable question of how valid any approach can be that gives priority to a historic model over actual invention. 'I am willing to accept the undertaking if I can, by doing so, liberate people from this argument and orientate them towards the actual music,' says Stravinsky. Well. . . .

Is *The Rake's Progress* one of Stravinsky's masterpieces? There is no simple answer. The work benefits, of course, from the general overvaluation of opera as such and has given rise to a corpus of commentary such as no non-theatrical work would arouse. But opera as such was never the field in which Stravinsky had his great successes, nothing to compare with what he achieved in the field of religious music. The fact is that his pure and hard-grained melody leans to the hieratic rather than the dramatic, and that he himself refuses a straight one-to-one relationship with material of a psychological nature and is incapable of even that minimum of hysteria essential to the musical and scenic representation of emotion. That lofty distancing of the musical image from the affective image called up by the text, allowing the pure music-structure to speak for itself, is precisely what arouses our admiration, and we see it most frequently in his religious works. Opera on the other hand is not a matter of 'lofty distancing' and 'pure musical structures'. Opera is made 'impure' by the fact that it accepts — takes, indeed, for granted — an element of musical miming.

This aspect of opera went against the grain, and to avoid this, Stravinsky always took refuge behind some already existing stylistic model when writing an opera, allowing the model a much greater influence on his musical language than in most of his purely instrumental works. How successful he was in *Mavra*, where he approached the archetypal Russian comic opera by indulging in a deliberate stylistic prejudice, is a matter of debate; but in *The Rake's Progress* he employed, as it were verbatim, not only the spirit but the letter — the actual clauses and organization — of his chosen model. Moreover this model was not simply an age or a genre, but an individual composer (Mozart) and often an individual work (*Così fan tutte*). Stravinsky did not even *employ* this model for his own artistic purposes, as he had done felicitously elsewhere, wittily and sometimes cynically: he confined himself to simply 'following' it, so that *The Rake's Progress* seems, musically, to reinstate the 'chart' of a Mozart opera rather than to revive 'a number-opera of the Gluckian or Mozartian type'. Strangely enough it is Auden's and Kallman's libretto (in which Stravinsky himself had a considerable hand, we must remember) that has the archetypal dimension, and it is as though the libretto occupied the whole stage, with the music no more than doubling it. . . . Thus the music, for all its skilful handling of stereotypes and disposing of figuration, seems reduced to a certain impersonality. Stravinsky of course often uses deliberately 'depersonalised' figuration, especially melodic, in which case he will give the passage his own personal character by some feature either in the orchestra or in the harmony however simple, such as a 'wrong bass' chord, in which, nevertheless the constituents are 'layered' in his own inimitable fashion. Such things, however, are rare in *The Rake*, either in the vocal or the orchestral parts. This sleek musical language is sometimes marked by a purely cultural reference or an association with one of the composer's earlier works. Anne's important aria in Act 1, for instance, contains distant echoes of *The Nightingale*, even of *Mavra*, and the same is true of the big duet for Anne and Tom in Act 2, while at the end of Scene 2 the orchestra appears in the court dress worn by eighteenth-century 'Overtures'. There is a vacuousness about the immaculate good manners of these acts of homage to the past, and it makes itself felt even in the best melodies such as, for example, that given to the melancholy cornet at the opening of Act 2. As soon as this melody is taken over by the voice, it loses its *mood* and even becomes disturbing in 'O heart, be stronger'. Scene 2, on the other hand, is an excellent operatic moment, strictly handled, especially in the duet for Tom and Anne and Baba's violent interruptions leading up to the excited crowd chorus.

Act 3 is the most developed and the best of the three. Stravinsky's music is more strongly engaged in the dramatic development here. Though still keeping his distance, he does at least drop his smooth, impersonal mask, preserving simply the livery of Mozart and Bach, or the garments of Apollo or Don Giovanni, under which we never fail to recognize him. The auction, in which the ruined Tom's possessions are scattered to the four winds, is conducted at a hectic pace by Sellem, a new version by Auden and Kallman of the 'notary' who often plays a part in Mozart's operas. Stravinsky makes him a countertenor. The instrumental introduction (strings, without double basses) to Scene 2, in the cemetery, carries us back to *Orpheus* and the Bach-style 'Air de danse' for two oboes, Stravinsky thus continuing to make his appearance in self-quotations and new versions of old procedures. The card-game has a bitonal harpsichord accompaniment, one of the chord-components being lowered a semitone as in *Petrushka*.

Scene 3, in Bedlam, is musically the most attractive in its rather pre-Raphaelite way, with its orchestral prelude (echoes of *Apollo*) the big duet for Tom — as Adonis — and Anne, and finally Anne's simple and serene lullaby, marked by intervals of the fourth and the third:

Ex. 90

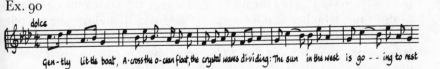

Gen-tly lit-tle boat, A-cross the o-cean float, the crystal waves di-vi-ding: The sun in the west is go - - ing to rest

As in *Don Giovanni*, there is a final quintet which dispels the gloom o
the last scene by its high spirits and delivers the 'moral of the story':

> For idle hands
> And hearts and minds
> The Devil finds
> A work to do
> A work, dear Sir, fair Madam
> For you and you. . . .

The Rake made great progress in the world, the high points of which
were the first performance, in Venice, on 11 September 1951,
conducted by Stravinsky, with the chorus and orchestra of La Scala;
Ingmar Bergman's production at the Stockholm Opera in 1961, much
loved by the composer himself, who met Bergman on this occasion; the
first performance in America, at the Metropolitan Opera on 14 May
1953; the revival by the Glyndebourne Opera at the Edinburgh
Festival on 25 August 1953; and the Paris performances in November
1980 (Festival d'Automne) with Bernard Haitink conducting the
Orchestre de Paris and the Glyndebourne Chorus, producer John Cox,
with exquisite sets by David Hockney. Vera Stravinsky's proud and
touching account of the social splendours of the first night in Venice,
entitled 'La prima assoluta', appeared in *Themes and Episodes*. The cast
at La Fenice on that occasion was the following: Anne — Elisabeth
Schwarzkopf; Tom — Robert Rounseville; Nick Shadow — Otakar
Kraus; Truelove — Rafael Arié; Baba — Jennie Tourel; Sellem —
Hugues Cuénod. The production was by Carl Ebert, the rehearsals (at
La Scala) were supervised by Ferdinand Leitner. Auden and Kallman
were given the role of 'consultants' and rather poorly paid.

The audience of La Fenice — in fact the *crème de la crème* of the smart
world from all over Europe — gave Stravinsky, whose conducting was
masterly, a great ovation.

Despite its impeccable construction, its perfect scenic and musical
balance and its unquestionable musical elegance, *The Rake's Progress* is a
crisis work. The impression of a *lost self*, the absence of that personal
note that was present and powerful even in *Pulcinella* suggests, almost
painfully, to the listener the impasse in which Stravinsky found himself
at this time, whether or not he was conscious of it, and despite his self-
assurance while he was composing the work. Even the tonal bases of his
language seem in the *The Rake* to be somehow off-centre in their almost
desperate affirmation. It is as though something vital has gone astray,

has got lost in the very effort of looking for and outbidding itself. Did Stravinsky feel 'threatened'? Was he already listening for 'other voices'? No, not yet. What, then, is the explanation of that particular feeling of unease that today's listeners may well feel when they hear *The Rake's Progress*? There is something of an artistic enigma in this but it is certainly not a matter of mere chance.

X

On the Verge of Fertile Land

IN JULY 1951 Schoenberg died in Hollywood, and a telegram was immediately despatched to his wife: 'Deeply shocked by saddening news of terrible blow inflicted to whole musical world by loss Arnold Schoenberg. Please accept my heartfelt sympathy. Igor Stravinsky.' Stravinsky was 'silent the whole day'. They had lived next door to each other for eleven years without ever meeting. Schoenberg's death finally broke this negative bond between them — 'the forty-year, antinomical coupling of their names.'[1] But was that all?

Anyone who is aware of the almost physical antipathy that Stravinsky felt for Schoenberg, of the radical opposition between their attitudes, of Schoenberg's choral *Satire* aimed at Stravinsky and of the occasions on which Stravinsky did not fail to repay the Viennese composer in the same coin, will also be aware that this antagonism did not exclude a feeling of mutual respect. Even so, we ask ourselves what could Schoenberg's death mean to Stravinsky beyond the sincere and spontaneous gesture of a telegram? One need not embark on theories about Stravinsky's unconscious in order to recognize the importance to him of the *physical* disappearance of the man who invented serialism: although Stravinsky was not yet aware of it, that disappearance opened up a new possibility. As Eric Walter White perceptively remarks, 'the three chief Viennese serialists were all now dead and so their contributions to serialism could at last be considered in historical perspective'. In such a context were Stravinsky's meeting with Robert Craft and the immediate confidence and seriousness of their musical relationship merely a coincidence? When Craft consulted Schoenberg at Los Angeles in July 1950 about *Pierrot Lunaire*, which he was to conduct in one of his New York concerts, he avoided mentioning the fact to Stravinsky, who was happily at work on *The Rake's Progress*. When Craft's New York venture came to financial grief and he finally settled — at Stravinsky's invitation — in Hollywood, he started conducting works by Schoenberg, Berg and Webern and Bartók, as well as Stravinsky, at his Los Angeles concerts. Stravinsky enjoyed these 'Evenings on the Roof', as the concerts were called, saying that they reminded him of the 'Soirées de musique contemporaine' that he used to attend as a young man in St Petersburg. Partly thanks to Stravinsky's support, these 'Evenings' quickly acquired great prestige. They also gave the composer frequent opportunities to hear not only the works of the Second Viennese School but, later, Boulez, Stockhausen and others of their contemporaries whose music was programmed with 'rare' Renaissance and Baroque works. 'The first work that made a deep impression on Stravinsky,' Craft writes in *Dix Ans avec Stravinsky*, 'was Webern's quartet op. 22, which he heard several times in January and February 1952.' And it was doubtless owing to these impressions and the renewing of his contact with Europe and its 'new music', that Stravinsky 'gradually came to believe that the serial system was a usable means of musical composition'.

Between 1952 and 1955 he listened to a great deal of Webern. Craft's part in this gradual discovery of serialism was without doubt an essential, but not a decisive one.

The fact that my arrival coincided with a sudden and mysterious interest in the three Viennese composers has made me considered as Stravinsky's evil genius, responsible for his evolution in their direction, his 'fall into Webernism', as if anyone but Stravinsky could be responsible for Stravinsky's evolutions! Naturally the explanation of this evolution is in his actual music. *The Rake's Progress* was an end. He said so himself when he finished the opera.[2]

Stravinsky was to advance in this new field with the prudence of a fox (his totem animal) and, paradoxical as it may seem to post-Webernians in Europe, without abandoning — at least until his most radical works, *Threni* and *Movements*, written in 1957 and 1958 — the principle of 'polarity', if not of tonality. And it was quite natural for him to return to this principle, at least partially, in *Requiem Canticles*.

The importance of Stravinsky's stylistic mutation in favour of serialism does not lie in his limited borrowings from the Viennese School but in the fact that they enabled him to find himself again. In *Orpheus* and *The Rake's Progress* his identity was, as it were, threatened and there are passages in *The Rake* where the listener might find himself wondering, uncomfortably, 'Who is that by?' But the moment we hear the *Cantata*, the *Septet* or any of the works that followed, we are unmistakably back with the Stravinsky we have always known. That is the Stravinsky paradox, the most profoundly puzzling thing about him — a paradox unmistakably confirmed by the works written after 1951.

The *Cantata* for soprano, tenor, women's chorus and instrumental ensemble (2 flutes, 2 oboes and cello) was begun in April 1951 and

finished in August 1952, an unusually long period partly due to
Stravinsky's visits to Europe mentioned above. Writing of the first
performance, given by the Los Angeles Chamber Symphony Orchestra, Stravinsky said that after *The Rake's Progress* he had a great desire to
compose another English text 'but this time in a purer, not dramatic
form' — words that suggest a need for something more *interior*, a
healthy reaction in any composer after writing an opera. With this in
mind he chose a number of anonymous fifteenth- and sixteenth-century
English texts, 'verses which attracted me not only for their great beauty
and their compelling syllabification, but for their construction, which
suggested musical construction'.

Stravinsky, with his usual precision, called these poems 'semi-
sacred', and the religious feeling which they express is both familiar
and distant, popular and elaborate. The fourth, 'Westron Wind', is an
ordinary love-poem, in which love is symbolized by the wind, and it is
placed in its sacred context much as 'Surge, Aquilo', from the *Song of
Songs*, was later to be placed in the context of *Canticum Sacrum*. The
whole work is built on a symmetrical plan, as shown below:

Ex. 91

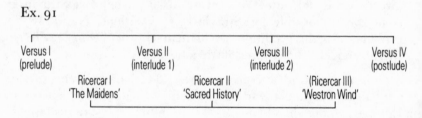

This 'odd' symmetry was much favoured by Stravinsky, as we shall see
later. It implies a *centre* to which particular importance is attached and
wings that overlap each other on the principle of alternation. Thus
'Westron Wind' may be thought of as a third *ricercar* (despite the fact
that it is not so called, and despite its non-religious character)
inasmuch as it is a vocal synthesis (soprano *and* tenor) of the two
preceding *ricercari* for soprano and tenor respectively. Stravinsky gives
Versus I, II and III to the chorus, who have exactly the same musical
material but with shifting rhythmic and melodic shapes. The most
developed piece is 'The Sacred History', an Elizabethan text which
occupies a central position and is serial in structure.

The different Versus-numbers make use of the 'Lyke-Wake Dirge',
the lines of which are repeated by twos, the lament implied by the title
being allegorical. The chorus's modal couplets have short introductions in the Phrygian mode. The number of bars is in each case the

same, seven bars' introduction and seventeen bars' chorus. The polyphony is simple, in contrary motion, the manner tranquil and the colour transparent: 'This ae nighte, this ae nighte,/ every nighte and alle,/fire and fleet and candlelighte,/ and Christe receive thy soule'.

'The Maidens came', for soprano solo and quintet, is the first *ricercar* — a term used by Stravinsky in its old sense of a 'researched' piece in an elaborate polyphonic style. In the first section there is a canon by contrary motion between cor anglais and flute, and in the second, between voice and flute. All the sections are canonic, the last being a recitative on the charmingly naïve words, 'Most puissant and victorious Elizabeth, let us pray the King of Heaven, Christ Eternal. . . . Grant them a place to sing eternally, Amen.'

The score shows how much Stravinsky still, and indeed always, thinks in modal and diatonic terms (emphasized by strong cadences).* This is just as true for the *ricercari* as for 'The Sacred History' itself, on the poem, 'To-morrow shall be my dancing day', and in spite of its particular structure.

'The Sacred History' is the centre of gravity of the work and the first example in Stravinsky of a serial type of organization. We know that during January and February 1952 he listened a great deal to Webern's Quartet op. 22, and this is exactly when he was composing 'The Sacred History' (February 1952). The 'series' underlying this piece is itself tonal-modal, being, one might say, in C major/minor:

Ex. 92

The question of its tonal character does not primarily concern us here, as we have seen that Stravinsky was still — and was to remain — 'unaligned' on the *principle* of atonality and was never to consider the serial factor as an overriding element in that principle. What is, on the other hand, of primary importance, and distinguishes Stravinsky's series from mere thematic material, is the fact that he treats it in the four 'classical' ways originated by Schoenberg: original form (Or), retrograde (R), inversion (I) and inversion of the retrograde (RI). This serial structure appears in its four basic forms in the first tenor solo:

*In his valuable detailed analysis of 'The Sacred History', printed in *Dix Ans avec Stravinsky*, Craft observes that 'the pupils of Schoenberg have formulated their criticism, according to which 'The Sacred History' is the very antithesis of functional harmony. This is exact. It evokes a period during which harmony depended upon counterpoint and had no function in Schoenberg's sense. . . .'

Ex. 93

Canons between voices and instruments and *ritornelli* will now alternate according to a principle of very delicately adjusted repetition and variations. Of the nine canons the odd numbers are identical, while the even introduce different associations and transpositions of serial forms. Apart from a few rhythmic variants the *ritornelli* remain identical. Here the perpetual return of the line, 'To call, to call my true love to my dance,' has an obsessive character. Is this dance to be understood here as an allegory of the life and passion of Christ? We know that for Stravinsky there was a close link between dance and religion, and it seems certain that this Elizabethan text struck him for its allegorical echoes as much as for its poetic beauty.

After 'The Sacred History' the simple and noble melodic line of Versus III returns, close again to Bach but very different from the *fabricated*, literal Bach of the oboes in *Orpheus*. Here we have something quintessentially Bach-like; and Klemperer, who saw a lot of Stravinsky in Los Angeles during the early Fifties, recalls that the composer used to play the 'Forty-Eight' every day.

With 'Westron Wind', on the other hand, we find ourselves back in this earlier, superseded Bach world, with its accompaniment figures in C minor for the cello and the flute and its repeated notes, which Craft compares to the 'Danse des bacchantes' in *Orpheus*. The effect on the listener, though, is no longer the same. Something has changed, something in the strange context of the ensemble. . . . The last Versus forms a postlude, bringing the work to an unexpected end with a six-four chord in A major which seems not so much a conclusion as a final enigma.

The *Cantata* is a long work, lasting half an hour, and its 'bare' style is a very long way from the seductions of *The Rake's Progress*. It has a name for austerity, not to say dullness and is virtually never performed. It is nevertheless an important piece, not simply for the fact of its being a key-work in Stravinsky's development and paradoxically combining new ideas with an insistence on elements of the past, but for its actual beauty. The music hovers tranquilly, as though belonging to another sphere and its ambiguous features, its slowly distilled 'white' polyphony and its hermetic lyricism demand to be revealed.

*

Having finished 'To-morrow shall be my dancing day', Stravinsky left for Europe, where he heard — for the first time in his life! — both *Erwartung* and *Wozzeck* at the 'Festival de l'Oeuvre du xxe siècle' in the Théâtre des Champs Elysées, Paris. Returning from Europe, he set to work on his *Septet,* commissioned by the Dumbarton Oaks Research Library and finished it in February 1953. It was to have its first performance on 23 January 1954 at Dumbarton Oaks, under the composer's own direction, but was no more than a *succès d'estime.* Here in fact, at the very height of his career, came another renunciation similar to that which followed the *Sacre.* At over seventy, with the success of *The Rake* still fresh in his mind, Stravinsky abandoned the style to which he had accustomed his admirers in order to follow his own inner promptings. It was a turning-point indeed, but not yet an obvious one. It was only with *Canticum Sacrum* that its full importance became clear and, indeed, a matter of 'scandal'.

The *Septet* is in three movements, the first of which has only the metronome marking crotchet = 88, which corresponds to an *allegro moderato.* Written in two weeks, it belongs to the same 'Bachian' aesthetic as the *Dumbarton Oaks* concerto written fifteen years earlier on the same spot. The very 'straightforward' clarinet theme is stated at the same time as its rhythmic augmentation and, reduced by a beat, its inversion in the horn appears exclusively in equal rhythmic note-values. A careful listener will discern the composer's search for a new language both here and in the figures at ⟨3⟩, just before ⟨4⟩ (but what makes one suddenly think of the 'tour de passe-passe' in *Petrushka?*) and again at ⟨12⟩:

Ex. 94

Notice the harmonic 'contradictions' especially in the piano part where the fourths and sixths in D major and C major respectively hardly conform to Schoenberg's rules, it must be admitted. . . . In the central 'Passacaglia' Stravinsky takes the decisive step towards what will eventually become, through Webern, his own brand of serialism. The serial material here consists of sixteen notes, only eight of which are not repeated, the first five being a transposition of the first five notes of the principal theme of the first movement, thus forming a cyclic link which will also include the third movement.

What immediately strike the listener are the 'boldness' and delicacy with which the composer handles this material, creating nothing less than a *Klangfarbenmelodie* in which the timbres, which change from one cell to the next, are almost as important to the musical development as the pitches. Dynamic intensity remains at a neutral *mezzo piano*, the articulation of the beginning and the end of each phrase being differentiated by the manner of attack:

Ex. 95

This exposition, which is thematic only in an ambiguous way, is to be followed by nine variations, so that what may be called the 'person-theme' is about to become 'structure-theme', simply a *condition* of future play. Even so it is still recognizable in its original form which is in fact that of a *passacaglia*, a form used by many composers (including Webern) as the framework for a first exploration of unknown territory. Variation 1, for woodwinds, is rhythmical, with the theme in the bass (violoncello, piano). Var. 2 has the *passacaglia* theme in long note-values in the violoncello underpinning a brief crop of canons at the octave (violin), at the fifth (viola) and at the minor seventh (clarinet). In Var. 3 the piano has both the original and the inversion of the series, in a radical rhythmic diminution, and then their retrogrades. Var. 4 is based on the mirror inversion of the series and its various symmetries, while Var. 5 is, in contrast, asymmetrical and unexpected. Just as Beethoven introduced a 'foreign body' into the third of his *Diabelli Variations*, so Stravinsky introduces here *seven bars* of the polarizing note A, to which he even adds a lower fifth, thereby producing — in this context and this 'density of time' — a quite astonishing effect. . . . The third movement is entitled 'Gigue' — possibly a tribute to Schoenberg's op. 25* after his death. The writing here is even more radical and unusual. What Stravinsky does, in effect, is to construct from the eight different notes in his basic series two modes, each of whose two tetrachords are superimposable. These he places above each corresponding instrumental entry:

Ex. 96

In any case Stravinsky uses the notes of these 'series' in their original thematic, not modal, order.

The four sections of this movement consist of four fugues. The first of these is given to the three strings, the second to the three winds and the piano; this has its own three-part fugue which turns out to be none other than the first string fugue! The third, again for strings, is on the inversion of the original subject, with the different series inverted and transposed in consequence. Like the second, the fourth is a double fugue, for piano and winds, using not only the inversion of the subject but also its retrograde. The piano is given what was previously the strings' part, while the winds transpose the subject and transform its rhythmic values. This comes to a climax in the triple *stretto* of the subject, its inversion and retrograde, entrusted to the piano and the strings, which only rejoin the ensemble for the conclusion of the work, in which a number of contradictory 'tonics' are superimposed on each other.

*

Stravinsky's time during the 1950s was divided between quiet periods of composing in Hollywood and the busy routine of concert tours all over the world, chronicled with much picturesque detail by Robert Craft. Whether it was in Japan, Yugoslavia, Portugal, Mexico, or at home in the United States the inseparable trio of Stravinsky, his wife and Robert Craft spent all their time between rehearsals, concerts and frequent dinners with friendly local personalities, in sightseeing. Take the single example of a day in Madrid — a visit to the Prado in the

*It was in the 'Walzer' of Schoenberg's op. 23 that the twelve-tone series made its first 'official' appearance. The 'Gigue' belongs to op. 25 where dodecaphony seems to achieve the status of a grammar.

morning, an expedition to the Escurial in the afternoon in the company of a nephew of Alfonso XIII (an old admirer); then back to Madrid and on to a visit to the writer, Ortega y Gasset, during which two bottles of whisky were drunk, followed by an evening of flamenco music in a private club, from midnight to 2 a.m. . . .

Once again Stravinsky found himself moving, as in his old European days, from one palace to another, always staying — as he did on principle — in the very best hotels. This was for a number of reasons, all of which were compelling in his eyes — to satisfy his taste for comfort, to escape from his countless admirers and to spite the tax-man, hotel-bills being totally deductible as 'expenses'. Stravinsky's meanness — and his extreme generosity in a number of unpredictable cases, and towards his own family — was proverbial, and he was often the first to make fun of it. Every piece of string was carefully untied, every unfranked stamp carefully removed from its envelope; no unsolicited letter was answered unless accompanied by a stamped envelope; and a whole correspondence would be devoted to reclaiming a debt, however tiny. One evening in 1955, in Seville, he was approached by the Cathedral organist, aware that the composer had just been awarded the Sibelius Prize of 18,000 dollars. 'Estravinsky? Estravinsky? . . . You must be rich now . . . the Esibelius Prize.' And the composer, scenting a request for money: 'I may be rich, *mon père*, but I am very mean'. (*Themes and Episodes*, Robert Craft's diary)

Life in California, in contrast, was quiet, strictly regulated and, despite various friendly visits and parties, all but retired. Apart from some members of his family (his daughter Milena and her husband, André Marion) and his lawyers Sapiro and Montapert, who had become intimates, Stravinsky's close friends could be counted on the fingers of both hands.

Stravinsky's close friendship with Aldous Huxley was enriching to both men. They met through Victoria Ocampo in 1925, but saw little of each other until the war years when Stravinsky arrived in Hollywood and their sympathy grew with a sometimes daily exchange of visits. Huxley was fascinated and amused by Stravinsky's gaiety and caustic wit, his curiosity, and the decisiveness of his judgments, which were for the most part severe and sometimes unjust, like his violent prejudices. Added to these was his enormous culture, served by a prodigious memory and, above all, the understanding that he had of his own creative processes. Huxley himself was a famous polymath as well as a literary genius, and endlessly generous in sharing his knowledge. What charmed Stravinsky in him were his unfailing personal and intellectual courtesy, his kindness, his modesty and his supreme mastery of the art of conversation, that 'intellectual charity' which, according to the composer, led him to take it for granted that his partner was as well-informed as himself. 'Aldous Huxley is the most aristocratic man I have ever known', he says in *Dialogues*, 'and I do not mean in the sense of birth'. Huxley's taste for understatement could not fail to hypnotize the Russian in Stravinsky. When his Hollywood house and all its contents, including a number of important manuscripts were destroyed by a fire, Huxley's only comment was, 'Well, you know, it *is* inconvenient'. (*Dialogues and a Diary*)

Aldous Huxley, Christopher Isherwood and the very literary 'pastor', Gerald Heard, made up Stravinsky's trio of friends during the Fifties in Hollywood. Isherwood's 'snapshots' of the composer call him up very clearly. 'Stravinsky was physically adorable . . . so small that one wanted to protect him. . . . The first time I saw him in his house he said "Shall we listen to my *Mass* before we get drunk?"', while Stravinsky remembered in *Dialogues and a Diary*:

We have often been drunk together — as often as once a week in the early Fifties, I should think — and in such different climes as Sequoia Park and Santa Monica beach. On Christopher's first visit to my home he fell asleep when someone started to play a record of my music. My affection for him began with that incident. . . .

Life, however, was relatively quiet, as we have said, and evenings at the cinema, listening to records and games of Chinese chess or Scrabble with Vera were more frequent than visits to or from friends. (The few film-star parties attended by the Stravinskys bored the composer to extinction and were quickly banished from their existence.)

At home Stravinsky was called 'Maestro' and the same practice was followed by members of his immediate entourage: secretaries, impresarios, publishers and even personal friends. His wife, always known as 'Madame', devoted her time to painting, and from the Fifties onwards, she had a number of important personal exhibitions in the USA and in Europe (the Obelisco gallery in Rome, the Cavallino in Venice etc.). Craft on the other hand very soon embarked on a detailed journal of his life in Hollywood with Stravinsky and, from 1957 onwards, was busy with the 'conversations' to which we shall return.

In fact Craft has given a very clear picture of Stravinsky's life at 1260 North Wetherly Drive during these years in his *Dix Ans avec Stravinsky*:

Once he has started a work, Stravinsky follows the routine of Apollo. At such times, I don't think he ever really manages to separate himself from his work, even when he is physically absent from it, for he eats at fixed times, has his siesta after lunch, and tea in the afternoon. When he is composing, 'the time-table' is one of his favourite phrases. There is one 'time-table' for composing, another for his health, depending on what time of day it is, what day, what month, what year . . . and there's also a certain amount of work avoidance: lingering after breakfast in his dressing-gown and beret to feed the parakeets, holding the seed between his lips, like the Indians. Then the post arrives, and anything, no matter how futile, will give him an excuse. In the evening the horrible attraction of the cinema is a constant menace. Stravinsky can find reasons for justifying his passion for Westerns and the films of Cecil B. de Mille by quoting complicated formulas from theatre criticism; but he has a deep love of animal films, photos of landscapes, huge productions and melodrama. . . . He has a physical revulsion just at the sight of a piece of meat which is too fat, and the smell of cooking-oil puts him in a temper. The same physical reaction overwhelms him when he has to listen to a piece of music which is too rich, with too much orchestral flab. Seeing Stravinsky eat makes you understand why he says his music is 'made solely of bones'; and why he insists that you play it *secco, non vibrato, senza espressivo. . . .*

Stravinsky writes on large pieces of unlined manila paper, pinned on to a cork board which rests on the front of his upright piano. The piano is muted, covered with felt: Stravinsky says he needs to hear vibrations rather than sound. The piano is the centre of all discussions about music. The composer rushes over to it when he wants to demonstrate a detail, or put an end to an abstract discussion . . .

The corpus of writings arising from the association between Craft and Stravinsky consists of two kinds of texts, as listed in the bibliography on p. 324: Craft's conversations with the composer and his own personal diaries, the two often appearing together in the same publication. The material, which is quite considerable, is extremely interesting since it gives a discontinuous, but often extremely detailed account of the last twenty years of Stravinsky's life both in Hollywood and on the concert tours on which Craft accompanied the composer as assistant conductor.

The first *Conversations* date from 1957, when Stravinsky was seventy-four. They consist of questions put by Craft, sometimes even prompted by Stravinsky, and the composer's replies, apparently jotted down on slips of paper in Russian, French or English or, more frequently, given orally, their deciphering and formulation, if not expansion, falling to Craft. There has been much questioning of the 'authenticity' of these texts although this has seldom — with a few exceptions — been publicly contested. It is a subject that demands some discussion.

Stravinsky virtually never wrote anything; writing was an activity for which he felt no inclination. He always made use of a 'third party', whether it was Walter Nouvel for *Chronicle*, or Souvtchinsky (very scantily) and Roland-Manuel (very widely and to a point beyond simply 'transcribing an idea') for *Poetics of Music*. Should one, or should one not, regard *Poetics of Music* as 'authentic', knowing, as we do, that not a single word of it was written by Stravinsky? The musical world seems not really to have asked itself that question. The answer must remain doubtful inasmuch as the ideas are indeed Stravinsky's, though the writer gives them a certain tone and orientation by the way in which he formulates and develops them. In spite of this the fact that the final text was approved and signed by Stravinsky gives it undeniable status as a *document*.

What is the position with regard to the 'dialogues' with Craft? In March 1958 Stravinsky wrote to Deborah Ishlon, who was at that time his agent, and Craft himself has published the letter,[3] in which the composer says unambiguously, ' . . . He [Craft] did write the book [*Conversations*], it is his language, his presentation, his imagination, his memory [. . .] It's not a question of simple ghost-writing but of somebody who is to a large extent creating me. . . .' Is this 'creation' faithful or deforming? That seems to be the real question. It may be that Stravinsky's 'presence' in these books diminishes with the years and, after the age of eighty, his part is in most cases essentially that of a catalyst — silent and perhaps distant — of words that have been in fact delegated. It may even be that passages dealing with events of the day — literary discussions, opinions about other composers or disputes with the American press — owe not only their formulation but their presence in the text to Craft. The fact remains that the whole collection of these publications* contains a mass of invaluable information and considerations, both biographical and musical. They should, however, be read with the same circumspection and the same reserves as apply in the case of the *Poetics of Music*. Such critical attitudes would also imply considerable familiarity with these texts, which are often repeated and/or republished from one collection or book to another.† Seen from

*For their different titles often quoted in this book, see Bibliographical Sources.

†See also on this subject a severe article by Kathryn Bailey — whose conclusions, however, are not of much weight — in which she makes a brave attempt to establish a list of these doublings in 'Studies in Music' no. 3, University of West Ontario, 1978.

this angle the texts signed jointly by Stravinsky and Craft constitute a corpus that is vitally important for the information that it provides on the last decades of Stravinsky's life.

Robert Craft's *Diaries* obviously present no problems of attribution. They contain interesting 'reporting' and also the author's own, personal reflections on Stravinsky's life, both public and private, during these last years. Meticulous in their attention to detail, though published fragmentarily, they form a separate section in most of the collections of *Conversations*. They are completed by *The Chronicle of a Friendship*, already quoted, which covers the whole period of Craft's association with Stravinsky, from 1948 to 1971, often brief extracts worked into year-by-year résumés including a number of diary-fragments already published in the *Conversations*. Finally we have *Stravinsky in pictures and documents*, an extremely interesting collection of biographical pieces, signed by Robert Craft as well as Vera Stravinsky. This traces Stravinsky's life from childhood to death by means of texts, documents, pictures, letters and often unpublished material from the composer's private archive, to which only the two authors had access.

*

The *Three Songs from William Shakespeare* for mezzo-soprano, flute, clarinet and viola were composed during the autumn of 1953, on Stravinsky's return from a concert tour in Latin America, and were intended for the 'Evenings on the Roof' concerts in Los Angeles, where Robert Craft conducted the first performance on 8 March 1954. The first song is based on Sonnet no. 8, 'Musick to heare'; the second on Ariel's song 'Full fathom five' from *The Tempest*; and the third is the 'Cuckoo' from *Love's Labour's Lost*.

These appear to me some of Stravinsky's most important chamber works, for here he seems to *abolish history* and to achieve a style that is independent not only of any model but of any pre-existing musical idiom. He manages to do this, oddly enough, by juxtaposing two elementary pieces of material, one tonal and the other serial, which appear to cancel each other out in the actual structure. In the first song the voice-line and that of the flute, which precedes it, state a four-note series, first in its original form (a) and then its retrograde, half of which is identical with the original (a1). (Ex. 97)

Meanwhile the accompaniment-figures in the clarinet and viola consist of repetitions, ascending and descending, of the first five notes of the scale of C major. . . . Rather elementary, it may seem — but very effective, since they carry us into a timeless world. Schoenberg is dead,

Ex. 97

and so is Orpheus. . . . It is as though music were inventing itself here and now, free of all the weight of the past.

In 'Full fathom five' this sense of an 'historical void' is accentuated still further. It opens with a *motto*, unbarred, consisting of seven notes arranged in triple canon at the fifth and at the octave, by diminution (a) and double-diminution (b) with the bass:

Ex. 98

This is indeed music to which Shakespeare's words — on a father's death — can be applied:

> Nothing of him that doth fade
> But doth suffer a sea-change
> Into something rich and strange. . . .

The more strongly affirmed harmonic pole in the third song ('When daisies pied') has already been prepared in 'Full fathom five' — it crystallizes primarily round B flat/E flat. Although the language here is diatonic, the material is developed serially inasmuch as the retrograde figures so largely. Here therefore, paradoxically, Stravinsky 'returns to history', his own history (and specifically to the works that he wrote in 1913–14, *Pribaoutki* and the *Three Japanese Lyrics*), in the airy tiering of polyphonic outlines and even in the instrumental colour. It was not, in fact, by chance that at the time when he was writing the Shakespeare songs (1953–54), he also regrouped and rescored four songs written forty years earlier, including the 'Chant dissident'. But the 'time-transparency' and the extreme fragility of the musical figures in the Shakespeare songs, their historical quite as much as their tonal 'weightlessness', relate them primarily to Webern. Surely by their elliptical, fugitive character they belong to the poetics of the *captured moment* which Webern revealed to the West. As Stravinsky says in *Memories and Commentaries*, Webern 'is the discoverer of a new distance between the musical object and ourselves and, therefore, of a new measure of musical time; as such he is supremely important'.

*

Did the success of *The Rake's Progress* mean that Stravinsky would soon write another opera? He did in fact plan one, but it never came to anything, and for a purely objective reason — a reason provided, possibly, by fate — namely the death of the librettist. Yet can we be sure that had Dylan Thomas lived and written the text for the new opera, Stravinsky would have composed it? It may be questioned whether the musical path on which Stravinsky was now entering could have led to any opera. Thomas, in fact, died and Stravinsky's next work was dedicated to his memory — it was a short, serial religious piece.

The meeting between Dylan Thomas and Stravinsky in 1953 was arranged by the film producer Michael Powell: they were to collaborate in a film on the *Odyssey*, a sort of 'masque', in Stravinsky's idiom. The plan came to nothing owing to lack of financial support. But when, in May 1953, the University of Boston, which had just produced *The Rake*, was planning to commission another opera from Stravinsky, his choice of a librettist was Dylan Thomas. 'As soon as I saw him,' Stravinsky was to write, 'I knew that the only thing to do was to love him. He was nervous, however, chain-smoking the whole time, and he complained of severe gout pains. . . . His face and skin had the colour and bloated appearance of too much drinking.' John Malcolm Brinnin, who saw Thomas after his meeting with Stravinsky in Boston, says in his *Dylan Thomas in America* 'that he had never seen him in such a bubbling state of creative excitement'. He and Stravinsky were going to re-create the world — the opera was to be about a single man and a single woman living on earth. They might be visitors from outer space finding themselves by some cosmic accident on an Earth recently devastated and reduced to silence by total war; or they might be human survivors of an atomic catastrophe. In either case they would be reliving the experience of the first man and woman and creating a new cosmogony. . . .

Stravinsky appears to have wanted something simpler. Thomas was to come to Hollywood — as Auden had come — to discuss the whole project at leisure. To avoid putting him up on the drawing-room sofa, Stravinsky planned to have a guest-room built. 'I expected a telegram from him announcing the hour of his aeroplane. On November 9 the telegram came. It said he was dead. All I could do was cry.' (*Conversations*)

In memoriam Dylan Thomas for tenor, string quartet and four trombones was composed in February-March 1954 and first performed on 20 September that year in Los Angeles, at the 'Monday Evenings Concerts' which succeeded the 'Evenings on the Roof'. The text chosen by the composer was: 'Do not go gentle into that good night', which Dylan Thomas had written in memory of his father. It is a cry of impotent anger against death, interrupted by repetitions of 'Rage, rage against the dying of the light'.

The work is short, lasting slightly more than six minutes, and tripartite in form, the tenor's central chant being framed by an instrumental prelude and postlude entitled 'Dirge-Canons'. These resemble the antiphonal polyphonic pieces of the Renaissance, brass alternating with strings, the two only combining in the final bars of the work. *In memoriam Dylan Thomas* is entirely serial but, like the composer's preceding works, not in any sense dodecaphonic, Stravinsky using a series of only five notes covering the span of a major third in broken semitones. Despite the chromatic nature of the actual material, its treatment is if anything modal in style. Here are the four forms of the series used by Stravinsky:

Ex. 99

This type of series is famous among composers for the formal combinations and transpositions that it permits, giving rise to a whole play of metamorphoses and identities; and it was almost certainly from Webern, who makes much use of it as a 'fragment' of the chromatic whole, that Stravinsky took the idea of semitones circling round a dissymmetrical axis. But the actual *treatment* is wholly, and indeed typically, Stravinskian.

Delighted with his serial discoveries the composer noted in the score the different forms of the series that he uses, having probably forgotten to remove these glosses (and a number of errors with them):

Ex. 100

The original form and its inversion can be seen in the second and fourth parts, in canon at the octave, the final note of one becoming a pivot and forming the first note of the transposed form of the other. The retrograde and its inversion follow in the third trombone part, the first trombone answering with the original form transposed an augmented fourth, thus making the deployment asymmetrical.

The strings make their entry, tied to the last note of the brass, with, first, a canon at the octave between the inversion (1st violin) and the retrograde (viola), by asymmetrical augmentation of note-values, followed by the original form (2nd violin), which is answered by the retrograde of the inversion, transposed (cello). This string sequence ends with a 'sham C major' cadence, so to speak, which — paradoxically — is the strict *result* of the serial contrapuntal lines pursued to their end. During the short development, in which the trombones are given other polyphonic configurations of the series, the strings' counterpoint returns exactly as before and serves as a *ritornello*.

The central 'Song', for tenor and strings, exhibits the same strictness in the handling of the series, the voice being given first the inversion and the retrograde forms which are made to overlap by transposing an augmented fourth (a very Webern-like idea) and then a transposition of the inversion of the retrograde. The line 'Rage, rage . . .' which serves as a *ritornello* — if one can use the word for such a cry of despair — remains musically unchanged, being built on the inversion of the series. Stravinsky's handling of English prosody throughout the 'Song' is a striking feature, especially his respect for tonic accents, as shown in the following beautiful phrase:

Ex. 101

Grave men, near death, who see with blinding sight Blind – ing of the light

In the 'Postlude' the strings are given the trombones' music, and vice-versa, with the transpositions and permutations of the serial forms dictated by a sense of harmony quite as much as counterpoint. The trombones arrive at the same cadence as the strings — C major with an added second (E and D simultaneously) — before they combine in the last four bars on an expansion of the same chord, which is given an extraordinary metallic timbre.

With *In memoriam Dylan Thomas* Stravinsky enters his final creative phase, which was devoted above all else to religious works. Serialism opened up for him an ordered, precise world where he could, in a new way, spread the search to which his whole life was devoted, a search that was both aesthetic and spiritual.

*

The year 1954 marked the beginning of a great period for Stravinsky. While *In memoriam* was still being rehearsed — Craft was to conduct the first performance on 20 September — the composer was already at work on a large commission from Lincoln Kirstein for Balanchine, a commission that he had been given long before Dylan Thomas's death. It was to be the third ballet in his 'second trilogy', with *Apollo* and *Orpheus*, but entirely different from both in language and conception, having in fact no 'subject', mythological or otherwise. *Agon* is the Greek for struggle or contest, and this was the title of the new ballet, decided on by Stravinsky in August 1954. He was already halfway through this when, in December of the same year, he accepted a commission from the Director of the Venice Biennale, Alessandro Piovesan, for a Passion according to Saint Mark. The work on *Agon* was not held up by this new commission but by a series of concert tours at the beginning of 1955, the United States in January and February and Switzerland and Germany in the spring. In the meantime he composed his *Greeting Prelude* for Pierre Monteux's eightieth birthday, a *musikalischer Spass* on 'Happy birthday to you!' for a large orchestra, though lasting less than a minute. Even for this small piece Stravinsky, who hated waste of any kind, made use of material planned for an earlier work. He twice changed his mind about Monteux, the 'godfather' of the *Sacre*, speaking of him in 1920 as a 'vain and petty person'. This was in a letter to Ansermet, who was also in due time to go out of favour. The war and exile in America brought Stravinsky and Monteux together again and Monteux, who was then chief conductor of the San Francisco Philharmonic, often invited Stravinsky to conduct. In 1960, several years after he had written the *Greeting Prelude*, Stravinsky was again, for some unknown reason, to refer very offensively to Monteux ('son-of-a-bitch, *c'est-à-dire* son of Monteux') in a conversation reported by Paul Horgan.[4] However that may be, *Greeting Prelude* was first performed by the Boston Symphony Orchestra under Charles Munch, on 4 April, 1955.

It was not until the beginning of the summer that Stravinsky really got down to work on what was to be not a 'Passion' but a musical panegyric, *Canticum Sacrum*, which he quickly completed in November of the same year.

XI

Urbi Venetiae

VENICE, THE CROSSROADS at which the Latin and Slav, the Catholic and the Byzantine worlds meet, was the city that Stravinsky loved above all others although he never lived there. It was a kind of fetish-town to him, the place where the paths of his travels over the world seemed to converge and where he kept returning from the days of Diaghilev to his own old age, the place where he was finally to be buried. It was also the scene of some of his great successes — the *Sonata* which he played with his 'miraculously' cured finger, in 1925; the performance of his *Capriccio* with his son Soulima in 1934; the triumph of *The Rake's Progress* in 1952. But Venice was to be, first and foremost, the scene of the magnificent occasions when the three greatest of his last religious works were performed: *Canticum Sacrum* in San Marco, *Threni* in the Scuola di San Rocco and *Requiem Canticles* in the basilica of San Giovanni e Paolo, on the day of his funeral.

At the beginning of 1955 Stravinsky studied the acoustic qualities of a number of great Venetian churches — the Frari and Santa Maria della Salute among them — but what really interested him was San Marco itself, where no orchestral music had been played for centuries. *Canticum Sacrum* was already completed on 10 August 1956, when the composer was received by the patriarch, Cardinal Roncalli — the future Pope John XXIII — who gave the necessary permission. But even before this, while he was still working on the new piece, he seems to have been confident of obtaining this permission, for the architecture of the basilica forms, as it were, part of the musical structure.

Canticum Sacrum is Stravinsky's personal act of homage to the city to which he was so devoted and to its glorious musical past. The bare, austere style that Stravinsky used for the majority of his religious works throughout his life is here, as it were, modified by the splendours of Renaissance music and takes on the Venetian reds and golds with which San Marco itself glows.

Canticum Sacrum ad honorem Sancti Marci Nominis — to give the work its full title — is for tenor and baritone solo, mixed chorus, orchestra (without horns, tubas, violins or violoncellos) and organ. The text is taken from the following passages of the Vulgate:

1. Gospel according to St Mark: XVI, 15.
2. Song of Songs: IV, 16; V, 1.
3. Deuteronomy: VI, 5.
   First Epistle of St John: IV, 7.
   Psalms: 124, 1; 130, 4, 5 and 6; 115, 10.
4. Gospel according to St Mark: IX, 22–23.
5. Gospel according to St Mark: VII, 20.

The work opens with a *dedicatio* sung by the tenor and the baritone accompanied by three trombones — 'Urbi Venetiae, in laude Sancti sui Presidis, Beati Marci Apostoli'. This page is archaic in character, modal and linear, and the predominating fourths and fifths in the harmony seem, as in the earliest days of music, to result from the very narrow-spanned polyphony of the voices and instruments. After passing through this narrow entrance-porch we find ourselves, as it were, in a five-chambered building.

Most discussions of *Canticum Sacrum* attach great importance to the 'Greek cross' symmetry of these five movements, which by analogy, they relate to the five domes of the basilica, no doubt correctly. In any case these were symmetries which favoured Stravinsky's designs, including also the exact 'miror' symmetry at each extreme. Despite the fact that some parts of the work are serial and others are not, this is in fact one of the most unified of his compositions.

The serial movements are the second, the third and the fourth. The middle movement, which is also the most developed, is itself divided into three parts. Although the first and fifth movements are not serial, they obey a fundamental serial principle, the last being the exact retrograde of the first, note by note and rhythm by rhythm.

Ex. 102

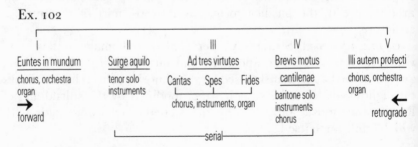

The meaning and symbolism of the Vulgate texts coincide with though they do not, as I see it, dictate this plan: it is a case of a structural accord existing between what is 'signifying' and what is 'signified', rather than of an attempt to subordinate form to 'content'. The first piece, 'Euntes in mundum praedicare', is Christ's exhortation to his disciples to 'go into all the world and preach the gospel', and the last (its exact retrograde) marks its fulfilment ('Illi autem profecti praedicaverunt ubique'). The central pieces, which are concerned with the three theological virtues, employ the strictest polyphonic forms within a serial framework — four-part canonic *ricercari* and various canons. These pieces are flanked on either side by more 'lyrical' texts — a love-song from the 'Song of Songs' and a *scena*, for baritone solo and chorus, relating the miracle of the curing of the deaf-mute.

The vertical writing in the 'mirror' pieces, 'Euntes in mundum' and 'Illi autem profecti', achieves both strength (by its solid harmonic foundations) and lightness (by the transparency of the brass-writing) which supports the chorus without overwhelming them. The harmony is very characteristic of Stravinsky, lay-out and instrumentation recalling the Renaissance masters, and in particular the Gabrielis (Andrea, in fact, rather than Giovanni) to whom he thus pays homage on the very spot where they established their claim to fame. The low B flat on which the whole construction rests is anchored deeply by the bassoons, the double bassoon and the double basses. On this foundation the brass divide into two harmonic layers — one in B flat major (without the fifth) in the trombones and the other in B minor. Harmonically speaking, this can be read in a number of different ways — for instance, the chord of B flat major can be understood as a chord of G minor without its fundamental, though it is rather difficult to hear a tonality where there is no tonic. The effect is not so much that of two minor tonalities as of a simultaneous major and minor, the B flat being in any case strongly emphasized. This is surely another case in which it is a mistake to interpret separately the elements of what is in fact a single phenomenon, a *block*.

Not that this block remains static. It is alive in the repeated notes of the brass: heavy in construction, it is light in its traversing of time, it throbs and creates a vibrating space. It is twice broken off by the distant sonority of the organ, which comes from a higher level and is supported by the orchestral basses, in a short *ritornello* every polyphonic layer of which employs its own modal fragment each of a different length. The top and bottom parts have shifted minims, the 'tenor' moves in dotted minims and the 'alto' proceeds by free irregular groupings. The three choruses, separated by two organ interludes (a single symmetrical sequence), reappear in exact retrograde at the end of the work, as

explained above. A few felicitous shifts and rhythmic modifications
prevent the mirror-process from becoming too rigidly mechanical and
establish it as a jubilant response to the exhortation of the opening.

The second movement, 'Surge Aquilo' (Rise, north wind) is a hymn
to profane love, serial in language, within the precincts of the basilica!
In contrast to the powerful mass of voices used in the first movement,
the tenor soloist is accompanied here by flute, cor anglais and harp,
sparingly assisted by a few chords in harmonics in three double-basses.
In his excellent analysis of the work Craft describes this piece as 'a
stylised lyrical hymn, which from the musical point of view is equally
stylised in its classical formalism and its use of both vocal and
instrumental virtuosity'.[1]

Stravinsky's series is deployed horizontally, primarily in the melodic
line but also controlling the harmony. This is very clear in the vertical
re-grouping of the twelve notes in three chords:

Ex. 103

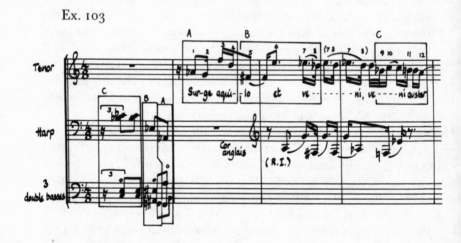

After this vertical statement of the series by the instruments in three
permuted segments C-B-A, the tenor sings the original, horizontal form
of the series (Ex. 103). It is followed by its retrograde, first fragmentary
and then complete, while the flute is given the complete retrograde
transposed a minor third up. . . . It would be tedious here to describe in
detail the various serial procedures, with their innumerable ingen-
uities, mirror-versions and rhythmic configurations. But it is worth
pointing out the deliberate repetitions of certain fragments (starting
with the initial 'Veni'). This creates centres of attraction and fugitive
polarizations quite alien to the spirit of Viennese 'dodecaphony', the

aim of which is to eliminate such poles (although even Schoenberg and Berg sometimes cheat and craftily 'bend' the rules). Some writers have discovered 'tonal tendencies' in the actual structure of Stravinsky's series, but these seem to be no more than apparent, and are easily explained by the persistence of traditional methods of analysis. The listener, on the other hand, is very aware of these repeated oscillations, which are not so much tonal as *polar*.

The central part of the work, 'Ad Tres Virtutes Hortationes', is symbolical. It is devoted, as mentioned above, to the three theological virtues. For structural reasons, they appear in inverse order: Charity (Love), Hope, Faith. But the striking feature, apart from the symmetry of the overall form and its exponents (see Ex. 102), is the dissymmetry in the detail, which causes the attentive listener repeated surprises.

'Caritas' opens with a *ritornello* for organ solo, analogous in character and tempo to earlier examples, but here both serial and homophonic. It states the retrograde inversion of a new series, close to the first series but different:

Ex. 104

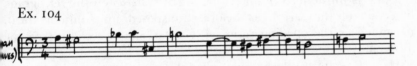

The instrumental section that follows is led by the cor anglais and is full of diatonic oscillations. The whole of Stravinsky can be found in the

Ex. 105

strange and fascinating contradiction between this diatonicism and the implacable rigour of the serial writing. A quadruple canon between the tenor, the bass trumpet, the altos and the sopranos; in which the original is transposed, respectively, up a major third, down a minor third, its inversion down a fourth and the original an augmented fourth, is to be found here. (Ex. 105)

This polyphonic web, which seems to belong to another age, is twice interrupted by a simple, marvellous 'cadence'. All Stravinsky needs to create surprise and to suspend time's flow is a single moment and two rising notes in the voice-part:

Ex. 106

'Spes' is introduced by the ritual organ *ritornello* on the retrograde inversion of the series, as before, transposed up a minor third, inasmuch as the opening series of 'Caritas' may be considered the 'original'.

Here the soloists alternate antiphonally with the women's voices of the chorus. The two-part polyphony — *punctum contra punctum* — is only occasionally punctuated by the instruments. The passage recalls certain primitive polyphonies in the Byzantine rite, the soloists playing a part analogous to that of the deacons. The whole piece is dominated by the retrograde and the inverted retrograde of the series.

'Fides' is the most impressive of these central pieces, if only for the vocal writing. It starts with the serial *ritornello* in the organ (transposed up a tone) firmly rooted in the bottom register. First we hear the chorus's 'credidi', a semitone oscillation, repeated five times with changing rhythmic and prosodic grouping (4+2, 2+2, 10+2 etc):

Ex. 107

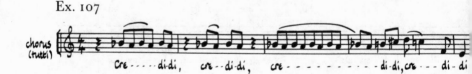

An exchange between the four trumpets and a choral response ('credidi') in turn sets in motion a serial development (retrograde of the

inversion) starting with the two notes of Ex. 107, and the piece
culminates in a big polyphonic passage, with the first trumpet and the
bass and double-bass trombones providing a kind of barbarous, highly
effective counterpoint. Stravinsky had prudently allowed the violas to
double the four choral parts *ad libitum*, though Craft observed that in
Venice advantage was not taken of this doubling, and this improved
both the balance and the harmonic clarity. The piece continues with a
three-part canon between the organ and two trumpets on the semitonal
oscillation of 'credidi' and its serial issue (still the inversion of the
retrograde). The piece ends with the same series again as *ritornello*,
though not this time in the organ (which has taken part in the last
canon) but in the violas and double-basses.

The fourth part, 'Brevis Motus Cantilenae' opens with a vigorous
attack in the violas, introducing the baritone's dramatic narrative
'Jesus autem ait illi', which the chorus echoes *pianissimo*. This is a
striking effect, and the more so because the musical 'echo' is reinforced
by the acoustics of the basilica. The Gabrielis had made use of this
effect, and Stravinsky was only following the masters of the Venetian
School in writing 'for' St Mark's.

The unaccompanied canonic chorus that follows makes use of all the
four serial forms: original in the tenor, retrograde and inversion in the
altos and basses, inversion of the retrograde in the sopranos. The
forward impetus suddenly slows down, leaving the baritone solo to
utter a final supplication which culminates in the glacial cry 'Credo,
Domine, adjuva incredulitatem meam', punctuated by pizzicato
strings. Here one-crotchet rests alternate with two-crotchet, followed
systematically by three- and five-quaver rests:

Ex. 108

The fifth part opens with the last chord of the first part, of which it is
the retrograde; and it ends *pianissimo* with a marvellous 'Amen' and the
closing/opening double chord of B flat – B minor in the brass, as final
and unemotional as the falling of a knife.

The first performance of *Canticum Sacrum* was conducted in St Mark's
by the composer on 13 September 1956 and was a milestone in the
public musical life of our time. The present author was fortunate

enough to attend both the performance and the rehearsals, which were conducted swiftly and efficiently by this youthful seventy-five year old wearing a towel round his neck like a tennis-player. It was the first occasion on which Stravinsky was called upon to conduct a major *serial* work in Europe before a very large audience. Moreover Cardinal Roncalli had ordered loudspeakers to be put up in the Piazza so that, on this golden September evening, the performance was heard not only by the three thousand who had the privilege of being actually inside the building but by the Venetians themselves and the tourists. One had never seen St Mark's looking like this before: its sombre gold mosaics were lit up by the little flames of thousands of votive lamps arranged along the cornices. In the audience were professional musicians, personal friends from all over the world, admirers, followers, or simply 'socialites'. When the tenor soloist, Gérard Souzay, embarked on the 'Surge Aquilo', with its garlands of small poisonous flowers in the harp and the double-basses, a shudder passed through the crowd. The ruthless serial counterpoint and the battering of the deep brass and the *tromba bassa* did the rest, paralysing the audience with something very like fear. There was no doubt about the 'scandal', but this time it was a *silent* scandal, muzzled by the ban on any kind of demonstration in a sacred building. But what a feast for the spirit! Stravinsky at seventy-five, younger than ever, foxing his adorers with the same provocation as in 1913. And indeed was this audience any different from that of the first night of the *Sacre*? an audience of regulars, used to a style and a personality that they thought inseparable from a never-to-change Stravinsky. As in 1913, Stravinsky simply produced something different — different from what was expected of him. Was this a genuine revolution or simply a 'scandal', a flash in the pan? *Canticum Sacrum*, like the *Sacre*, soon made its way in the world. It was not long after the first performance that Craft was conducting the work at the Concerts du Domaine Musical in Paris and Stravinsky himself in Rome, at the end of November — and in both cases it was a triumph.

In Piazza San Marco, on the other hand — which for once lived up to its description as 'le plus beau salon du monde' — the crowd was openly hostile and there were cries of 'Profanazione!' — sacrilege. There was no longer that feeling for the avant-garde which the Venetian public had had when Monteverdi supervised the music at St Mark's — *Time* magazine even spoke of 'Murder in the Cathedral', though no one seems to have been worried by this headline except T. S. Eliot himself, who was horrified to think that this title might have been used to wound his friend.

Meanwhile, indifferent to this 'sound and fury', Stravinsky went on quietly composing in Venice, busy with the commission that had been interrupted by *Canticum Sacrum*. Every morning since the summer he had shut himself up in the night-club of his hotel, the Bauer-Grünwald, where at the *pink* piano and in an atmosphere of stale cigar-smoke, he sat composing *Agon*.

Canticum Sacrum had — *et nunc erudimini!* — two performances on that evening of 13 September 1956. And between the two there was another Stravinsky *première*, his *Canonic Variations on the Chorale 'Vom Himmel Hoch'*, recomposed after Bach (a highly speculative polyphonic work which J. S. Bach composed for his entry, in 1747, into the 'Sozietät der Musikalischen Wissenschaften', of which Handel and Telemann were already members). Did Stravinsky find the company flattering? He wanted in any case to complete the Venice programme with something that was neither an earlier work of his own — which would not have gone well with the first performance of *Canticum Sacrum* — nor a baroque work from the repertory. These variations were in fact written specially for the occasion. Like a good professional, he wrote them for the same forces as those of *Canticum Sacrum* — the brass (three trumpets and three trombones instead of the four of *Canticum Sacrum*) playing the major role, with woodwinds and harp for the most delicate contrapuntal passages.

As in *Pulcinella*, the original text is here 'redistributed' to form a real re-composition of the whole, something much more than a simple 'instrumentation'. The result is, in fact, another masterpiece, a miracle of delicacy, economy and ingenious contrasts, with characteristically Stravinskian re-lighting and re-arranging of the polyphonic texture — all inspired by one of Bach's most complex organ-works. Stravinsky signed his manuscript with the words: *Mit Genehmigung des Meisters* (as authorized by the Master).

The chorale itself — the Christmas carol 'Vom Himmel hoch da komm' ich her' — does not occur in Bach's organ-text, but Stravinsky places it at the top of his *Canonic Variations*, giving it the important place that it occupies in the *Christmas Oratorio*. Another important modification is the introduction of unison choruses for the theme of the chorale from the second to the fifth variation, which is in two polyphonic parts. A further modification is no less radical: whereas all Bach's variations are in C major, Stravinsky recomposes his according to a logical tonal plan, from tonic to dominant and, unable to resist the temptation to break the symmetry, he includes a D flat major (no. 3) forming the 'odd man out' among the variations.

It is impossible to recommend too strongly a study of this magnificent score and a comparison with the original in, for instance, Walcha's knife-sharp recording, in which the phrasing and the highlighting of the different timbres are not unlike Stravinsky in spirit. The *Canonic Variations* had an *avant première* at the Ojai Festival in California, under Robert Craft.

*

After Venice Stravinsky toured, first Switzerland and then Germany. On 2 October in Berlin, just at the end of the first movement of the *Symphony in C*, he felt a blinding pain and became unconscious for a few moments. According to the orchestral players it seems he was somehow able to complete the movement, after a short interruption, but he partially lost the ability to speak and was unable to write his own name. He nevertheless refused to see a doctor and next day received Hermann Scherchen, 'with whom he drank *Sekt* and ate goose liver and apple strudel',[2] before flying to Munich. There, however, faced by the continuing difficulty of co-ordinating his movements and the relative immobility of his left side, he eventually agreed to enter hospital, leaving Craft to conduct the remainder of the tour. He was back at the end of November, however, to conduct *Canticum Sacrum* in Rome. The relatively slight attack in Berlin was followed by a thrombo-phlebitis in January 1957, leaving him with some difficulty in moving his left leg. Henceforward Stravinsky was to be permanently under medical supervision, obliged to undergo periodical examinations and treatments, particularly with anti-coagulants. But he still continued to compose and to conduct, to drink whisky and to smoke as before.

This was the background against which he completed *Agon*, a ballet for twelve dancers, commissioned by Lincoln Kirstein for the New York City Ballet. Craft conducted the first concert-performance on 17 June 1957 (Stravinsky's seventy-fifth birthday) at Los Angeles, and also the stage performance in New York on 1 December. Balanchine's choreography of the piece is unquestionably the most beautiful ever created by this 'prince of the dance'. In the programme of that memorable evening Balanchine wrote that the work was 'planned by Stravinsky and myself for twelve of our most highly qualified technicians. It has no plot but the dance itself; it is not so much a combat or a competition (the two possible meanings of the Greek word ἀγών) as a construction measured out in space, brought to life by bodies moving in accordance with certain schemes or sequences of rhythms and melodies.'

The order of the work is as follows:

I. 1. Pas de quatre (4 men)
    2. Double pas de quatre (8 women)
    3. Triple pas de quatre (4 men, 8 women)

    Prelude

    [First Pas de trois (1 man, 2 women)]
II. 1. Sarabande (1 man)
    2. Gaillarde (1 man)
    3. Coda (1 man, 2 women)

    Interlude

III. [Second Pas de trois (2 men, 1 woman)]
    1. Bransle simple (2 men)
    2. Bransle gay (1 woman)
    3. Bransle du Poitou (2 men, 1 woman)

    Interlude

IV. Pas de deux (1 man, 1 woman)
    Four Duos (4 men, 4 women)
    Four Trios (4 men, 8 women)

As the dance-titles show, *Agon* is based on French seventeenth-century *ballets de cour*. While engaged on the composition Stravinsky cast an expert eye through the pages of Lauze's *Apologie de la Danse* (1623). But the different numbers of *Agon* 'evoke court dances as much as a Cubist picture evokes a pipe or a guitar':[3] they are no more than structural frames 'as yet unfilled' with music, and in exactly the same way a breath of *grand siècle* classicism can be felt in the delightful modal cadences of the 'Interludes'.

The composition-dates of the various parts of *Agon* are certainly important. The opening fanfare dates from 1953, and the first half of the work — ending at the Coda following the 'Gaillarde' — from the first half of 1954. Stravinsky went back to the work in Hollywood in 1956, after *Canticum Sacrum*, continued working on it in Venice (in the night-club of the Bauer-Grünwald) during the summer of 1956 and finished it in the USA in 1957. The two-year break right in the middle of the work coincided with an important development in the direction of serialism in the composer's musical language, crystallized by *Canticum Sacrum*. There is certainly a whole world of difference between the various series in the *Cantata* (or *In Memoriam*), with which the first half of *Agon* belongs, and the radical twelve-tone series of the second half. But as we shall see, Stravinsky took care to erase these differences in the writing, so that the minimum conditions of formal unity ensure that the overall *structure* welds the different parts of the work into a convincing whole, tones down their discrepancies and highlights their organic relationships.

Henri Pousseur's extremely detailed analysis of the harmonic aspects (horizontal and vertical) of *Agon* is as thorough as Boulez's analysis of the rhythms of the *Sacre*. The characteristic that these two analyses have in common is their 'engagement' in a contemporary problem, the fact (already mentioned) that each was dictated and *dated* by the questions that were puzzling each of these composers in their own writing. It is significant that Stravinsky's should have been the chosen field for these sound reflections, with two major works of his separated by forty years. Quite apart from its immediate object, Pousseur's study reveals the potential discoveries that exist in *all* Stravinsky's music both now and in the future. The author quotes chapter and verse to disprove the generally accepted, much repeated idea of the 'weakness' of Stravinsky's late works. The specialist reader should study Pousseur's text in its entirety.[4] All that we can do is to emphasize the importance of a number of *constants* that Pousseur establishes between Stravinsky and Webern on the one hand and between the serial and strictly speaking non-serial parts of *Agon* on the other.

For instance, Pousseur points to the astonishing similarity between Stravinsky's serial writing and Webern's in the 'Pas de deux', a similarity that even includes the material itself (Webern's series). Once this has been made clear, Pousseur analyses a passage from the first period of the work's composition — the Fanfare (a) with which *Agon* begins and ends and compares it with one of Webern's most celebrated series, that of op. 30 (b), to try to extract a formative principle common to both composers at the interval level (we are dealing here with one of the fundamental cells of the whole work). (Ex. 109)

Pousseur is able to demonstrate not only Stravinsky's relationship to chromaticism but also Webern's relationship to diatonicism, by rigorously examining this central formative cell in particular (b, c — a'): 'It is indeed the matter of a perfect major-minor chord, a figure very much favoured by Webern in his last works.' Pousseur's investigation is supported by numerous examples and his conclusion is important for composers today: 'It is clear that Webern wanted once again to have the use of harmonic *characterizers* and *differentiators* which *on a larger scale* he had lacked for too long, even if very early on his employment of all non-heavy consonant intervals (thirds, fourths,

Ex. 109

sixths) revealed a concern with counter-balance and — at a lower level — with attenuation of excessive chromatic neutralisations.' All Stravinsky's work that can in any sense be called tonal certainly shows him manipulating these 'harmonic differentiators' so totally absent from post-Webernian music; but they take on a more modern meaning in his *serial* works, because there they can be seen fulfilling their function *within the chromatic total.* One could say that at the time of writing *Agon*, Stravinsky was the only composer to make use of them.

Although *Agon* contains a number of series, they all function on the same principle of the permutation of diatonic and chromatic intervals, which allows the composer to adapt them to the maximum number of structural contexts and at the same time to impose a unity on them. The series in the intermediate Coda (the point at which the composer gave up working on *Agon* and started *Canticum Sacrum*) is a very Webernian 'permutation' of the notes of the chromatic scale, and it is used both horizontally and vertically in all the traditional forms (retrograde, inverted retrograde etc.).

In the second 'Pas de trois' the series is more diatonic in character: the 'Bransle simple' and the 'Bransle double' (or 'du Poitou') is based on a six-note series (a), which is supplemented in the second dance by a further series (a') to complete the chromatic scale. The central part, the 'Bransle gay', is also called 'Variation for the castanets', which provide a regular rhythmic pedal independent of the shifting rhythm, with which it does not synchronize. This is based on a series of displaced or 'reverted' notes (b) close to the previous series (Ex. 110):

Ex. 110

We have already mentioned the series of the 'Pas de deux', which is serially one of the most elaborate numbers and, as Pousseur says, very Webernian in character. It offers many possibilities for combinations, 'broadening' its chromatic intervals in the masculine Variation (bars 463 sqq.) and remaining long undecided around its two first notes. The chromatic serial form of the feminine Variation returns to something more like the 'Pas de deux'. This is the canonic development, by augmentation, for three flutes (the string accompaniment providing the notes needed to complete the chromatic total):

Ex. 111

The opening and closing 'Fanfare' on the one hand and the 'Prelude' and two 'Interludes' on the other make use of textual repetition as simple but effective 'markers' to assist the listener's memory and also as unifying factors.

'*Agon* is an astonishing work coming from a man of seventy-five', as Craft says in the very clear analysis that he, too, has made of the work. And he concludes: 'When one compares this score and *Orpheus* (written ten years earlier), *Agon* really seems to be the work of a young composer.'

*

In 1957 Stravinsky celebrated his seventy-fifth birthday and the occasion was marked by a number of celebratory concerts, notably one in Lon-

Angeles with *Agon* and *Canticum Sacrum* and Aldous Huxley reading an 'address' to the composer, and a performance of *The Rake's Progress* at the Santa Fé opera-house, a bold new venture created and directed by John Crosby. In the same year Stravinsky was elected a Fellow of the American Academy of Arts and Letters; and he paid a visit to Darting-ton, where William Glock's summer school continued the inspired work that he was doing for contemporary music at the BBC. In October Stravinsky visited first Venice and then Paris, where he conducted *Agon* at the Concerts du Domaine Musical, sat for Giacometti, saw Boulez and Souvtchinsky whom he had met again in 1956 after almost twenty years. He was then the guest of Prince Fürstenberg at Donaueschingen, where he conducted *Agon* at the annual festival of contemporary music.

The major event of the year 1957 was the composition of *Threni*, which Stravinsky began at the end of August in Venice, in the same night-club of the Bauer-Grünwald where he had written parts of *Agon*. He worked disconnectedly on the new composition, but he was in a hurry to complete it, which he did in the following March (1958). In Venice again, he conducted its first performance on 23 September that year in the Scuola di San Rocco, beneath Tintoretto's ceilings. *Threni* had been commissioned by Rolf Liebermann, who was at that time Director of Norddeutsche Rundfunk in Hamburg, and in his memoirs he gives an account of the rather strange negotiations involved:

I offered him 10,000 dollars which he made no difficulty about accepting. But at seven o'clock the next morning I was awoken by a telephone call from our mutual friend Nicolas Nabokov. 'Look', he said, 'Igor has not slept a wink: he wants another thousand dollars and daren't ask you.' It would have been silly to miss a new work by Stravinsky for want of a sum that our rich Hamburg patrons could collect in a few minutes and during the course of the morning the additional thousand dollars was found. Igor was so delighted that he invited us to the best restaurant in the town and ordered cases of champagne and mountains of caviar. This accounted for the thousand dollars, but he had obtained satisfaction.

The result of this haggling and this Russian-style banquet was the most austere, the most noble and the most imposing of all the composer's religious works.

The text of *Threni, id est lamentationes Jeremiae prophetae* is taken from the Lamentations of Jeremiah which form the Tenebrae lessons of Holy Week written, according to tradition, by the prophet's own hand. They are a song of grief for the City and the Temple of Jerusalem, destroyed by the Babylonians. 'Plorans ploravit in nocte et lacrimae ejus in maxillis ejus': the weeping City is to be understood as an allegory of a mourning, grieving humanity.

Among the Lamentations (which he calls 'elegies') Stravinsky selected fragments of the first, the third and the fifth (the Prayer of Jeremiah). The plan of the work resembles that of *Canticum Sacrum*, being both symmetrical and uneven, and the central 'Elegy' is itself tripartite. The Hebrew letters *aleph, beth, he, caph* etc., are incorporated in the musical setting, in the traditional manner, figuring like initial capitals at the beginning of each verse of Elegies 1 and 3.

Ex. 112

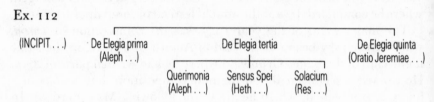

The forces employed in *Threni* are larger than those used by Stravinsky in any other religious work: six soloists (soprano, contralto, two tenors, bass, *basso profondo*), mixed choirs and full orchestra (in which a sarrusophone replaces the bassoons and a bugle the trumpets). But Stravinsky uses his instruments either in small groups or else as soloists, as so many voices in a lucid polyphony or as infinitely multi- coloured accompaniment to the voices, which dominate the whole work.

Threni, says André Souris, 'is not only Stravinsky's first completely serial work, but one of the peaks of his religious output. Monumental in size, tragic in character and hieratic in form, it is a witness to the profound faith of the composer and also to the powerful renaissance of his genius.'

Unlike his earlier 'progressively serial' works, *Threni* has a single twelve-tone series, the basic forms of which are given below:

Ex. 113

The 'Introduction', which is proclaimed in the manner of the deacons in the Byzantine rite, is based on the original form of the series and its inversion, as seen in Ex. 114. If the non-specialist reader plays this on the piano, he will immediately be aware of the horizontal, archaic character of the serial process:

Ex. 114

As André Souris observes: 'There is in fact only one series, but there is nothing systematic about its melodic treatment and the intervals are all given the same expressive (or symbolical) significance that they have had since the Renaissance.' The semitonal melismatic oscillations in the voices, like those in *Canticum Sacrum*, belong to the same tradition.

The first Elegy begins with the word 'Aleph' heard in one choral entry after another, and it has a doubly alternating symbolical plan.

The rhythmic sequences spoken by the chorus were something new in Stravinsky, except for four isolated instances in *Les Noces*, and their unchanging *sotto voce* recalls the 'Credo' of the *Mass* where the pitch is given exactly, but the intention is identical. The same words are constantly repeated by the women's chorus, where they are sung, and are accompanied by the strings; the tenor solo and the bugle engage in an archaic-sounding contrapuntal duet. On the letter 'Beth' the chorus assumes a role which is no longer inaugural but conclusive; this is followed by an intermezzo which Stravinsky called 'Diphona', which serves as a 'refrain' and is performed by two unaccompanied tenor soloists. The letter 'He' opens a second part, analogous to the first in both material and form — spoken chorus, women's choir, tenor solo with bugle, and 'Diphona II' for the two tenors, on this occasion based on a transposition (down a semitone) of the retrograde of the series, and with new rhythms. A third choral sequence follows without a break and ends with the tenor and the bugle. For the 'Diphona' the composer uses the four forms of the series in a free, unbarred polyphony, since the bar-line would in this case diminish the astonishing rhythmic autonomy of the participants.

In the first part of the third 'Elegy' — 'Querimonia' — the Hebrew letters are used vertically (harmonically), either framing or punctuating the sequences of the four male soloists. The architecture of the piece follows a polyphonic progression from monody to two-, three- and finally four-part canons between the solo voices. Again there are no bar-lines, this being an essentially horizontal structure going back to mediaeval models.

The second part of this third Elegy, 'Sensus Spei', is the most elaborate, and it forms the heart of the work. Stravinsky uses differing and alternating groupings of the solo voices, the chorus and the orchestra in magnificent polyphonic sequences. Here the Hebrew letters are treated as blocks, real 'sound-objects', the attack, the consistency and the resonance of each carefully studied. The animated tempo, the rapid scansion of the text and the bursts of chord-letters breaking up the syllabic murmur in the background all recall *Les Noces*, often to a startling degree. Each of these two works seems to throw light on the other, 'Sensus Spei' revealing the liturgical character of *Les Noces* and *Les Noces* revealing 'Sensus Spei' as a savagely austere hymn of hope and joy. The 'coincidences' — but are they coincidences? — go as far as almost exact reminiscence, even in the vocal writing between falsetto and *basso profondo* — the chorus's ascending sixth on the Hebrew letter Lamed with piano and drums murmuring. (Ex. 115)

After the block constructions, after the soloists' syllabic chant and the choral heterophonies, the strongly contrasted and powerfully rhythmic writing of 'Sensus Spei', the next piece, 'Solacium', forms a complete contrast. Here we have the lament of the women of the City, soprano and contralto soloists answered by the two male soloists and then by an astonishing eight-part polyphonic chorus. The system of serial derivations that Stravinsky uses here is close to — if not actually inspired by — that used by Berg in *Lulu*. Stravinsky takes the odd-number notes of the retrograde of the inversion of the original series in mounting order and follows them with the even-numbered notes in falling order — 1, 3, 5, 7, 9, 11, 12, 10, 8, 6, 4, 2 (transposed an

Ex. 115

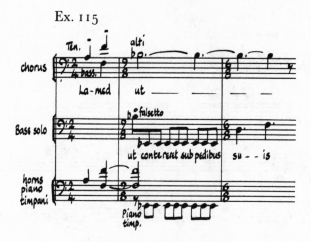

augmented fourth). Another series is derived by triple subtractions in three four-note segments: 12, 9, 6, 3/ 11, 8, 5, 2/ 10, 7, 4, 1 — giving the following series (to be compared with the original):

Ex. 116

The last words of the Prayer of Jeremiah might serve as a motto for Stravinsky's whole artistic career: 'Innova dies nostros sicut a principio'. First separately and then together, the choirs and the soloists, supported by the four horns, raise their voices to give the work its crowning glory. By dividing the four serial forms and their transpositions between the voices and the brass Stravinsky reaches the configuration shown in Ex. 117.

Most commentators have drawn attention to the tonal look of this passage, and not without reason. It is surely, however, something quite different from a 'tonal polarization of the twelve-note series', as described by Roman Vlad in his *Strawinsky* (pp. 215–17), but rather a singularly apt use of what Pousseur, in speaking of Webern, calls 'harmonic differentiators', such as we have already observed in *Agon*. In this instance, in fact, these 'simple frequency relations' — which Stravinsky never ceased to use — assume, in the context of the complex frequency relations of serial writing, an articulating function *against* a possible chromatic entropy.

Ex. 117

The Venice performance of *Threni* was followed by others in New York, in Switzerland, Germany and France, all conducted by the composer. The Paris performance in the Salle Pleyel was one of the Concerts du Domaine Musical, which makes it all the more surprising that the music was insufficiently rehearsed. Stravinsky not only refused to return to the platform to take his bow at the end of the work but swore that he would never conduct in Paris again. Even so this performance provoked an extremely penetrating and admiring criticism by the writer Michel Butor (published two years later in *Arts*) and a passionate statement of adhesion to the 'new' Stravinsky on the part of Boris de Schloezer, who wrote a letter of gratitude to the composer and received a signed photograph in return. In an interview published in the *Nouvelle Revue Française* in 1959 Boris de Schloezer declared to the present writer — 'For me this is one of the few great modern religious works. Its extreme severity in no way limits it, on the contrary, its asceticism is one of the reasons of its expressive power. There is no compromise with the outside world, no compromise with pleasing the listener: the music could be performed at the actual office of Tenebrae, and its proper setting is a Romanesque cathedral — not because there is anything affectedly 'archaic' about it, but because its contemporary language is a means of regaining the purity and severity of Romanesque architecture.'

*

Even before he had finished work on *Threni* Stravinsky received another commission through Nicolas Nabokov, and immediately accepted it. This was for a work for piano and orchestra and was the future

Movements. The fee offered for this by the Swiss pianist Margrit Weber was 15,000 dollars to be paid, according to Vera Stravinsky and Robert Craft, directly into the numbered bank-account of the composer or his wife, at Basle.

Having in this way avoided, for once, the American tax authorities, Stravinsky observed his contract most scrupulously, even offering to return his advance should the pianist find his writing too disconcerting. . . . She, however, was unabashed, met Stravinsky, corrected the score with him and then worked on it with him for several days in Venice. They gave the first performance together in the Town Hall, New York, on 10 January 1960 at a concert organized by Stravinsky himself, of which we shall be saying more later.

Movements is certainly Stravinsky's most elaborate serial work, and he was extremely proud of it:

> *Movements* are the most advanced music from the point of view of construction of anything I have composed. No theorist could determine the spelling of the note order in, for example, the flute solo near the beginning. . . . (*Memories and Commentaries*)

In fact they can. In *Movements* the series is treated essentially in segments of 6, 4, 3 notes, both vertically and horizontally; and it employs a limited number of transpositions, odd-numbered as far as the original form is concerned (3, 5, 7, 9, 11), particularly in the famous flute passage quoted by Stravinsky (see E. W. White, *Stravinsky* p. 506):

Ex. 118

The overlapping of these segments arising both from the original and its inversion, lends partial credibility to the composer's slightly puerile challenge. The interest of the work lies, of course, in the speculative rigour of the music and not in the difficulty that it presents to the analyst —and that only in so far as this rigour is perceptible to the ear. In fact the listener has the impression of 'hearing' the glitter of the different facets of a crystal of sound, and Stravinsky himself employed this crystal-imagery to convey the radiation of the serial structure in all directions.

Movements is equally elegant from the rhythmic point of view, something of which Stravinsky was equally proud. 'I should say, too, that its rhythmic language is also the most advanced I have so far employed; perhaps some listeners might even detect a hint of serialism in it too,' and, later, 'each section of the piece is confined to a certain range of instrumental timbre . . .'

The work is orchestrated for two flutes, oboe, cor anglais, clarinet, bass clarinet, bassoon, two trumpets, three trombones, harp, celesta and a small body of strings. It is essentially contrapuntal — perhaps Stravinsky's most elaborate contrapuntal work, in fact — and there are absolutely no *tutti*, except for the last four bars of the fourth part. The piano has not, properly speaking, a *concertante* role, but forms part of the orchestra, standing out by its timbre and its cleanness of attack rather than by any virtuoso display.

Each of the five parts of *Movements* belongs to a polyphonic type — canons, serial mirror-pieces etc. — combined with long held notes playing the role of 'axes'. The perpetually shifting instrumental configurations form a kind of ingenious structural *Klangfarbenmelodie*. Stravinsky originally planned to have purely orchestral 'interludes' between the parts, but in the final version these few intermediate bars in which the soloist is silent, are placed, unidentified by name, like final *clausulae* at the end of each piece. They are some of the most beautiful moments in the work.

Listeners accustomed to Stravinsky's earlier styles can hardly fail to find *Movements* a 'difficult' piece. But anyone who recalls Balanchine's choreography for his 1963 ballet — with Susan Farrell and Jacques d'Amboise flanked by an 'orchestra' of six long-legged girls — will have had no difficulties in understanding the music. This may indeed have been the single occasion on which dancing gave a completely faithful *visual* account of the web of lines, timbres and rhythms without at the same time surrendering its autonomy. It is certainly one of the great choreographer's masterpieces.

*

Epitaphium for flute, clarinet and harp was composed this same year (1959) after the death in April of Prince Max Egon zu Fürstenberg, owner of Schloss Donaueschingen and patron of the annual festival of contemporary music, whose guest Stravinsky had been in 1957 and 1958.[6]

According to the composer this piece, which only lasts one minute and sixteen seconds, started in his mind,

with a melodic-harmonic phrase. I certainly did not (and never do) begin with a purely serial idea and, in fact, when I began I did not know, or care, whether all twelve notes would be used. After I had written about half the first phrase, I saw its serial pattern and then perhaps I began to work towards that pattern. . . . There are four short antiphonal strophes for the harp, and four for the wind duet, and each strophe is a complete order of the series. (*Memories and Commentaries*)

This is the series:

Ex. 119

The first performance of *Epitaphium* was given on 17 October 1959 in one of three concerts in memory of Prince Max Egon at Donaueschingen.

Double-Canon, Raoul Dufy in memoriam for string quartet also belongs to the same year and is of almost exactly the same length (one minute and about fifteen seconds). Stravinsky and Dufy never met and Dufy's death was not the occasion of this piece, which was composed in Venice in September 1959 in answer to a private request for an autograph. The canons, first between the violins and then between viola and cello, are strict and employ the different forms of the following series:

Ex. 120

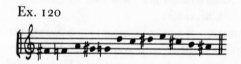

If the serialism of *Epitaphium* is fairly conventional, not to say academic, the same cannot be said of *Double-Canon*. What seems remarkable about this minute piece is its completely *timeless* character, which it shares with the *Shakespeare Songs*. This is due as much to the actual material as to its handling — a very symmetrical and 'consonant' series of overlapping thirds 1–3, 2–4, 7–8, 9–10, the central interval being a fifth, as shown in Ex. 120. Dateless, but timeless too in the sense that the piece can be endlessly repeated (it has to be played twice, in any case, without a break).

*

Stravinsky's interest in Carlo Gesualdo da Venosa (1561–1613), prince, murderer and inspired composer of vocal music, dates from the early 1950s. Having obtained photocopies of the *Sacrae Cantiones*, he decided to complete the missing sextus and bass parts of the last piece in the collection, 'Illumina nos', and have it performed in September 1956 in St Mark's with *Canticum Sacrum*. But the Venetians, who had once given Monteverdi a pauper's burial at the Frari because he was a *Cremonese*, absolutely refused to have this *Neapolitan* in their basilica. . . . The plan had to be waived; but it was nevertheless during this last stay in Venice, in September 1959, that Stravinsky returned to his work on Gesualdo, realizing (as he had done with the motet 'Illumina nos') the quintus, sextus and bass parts of the motets 'Assumpta est Maria' and 'Da pacem Domine'. According to Craft, the missing parts of the first piece were canons *in diapason e diapente* (at the octave and the fifth), those of the second *in diapente* only — and therefore, surely, 'understood' rather than 'missing', so that Stravinsky had only to compose the bass. In any case, as Craft observed in his preface to the work (which is dedicated to him): 'Stravinsky has not attempted a reconstruction. In fact, he seems to have avoided what in certain circumstances might appear to be the prescribed solution. What he has done is to re-compose everything from the viewpoint of what he has added. The result is not pure Gesualdo but a fusion of the two composers.' Much more radical is the composition for instruments (two clarinets, two bassoons, brass and strings) of three madrigals from Gesualdo's Books V and VI, 'Asciugate i begli occhi', 'Ma tu cagion di quella' and 'Beltà poi che t'assenti'. This *Monumentum pro Gesualdo*, as Stravinsky called it, was written in 1960 in California.

The transformation of a purely vocal into a purely instrumental piece could not fail to be radical, and was in fact totally Stravinskian with sharp, demi-staccato attacks, muted horns and 'unorthodox' instrumental layering etc. This magnificent 're-reading' of Gesualdo was given its first performance on 27 September 1960 in the Doge's Palace in Venice under the direction of the composer, who had to be hoisted up to the Sala Grande, on a sort of portable chair like some mediaeval instrument of torture, owing to the extreme steepness of the Scalone dei Giganti. This work was also choreographed by Balanchine for seven couples of dancers.

*

These years divided between composition and concert tours were, as we have seen, extraordinarily productive and intense. During 1959 Stravinsky visited Honolulu and Manila (March), Hong Kong and

Japan (April) where he visited Tokyo and Kyoto and saw the chief historical sites of the country; and he was in Italy during the autumn, returning to New York on the *Liberté* at the end of December. Early in January 1960 he planned with Craft three large concerts for his own benefit, one at Carnegie Hall and the other two at Town Hall, where *Movements* had its first performance. Despite Stravinsky's careful personal supervision of the box office (there were absolutely no invitations beyond those extended — grudgingly — to the critics), the financial result of the whole undertaking, which had been exhausting for everyone except apparently Stravinsky, was disastrous, though the success was enormous. His spirits damped by this financial setback, Stravinsky retired to Hollywood and began composing *A Sermon, a Narrative and a Prayer*, a cantata commissioned some time before by his friend Paul Sacher for the Basler Kammerorchester. The work was interrupted, however, by a major tour of Latin America, where Stravinsky found the enormous fees irresistible. Despite his cerebral attack at the beginning of the year, which resulted in a permanent though relatively mild disability on his left side, Stravinsky shared with Craft the conducting in Mexico, Peru, Chile and Argentina. The tour was hardly finished when he and his wife set out again for a two-month visit to Venice and the first performance of *Monumentum pro Gesualdo*. There was an *acqua alta* in Venice on 15 October 1960. With water nineteen inches deep in the salon of the Bauer-Grünwald hotel, Stravinsky had to be carried out in the arms of one of the porters — all of which gave him the title of his next work, *The Flood*. Before that, however, he returned to his cantata for Basle, the score of which was finished in Hollywood on 31 January 1961.

A Sermon, a Narrative and a Prayer is for alto and tenor soloists, narrator, chorus and orchestra and is dedicated to Paul Sacher. Though one of the most endearing of Stravinsky's 'last period' pieces, it is not often performed. Its theme is Faith, Hope and Charity and the text of the two first parts — 'Sermon' and 'Narrative' — are taken respectively from St Paul's Epistles and the Acts of the Apostles in the superb English of the Authorized Version. The final prayer comes from the seventeenth-century playwright Thomas Dekker:

We are saved by hope, but hope that is seen is not hope. . . . The substance of things hoped for, the evidence of things not seen, is Faith.

'Narrative', which is the centre and heart of the work, introduces the Narrator and the two soloists, while the chorus is silent. It relates, in

words taken from the Acts, the stoning of St Stephen who by faith and
hope achieved charity and prayed for his murderers. Narrator and
soloists alternate with each other and twice coincide exactly on the
name 'Stephen':

Ex. 121

'Narrative' is a perfect example of one musical conception of the
sacred. No hint of pathos, no trace of 'expressiveness' is permitted, only
a few hieratic conventions of grief, as changeless as those found in ikons.
Any note of the theatrical, any suggestion of romanticism or realism in
the handling of such a theme would constitute an outrage; and
Stravinsky is possibly the only twentieth-century composer capable of
mastering not only a text of this kind but, even more importantly, the
perilous musical form of a *scena* with narrative. . . .

Finally, the 'Prayer' is a polyphonic structure for soloists, chorus and
orchestra (with three tam-tams added), but the Narrator is silent. All
the serial forms are unfolded here to give the work a solemn climax.

In *A Sermon, a Narrative and a Prayer* Stravinsky attaches the greatest
importance to the *word*. Narrator, soloists and chorus take it in turns to
carry the 'word' through every stage of musical composition, from free
narration to rhythmic declamation, with and without fixed pitches, and
finally to song properly so called.

*

The Flood is a 'musical play' for tenor and two bass soloists, mixed
chorus (no basses) and large orchestra and includes some verbal
narrative. The text is taken from the mediaeval miracle-plays of
Chester and York and the book of Genesis, and was chosen and
prepared by Robert Craft. The work was commissioned by CBS
Television and had its first performance on the CBS network on 14 June
1962. It is a composite work in which music alternates with drama,
narrative and dance. Stravinsky makes a clear distinction between the
celestial and the human characters, the former singing and the latter
(the Narrator or Caller and Noah and his family) speaking. The
obvious problem was the voice of God. Stravinsky, it will be remem-

bered, thought it inconceivable to entrust this to a single singer in *Babel* and therefore used the chorus. Here he uses two bass soloists (hence the absence of basses in the chorus) — an example of the intellectual rigour with which he determined his 'programme', both conceptual and musical. The dance episodes — 'The Building of the Ark' and the actual Flood — were entrusted to Balanchine. 'Working Notes for *The Flood*', published by Robert Craft in *Dialogues and a Diary*, provides an account of Stravinsky's work-sessions with Balanchine, in which the veritable 'flood' of ideas reveals the two Russians' astonishing sense of theatre and the ease with which they adapted themselves to a new medium. According to Stravinsky, television 'visually offers every advantage over stage opera, but the saving of musical time interests me more than anything visual. This new musical economy was the one specific of the medium guiding my conception of *The Flood*. Because the succession of visualizations can be instantaneous, the composer may dispense with the afflatus of overtures, connecting episodes, curtain music. . .' (*Dialogues and a Diary*)

The plan of the work is as follows:

Prelude
  1. Introduction (orchestra)
  2. Te Deum (chorus)
  3. Melodrama (Narrator)
  4. The Word of God (two basses)
  5. Aria (Lucifer)
  6. Melodrama (Narrator)
  7. The Word of God (conclusion)
The Building of the Ark
  Dance
The Catalogue of the Animals
  Melodrama (Noah and the Caller)
The Comedy
  Melodrama (Noah with his wife and sons)
The Flood
  Dance
The Covenant of the Rainbow
  1. The Word of God (2 basses)
  2. Melodrama (Noah)
  3. Return of the instrumental introduction
  4. Aria (Lucifer)
  5. Sanctus (chorus)

The 'new musical economy specific to the medium' (all within the space of twenty-four minutes) was greatly favoured by the serial structure of the work, and particularly by the *athematic* character of the music which this implied (something, we must insist, characteristic of all Stravinsky's music since the *Sacre* and the small works composed before 1920, immediately distinguishing his music from that of the German tradition — theme and development — and forming one more, perhaps paradoxical, link with Webern).

The following is the serial chart of *The Flood*:

Ex. 122

The opening chord of the work is composed of all twelve notes of the chromatic scale arranged in layers of fifths, an interval not very frequently used in the work itself.

The most impressive number in the work is the Flood itself, a conception both instrumental and choreographic and constructed round a *sonority* emanating from two sources — a magnificent vertical serial configuration and the horizontal unfolding of the series in the flutes *flatterzunge* with the violins and some of the brass. Stravinsky uses devices of successive, sound by sound, serial addition and subtraction rather like the 'serial rotation' in Stockhausen's *Klavierstück IX*. This 'musical downpour' really is illustrative music, whatever Stravinsky may say, but how successful it is simply as sound! He was always on the look-out for 'unusual sounds' for his music and this is certainly a magnificent specimen.

The word 'specimen' in fact suggests the limitations of *The Flood*, a work which is perpetually interrupted by the melodramas (the least interesting parts), and — obviously — by the swift succession of different 'sound-frames' corresponding to the changes of visual frame, of which the listener is always vaguely aware. The purely instrumental numbers, 'The Building of the Ark' and 'The Flood', are the most successful pieces in the score.

The television production — which Stravinsky never saw — commissioned and financed jointly by CBS and a shampoo company

(Oh America . . .) surrounded by shots of the said product (accompanied by its own 'music') was pretty bizarre. Balanchine's choreography seemed out of place in this context and in the restricting framework of the small screen.

Rolf Liebermann's idea of staging the work at the Hamburg Opera with Gunther Rennert as producer and Peter Van Dyk as choreographer, proved not much more successful and the music suffered. Although the sets were eventually Theo Otto's, Liebermann's original idea had been to get Chagall to do both sets and costumes. Chagall agreed, but Nicolas Nabokov had difficulty in arranging the Paris meeting between the two men in late 1960, and although Chagall came specially from Reims and Liebermann from Hamburg, it was a failure. There was a lunch-party that day at the Boule d'Or, at which Stravinsky, Souvtchinsky, François Michel and Craft drank two bottles of vodka, three bottles of claret, and two bottles of Dom Pérignon, not to speak of the calvados. Stravinsky was expected at 5.30, but at 6.30 his wife telephoned to say that he was completely drunk and that it was impossible to wake him. 'I went to bed rather sad that night,' Liebermann wrote in his memoirs,

> but at 2 a.m. the telephone rang: Stravinsky had woken and was terribly thirsty. He wanted to have a drink with me. And there he was at his hotel, busying himself with two bottles of Dom Pérignon which were already on ice. I made a last effort to arrange things. 'Look, Igor, ring Chagall or send him a line. . . .' 'Quite out of the question,' he said, cutting me short, 'I don't want any sets by that *con*.'

*

Stravinsky's meeting with Ingmar Bergman was quite a different matter — the happiest of all his relationships with the theatre, according to the composer. Bergman in fact produced *The Rake's Progress* at the Royal Opera House in Stockholm and the composer attended the performance on 13 September 1961 before giving a concert of his own on the 24th. Craft's diary contains the following account:

> I have never seen I.S. so moved by a performance of a work of his — in fact, one seldom sees him not angry — and this in spite of large cuts and legions of places in which the direction is at loggerheads with the libretto. . . . Arias are sung to the audience, stage front, and so are actionless ensembles, such as the quartet and trio in the first scene. But Bergman makes singers move their arms and eyes as they have

never moved them before. . . . Contact is immediate, and as soon as he talks — fluent English — his hands become lively and expressive. . . . He says with passion that 'the artist has only to discover what to do and with all his strength purify the doing'. . . . When I.S. asks what initially attracted him to *The Rake*, Bergman says 'A bad performance'. (*Dialogues and a Diary*)

After Stockholm the trio — Stravinsky, his wife and Robert Craft — continued their perambulations via Berlin, Belgrade, Zürich and London and thence to Australia, and Tahiti. Egypt and New Zealand followed at the end of the year. In London Stravinsky saw his friend T. S. Eliot, as always, and during this meeting the poet, whose publisher had asked him for a new collection of English hymns, suggested that Stravinsky might set some lines of his. This was the origin of *Anthem* or *The Dove descending breaks the air* — an unaccompanied choral setting of an essentially religious poem, the last of the *Four Quartets*, worthy to be set beside the best Elizabethan models. Once again we have an 'extra-historical' work which, despite its serial language, can be compared with the thirty-year old *Credo* and *Pater Noster* without any stylistic discontinuity being discernible. The serial forms criss-cross as they move from one voice to the next. . . .

XII

Looking in the Glass

IN 1962 STRAVINSKY kept his eightieth birthday, which was much celebrated. The year began with an invitation to the White House, arranged (it seems) by Nicolas Nabokov. As well as Stravinsky and his wife, President Kennedy's 'small party' consisted of Robert Craft, Nabokov, Leonard Bernstein and his wife, Goddard Lieberson (president of CBS), the Arthur Schlesingers, the Pierre Salingers and, among others, Jacqueline Kennedy's sister, Lee Radziwill and her schoolfriend Helen Chavchavadze. The dinner took place on 18 January 1962 and was severely formal; but it seems to have ended badly in that Stravinsky soon got drunk and had to leave early. . . .

One of the most important celebrations of this memorable year was that organized by Rolf Liebermann at the Hamburg Opera on the composer's actual birthday, 18 June. For that occasion Liebermann engaged the New York City Ballet, led by Balanchine, to perform Stravinsky's three 'Greek ballets' — *Apollo Musagetes*, *Orpheus* and *Agon*. That evening Stravinsky was given one of the warmest ovations of his life from the audience and the whole company on stage.

Stravinsky's visit to the USSR the same year, after an exile of half a century, was certainly the most striking event of his old age. A delegation of Russian musicians, led by Khrennikov, had already invited him in June 1961 to conduct in Russia on the occasion of his eightieth birthday, and this invitation was repeated by the Soviet authorities. At first he felt the inevitable resonances of such a visit disturbing; but while he still vacillated, bombarded with contradictory advice by his Russian friends in America, a desire to accept crystallized within him. The official organization of the visit, according to the State Department's scheme of cultural exchanges, took a long time. It was then decided by the composer's general staff to organize the visit on an entirely private footing, with all the details, financial and otherwise, entrusted to the well-known New York impresario Sol Hurok.*

*According to Lillian Libman's detailed account of the preparations for this incredibly complex undertaking, Hurok, aware of the publicity value of 'managing' this visit, even

Stravinsky shared the conducting in Moscow and Leningrad with Craft (the planned concert in Kiev was abandoned). Apart from the inevitable *Sacre*, *Firebird* and *Petrushka*, the programmes included *Symphony in Three Movements*, *Orpheus*, *Ode*, *Capriccio*, *Le Baiser de la fée* and *Fireworks* (with the *Song of the Volga boatmen* as an encore). These, it will be noticed, were all old works and none of them religious in character.

Lillian Libman, who worked for the Hurok agency, now began to deal increasingly with Stravinsky's contracts and other administrative affairs, even giving up her own New York office and devoting a great deal of her time to the composer, both at his home and on tour. It is impossible to disregard her book, quoted below, as a source of information about the composer's life after 1959–60, and it often contradicts — to say the very least — Craft's accounts.

The preparations for the Russian visit are given in detail by Lillian Libman, while Robert Craft's *Diaries* describe the visit itself, concentrating more on the day-to-day events than on the musical programme. The story is included in both *Dialogues and a Diary* and *The Chronicle of a Friendship* and it provides first-hand evidence of the feelings and reactions of Stravinsky and his wife in Russia and on the realities of Soviet life as they may have appeared to a young American.

The trio left Paris on 21 September 1962 at the end of a tour which had taken them to Brazzaville and Johannesburg, Rome, Germany and Israel. At Moscow airport Stravinsky was met by Khrennikov and Karaev, by his niece Xenia Yurevna, who had come from Leningrad, and among others by Maria Yudina, a piano professor at the Conservatoire and fanatical propagandist of Stravinsky's music and contemporary music in general, not an easy role in the Soviet Union. Rehearsals for the first concert, at which Stravinsky was to conduct *Ode* and *Orpheus* (a strange choice) and Craft the *Sacre*, began the next day. At one of the rehearsals the conductor Rozhdestvensky presented Stravinsky with an autograph of Debussy's — the dedication to him of the second book of the *Préludes* [for piano] 'et surtout pour amuser mon ami Igor Stravinsky, ton ami Claude Debussy, juin 1913' (and particularly to amuse my friend Igor Stravinsky, your friend Claude Debussy, June 1913). At the end of the concert, which was packed and endlessly applauded, Stravinsky said to the audience: 'You see a very happy man.'

---

reimbursed Stravinsky in dollars for the loss represented by the difference between the roubles offered by the Russians and the composer's performing fees. (L. Libman, *And Music at the Close — Stravinsky's Last Years*, New York, 1972). It is through her we learn that on his visit to his native land Stravinsky was in fact 'presented' by a big theatrical and concert agency, and received fees for his appearances.

Meanwhile the 'trio' had seen *Boris Godunov* at the Bolshoi, visited the Kremlin, and attended an official performance of *Petrushka, Orpheus* and *Firebird* by the ballet-company of the Maly Theatre, who had come specially from Leningrad. Khrushchev, Kosygin and Suslov were present at this performance. There was a ceaseless round of official receptions and private visits to all the places that Stravinsky and his wife remembered from their youth. On 1 October the Minister of Culture Mme Furtseva ('an attractive blonde' according to Craft), gave a reception in their honour attended by Shostakovich and Khachaturian. With the help of vodka the dinner was very animated — though the Soviet composers remained guarded in their remarks about the problems of contemporary music. Stravinsky is recorded as having said:

A man has one birthplace, one fatherland, one country — he *can* have only one country — and the place of his birth is the most important factor in his life. I regret that circumstances separated me from my fatherland, that I did not bring my works to birth there and, above all, that I was not there to help the new Soviet Union create its new music. But I did not leave Russia only by my own will, even though I admit that I disliked much in my Russia and in Russia generally —but the right to criticize Russia is mine, because Russia is mine and because I love it. I do not give any foreigner that right. (*Dialogues and a Diary*)

From the first moment of their arrival in Moscow the Stravinskys seem to have bridged the gap which separated the world in which they now found themselves from the very different world of their childhood, and in Leningrad this feeling of familiarity became even stronger. There they met a daughter of Balmont's, a nephew of Diaghilev's and most important of all, Rimsky-Korsakov's son Vladimir, whom Stravinsky did not at first recognize and who was reduced to tears. Everywhere in Leningrad they kept coming on places familiar from their young days — the Nevsky Prospekt, the Winter Palace. . . . When they went to the Kryukov Canal, where Stravinsky spent his childhood, the composer fell silent, but when he saw the Conservatoire and the Mariinsky Theatre round the corner, an involuntary 'Glazunov!' escaped him.

At the Composers' Union there was a Stravinsky Exhibition which they visited with Maria Yudina, who a few moments later played the piano part in the *Septet*.

The Leningrad concert on 8 October consisted of *Le Baiser de la fée*, *Fireworks* and *Firebird*. Before starting, Stravinsky told the audience: 'Sixty-nine years ago I sat with my mother in that corner at a concert conducted by Napravnik to mourn the death of Tchaikovsky. Now I am conducting in the same hall. I am very happy.' This moving little speech

was 'even more of a success than the music', acccording to Craft.
(*Dialogues and a Diary*)

Back in Moscow the trio were received on 11 October by Khrushchev in the Kremlin. To the great relief of both parties the conversation
did not touch on either music or politics, but was entirely about 'Nikita
Sergeevich's' recent visit to Turkestan, about which he was delighted to
talk. For his part Stravinsky said how beautiful he found Moscow and,
as they left, there was a new invitation to spend a holiday in a *dacha* in
the Crimea. Craft felt sure that to be recognized and acclaimed as a
Russian in Russia, and to be played there, had been more important to
Stravinsky than anything else during the years he had known him.

By a charming contrast Stravinsky was hardly back from Russia that
October when he received the title of 'Cavaliere di San Silvestro' from
Pope John XXIII, his old friend from the days of *Canticum Sacrum*. A
year later Stravinsky was invested with the insignia of the Order in the
cathedral of Santa Fé by the archbishop.

*

He never stopped working . . . and Vera Stravinsky gives the following
account to a Moscow cousin on her return to Hollywood:

> He composes at a tacky-sounding and usually out-of-tune upright
> piano that has been muted and dampened with felt. . . . Although
> the studio is soundproofed and the door tightly closed, little noises as
> though from mice on the keyboard penetrate the next room. A
> plywood drawing-board is fixed to the music-rack and to it are
> clipped quarto-size strips of thick white paper. These are used for the
> pencil- sketch manuscript. A few smaller sheets of paper are pinned
> to the board around this central manuscript, like sputniks. They are
> the navigation charts of serial orders, the transportation tables, the
> calculations of permutations — 'here the twelfth note becomes the
> second note . . .' and so forth. A kind of surgeon's operating-table
> stands to the side of the piano, the cutlery in this case being colored
> pencils, gums, stopwatches, electric pencil-sharpeners (they sound
> unpleasantly like lawn-mowers), electric metronomes, and the
> styluses with which Igor draws the staves and of which he is the
> patented inventor. (*Themes and Episodes*)

At home Stravinsky regularly devoted the mornings to composition,
sometimes returning to work in the late afternoon. Concert-tours interrupted this routine, but it often happened that he was obsessed by an idea
until he had mastered it. Liebermann in his memoirs, recalls an 'unforgettable' duel — 'Igor struggling with sheets of toilet paper, from the

lavatory of the aircraft, to work out a twelve-tone series and trying to un-
ravel the knot of a new work. This real battle between the artist and his
material lasted three hours, and it is not hard to imagine Stravinsky's delight when he at last discovered his series a few minutes before landing.'

Was this the series of *Abraham and Isaac*? Passing through Oxford ten
years earlier, he had had passages of the Bible read to him in Hebrew
with the old scansion by his friend the philosopher Isaiah Berlin and,
word-rhythms being — as we have said — the most powerful 'starter' of
musical ideas for Stravinsky, he conceived a wish to compose a work in
this ancient language. When did he start sketching *Abraham and Isaac*? We
know that he began actually composing it on 2 April 1962 at Santa Fé and
went on with it during the autumn in Venice. In the meanwhile he had
visited Israel, where the work was definitely commissioned — though
Stravinsky presented his fee to a local foundation and dedicated the work
'to the people of the State of Israel', in gratitude for the welcome he had
received on his visit. The first performance took place at the Israel
Festival in Jerusalem on 23 August 1963, with Robert Craft conducting.

The composition of *Abraham and Isaac* was interrupted by the visit to
Russia, where Stravinsky replied to an 'ill-advised' question on Soviet
Television about his next work — 'A biblical cantata,' he said, 'in
Hebrew, for the people of Israel.' This quickly brought the programme
to a chilly end. . . .

The work was completed in Hollywood in January-February 1963.
Hebrew was the sixth language to be set by Stravinsky, and he set it
with much care and such precision that specialists all agree that in this
work ancient Hebrew became for the composer a kind of pre-mother-
tongue, like Old Slavonic. In fact he banned all translations of the text.

Abraham and Isaac is written for high baritone (the French *baryton
Martin*) and chamber orchestra — single woodwinds, but two bassoons,
brass sextet (including a tuba) and strings. The text is taken from
Genesis XXII, Abraham's sacrifice of his son Isaac. The series which
organizes the work is the following:

Ex. 123

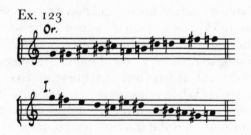

STRAVINSKY

294

Immediately striking is its upward direction (modifiable, of course, but this is how Stravinsky 'thinks' it) and the fact that none of the intervals is larger than a major third — presumably because the voice has the most important part, and Stravinsky wanted to give it a chant-like character. He did not always observe this strictly, but it was the basic conception of the material. There are, altogether, seven parts (Stravinsky first said five, then six) if we count the Coda. The use of the tuba is astonishing throughout, both in conjunction with other bass instruments (in the first part, with bass trombone and bass clarinet) and even more so in opposing registers (trumpet and tuba in the central 'Sacrifice of Abraham'); and in the next part, flute and tuba. The ensembles are written with a light hand and never threaten the solo voice.

For the first performance Stravinsky published a programme-note which also appears, slightly altered, in *Themes and Episodes*:

The six parts, including one purely orchestral movement, are performed without interruption, but they are distinguished by changes to successively slower pulsations. Nineteen verses are used, and they are comprised in ten musical units. Though the verses are sometimes expressed in dialogue form in the Bible, my setting does not impersonate the protagonists, but tells the whole story through the baritone-narrator. . . . No translation of the Hebrew should be attempted, the Hebrew syllables, both as accentuation and timbre, being a principal and fixed element of the music. . . . I do not wish the listener any luck in discovering musical descriptions or illustrations; to my knowledge none was composed, and as I see it the notes themselves are the end of the road. . . .

*

With the deaths of Aldous Huxley and John F. Kennedy — both on 22 November 1963 — Stravinsky lost a close friend and a man for whom he felt a deep sympathy, though he was not close to him. The assassination of President Kennedy stirred his indignation: it was something he felt 'should not too quickly be forgotten' — hence the sense of a kind of protest in his short (one and a half minutes) *Elegy for J. F. K.* for baritone and three clarinets, written a few months after the tragedy.

Auden wrote the text, at Stravinsky's request, and its rhetoric is quite Elizabethan in style: 'When a just man dies, lamentation and praise, sorrow and joy are one.' Apart from the elegiac character established by the three clarinets, and the tranquil tempo, there is no attempt at illustration in Stravinsky's music, which is concerned essentially with

what is really significant, namely the prosody and the *musical* sense of
the words. 'Sorrow' and 'joy' are thus presented as equivalent on the
plane of expression, 'joy' standing out by its very brevity and
dominating the listener's attention, an ambiguous, not to say uncom-
fortable impression emphasized by the repetition of this first line at the
end of the piece.

Apart from this ambiguity *Elegy for J.F.K.* — a typically Stravinskian
haiku — is impressive for the delicacy of the instrumental writing
(superb handling of the different registers of the clarinet) and the
transparent contrapuntal writing. The series of the work contains three
tritones:

Ex. 124

*

In 1963 Stravinsky was already working at Santa Fé on a set of
orchestral variations which he finished in October 1964 and dedicated
to Aldous Huxley. 'Although they are remote from my dear friend's
musical tastes, I cannot prevent myself from dedicating them to his
memory.' (*Themes and Episodes*)

The extreme brevity of *Elegy*, *Double-Canon* and of the lively *Fanfare
for a new theater* (two trumpets, 30 seconds!) composed for Balanchine on
the occasion of the opening of the Lincoln Center in New York, might
suggest that Stravinsky's creative powers were wearing thin and that
from now on he would be speaking in musical monosyllables. Far from
this being the case, however, he was still to write three masterpieces,
each carefully architected and each a remarkable example of its genre:
Variations, Introitus and *Requiem Canticles*.

Variations for orchestra (the Huxley variations mentioned above) were
begun in July 1963, finished in October 1964, and first performed on 17
April 1965 in Chicago. Fresh, ingenious and — particularly rhythmically — alive, they deserve to be more often performed. Any admirer of
Stravinsky should give them a careful hearing, first without and then
with a score, in order to appreciate all their subtleties.

A number of his recent works were 'extra-historical' in character, but
these *Variations* show the composer apparently alive to the most recent
events of the early Sixties and accepting an astonishing challenge —

that of Stockhausen, or so it would seem from an examination of the three 12-part variations. These are, in fact, a working of a rhythm that has a strange, if distant resemblance to that of *Gruppen*. All of the 'formants' — twelve solo violins in the first variation, ten violas and two double-basses in the second, eleven woodwinds and one horn in the third — pulsate in their own, ingeniously evolving rhythms, systematically 'super-modulated' by a metric framework of $\frac{4+3+5}{8}$ repeated four times: an 'isometry' enclosing the 'isorhythmy' of the twelve parts concerned.* Observe the septuplets of the first violin, the triplets of the third, the independence of the fifth, the asymmetries of the seventh, the semiquavers of the ninth and tenth, the crotchets of the eleventh and the even quavers of the twelfth — all individual *patterns* which persist in the two other variations, but redistributed among the instruments and at different serial pitches. (Ex. 125)

What was the purpose of this arrangement? For Stockhausen the answer was clear — in order to *form* the timbres from precise 'rhythmic formants', inasmuch as timbre is a function of the distribution of sound in time. That was certainly not Stravinsky's original idea, so much as a result of the way he wrote. Stravinsky's piece was primarily a *research into rhythm* (not unlike Messiaen's *Chronochromie*, to which these *Variations* also bear a certain resemblance e.g. the 'Epode' for eighteen solo violins) which finished up by having an effect on the *timbre*. The sound-effect is certainly remarkable. . . .

In the *interludes* — if this is what we should call the firmly engraved polyphonic passages between the variations — the instrumental pairings are shifting, the counterpoint of timbres as biting as acid and the rhythmic transformations are amazingly plastic, set in high relief. The penultimate interlude has all the look of a *fugato* though it does not have the actual structure; but the listener's attention is drawn in that direction by the logical consistency of both the serial and the rhythmic manipulations. The work ends with a violent *postlude*, all contrasts and surprises, with the bass clarinet adding at the very last moment the single note (G sharp) missing from the obligatory twelve.

The year 1965 opened with the death on 4 January of another friend: T. S. Eliot. A mutual respect and a deep attachment untouched by any note of familiarity linked these two elderly artists, both well aware of their worth and their authority. A few days after Eliot's death Stravinsky started *Introitus* in his memory, finishing it in a month. This is one of his most elliptical works. It has a monastic simplicity, consisting merely of a Requiem chant, in the four basic serial forms, sung by a male-voice chorus. The words, which are alternately sung

Ex. 125

*Compare the score of *Gruppen* and Stockhausen's famous article, already quoted. The 'super-modulating' elements in *Gruppen* are of course the three orchestras entrusted with the formants, in order to play them at *different tempi* and so create musical spectres in constant transformation.

and spoken, are given their funeral rhythm by a handful of instruments
— viola and double-bass, harp, piano, two tam-tams and *timpani coperti*
(muffled drums).

The tenors are given the original and the retrograde of the series:

Ex. 126

An instrumental counterpoint (on the retrograde shared between the
two parts) provides a short interlude, after which the basses sing the
inversion and the retrograde of the inversion transposed a tone. The
voices meet at the end. The muffled *timpani* are so tuned that, as the
work unfolds, they follow the pitches of the series.

The timbre of the work is most impressive — a funeral toll
constructed of almost nothing, but with a feeling for the sound-
material that age seems to have made even more acute. The use of harp,
piano and tam-tams together is comparable to the final tolling in *Les
Noces*.

*

Early in 1965 the shooting of two films about Stravinsky began: one by
Richard Leacock at the suggestion of Liebermann and the other for
CBS, directed by David Oppenheimer, to be made as he went on tour.
At the same time Stravinsky accepted what was to be his last
commission, from the son of Mrs Helen Buchanan Seeger who had left
a legacy to the Music Department of Princeton University. This was to
be a Requiem in her memory and Stravinsky started work on it before
he left Hollywood for Paris and Poland via Chicago and New York — a
tour described in great detail by Robert Craft in *The Chronicle of a
Friendship*.

In Paris Stravinsky called on Giacometti in his studio in rue
Hippolyte-Maindron and saw him again two days later, when
Giacometti returned the call, armed with his drawing-block, at the
composer's hotel near the Champs-Elysées. The portraits that
Giacometti made are marvellously accurate in their 'multi-linearity'.
The same day Stravinsky lunched with Henri Michaux, who dazzled
him by the brilliance of his conversation.

Switzerland was the next leg of his tour and there, for the benefit of the CBS cameramen who were his constant companions, he returned first to 'Les Tilleuls' — the pension where he had written the *Sacre* — and then to the villa 'La Pervenche'. In Warsaw, where he arrived on 23 May, he conducted for the cameras short fragments of the *Sacre* — which had really become too exhausting for him — and a concert-performance of the *Symphony of Psalms*.

Back in Paris again he attended the Béjart Company's Stravinsky evening at the Opéra, conducted by Boulez. Was the choreography on that occasion as bad as Craft says, at great length, in *The Chronicle of a Friendship*? No doubt the whole stage-conception of *Les Noces* was over-elaborate and neo-academic in style, and presented a picture of Russia that rather recalled the World Exhibition of 1937. *Renard*, on the other hand, was delightful, with the company arriving in a Hispano-Suiza and Claire Motte as an 'Art Déco' Renard. (Why was the part played by a woman? simply because Renard, in Russian, *is* a woman.) The *Sacre* was Béjart's *Sacre*, with a magnificently bold choreography in which the sexes were separated — men in the first part, women in the second — and met only in the 'Danse sacrale', but then with incredible violence.

Before going back to Hollywood Stravinsky went to Rome, where he was received and decorated by the Pope. He returned to a new house, which he had bought from Baroness Erlanger, quite close to his former home. This was redecorated and soon had its own swimming-pool though it was never used by Stravinsky, who had had a horror of water since his childhood. In Los Angeles the summer of 1965 was appallingly hot and humid, and Stravinsky dreaded his last recording sessions (*Pulcinella* and *Le Baiser de la fée*, the Huxley *Variations* being judged unsuitable for pressing). Despite these conditions Stravinsky's agents were still actively on the look-out for interesting concerts at which he could share the conducting with Craft, since the actual requests that he received, though numerous, were seldom satisfactory to him from the financial point of view.

The list of prospective concerts, and the contracts that his agents were instructed to negotiate, with increasingly demanding clauses attached and at increasingly high fees, is an impressive one. Having exhausted the great European musical centres and the Latin American capitals, his agents now started combing the major towns and orchestras of the United States. What drove Stravinsky at over eighty to continue conducting when the sheer physical effort involved became more and more exhausting? He had been anxious to establish 'model' interpretations of his works for other conductors, but this had no longer

any point in the concert hall. Was it a need to 'communicate' directly
with his public? As he very well knew, all the public wanted belonged to
the realm of the anecdotal. It was not his musical interpretations that
interested them, and in any case these were by now unreliable,
tentative and even embarrassing. What they wanted was quite clearly
the *spectacle* of this old man on the podium and the chance of being able
to say: 'I was at the last concert conducted by Stravinsky.' Of course
there were a number of intermediary figures between him and the
public who stood to gain from his continuing to conduct, but these
could never have forced him to do so against his will. It was still
Stravinsky who was in command, and who cancelled when it suited
him. Robert Craft was necessarily called upon to share the conducting
in programmes where Stravinsky appeared in only one or two works,
and obviously his conducting career was organically linked to Stravinsky's. This clearly concerned him, but for reasons that were musical
rather than material, since the fees that he received from Stravinsky
were reckoned very parsimoniously and represented a relatively small
fraction of the total sum. In fact it was always the composer himself who
seems to have insisted on continuing this lucrative activity which he
had begun forty years earlier and never abandoned. His obsession with
money lasted until his death and he devoted all his remaining strength
to his concerts — despite the taxman's merciless levy on his fees.

It was only after 1966 that, owing to his steadily declining health, his
activities as conductor were replaced by the simple 'presence of the
composer' at the concerts conducted by Craft — and even that brought
in increasingly spectacular fees, sometimes amounting to as much as
ten thousand dollars. . . .

More than being a big and risky financial operation, the contract
with CBS for the recording of his complete works was meant to have a
real significance as a definitive statement of the composer's conception
of his own works at the end of his life — for the edification of future
generations.

These recordings* were naturally subject to serious limitations due

---

*The present writer witnessed one of them (*Apollo Musagetes*) in New York in 1964.
Craft prepared the orchestra within the strict time-limits imposed by American union
demands, and Stravinsky then arrived supported by Craft and John McLure (the
artistic director in charge of the series), and conducted, imposing his own tempo,
altering a few details and emphasizing a small point here and there. Then the whisky
was brought, in the cardboard beakers used in New York during working hours, and
consumed while listening to the play-back. Considering the short time allowed by
American labour-laws, it was a more than decent performance, thanks to the
professionalism of all concerned, the competence of the players, Craft's good
knowledge of the scores and, in the last resort, the vigilance of the composer himself.

to the composer's age and extreme exhaustion; but although Craft played an increasingly large supportive role, the stake in this almost tragic challenge is a document which is now there as a point of reference.

When the difficult session of recordings in August 1965 was over, Stravinsky was faced with the prospect of a concert at the Hollywood Bowl, with an audience of 10,000, on 2 September, enormously testing in the exceptional heat and humidity of that season in Los Angeles. Stravinsky, however gave gallant performances of *Fireworks*, *Scherzo à la russe* and the *Firebird* suite. The very next day he set off with his wife and Craft for Hamburg via New York, to complete Liebermann's television film. Back in New York he was on the point of cancelling his Cincinnati concerts but still dined in a fashionable restaurant, saw *Hello Dolly* and gaily, it seems, kept his engagements in Cincinnati on 15 and 16 October. Returning to Hollywood, he picked up his work on the *Requiem Canticles* where he had left it, finished the piece the following summer and attended the first performance, with Craft conducting, at Princeton on 8 October 1966.

*

Requiem Canticles is written for contralto and bass, chorus and orchestra (with four flutes and four horns, no oboes and no clarinets, large percussion section, harp, celesta, bells, piano and strings). With the exception of *The Owl and the Pussycat*, a small 'two-part invention' for voice and piano to words by Edward Lear, written when he was finishing the *Requiem Canticles*, and the arrangement of two Hugo Wolf songs (to be discussed later), this was Stravinsky's last piece — and his last masterpiece.

The text consists of brief extracts from the most important parts of the Catholic Requiem Mass. The formal plan, like that of all his big recent works (*Agon*, *Threni*, *Canticum Sacrum*) is symmetrical. It comprises six vocal parts, flanked by a 'Prelude' and 'Postlude' and arranged round a central instrumental 'Interlude'.

Ex. 127

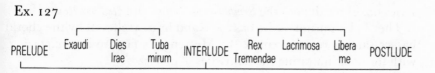

The work is built, exceptionally, not on one series but on two:

Ex. 128

As so often with Stravinsky, the first of these is diatonic in character owing to the number of major seconds, a minor seventh and two fifths. To make up for this, the second series is not only more chromatic but — in its original form — more angular and more 'dramatic', with its two rising major sevenths. This second series is the basis of the 'Prelude', which is for strings only. The rhythm — an isochronous pulsation — is super-defined by the metre that divides it up into shifting proportions: 5 (−1)/16, 7/16, 5/16, 2/8 (= 5/16) and so forth, this last proportion indicating a group of five semi-quavers in the bass against two quavers in the solo violin — something that Stravinsky had never done before. An eloquent 5/16 bar's rest separates this motto from its subsequent rhythmic development, which becomes increasingly complex with the increasing number of instrumental entries. The return to strings only takes place on the following sequence of proportions 4 (−1)/16, 5/16, 7/16, 5/16, 4/16, 5/16, 6/16, 2/16 — evidence that Stravinsky never lost his rhythmic awareness and still remembered the *Sacre*!

'Exaudi' brings a crude opposition between horizontal (harp) and vertical (orchestral chords) dimensions, with the 'diagonal' dimension of the choral polyphony between them. In the choral part (no basses) the vertical clumpings of the first series alternate by twos.

In the 'Dies irae' the divine wrath is symbolized by a *fortissimo* explosion of piano and strings followed by the exclamation of the chorus, which is immediately echoed. The binary rhythmic *parlando sotto voce* in the next part, and the ternary piano accompaniment (on series no. 2) recall both the *Symphony of Psalms* and *Oedipus Rex*.

The 'Tuba mirum' is for bass solo and brass (relieved by the choral basses) and is reminiscent of the Messenger's fanfare in *Oedipus Rex*, with the voice imitating the flourishes of the brass.

One of the most beautiful episodes in *Requiem Canticles* is the instrumental 'Interlude'. Here the harmony goes back to the 'old Stravinsky' of the *Symphonies of Wind Instruments*, which seems at first to be 'polytonal', but is nothing of the kind. The fifth with the 'wrong bass' might be said to be one of the composer's fingerprints, as is the writing for the four flutes in the bottom register, which produces a unique sonority.

'Rex Tremendae' is a true, archaistic polyphony, in four choral parts which the brass duplicate (but in a ragged fashion); wind instruments and strings form harmonic *ritornelli* in repeated notes.

'Lacrimosa' sets the solo contralto voice in a kind of wide spatial frame bounded by the double-bassoon at one extreme and the piccolo at the other. The voice becomes progressively freer as the instruments settle into static chords.

In 'Libera me' four solo voices from the chorus are matched against the rest of the chorus, which speaks, supported by the chords of four horns (perhaps originally a harmonium, replaced by Stravinsky at the last minute). It is hard to conceive a simpler *and* more effective device than this, which leaves the listener uncertain as to whether what he hears is being spoken or sung — an almost frightening, catacomb-like chant:

Ex. 129

The final 'Postlude' is Stravinsky's farewell to music, and its unique sonorities recall the enigmatic sound with which *Les Noces* ends. Funeral bells they may be, but wholly unlike the heavy, solemn, 'tolling' for Titurel. . . . These are small crystalline bells that float timelessly above the Laguna dei Morti.

The polyphony is divided, note by note, between vibraphone, tubular bells and celesta, which form chords that have no locus and no time. A single held horn-note supports this airy structure.

Requiem Canticles are memories . . . as though in his old age the composer were casting a keen glance over the past, reviewing and evoking all his music. In the 'Prelude' it is the continuous-discontinuous pulsations of the *Sacre*; in 'Exaudi' the hovering polyphony of *Symphony of Psalms*; in 'Dies Irae' the wild sound of the cimbalom of *Renard*; in 'Tuba mirum' the icy fanfares of *Oedipus Rex*; in the 'Interlude' the 'Chorale' of the *Symphonies* in memory of Debussy; in 'Lacrimosa' the intonation of the 'Chant dissident'; in 'Libera me' the murmured chanting of the *Mass* — and finally in the 'Postlude' the timeless, siteless bell of *Les Noces*. As André Souris says in his summing-up, 'of all his works this is the one that stands above and beyond analysis, because in it are concentrated all the forces which lie behind the vast, universally relevant work of one of the greatest of all creative artists'.

*

In May 1968, in San Francisco, Stravinsky completed his last finished act as a composer, orchestrating for a small ensemble two religious songs from Hugo Wolf's *Spanisches Liederbuch* — 'Herr, was trägt der Boden hier?' and 'Wunden trägst Du'. Done as it were in a state of grace, this orchestration has the familiar Stravinsky hallmark, a sonority of its own achieved by bold and subtle layering of harmonies and instruments. Stravinsky, according to Craft, wanted to say something about death and felt that he was no longer able to compose it himself.

During 1966 there were concerts in Saint Louis, Los Angeles, Athens, Lisbon, New York (a big Stravinsky Festival) and once again at the Hollywood Bowl. After that, however, there was a marked slowing-down of his activity as conductor. At North Wetherly Drive he finished *Requiem Canticles* and *The Owl and the Pussycat*. Among the few friends he still saw were Lawrence Morton, Miranda Levi and a number of visitors from New York, particularly his daughter Milena, his son-in-law André Marion and his lawyer, William Montapert — though with these last three he was soon to quarrel irretrievably. Visitors from abroad became less frequent, though Yevtushenko came and recited his poems and was followed later by Margot Fonteyn, who brought with her a Nureyev bursting with youth, all in white and wearing tennis-shoes.

After the first performance of *Requiem Canticles*, at Princeton, the physicist, Dr Robert Oppenheimer, asked for the work to be played at his own funeral, a wish that was granted only a few months later. The charm, devotion and efficiency of a new secretary — Marilyn Stalvey, wife of Dorrance Stalvey, a composer who also directed the 'Monday Evening Concerts', assured the tranquil running of his household.

Stravinsky made his last public appearances in 1967, and after a concert in Chicago and another in Miami he made his last record —the 1945 'Suite' from *Firebird* — and gave what was to be his last public concert in the Massey Hall at Toronto, where he conducted — for the first and last time, sitting — the 'Suite' from *Pulcinella*.

There were important visits in 1967, his son Theodore coming in March from Geneva and Pierre Souvtchinsky at the end of October from Paris. In August he suffered, while in New York, from an open ulcer which made him lose a lot of blood. Recovering from this at the Cedars of Lebanon Hospital, he was troubled with a bladder infection. In November his left hand suddenly turned black after circulatory trouble, and his general condition grew worse. At the Mount Sinai Hospital in Los Angeles he could still be resuscitated even at his worst by a dose of that best of all vaso-dilatories, whisky. He himself could hardly believe it until the moment when Craft opened the bottle in front of him. The head nurse offered him the whisky with a straw but 'he threw away the straw and, with inimitable Stravinskian panache, clinked his cardboard beaker with mine'. At the end of November his hand was no longer discoloured and he got up, ready to leave. 'How much does all this cost?' he asked and Craft comments: 'In all these weeks nothing has sounded so cheering. Stravinsky is back in the decimal system. Thank God' (*Chronicle of a Friendship*).

From that time onward, though, Stravinsky's health gradually got worse, and doctors and nurses became part of his daily existence. Not that this was anything new as far as doctors were concerned! He had always been surrounded by them, and rather enjoyed it. His medicine-cupboard at home, with everything carefully labelled, was generally agreed by his friends to be a regular chemist's shop. The present author saw him taking pills with a bumper of whisky on the Campo San Fantin during the interval of a concert in the Fenice. At home he made a note of the times of his various medications — 'took one pill *marron*' and so forth; and the list of his doctors — apart from the regular Dr Edel in Hollywood and Drs Lewithin and Lax in New York — totalled, according to Craft, something like eighty.

Despite his incredible vitality Stravinsky, after 1968, was a very ailing old man. The Sunday expeditions to some smart Hollywood

restaurant and the visits to the cinema — always very popular with him
— became much less frequent and were replaced by listening to
gramophone records after dinner. These evening sessions, arranged by
Craft who also chose the programmes, were the great joy of Stravinsky's last years. It was with Craft that he enjoyed listening, the two of
them often following in the score, bar by bar — especially Beethoven
quartets, to which he listened greedily almost every evening.

Concerts given 'with the composer in attendance' took the place of
'real' ones, and even these were infrequent and exclusively in the USA,
particularly California. In Europe no concert-organizer would have
dreamed of paying him to attend, and no concert-goer would pay
simply to see him. In October 1968 his doctors allowed him to cross the
Atlantic. In Switzerland he visited his bank in Basle, saw Wagner's
Triebschen at Lucerne and in Geneva his son Theodore presented him
with the original manuscript of the Sacre, beautifully bound. With his
wife and, as always, Robert Craft, he then went to Paris where he
stayed at the Ritz and attended, more or less incognito, a performance
of the Sacre at the Opéra. Apart from that he saw his friends
Souvtchinsky, Nabokov and Nadia Boulanger and went to some
concerts of contemporary music.

At New York in the spring of 1969 he was still working an hour a day
in spite of having had two serious operations on his legs for removal of
blood clots. First in Hollywood and then at the Hotel Pierre in New
York he orchestrated four preludes and fugues from the 'Forty-Eight'
— the E minor, B minor and C sharp minor from the first book, and the
D minor from the second. The orchestrations, however, for strings and
wind, were neither played nor published — Craft had asked (with
Nabokov's consent) that they should be removed from the programme
of the Berlin Festival on the grounds that 'too little — if indeed
anything — of Stravinsky can be discerned in them as they stand'. (The
Chronicle of a Friendship)

At the end of 1969 life in Hollywood had become too difficult and
complicated for what was now in fact a staff of nurses in charge of an
invalid, and it was decided to move to New York. The choice was Essex
House, a luxurious building on Central Park South, combining the
comfort of a private house with the services of a large hotel. Nabokov
and Auden came to visit their old friend, and the gramophone evenings
continued.

In April 1970 Stravinsky was hurriedly moved to the Lennox Hill
Hospital in New York, suffering from double pneumonia and, apparently, cardiac weakness, and declared by the press to be 'in a critical
condition'. But he recovered enough to see his son Theodore and to

listen to Boulez's *Sonatine*, which he had sufficient strength to make malicious comments about. In fact his doctors, declaring that he would benefit from 'a change of air', authorized another visit to Europe and the 'trio', with Lillian Libman added to the party, settled in the Hôtel Royal at Evian, where his son Theodore and his grand-daughter Kitty, as well as his niece Xenia from Moscow, all visited him. Souvtchinsky also came, and the two of them paid a visit to Clarens. But whether in his bed, in his wheel-chair pushed by nurses, or in the new Lincoln motor car sent from New York by boat, Stravinsky seemed a shadowy figure indifferent to his surroundings, fragile, silent and absent-looking, having virtually lost his memory. One of the few outsiders who was admitted was Lord Snowdon, who took a number of poignant photographs.

By the end of April the party was back in New York, and in December of that year Vera Stravinsky bought an apartment on Fifth Avenue, at the corner of 73rd Street. Alterations and decorations were a long and costly business and in the meantime Stravinsky's health took a further turn for the worse. By mid-March he was back in the same room in the same hospital as the year before, with a return of pulmonary oedema. He was treated according to Craft, 'like something on a production-chain in a factory, his chest covered with electrodes, his trachea blocked by a breathing-machine and his nostrils by plastic oxygen-tubes' (Diary of 18 March). After a slight improvement in his condition he was moved back to his new apartment on 30 March; and surrounded by his wife, his faithful nurses and Dr Lax, and a whole arsenal of therapeutic weaponry, he was kept alive for a few days longer. He died, unconscious, in the small hours of 6 April.

*

A few hours after his solitary, almost secret death the public demise of the great composer was under way. Stravinsky had always had a horror of talking about death and had never really considered where he wished to be buried. A year earlier, however, his close friends had thought of Venice, and when the moment arrived, this seemed the natural choice and was immediately adopted. Apart from sentimental reasons — Venice was Stravinsky's favourite town — there were diplomatic considerations to be taken into account. The Soviet Ambassador in Washington expressed the wish that Stravinsky's body should be taken back to Russia, whereas he had in fact been an American citizen for thirty years — it was therefore essential to find another solution which would offend neither of the two parties. Vera

Stravinsky also felt strongly that Stravinsky belonged to the whole world.

The funeral ceremony in New York took place at one of the innumerable 'funeral homes', at the corner of Madison Avenue and 81st Street. The official ceremony there was preceded by two others, both held in the evening and both restricted to the family and very close friends such as Balanchine, Theodore and Soulima Stravinsky, and Milena and André Marion who had immediately flown to New York. They were not, however, invited to the Fifth Avenue apartment owing to the difficult relations between them and Vera Stravinsky. At the solemn service on Good Friday afternoon in the mortuary chapel they were seated on the left, while Vera Stravinsky, Robert Craft, Rita Christensen (Stravinsky's favourite nurse) and Natasha Nabokov were on the right. The carefully sifted congregation included Artur Rubinstein, Stokowsky, Isaac Stern; the composers Carter, Sessions, Babbitt and Spies; and the representatives of President Nixon (Michael Straight) and Nikita Khrushchev (the cultural attaché, Anatole Dyushev) and of the French and Italian embassies. The mortuary chapel held only 200, but there was a large, silent crowd outside, which included the present writer and the composer Berio.

Meanwhile Lillian Libman was organizing Stravinsky's solemn funeral in Venice, which was to take place on 15 April: transportation of the coffin via Rome, the Mass in San Giovanni e Paolo, the performance of the *Requiem Canticles* by the chorus and orchestra of the RAI under Craft and the funeral gondola-procession.

Stravinsky's body, accompanied by his wife, arrived in Venice on 13 April and was placed next day in the Chapel of the Rosary in San Giovanni e Paolo, beneath the Veronese ceilings, and taken to the middle of the nave on the morning of the funeral. After a Mass for the poor, Vera Stravinsky arrived on Nicolas Nabokov's arm and all the members of the family occupied their specially reserved — and separated — seats. Alessandro Scarlatti's *Missa pro defunctis* was followed by an oration by the Mayor of Venice, after which Craft conducted the *Requiem Canticles*. The Orthodox ceremony began at 12.30, presided over by the Archimandrite Malissianos, and the chants of the Greek rite were interspersed with three organ pieces by Andrea Gabrieli. This was an occasion on which Venice performed her role as the ultimate reconciler of civilizations and rites, Byzantium linked to the Latin world beneath the stone eyes of the Doges whose tombs stand here. . . .

The procession to the island of San Michele was headed by the

Archimandrite, followed by the funeral gondola and others containing members of the family. In the cemetery itself the plot chosen was in the corner reserved for the Orthodox, a few steps away from Diaghilev's grave.

The absolute simplicity of Stravinsky's grave contrasted strangely with the imposing funeral that Venice had given him. Diaghilev's carries the inscription 'Venise, inspiratrice éternelle de nos apaise-ments', which would no doubt have prompted an ironical comment from Stravinsky, whose own grave bears nothing but a name and two dates engraved by the sculptor Manzù, and a small cross — of pure gold.

REFERENCES

I *Keys to Stravinsky*

1. Pierre Boulez, 'Stravinsky demeure' in *Relevés d'apprenti* (Paris: 1979).
2. Henri Pousseur, 'Stravinsky selon Webern selon Stravinsky' in *Musique en jeu*, nos. 4 and 5 (Paris).
3. Arthur Gold and Robert Fitzdale, *Misia* (Paris: 1981).
4. Boris de Schloezer, *Igor Stravinsky* (Paris 1929).
5. Pierre Souvtchinsky, *Das Wunder des 'Sacre du Printemps'* (Cologne: 1963).
6. See Boulez, *Penser la musique aujourd'hui*; Stockhausen, *Texte* (Cologne); Pousseur, 'Stravinsky selon Webern selon Stravinsky' *op. cit.*
7. Roland Barthes, '*Leçon*' (inaugural lecture at the Collège de France) (Paris: 1978).
8. André Souris, 'Debussy et Stravinsky' in *Conditions de la musique* (Paris: 1976).

II *Apprenticeship*

1. Vera Stravinsky and Robert Craft, *Stravinsky in Pictures and Documents* (London: 1978) — referred to in future as VS/RC.
2. VS/RC, p. 20.
3. VS/RC, p. 48.
4. VS/RC, pp. 50–51.
5. André Schaeffner, *Stravinsky* (Paris: 1951).

III *With the 'Ballets russes'*

1. Alexandre Benois, *Reminiscences of the Russian Ballet* (London: 1941).
2. See André Boucourechliev, *Beethoven* (Paris: 1963).
3. Michel Philippot, *Igor Stravinsky* (Paris: 1965).
4. Gennadi Rozhdestvensky in *Igor Stravinsky: stat'i i materialy* (Moscow: 1973).
5. Louis Laloy, *La Musique retrouvée* (Paris: 1928).
6. Letter published in VS/RC, p. 605.
7. Pierre Boulez, 'Trajectoires' in *Relevés d'apprenti, op. cit.*

IV *Le Sacre du Printemps*

1. Interview with the *Daily Mail*, 13 February 1913 (quoted in VS/RC, p. 95). Stravinsky was very fond of this English title, *The Crowning of Spring*, which was eventually replaced by *The Rite of Spring*.

2. According to Stravinsky's Russian manuscript reproduced in VS/RC, p. 78, here translated literally (Craft's and my own translations are almost identical).

3. Same text.

4. The whole English text is given in VS/RC, p. 75.

5. Published in VS/RC.

6. July 27, 1913 (quoted in VS/RC, p. 104).

7. See also the article by B. Yarustovsky, in *Stat'i i materialy, op cit.*

8. See Stockhausen, '... Wie die Zeit vergeht...' in *Die Reihe*, no. 3 (Vienna).

V *Critical Years*

1. Romain Rolland, *Journal des Années de Guerre* (Paris: 1952).

2. Richard Buckle, *Diaghilev* (Paris: 1980).

3. Boris Asafiev, *Kniga o Stravinskom* (*A Book about Stravinsky*) (Leningrad: 1929).

4. *Op. cit.*

5. Jean Hugo, *Avant d'oublier* (Paris: 1976).

VI *Between the Wars 1*

1. Given in VS/RC.

2. Paul Morand, *L'Allure de Chanel* (Paris: 1976).

3. VS/RC.

4. 'Les Six' was a name invented by the critic Henri Collet for the group of composers Auric, Poulenc, Milhaud, Honegger and Germaine Tailleferre. The sixth, Louis Durey, had retired at the time of *Les Mariés de la Tour Eiffel*.

5. Georges Auric, *Quand j'étais là* (Paris: 1979).

6. VS/RC.

7. *Ibid.*

8. In *Dix Ans avec Stravinsky* (Monaco: 1958).

9. Quoted in VS/RC.

10. Letter to Ramuz of 29 July 1925, quoted (in English) in VS/RC, p. 258.

11. VS/RC, p. 263.

12. A. Schaeffner, *op. cit.* There is an even more detailed chronology of the composition of *Oedipus Rex* in VS/RC.

13. Arthur Gold and Robert Fitzdale, *op. cit.* But this version of the story is not the same as that given in R. Buckle's *Diaghilev*.

VII *Between the Wars 2*

1. André Souris, in *op. cit.* 'Le sens du sacré dans la musique de Stravinsky'.

2. VS/RC, pp. 349-350.

322 STRAVINSKY

VIII *Refuge in Exile*

1. These corrections of the generally accepted chronology, according to which the work was finished after *Scènes de ballet*, are given in VS/RC, p. 373.
2. The plan found in Stravinsky's papers is given in VS/RC, p. 374.

IX *Characters in Search of an Author*

1. Nicolas Nabokov, *Cosmopolite* (Paris: 1975).
2. André Boucourechliev, *op. cit.*
3. André Souris, *op. cit.*
4. Robert Craft, *The Chronicle of a Friendship*, 1948–1971 (London: 1972), pp. 4–5.
5. *Dix Ans avec Stravinsky, op. cit.*

X *On the Verge of Fertile Land*

1. Telegram and quotation in VS/RC, p. 411.
2. *Dix Ans avec Stravinsky, op. cit.*
3. VS/RC, p. 438.
4. Paul Horgan, *Encounters with Stravinsky* (New York: 1972).

XI *Urbi Venetiae*

1. In *Dix Ans avec Stravinsky*, 'Une Cantate pour Saint Marc'.
2. VS/RC, p. 435.
3. Quoted by E. W. White, *Stravinsky* p. 493.
4. H. Pousseur, *op. cit.*
5. In *Dix Ans avec Stravinsky*, 'Un Ballet pour douze danseurs'.
6. Prince Joachim, the son of Max-Egon, has continued the tradition of these *Musiktage*.

LIST OF WORKS

Abbreviations
arr.: *arrangement*
bar.: *baritone*
bibl.: *bibliography*
ch.: *chamber*
facs.: *facsimile*
inst.: *instrumental, instruments*
lg.: *large*
ms.: *manuscript*
mus.: *music, musicians*
orch.: *orchestra*
perc.: *percussion*
pub.: *published by*
qt.: *quartet*
red.: *reduced*
rev.: *revision*
sol.: *soloist*
sopr.: *soprano*
sc.: *scene*
st.: *storyline*
ten.: *tenor*
trans.: *transcription*
ver.: *version*
Russian title: [ ]

Publishers
AMP: Associated Music Publishers
Bf.: Belaieff
Bes.: Bessel
B. & H.: Boosey & Hawkes
Br.: Breitkopf & Härtel
Chp.: Chappell
C.: Chester
F.: Faber and Faber
H.: Hansen
Jurg.: Jurgensen
ERM: Edition Russe de Musique
Sch.: Schott.

I *Theatrical Works*

L'OISEAU DE FEU [*Zhar-ptitza*] (*Firebird*) 1909–1910
Ballet in 2 sc. for lg. orch. St. by Fokine based on a Russian legend.
  Pub. Jurg., 1910, then Sch. Concert *Suites*. See under *Orchestral Works* Misc. arr.
PETROUCHKA (*Petrushka*) 1910–1911
Ballet in 4 sc. for lg. orch. St. by A. Benois [and Stravinsky].
  Pub. ERM, 1912; rev. 1946, B. & H., 1947. Trans. see under *Piano Works*.
LE SACRE DU PRINTEMPS [*Vesna Sviashchennaya*] (*The Rite of Spring*) 1911–1913
'Scenes of Pagan Russia', ballet in 2 sc. for lg. orch. St. by N. Roerich and I. Stravinsky.
  Pub. ERM, 1921, then B. & H. Trans. see under *Piano Works*. Sketches: Facs. pub. B. & H., 1969.
LE ROSSIGNOL [*Solovei*] (*The Nightingale*) I, 1908–1909; II–III, 1913–1914
Lyrical tale in 3 acts for sol., chorus and orch. Libretto by Stepan Mitusov [and Stravinsky] based on Hans Andersen.
  Pub. ERM, 1923; B. & H., 1947, rev. 1962.
RENARD [*Baika*] 1915–1916
'Burlesque tale for acting and singing' for 2 ten., 2 basses and small orch. Text by Stravinsky based on Russian folk-tales.
  Originally published by Henn. Now copyright to C.
CHANT DU ROSSIGNOL [*Pesnia Solovia*] (*Nightingale's song*) 1917
Ballet based on *The Nightingale* for lg. orch.
  Pub. ERM, 1921, then B. & H.
HISTOIRE DU SOLDAT (*The Soldier's Tale*) 1918
'To be read, played and danced' for 3 actors, 1 female dancer and 7 instr. Text by C. F. Ramuz.
  Pub. C., 1924.
PULCINELLA 1919–1920
Ballet with singing, for ch. orch., based on Pergolesi and others.
  Pub. ERM, then B. & H.
MAVRA 1921–1922
Opéra-bouffe, libretto by B. Kochno based on 'The little house at Kolomna' by Pushkin.
  Pub. ERM, 1925; B. & H., 1947.
LES NOCES [*Svadebka*] (*The Wedding*) Non-instr. part 1914–1917; definitive version 1923
'Russian choreographic sc.' for sol. voices, chorus, 4 pianos and perc. Text by Stravinsky based on Russian folktales.
  Pub. C., 1923. Various unfinished inst. ver.
OEDIPUS REX 1926–1927
Opera-oratorio for narrator, sol. voices, chorus and orch. Text by Jean Cocteau based on Sophocles, Latin ver. by J. Daniélou.
  Pub. ERM, 1927. Rev. 1948, B. & H. 1949.

APOLLON MUSAGÈTE (*Apollo Musagetes*) 1927–1928
Ballet in 2 sc. for string orch. St. by Stravinsky.
  Pub. ERM, 1928. Rev. 1947, B. & H. 1952.
LE BAISER DE LA FÉE (*The Fairy's Kiss*) 1928
Ballet in 4 sc. for orch. St. by Stravinsky based on Hans Christian Andersen
  (mus. based on num. pieces by Tchaikovsky).
  Pub. ERM, 1928. Rev. 1950, B. & H., 1952.
PERSEPHONE 1933–1934
Melodrama in 3 sc. for female narrator, ten. sol., chorus and orch. Text by
  André Gide.
  Pub. ERM, 1934; Rev. 1949, B. & H., 1950.
JEU DE CARTES (*Game of Cards*)
'Ballet in 3 deals' for orch. St. by M. Malaieff and Stravinsky.
  Pub. Sch., 1937.
CIRCUS POLKA 1942
'For a young elephant'. See under *Orchestral Works*.
SCÈNES DE BALLET 1944
Ballet for orch.
  Pub. Chp., 1944.
ORPHEUS 1947
Ballet in 3 sc. for orch.
  Pub. B. & H., 1948.
THE RAKE'S PROGRESS 1948–1951
Opera in 3 acts. Libretto by W. H. Auden and Chester Kallman.
  Pub. B. & H., 1951.
AGON 1953–1954, 1956–1957
Ballet for 12 dancers and orch.
  Pub. B. & H., 1957.
THE FLOOD 1961–1962
'Musical play' for actors, solo voices and orch. for television. Text by Robert
  Craft based on York and Chester Mystery Plays and Book of Genesis.
  Pub. B. & H., 1963.

2 *Orchestral Works*

SYMPHONY IN E FLAT MAJOR 1905–1907
  Pub. Jurg., 1914.
SCHERZO FANTASTIQUE 1907–1908
  Pub. Jurg., then Sch.
FIREWORKS 1908
  Pub. Sch., 1910.
CHANT FUNÈBRE 1908
  (in memory of Rimsky). Unpub. lost ms.
L'OISEAU DE FEU (*Firebird*)
  1st *Suite* for lg. orch. 1911. Pub. Jurg., 1912.

2nd *Suite* for red. orch. 1919. Pub. C.

3rd *Suite* for red. orch. 1945. Pub. Leeds, 1946–47.

RAGTIME 1918

For instr. ensemble.

Pub. Sirène, 1919; C., 1920.

SYMPHONIES OF WIND INSTRUMENTS 1920

For ensemble of 23 inst.

Pub. ERM, 1926; Rev. 1945–1947, B. & H.

SUITE NO. 2 1921

For small orch. Arr. of THREE EASY PIECES for piano duet and of FIVE EASY PIECES for piano duet No. 5.

Pub. C.

PULCINELLA: Suite for ch. orch. 1922

Pub. ERM, 1924; Rev. 1949, B. & H.

CONCERTO FOR PIANO AND WIND 1923–1924

Pub. ERM, 1936; Rev. 1950; B. & H., 1950.

SUITE NO. 1 1917–1925

For small orch. Arr. of FIVE EASY PIECES for piano duet, nos. 1–4.

Pub. C.

FOUR STUDIES FOR ORCHESTRA nos. 1–3 1914–1918; no. 4 1928

Arr. for orch. of THREE PIECES FOR STRING QUARTET and ETUDE FOR PIANOLA.

Pub. ERM, then B. & H.

CAPRICCIO FOR PIANO AND ORCHESTRA 1928–1929

Pub. ERM, 1930; Rev. 1949, B. & H., 1952.

CONCERTO FOR VIOLIN IN D MAJOR 1930

Pub. Sch., 1931.

DIVERTIMENTO 1934

Arr. of LE BAISER DE LA FÉE.

Pub. ERM, 1938; Rev. 1949, B. & H., 1950.

PRELUDIUM 1936–1937

For jazz group. Unpub. Reorch. 1953.

Pub. B. & H., 1968.

DUMBARTON OAKS CONCERTO IN E FLAT MAJOR 1937–1938

For ch. orch.

Pub. Sch., 1938.

SYMPHONY IN C 1939–1940

Pub. Sch., 1948.

DANSES CONCERTANTES 1941–1942

For ch. orch.

Pub. AMP, 1942.

CIRCUS POLKA 1942

Pub. AMP, 1944.

FOUR NORWEGIAN MOODS 1942

Pub. AMP. 1944.

ODE 1943

'Elegiac song in 4 parts'.
Pub. Sch., 1947.

SCHERZO À LA RUSSE 1944
For jazz group, unpub. Reorch. 1943–1944.
Pub. Chp., 1945.

SYMPHONY IN THREE MOVEMENTS 1942–1945
Pub. AMP, 1946.

EBONY CONCERTO 1945
For solo clarinet and jazz group.
Pub. Charling, 1946.

CONCERTO IN D 1946
For string orch.
Pub. B. & H., 1946.

CONCERTINO 1952
Arr. for 12 instr. of the piece of the same name for string quartet.
Pub. Hansen, 1953.

TANGO, 1953
Arr. for 19 instr. of TANGO for piano.
Pub. Mercury, 1954.

GREETING PRELUDE 1955
Arr. for lg. orch. of 'Happy Birthday to You' (for Pierre Monteux).
Pub. B. & H., 1960.

MOVEMENTS 1958–1960
For piano and orch.
Pub. B. & H., 1960.

EIGHT INSTRUMENTAL MINIATURES 1962
Arr. for 15 instr. of FIVE FINGERS (*Les Cinq doigts*) for piano.
Pub. C., 1963.

VARIATIONS 1963–4
PUB. B. & H., 1965.

3 *Choral Works*

CANTATA 1904
For chorus and piano, unpub. ms. lost.

ZVEZDOLIKI (*Le Roi des étoiles/King of the Stars*) 1911–1912
Cantata for male chorus and orch. Text by Balmont.
Pub. Jurg., 1913.

PODBLIUDNIA (*Soucoupes*/Saucers) 1914–1917 known as
FOUR RUSSIAN PEASANT SONGS: 1. 'Near the church of Tchigissakh';
2. 'Ovsen'; 3. 'The pike'; 4. 'Mr Potbelly'. For women's chorus. Text:
Russian popular songs.
Pub. Sch, 1930; C., 1932. Rev. for female chorus and 4 horns, 1954; C., 1958.

PATER NOSTER [*Otche nash*] for mixed church choir
1. Slavonic text 1926 Pub. ERM, 1932.

2. Latin text 1949 Pub. B. & H., 1949.

SYMPHONIE DES PSAUMES (*Symphony of Psalms*) 1930
For mixed church choir and orch. Texts: fragments of Psalms 38, 39; Psalm 150.
Pub. ERM, 1930–1932. Rev. 1948, B. & H., 1948.

CREDO [*Simvol veri*] For mixed church choir:
1. Slavonic text 1926 Pub. ERM, 1933.
2. Latin text 1949 Pub. B. & H., 1949.
3. Rev. of 1. 1964 Pub. B. & H., 1964.

AVE MARIA [*Bogoroditse Devo*] For mixed church choir:
1. Slavonic text 1934 Pub. ERM, 1934.
2. Latin text 1949 Pub. B. & H.

BABEL 1944
Cantata for narrator, men's chorus and orch. Text from Genesis XI, 1–9.
Pub. Sch., 1953.

MASS 1944–1948
For mixed choir and 10 instr. Latin text of the Mass.
Pub. B. & H., 1948.

CANTATA 1951–1952
For 2 sol., female chorus and instr. ens. Anonymous Elizabethan texts.
Pub. B. & H., 1952.

CANTICUM SACRUM AD HONOREM SANCTI MARCI NOMINIS 1956
For 2 sol., choir, organ, orch. Texts: Gospel according to St Mark; Song of Songs; Psalms; St John's Epistles (fragments).
Pub. B. & H., 1956.

THRENI, ID EST LAMENTATIONES JEREMIAE PROPHETAE 1957–1958
For 6 sol., choir and orch. Text: Lamentations for Good Friday (fragments); Jeremiah's prayer.
Pub. B. & H., 1958.

A SERMON, A NARRATIVE AND A PRAYER 1960–1961
Cantata for narrator, 2 sol., chorus and orch. Texts: The Epistles of St Paul, The Acts of the Apostles, Thomas Dekker.
Pub. B. & H., 1961.

ANTHEM: THE DOVE DESCENDING BREAKS THE AIR 1962
[Hymn] for mixed church choir. Text by T. S. Eliot.
Pub. B. & H., 1961.

INTROITUS (in memory of T. S. Eliot) 1965
For men's choir and inst. ens. Text of the Requiem Mass (fragment).
Pub. B. & H., 1965.

REQUIEM CANTICLES 1965–1966
For 2 sol., choir and orch. Text of the Requiem Mass (fragments).
Pub. B. & H., 1967.

4 *Vocal Works (other than choral)*

STORM-CLOUD [in Russian] 1902

Romance for voice and piano (Pushkin). Unpub. (Ms. in National Archives of Art and Literature, Moscow).

THE MUSHROOMS ARE GOING TO WAR [in Russian] 1904
For bass voice and piano (Kozma Proutkov) Unpub.

FAUN AND SHEPHERDESS [in Russian] 1906
Three melodies for mezzo-sopr. and orch. (Pushkin) 1. 'Shepherdess'; 2. 'Faun'; 3. 'River'.
Pub. Bf., 1908, then B. & H.

PASTORALE 1907
For voice and piano (no text).
Pub. Jurg., 1910, then C., and Sch. Vers. for voice and instr., 1923. Vers. for violin and piano, 1933.

TWO MELODIES [in Russian] 1908
For mezzo-sopr. and piano (Gorodetzky).
1. 'The Novice'; 2. 'Holy Dew'.
Pub. Jurg. [1912], B. & H., 1968.

TWO POEMS OF PAUL VERLAINE 1910
For bar. and piano. 1. 'Un grand sommeil noir' (A great black sleep); 2. 'La lune blanche' (The white moon).
Pub. Jurg., 1911, B. & H., 1954. Vers. for bar. and ch. orch. 1951, B. & H., 1953.

TWO POEMS OF KONSTANTIN BALMONT 1911
For sopr./ten. and piano. 1. 'Forget-me-not'; 2. 'The Pigeon'.
Pub. ERM, 1912, then B. & H. Vers. for bar. and ch. orch. 1954, B. & H.

TROIS POÈMES DE LA LYRIQUE JAPONAISE (*Three Japanese Lyrics*) 1912–1913
For sopr. and [piano] instr. ens. (Authors of texts = titles). 1. Akahito; 2. Mazatzumi; 3. Tsaraiuki.
Pub. ERM, 1934, then B. & H.

THREE LITTLE SONGS known as MEMORIES OF MY CHILDHOOD (*Souvenirs de mon enfance*) 1913 (Sketch 1906)
For voice and piano (Russian folksongs) 1. 'The Little Magpie'; 2. 'The Crow'; 3. 'Tchicher-Yacher'.
Pub. ERM, 1914, then B. & H. Transcribed for voice and ch. orch. 1919–1930, ERM, 1934, then B. & H.

PRIBAOUTKI 1914
For voice and instr. ens. (Popular Russian texts) 1. 'Kornilo'; 2. 'Natashka'; 3. 'Polkovnik' (The Colonel); 4. 'Staretz i zayatz' (The old man and the hare) (Translated by Ramuz as 1. 'L'Oncle Armand'; 2. 'Le Four'; 3. 'Le Colonel'; 4. 'Le Vieux et le lièvre'.
Pub. Henn, 1917, then C.

BERCEUSES DU CHAT (Cat's cradlesongs) 1915–1916
For voice and 3 clarinets. Texts: popular Russian songs, translated by C. F. Ramuz. 1. 'Sur le poêle' (On the stove); 2. 'Intérieur'; 3. 'Dodo' (Bye-byes); 4. 'Ce qu'il a, le chat' (What's wrong with the cat).
Pub. Henn, 1917 then C.

TROIS HISTOIRES POUR ENFANTS (Three stories for children) 1915–1917
  For voice and piano. Texts: popular Russian songs, translated by C. F.
  Ramuz. 1. 'Tilim-bom'; 2. 'Les Oies et les cygnes . . .' (The geese and the
  swans . . .); 'Chanson de l'ours' (Song of the bear).
  Pub. C., 1920. *Tilim-bom*, orch. vers. 1923, C.

BERCEUSE (Cradlesong) 1917
  For voice and piano (Stravinsky).
  Pub. in *Expositions and Developments* (see Bibliography).

QUATRE CHANTS RUSSES (Four Russian songs) 1918–1919
  For voice and piano. Texts: popular Russian songs, translated by C. F.
  Ramuz. 1. 'Canard' (Duck); 2. 'Chanson pour compter' (Counting
  song); 3. 'Le Moineau est assis' (The sparrow is perched); 4. 'Chant
  dissident' (Sectarian song).
  Pub. C., 1920.

PARASHA'S SONG 1922–1923
  Extract from *Mavra*. For voice and orch.

PETIT CANON POUR NADIA BOULANGER 1947
  For 2 ten. Unpub.

THREE SONGS FROM WILLIAM SHAKESPEARE 1953
  For mezzo-sopr., flute, clarinet, viola. 1. 'Musick to heare'; 2. 'Full
  fathom five'; 3. 'When daisies pied'.
  Pub. B. & H., 1954.

FOUR SONGS (*Quatre chants*) 1953–1954
  For voice and instr. ens. Arr. from QUATRE CHANTS RUSSES nos. 1 and 4,
  and TROIS HISTOIRES POUR ENFANTS nos. 1 and 2.
  Pub. C., 1955.

IN MEMORIAM DYLAN THOMAS 1954
  Funeral canons and song (Dylan Thomas), for ten., string quartet and 4
  trombones.
  Pub. B. & H., 1954.

ABRAHAM AND ISAAC 1962–1963
  Sacred ballet for bar. and ch. orch. Hebrew text of Book of Genesis.
  Pub. B. & H., 1965.

ELEGY FOR J.F.K. 1964
  For bar. (or mezzo-sopr.) voice and 3 clarinets (Auden).
  Pub. B. & H., 1964.

THE OWL AND THE PUSSYCAT 1966
  For voice and piano (Edward Lear).
  Pub. B. & H., 1967.

5 *Piano Works*

TARANTELLA 1898 Unpub. ms. in State Library, Leningrad.
SCHERZO 1902
  Pub. Faber, 1975.
SONATA IN F SHARP MINOR 1903–1904

Pub. Faber 1973.

FOUR STUDIES 1908
Pub. Jurg., 1910.

FLOWER WALTZ for 2 pianos. Unpub. ms. lost.

THREE EASY PIECES 1914–1915
For piano duet. 1. *March*; 2. *Valse*; 3. *Polka*.
Pub. Henn, 1917 then C.

SOUVENIR D'UNE MARCHE BOCHE (Memory of a Boche march) 1915
Pub. in *The Book of the Homeless*, Edith Wharton, Macmillan (London).

FIVE EASY PIECES 1916–1917
For piano duet. 1. *Andante*; 2. *Española*; 3. *Balalaika*; 4. *Napolitana*;
5. *Galop*.
Pub. Henn, 1917, then C.

VALSE POUR LES ENFANTS (Waltz for children) 1917
Pub. in *Le Figaro*, 21 May 1922, repr. in E. W. White (see Bibliography).

PIANO RAG MUSIC 1919
Pub. C., 1920.

LES CINQ DOIGTS (The five fingers)
Eight easy pieces.
Pub. C., 1921.

THREE MOVEMENTS FROM PETRUSHKA 1921
Pub. ERM, 1922, then B. & H.

SONATA 1924
Pub. ERM, 1925, then B. & H.

SERENADE IN A 1925
Pub. ERM, 1926 then B. & H.

CONCERTO 1931–1935
For two pianos (without orch.)
Pub. Sch., 1936.

TANGO 1940
Pub. Mercury, 1941.

SONATA 1943–1944
For two pianos.
Pub. Chp., 1945.

6 *Instrumental Works*

THREE PIECES FOR STRING QUARTET 1914
Pub. ERM, 1922, B. & H., 1947.

CANONS 1917 for 2 horns, Unpub.

ETUDE 1917
For pianola. Unpub. as score except as orchestrated as 4th piece in FOUR
STUDIES FOR ORCHESTRA. Piano roll pub. by Aeolian, 1917; reconstructed
by Rex Lawson, 1980.

DUO 1918 for 2 bassoons. Unpub.

SUITE of *Histoire du soldat* (*The Soldier's Tale*)

1. For instr. ens. 1918.
2. For violin, clarinet, piano. 1919.
Pub. C., 1920 and 1922.

THREE PIECES FOR SOLO CLARINET 1919
Pub., C., 1920.

CONCERTINO 1920 for string quartet.
Pub. Hansen, 1923.

OCTET 1922–1923 for wind instruments
Pub. ERM, 1924; rev. 1952; B. & H., 1952.

SUITE 1925
For violin and piano. Extracts/arr. from PULCINELLA.
Pub. ERM, 1926, then B. & H.

DUO CONCERTANT 1931–1932
Pub. ERM, 1933, then B. & H.

SUITE ITALIENNE 1932
Extr./arr. from PULCINELLA.
1. For violin and piano.
2. For cello and piano.
Pub. ERM, 1934, then B. & H.

RUSSIAN SONG 1937
Arr. of Parasha's song from MAVRA.
1. For violin and piano, collab. Dushkin.
2. For cello and piano, collab. D. Markhevich.
Pub. B. & H.

ELEGY 1944
For solo viola.
Pub. Chp., 1945.

SEPTET 1952–1953
Pub. B. & H., 1953.

EPITAPHIUM 1959
For flute, clarinet and harp.
Pub. B. & H., 1959.

DOUBLE-CANON (In memoriam Raoul Dufy) 1959.
Pub. B. & H., 1960.

FANFARE FOR A NEW THEATER 1964
For 2 trumpets.
Pub. B. & H., 1968.

7 Arrangements of Other Composers' Works

Grieg: KOBOLD 1909. For orchestra. Unpub.
Chopin: NOCTURNE in A Flat Major. VALSE BRILLANTE in E flat major 1909 for orchestra. Unpub.
Mussorgsky: KHOVANSHTCHINA 1913
Orchestrated fragments in collab. with M. Ravel.

Pub. Bessel, 1914.

SONG OF THE VOLGA BOATMEN 1917 For orch.
Pub. C., 1920.

Rouget de Lisle: LA MARSEILLAISE for orch. Unpub.

Tchaikovsky: SLEEPING BEAUTY 1921. Fragments for orch. Unpub.

THE STAR-SPANGLED BANNER 1941 For orch.
Pub. Mercury.

J. S. Bach: CANONIC VARIATIONS ON THE CHORALE 'VOM HIMMEL HOCH'
1956
For choir and orchestra.
Pub.B. & H., 1956.

Carlo Gesualdo da Venosa: TRES SACRAE CANTIONES 1957–1959
For church choir. Missing parts completed, recomposition.
1. *Da pacem*; 2. *Assumpta est Maria*; 3. *Illumina nos*.
Pub. B. & H., 1957.

MONUMENTUM PRO GESUALDO DA VENOSA 1960
Arr. of 3 madrigals for orch.
Pub. B. & H., 1960.

H. Wolf: TWO SACRED SONGS 1968
For Mezzo-sopr. and 9 inst.
Pub. B. & H., 1968.

(J. S. Bach: Preludes and Fugues of THE WELL-TEMPERED CLAVIER 1969
Unfinished orch. Unpub.)

SELECTED BIBLIOGRAPHICAL SOURCES

1 Stravinsky's works
Chronicle of my life, Victor Gollancz, London 1935.
Poétique musicale, Paris, Plon, 1952; *Poetics of Music in the Form of Six Lessons*, Harvard University Press, 1974.

2 Co-authored works by Stravinsky
Conversations with Igor Stravinsky, by Igor Stravinsky and Robert Craft, New York, Doubleday, 1959.
Memories and Commentaries, by Igor Stravinsky and Robert Craft, New York, Doubleday, 1960; London, Faber.
Expositions and Developments, by Igor Stravinsky and Robert Craft, New York, Doubleday, 1962; London, Faber, 1961.
Dialogues and a Diary, by Igor Stravinsky and Robert Craft, New York, Doubleday, 1963; London, Faber.
Themes and Episodes, by Igor Stravinsky and Robert Craft, New York, Knopf, 1966; London, Faber.
Retrospectives and a Conclusion, by Igor Stravinsky and Robert Craft, New York, Knopf, 1969. Revised edition titled *Themes and Conclusions*, London, Faber, 1978.

3 Books on Stravinsky
(The spelling of his name follows that of the book. After the composer settled in the USA he changed the spelling from Strawinsky to Stravinsky.)
A. CASELLA: *Igor Strawinsky*, Rome, Formiggini, 1926; enlarged ed. Brescia, La Scuola, 1951.
B. DE SCHLOEZER: *Igor Strawinsky*, Paris, Cl. Aveline, 1929.
I. GLEBOV (pseud. of B. Assafiev): *Kniga o Stravinskom*, Leningrad, Triton, 1929; republished under the name of B. Assafiev, Leningrad, Muzika, 1977; *Book on Stravinsky*, UMI Research P., 1982.
C. F. RAMUZ: *Souvenirs sur Igor Stravinsky*, Lausanne, Mermod, 1929.
P. COLLAER: *Strawinsky*, Brussels, Equilibre, 1930.
A. SCHAEFFNER: *Strawinsky*, Paris, Rieder, 1931.
G. F. MALIPIERO: *Stravinsky*, Venice, Cavallino, 1945.
E. W. WHITE: *Stravinsky: a critical survey*, London, Lehmann, 1947.
T. STRAWINSKY: *Le message d'Igor Strawinsky*, Lausanne, Librairie F. Rouge, 1948.
A. TANSMAN: *Igor Stravinsky*, Paris, Amiot-Dumont, 1949.
L. OLEGGINI: *Connaissance de Stravinsky*, Lausanne, Foetisch, 1952.
H. STROBEL: *Igor Strawinsky*, Zurich, Atlantis, 1956.

R. CRAFT with A. PIOVESAN and R. VLAD: *La Musiche religiose di Igor Stravinsky*, Venice, Lombroso, 1956.

H. H. STUCKENSCHMIDT: *Strawinsky und sein Jahrhundert*, Berlin, Akademie der Kunste, 1957.

R. VLAD: *Strawinsky*, Rome, Einaudi, 1958; Oxford University Press, 1985.

R. CRAFT: *Dix Ans avec Stravinsky*, Monaco, Editions du Rocher, 1958.

R. SIOHAN: *Stravinsky*, Paris 'Solfèges' coll. Ed. du Seuil, 1959.

I. VERCHININA: *Rannye baleti Stravinskovo* (Stravinsky's first ballets), Moscow, Naouka, 1962.

B. YARUSTOVSKY: *Igor Stravinsky*, Moscow, Sovietki Kompozitor, 1963.

M. PHILIPPOT: *Igor Stravinsky*, Paris, Seghers, 1965.

E. W. WHITE: *Stravinsky: the Composer and his Works*, London, Faber & Faber, 1966; enlarged ed. 1979.

R. CRAFT: *The Chronicle of a Friendship, 1948–1971*, New York, Knopf, 1972.

P. HORGAN: *Encounters with Stravinsky: a personal record*, New York, Farrar Straus, 1972.

L. LIBMAN: *And Music at the Close: Stravinsky's last years*, New York, Norton, 1972.

V. STRAVINSKY and R. CRAFT: *Stravinsky in pictures and documents*, New York, Simon & Schuster, 1979; London, Hutchinson, 1978.

4 Symposia, special issues of periodicals devoted to Stravinsky, Collections

La Revue musicale, No. on Igor Stravinsky, Paris, December 1923.

Cahiers de Belgique, No. on Igor Stravinsky, Brussels, December 1930.

Igor Stravinsky, M. Armitage, ed., New York, Schirmer, 1936.

La Revue musicale, No. on Igor Stravinsky, Paris, May-June 1939.

Dance Index: 'Stravinsky and the Theatre', vol. VI, no. 10–12, New York 1945.

Tempo, No. on Igor Stravinsky, London, summer 1948.

Stravinsky in the theatre, M. Lederman, ed. New York, Pelegrini, 1949–1951.

Musik der Zeit, No. on Igor Stravinsky, Bonn, 1952.

The Score, No. 20 on Igor Stravinsky, London, June 1957.

Avec Stravinsky: symposium (texts of Igor Stravinsky, R. Craft, P. Boulez, K. H. Stockhausen, etc.), Monaco, Editions du Rocher 1958.

The Musical Quarterly, No. XLVIII/3 on Igor Stravinsky, New York, 1962.

Stravinsky: a new appraisal of his work, P. H. Lang, ed., New York, Norton, 1963 (repub. from *The Musical Quarterly* mentioned above).

Tempo, No. 81 on Igor Stravinsky, London, spring-summer 1967.

Stravinsky, symposium, Paris, Hachette ('Génies et réalités'), 1968.

Perspectives on Schoenberg and Stravinsky, B. Boretz and Ed. Cone, ed., Princeton University Press, 1969.

Tempo: No. 97 on Stravinsky, London, 1971.

Les Cahiers canadiens de Musique, No. 4 on Stravinsky, 1972.

Musique en jeu, No. 4 on Stravinsky, Paris, Seuil, 1972.

I. F. Stravinsky: Stati, pisma, vosspominania (Articles, letters, memories), L. Kutateladze, ed., Leningrad, 1972.

I. Stravinsky: stati e materiali (Articles and material, incl. 62 letters by the composer), L. S. Dyachkova, ed., Moscow, 1973.

5 Articles on Stravinsky (in periodicals, encyclopedias etc.)

J. Rivière: 'Le Sacre du Printemps', in *Nouvelle Revue Française*, Paris, December 1913.

B. de Schloezer: 'Igor Stravinsky', in *La Revue musicale*, Paris, December 1923 (see under IV).

B. de Schloezer: Numerous articles of criticism on Stravinsky in *Nouvelle Revue Française*, 1921–1956.

A. Schaeffner: 'Igor Stravinsky: Critique et Thématique' in *La Revue musicale*, Paris, May-June 1939 (see under 4).

P. Souvtchinsky: 'La notion du temps et la musique', in *La Revue musicale*, Paris, May-June 1939 (see under 4).

P. Boulez: 'Trajectoires', in *Contrepoints*, no. 6, Paris, 1949, reprinted in *Relevés d'apprenti* (see under 6).

P. Boulez: 'Stravinsky demeure', in *Musique russe*, Paris, PUF, 1953, reprinted in *Relevés d'apprenti* (see under 6).

A. Schaeffner: 'Renard et l'époque russe de Stravinsky' in *Cahiers Renaud-Barrault*, Paris, 1953.

B. de Schloezer/A. Boucourechliev: 'Stravinsky hier et aujourd'hui', an interview, in *Nouvelle Revue Française*, Paris, March 1959.

Lawrence Morton: 'Stravinsky', in *Encyclopédie de la Musique*, Paris, Fasquelle, 1961.

A. Souris: 'Debussy et Stravinsky' (1962) in *Conditions de la musique* (see under 6).

P. Souvtchinsky: 'Das Wunder des "Sacre du Printemps"' in *Igor Stravinsky, Eine Sendereihe*, WDR, Cologne, 1963.

H. F. Redlich: 'Stravinsky' in *M.G.G.*, T. XII, 1965.

A. Schnittke: 'Ossobenosti orkhestrovovo gholossovedenya . . .' (Details of orchestral voice-conducting in Stravinsky's early works) in *Muzika i sovremennost*, Moscow, 1967.

A. Souris: 'Le sens du sacré dans la musique de Stravinsky' (1971) in *Conditions de la musique* (see under 6).

H. Pousseur: 'Stravinsky selon Webern selon Stravinsky', in *Musique en jeu*, no. 4 (see 4) and 5, Paris, Editions du Seuil, 1971.

E. W. White and Jeremy Noble: 'Stravinsky' in Grove's *Dictionary of Music*, London, Macmillan, 1980.

J. M. Vaccaro: 'La musique dans "l'Histoire du soldat"'; J. Jacquot: 'La genèse du texte et la représentation de 1918'; Myriam Louzoun: 'La voix et la gestuelle de la création d'une forme théâtrale (L'Histoire du soldat)' in *Les Voies de la Création Théâtrale*, no. 6, Paris, CNRS, 1978.

6 Works or collections containing texts on Stravinsky

J. Cocteau: *Le Coq et l'Arlequin*, Paris, 1918, repub. Stock, 1978.

T. W. ADORNO: *Philosophie de la nouvelle musique*, Part II: 'Stravinsky ou la restauration', Tübingen, 1949.

Musique russe (several authors), 2 vol. Paris, PUF, 1953.

N. NABOKOV: *Cosmopolite*, 1975. trans. Fr. Paris, Laffont, 1976.

P. BOULEZ: *Relevés d'apprenti*, Paris, Seuil, 1966.

A. SOURIS: *Conditions de la musique et autres écrits*, Paris, CNRS, 1976.

JEAN HUGO: *Avant d'oublier*, Paris, Fayard, 1976.

ROLF LIEBERMANN: *Actes et entractes*, Paris, Stock, 1976.

GEORGES AURIC: *Quand j'étais là*, Paris, Grasset, 1979.

RICHARD BUCKLE: *Diaghilev*, London, Weidenfeld & Nicolson, 1979.

The French edition of this book was in the press at the moment when *Stravinsky, études et témoignages*, appeared. This was edited by François Lesure and included articles by P. Souvtchinsky, P. Boulez, St. Jarocinski, L. Cyr, C. Deliège, Cl. Helffer. Published by Lattès, Paris, 1982.

INDEX OF WORKS AND WRITINGS BY STRAVINSKY

Note: Line entries in roman characters are musical works;
those in italics are literary works by the composer.

INDEX OF NAMES